Source Book of Proposed Music Notation Reforms

Arthur Wallbridge, *The Sequential System of Musical Notation*,
London, 1844.

Source Book of Proposed Music Notation Reforms

GARDNER READ

Music Reference Collection,
Number 11

Greenwood Press
New York • Westport, Connecticut • London

Library of Congress Cataloging-in-Publication Data

Read, Gardner, 1913-
  Source book of proposed music notation reforms.

  (Music reference collection, ISSN 0736-7740 ; no. 11)
  Bibliography: p.
  Includes index.
  1. Musical notation. I. Title. II. Series.
ML432.R29   1987   781'.24   86-14315
ISBN 0-313-25446-X (lib. bdg. : alk. paper)

Library of Congress Catalog Card Number: 86-14315
ISBN: 0-313-25446-X
ISSN: 0736-7740

First published in 1987

Greenwood Press, Inc.
88 Post Road West, Westport, Connecticut 06881

Printed in the United States of America

∞

The paper used in this book complies with the
Permanent Paper Standards issued by the National
Information Standards Organization (Z39.48-1984).

10 9 8 7 6 5 4 3 2 1

Quae visa, vera; quae non, veriora
(What you see is true; what you do
not see is more true).
—Latin proverb

Contents

Foreword

No one would have been better suited to collect and annotate
this compilation of forgotten systems of music notation than
Gardner Read. After singling out (in his widely used <u>Music
Notation: A Manual of Modern Practice</u>) what at present is
the accepted, common method of notating music, he now ac-
quaints us with the myriad of notational systems and devices
that did <u>not</u> find acceptance, even though they provide much
valuable insight into the problems of our era's so-called
traditional notation.

There have always been people who found flaws in the
music notational systems of their eras, and this book shows
how these urges to improve go back to the very beginnings of
music notation. However, the book pays special attention to
the nineteenth century and to much of the twentieth because
the proposals offered by our immediate predecessors are of
greatest interest to us. Many of the innovations shown here
are ingenious and some are even beautiful to look at; nevertheless, none of them, except for an occasional "local" notational device, succeeded.

One reason for the lack of success of these innovations
is that the new "alphabets" were mostly the work of non
musicians. For example, some were developed by scientists
in the field of acoustics. They considered it both illogical
and troublesome to have to work with a staff that does not
distinguish between half- and whole-steps or a system that
has no provisions for notating microtones. Others, working
with pulsation, found traditional notation too crude to be
able to show multimetrics or controlled ritardandi and acce-
lerandi. In short, relatively few of these notational innovations were geared toward practicing musicians. Instead.
they were used mostly for illustrations in scientific treatises or as almost abstract proposals in learned periodicals.

There also is, among practically all the innovators, a
strange disregard of graphic flexibility. Traditional notation operates with very simple basic symbols -- notes, accidentals, and staves -- yet it is capable of functioning sat-
isfactorily in spite of considerably different musical styles,
not to mention the huge variety of handwritings, from Bach
and before, through Beethoven, all the way to Stravinsky and
beyond. Most of the proposals for new notational systems in-

clude note-symbols and staves that are much too subtle and delicate to permit comparable adjustments.

In addition, there is a rather prosaic reason why the many new suggested notational systems have not been found acceptable by the musical community. Most musicians, after spending years since childhood to become experts in dealing with the complexities and shortcomings of traditional notation, are quite unwilling to learn new, unproven additional systems, especially since common-practice notation has enabled them to perform a vast range of music perfectly well.

Let's face it: Notational innovations become desirable, or in fact necessary, only when <u>music</u> becomes so much more complex or so completely different in approach and technique that traditional notation can no longer cope with it, which has been the case since the early 1950s when music required new notational symbols and systems. As a result, there has been an overproduction of new devices, including countless duplications or different interpretations of the same signs, with the invention everywhere of novel notation for three decades. Fortunately, a trend toward regaining standards, where appropriate, is underway.

May I stress that in spite of the many "roads not taken," most of the proposals shown in this book are full of fascinating ideas and give much food for thought. One thing is assured: Many of these ideas are quite likely to make us more aware of the general philosophy and the many details of our traditional notation than was possible before Gardner Read's monumental effort.

--Kurt Stone

Preface

This compendium chronologically lists, describes, and critically analyzes 391 of the innumerable notational systems proposed during the past three centuries. It is thus a repository of "roads not taken" and a historical survey of the many
attempts to improve upon or to supplant the standard procedure for writing down music, which has been in widespread use
since the early eighteenth century. A variety of locales provided the materials incorporated into these pages: Libraries
in this country and in England; books in several languages
on music notation, theory, and history; domestic and foreign
music journals; the United States Patent Office; privately
printed tracts; and personal correspondence. Wherever and
whenever possible, the original sources were consulted. When
this was not possible, this compiler relied on authoritative
secondary sources, principally references or analyses in previous publications.

To facilitate access to the detail of the systems that
follow, each chapter of this book maintains a similar descriptive pattern. The proposed reforms appear chronologically,
making it possible to trace the progress of experimentation
from its earliest known efflorescence to its most recent mani-
festations. Titles of all proposals appear in full, even when
they reach the extravagant lengths beloved of some European
theorists and historians. For all titles in a foreign language, an English equivalent (not necessarily a strict translation) follows, together with the place of invention or publication when known and its publisher.

The separate elements or technical features of each notational reform are then briefly described and illustrated in
the following order:

Staff: the standard pentagram, a modified arrangement of
the staff lines (whether fewer or more than five), or no
staff at all.

Clef signs or register symbols: traditional, especially devised, or omitted altogether.

Pitch symbols: conventional or uniquely shaped noteheads,
numerals, letters, or stenographic marks.

Key signatures, if pertinent to the reform and indicated
unconventionally.

Durational and rhythmic factors should the symbology depart
from common practice; otherwise, these are incorporated in
the illustration of pitch.
   Special signs proposed for rests and pauses.
   Unusual indications of meter and of tempo if these are included in the system proposal.
   Dynamic marks, ornamentation, or specific performance directives when outlined by the individual notator.

   For the great majority of the systems analyzed, a brief
transcription in standard notation (of either an existing
work or an illustrative passage devised by this compiler)
precedes its equivalent in the suggested new notation, allowing immediate assessment of the effectiveness of the proposal.
Certain systems lend themselves only to writing single-line
music (usually vocal); others -- those designed for keyboard
compositions, for instance -- can accommodate chord textures
of varying complexity. Each illustration, therefore, is tai-
lored to the specific character and intent of the reform under consideration, and each shows chromatic inflections and
different rhythmic constructs as handled by the particular
proposer. Most of the rhythmic figures are conventional, how
ever, simply because the proposed reform ignored the problem
of irregular rhythms. Where the systems seemed excessively
primitive or notably restricted in usefulness or where a key
element such as duration was unaccountably omitted in the inventor's presentation, no pictorial example appears.
   Several of the musical illustrations in conventional notation serve more than a single new system; the chorale melody
Ein' feste Burg ist unser Gott, for example, appears twenty
times in the book because it effectively serves to demonstrate
the feasibility of a number of the proposed systems. Likewise,
a brief excerpt from Schubert's C Minor piano sonata proved
to be ideal for illustrating several of the keyboard-oriented
proposals. Wherever known, the musical examples are identified; when the source of an illustration included by a reformer could not be verified, or else was devised by this
author, no titles appear.
   The sometimes inferior reproductive quality of certain
musical examples must be attributed to the poor condition of
the originals. Many older publications, particularly those
from the eighteenth and nineteenth centuries on deposit in
the various libraries visited, were literally falling apart,
or else the print was blurred or the paper had darkened with
age. Hence it was not possible in every instance to secure
clearly legible photographic copies. Despite these minor
challenges, the reader should nonetheless be able to decipher
the quotations without undue strain.
   Frequently a notational reform significantly altered both
the staff employed and its pitch symbology; it was necessary,
therefore, to place the reform arbitrarily in one chapter or
another. In general, however, each novel system appears in
the category in which it was considered to be more unorthodox
or more inventive.

The commentary that follows the presentation of each reform is highly subjective, this being the prerogative of the
researcher. Some may find the criticisms too harsh; others
may take issue with certain positive assessments. Careful
scrutiny by other scholars and notational aficionados may
lead to quite different conclusions and to contemporary ap-
plications far more practical than the reformers ever dreamed.
These, in turn, are the prerogatives of any serious student
of the proposed innovations in musical notation catalogued
in this book.

Acknowledgments

Were it not for the immensely rich resources of certain of the major music libraries in this country and in England, this survey of notational reforms might never have been brought to fruition. I am, therefore, greatly indebted to the following institutions and to their invariably helpful personnel, all of whom eased for me the long hours of arduous research, brought to my attention rare items of special interest, and offered many valuable suggestions for incorporation in the book in progress: Ruth Bleeker, music librarian, Boston Public Library; O. W. Neighbour, music librarian, British Library, London; J. J. Pot, president, Klavarskribo Foundation, Holland; Wayne Shirley, reference librarian, Music Division of The Library of Congress; Frank Campbell, chief of the music division, Lincoln Center Library for the Performing Arts, New York; M. J. Harrington, librarian, Royal Academy of Music, London; Christopher Bornet, reference librarian, Royal College of Music, London; Ruth Watanabe, head, Sibley Music Library, Eastman School of Music, Rochester, New York; and Maigery Anthea Baird, music librarian, University of London.

The favorable testimony of three loyal and supportive colleagues -- Samuel Adler, William Schuman, and Kurt Stone -- was instrumental in persuading the Ingram Merrill Foundation of New York to award me a research grant; their personal recommendations and the welcome support of the Foundation are gratefully acknowledged.

I am also indebted to composer Herbert Fromm for his generous assistance in translating many of the German proposal titles and accompanying texts. Finally, my heartfelt thanks to my wife for her editorial additions and subtractions in the preliminary drafts of this compendium and for scrupulously proofreading the final typescript.

Source Book of Proposed Music Notation Reforms

1.
The Search for Improved Notation: An Overview

If the shelves of the various libraries of Europe were searched, it would probably be found that for some centuries a new notation has appeared about every three or four years, each of which is called by its author "The" new notation, for he fondly thinks that it will become universal.

--C. F. Abdy Williams, The Story of Notation, 1903.

Contemporary composers are in almost universal agreement that our traditional system of music notation demands improvement; indeed, some advocate its outright replacement by alternative methods and techniques. These convictions are not, however, uniquely twentieth-century phenomena; they were shared by many musicians of the past who also sought to alter both the structure of notation and its individual components. Since roughly 1700, composers and theorists, pedagogues and amateur musicians have put forward with notable regularity proposals to simplify, to improve, or to supplant the prevailing system. It is the primary purpose of this compendium to trace the historical progress of these reforms and to assess their potential, if any, for incorporation into current notational practice.

Such a scrutiny is valid even though it is indisputable that -- far from improving the notation standardized at the time of each proposed reform or substituting a superior new method -- most innovations succeeded only in creating more problems for the performer than they solved. Almost without exception each proposal made its small ripple in the waters of Western music and thereafter quietly sank beneath those waters, some reforms barely surviving the lifetime of their creators.

It is an intriguing facet of our survey that many of the reforms to be illustrated were the brainchildren of amateurs. Philosophers and physicists, philanthropists and priests, pedagogues and paralegals, scientists and mathematicians, advocates and civil engineers -- all were responsible for adding to the repository of notational reforms analyzed in these pages. The improvement of the written language of musical expression seems to have been an irresistible challenge

to many whose professions lay partly or even wholly outside
the field of music. That these aficionados sometimes succeeded
more obviously in their proposed systems than the professionals adds yet another engaging dimension to this critical study.
     At this point we might well ask: What specifically were
the innumerable inventors of new notational systems attempting to accomplish? What were their primary objectives in pro-
posing new ways of writing down music? Why, indeed, should
any musician, professional or amateur, wish to displace the
traditional, accepted modes of musical notation?
     The solution is simple: What unites the three-century ros-
ter of notational reforms is the inventors' frustration with
then-current ways of notating music and their determination --
however misdirected at times -- to rid notation of its obvious deficiencies and ambiguities. As musicologist Percy
Scholes maintained: "The inventor of any reasonably thought
out reformed staff notation can claim that he is offering the
means of saving several years of music study or, alternative-
ly, of freeing students from reading difficulties in order
that they may devote themselves more completely to other aspects of their work. Yet apparently nothing can be done, and
the reading of music remains many times more difficult than
it has any need to be"(1). In addition, there were always
practitioners unable to resist the challenge of devising individual new methods of notating music, many believing that
their contrivances would one day take the place of traditional
notation.
     Let us grant without question the reformers' serious pur-
pose and sincere conviction that their methods possessed special and enduring merit. Let us also concede without argument
that traditional notation has always been in need of improvement. The continuing search for a simplified yet viable means
of writing down the music of our own time remains, as in former periods, a worthy goal and an essential process. Yet the
history of music notation during the past three centuries
often resembles the landscape Robert Hughes necrologizes in
his provocative survey of modern art: "The culture of the
twentieth century is littered with Utopian schemes"(2). So
far no reform has succeeded in leading notation from its perceived Dark Ages to enduring light.
     This failure to endure has plagued even notational inno-
vations greeted with notable enthusiasm and critical acclaim --
as were, for instance, the widely hailed reforms of the Mexi-
can theorist and composer Julian Carrillo. When his notational
theories were published in 1895, musicologists, performers,
conductors, and music critics all outdid each other in praise.
"To truly express himself in his music, Julian Carrillo invented the true musical notation"(3), one fervent admirer put
it, while another tossed this critical bouquet: "Carrillo
ought to have been born in place of Guido d'Arezzo so as to
have spared the world so many useless efforts accumulated
over the centuries"(4). Not to be outdone by his loyal supporters, Carrillo himself stated in his published manifesto:
"My musical notation . . . does humanity a service for which
one day it will be thankful"(5). That day, of course, has not
yet arrived, nor is it likely that it ever will. Yet Julian

Carrillo's reforms are no less pragmatic, certainly no more
unrealistic than many another system devised to rid notation
of its many faults and incongruities.

If indeed well-grounded innovations have not survived, we
need look no further than ordinary apathy and skepticism for
reasons. As reformer Josiah Warren wrote in 1860, "Traditional
bias, reverence for authorities, vested interests, professional
ambition and egotism, all stand in deadly array against any
attack upon the present system (or want of system). The inno-
vator must be prepared to meet all the opposition these ad-
verse influences can wield; and nothing short of the glaring
and positive advantages he offers to the public can justify,
for a moment, the remotest hope of success"(6). It is indeed
ironic that Warren's own system (see page 24) failed for the
very reasons he so succinctly enumerated -- as did countless
proposals before and after.

We must, however, blame not only the conservative community of musicians but also the novelty-loving reformers who
in "simplifying" compounded the very limitations and illogi-
calities they ostensibly sought to overcome. Emmanuel Winternitz in his admirable Musical Autographs from Monteverdi to
Hindemith conjectured that "If a learned visitor from Mars
were to become interested in our music, and if he were commissioned to devise an easy and consistent system of musical
notation, he would probably arrive at something quite different from the one we use today." Our reformers are not from
Mars, nor have they been commissioned to devise new systems
of notation. But what they have invented can all too frequently be characterized as "something quite different" -- without
being as demonstrably effective as traditional notation.

The system known as Klavarskribo, for instance (page 74),
is a universe away from mainstream notation, but is it actually any more practical? Is it really easier to learn, to
read, and to write, as the publishers of this novel method
maintain? They can, it must be admitted, point to many teachers of music -- principally in England and Europe -- who have
embraced the system wholeheartedly and who regularly teach it
to their pupils. But where are the contemporary composers who
use Klavarskribo consistently and with enthusiasm? Where are
the performers of modern music adept at reading it? How many
new works are published each year in this system? The issu-
ance of Bach inventions, Beethoven sonatas, and Chopin pre-
ludes in Klavarskribo does not, of course, guarantee equal
suitability for the printing of late twentieth-century music.

Too many aspiring notational innovators are kin to the
ancient Egyptian scribe who, according to author John Barth's
witty essay on post-modernist literature, sometime around
2000 B.C. set down this heartfelt plaint: "Would I had phrases
that are not known, utterances that are strange, in new language that has not been used, free from repetition, not an
utterance that has grown stale, which men of old have spoken"
(7). Substitute musical for literary terms, and this scribe's
basic motivations are those of many an inventor of new notational symbology.

Further lapses in the search for the "new language that
has not been used, free from repetition" will be detailed in

the following chapters. But even an overview of the roads not taken must note the wide neglect of valid elements in the common-practice notation that well served compositional styles as diverse as those of Mozart and Schoenberg, of Schubert and Bartók, of Beethoven and Ravel, of Haydn and Stravinsky. Traditional notation in each of these oeuvres was able without undue ambiguity to communicate the composer's individual musical thoughts and to provide clear performance directives for the player or singer, while still allowing for a certain amount of interpretive freedom.

Perhaps above all other shortfalls, most revisionists seem to have been unaware that certain basic conditions must be met before any proposed reform can succeed. One of the first attempts to codify these elements occurred in 1847, when the Fine Arts section of the Belgian Royal Academy of the Sciences outlined the principles of all the known notational reforms made to date, particularly those based on the use of numbers, letters, and stenographic symbols. They then sought to test the strength and weakness of each proposed system by applying its governing principles to every aspect of notation. On this basis they sought a consensus on a single new and acceptable method of notating music.

Joseph Raymondi, one of the participants in the survey, whose Examen critique des notations musicales (8) appeared nine years after the Belgian conclave, came out strongly in favor of improved notation, even though he wryly commented that "A better, more simplified notation will not make one's musical taste more refined, the voice more beautiful, nor the fingers more agile!" But it would, he was convinced, make the learning of music easier by using fewer and less complex symbols, such essential simplifications being, as he put it, "the locomotives of science." For some two centuries, Raymondi felt, reformers had assiduously pointed out the imperfections of conventional notation and then -- uninformed of proposals prior to their time -- were utterly convinced they alone could devise a better method.

To assess the potential of the various new notation systems known to him, Raymondi outlined what he considered to be the ten primary criteria for any notational reform:

1. To make clearer the function of the staff lines and spaces.
2. To obviate the need for ledger lines, thus keeping all the notes on the staff.
3. To make all octaves have the same relationship to the staff.
4. To abolish the profusion of clef signs.
5. To simplify, or abolish, the accidental signs.
6. To improve the visual aspects of duration.
7. To regulate the indications of measure.
8. To improve the notation of irregular rhythmic values.
9. To facilitate the writing down of music.
10. To make musical typography easier to print and to read.

Even twentieth-century notators would find little here to dispute.

Post-Raymondi by 110 years, Erhard Karkoschka's pioneering survey of twentieth-century notation, <u>Notation in New Music</u>, formulated still another lexicon of standards for any new system of notation:

1. It should possess all the possibilities of traditional notation.
2. It should not go against tradition without good reason.
3. It should have enough new technical possibilities to be able to represent the present stage of musical thinking.
4. It should be capable of presenting complicated structures in a simpler form than does present-day notation.
5. It should have a broad, neutral basis and avoid, if possible, representing any particular style.
6. It should make easier the transition to individual notation forms, e.g., approximate values and musical graphics.
7. It should have no difficulty in being able to represent more than twelve values [intervals] in an octave.
8. What the ear hears must be presented to the eye in such a way that two basic characteristics are taken into consideration: (a) The visual event must be apparent as the direct translation of the auditory event, requiring as few additional thought processes as possible and (b) the individual symbols and the totality of symbols must be formed on an optical basis; they must be "correct" in the visual-psychological sense (9).

At least one of Karkoschka's reform criteria was disputed by British musicologist Hugo Cole in his <u>Sounds and Signs</u> (10). It is a fallacy, he said, that graphic appeal to the eye is essential for a truthful notation. Moreover, simplification per se does not automatically produce a better method of writing down music. This Cole supported by pointing out that many languages -- English being a prime example -- are extremely complex and full of inconsistencies yet are completely efficient once mastered. Even so, Karkoschka's updating of Joseph Raymondi's precepts remains valid, though one might have minor reservations regarding one or the other of his standards.

That meaningful notational reform should not stray too far from the time-tested values of traditional notation is a point wisely taken. Karkoschka's well-expressed rationale for adherence to the proven virtues of our present system holds that "It has survived centuries of attempts at reform, and justifiably. In spite of certain inadequacies it has supported a many-sided musical culture, especially because it presented pitches and durations to the eye in such a way that the sound corresponded directly with the visual event even if the notation was not completely perfect"(11). It is precisely because many of the reforms to be discussed do not achieve this essential synthesis that they have failed to make a lasting impact on the development of notation.

Twentieth-century writers on music are by no means alone in their defense of the indisputable virtues of common-practice notation. We have already commented on Joseph Raymondi's examination of the systems invented before his time, in which he characterized some reforms as "bizarre" and certain others as "reasonable but impractical." A century later a tract entitled La superiorité de la notation usuelle by N. Collet (12) was quite evidently written to refute the exaggerated claims made by some reformers as to the superiority of their own proposals. Even today many composers believe, along with Roberto Gerhard, that traditional notation's very ambiguities are its saving grace. "Despite its undeniable shortcomings," Gerhard declared, "I am not for scrapping traditional notation in favor of diagrams, doodlings, or musikalische Graphik" (13). This composer's personal decision to tolerate the inadequacies of common-practice notation rather than to forge a radically new method of putting down his musical ideas is one that is shared by many of his contemporaries. These defenses of traditional notation cannot, of course, be labeled reactionary, any more than Erhard Karkoschka can be dubbed a philistine because he too extols the merits of our inherited notation while at the same time admitting the compelling necessity for its improvement.

The perceived merits of traditional notation assume even greater validity when measured against the inadequacies, inconsistencies, and downright fuzzy thinking exhibited in system after system devised by the notational reformers. Time and time again one sees imperfections of one element of conventional notation overcome at the expense of another crucial aspect of that notation. If the inventor has succeeded in eliminating the need for accidental signs, let us say, he has at the same time increased the difficulty of distinguishing one notehead from another. If he has devised a numerical or alphabetical method of identifying the various octaves of the piano keyboard, replacing the standard clef signs and 8va indicators, he may have confused the performer by an illogical sequence of those numerals or letters. If he has worked out a clever new manner of indicating durational values, he has more often than not made those distinctions too minute to be easily perceived. If he has invented an ingenious means of outlining one notational parameter, he has unaccountably neglected to consider an equally vital factor -- pitch, but not duration; an unorthodox staff, but no indication of register; individual note duration, but no rests. The list of such inconsistencies could be extended ad infinitum.

If they prove nothing else, however, the proposals to be surveyed attest to the lively imagination of their inventors and to the single-mindedness with which the reformers pursued their objectives. Even an impractical or bizarre innovation has a unique interest not to be devaluated by its failure as an accepted reform. (See Christian Huth's astonishing proposal on page   for a prime specimen.) From the extensive volume of notational chaff to be uncovered we can perhaps extract some kernels of potential value. Among the piles of discarded symbols, impossibly enlarged staves, and arcane stenographic codes, may repose some ideas appropriate for the continuing development of contemporary musical notation.

That this has already been accomplished to a limited degree can be verified by contrasting, let us say, Adolph Decher's 1875 proposal (page 30), or perhaps Hans Wagner's Verein-

fachte Notenschrift of 1888 (page   ), with Earle Brown's
advocacy of "time-notation" (a concept that equates space with
duration) in 1959. Or, even more strikingly, one might compare
the system known as Melographie (1855) of Juan Nepomuceno
Adorno (page 22), with Klavarskribo, invented in 1931 (page
74) -- all based on vertically constructed staves. Few contemporary notational techniques are without such forebears;
many an avant-garde symbol has only been reinvented by a musician of our own day.

Even this extensive survey of notational reform, however,
can be concerned only with innovations designed to improve or
substitute for conventional notation practice. We must turn
to Karkoschka's compendium or Kurt Stone's Music Notation in
the Twentieth Century (14) to study the completely new notation that has evolved from the radical aesthetic of our mid-
century avant-garde, who began to compose material that could
not be adequately recorded with any existing notation. Only
three times in the history of Western music, Stone holds, has
there been such a revolutionary need. First, when monody
evolved into polyphony around the tenth century, durational
notation became necessary; later, harmony took precedence over
linear procedures during the sixteenth and seventeenth centuries, and a score became imperative. Finally, when the conceptual opposites -- minutely strict determinism and deliber-
ate ambiguity and chance -- were both advanced in the middle
of the twentieth century, they brought forth the implicit
graphics, the action notation, and the various aleatoric devices unique to the new kinds of music now being composed. In
consequence, they do not fall within the purpose and scope of
this thesaurus of notational reform.

For the large corpus of music without unique avant-garde
demands, common-practice notation flourishes after three centuries of effort to revise, improve, or supplant it. "Despite
their ingeniousness and their merits," wrote music historian
Alexandre Lavignac, "each of these systems [of new notation],
up to the present, has not been able to demolish the old cus-
toms whose soundness appears impossible to disturb" (15).
Hardly the last word on the subject, of course, but Lavignac
has accurately summed up the present state of affairs. Traditional notation, we may be sure, is not about to be overthrown
-- only refined and its resources strengthened and enlarged.

"Changes will undoubtedly come, as long as music continues to be a living and advancing art, but they will come slow-
ly and gradually, as they have done in the past, and it is
probable that in its general structural principles our notation will last as long as our present system of music" (16).
Though the numerous reforms to be displayed may not remake
our present system of notation, we can each measure in our
own way the potential of what has already been proposed. Time,
we may be sure, will make the ultimate assessment.

NOTES

    1. Percy Scholes, ed., The Oxford Companion to Music,
tenth edition (London: Oxford University Press, 1970),
pp. 690-691.
    2. Robert Hughes, The Shock of the New (New York: Alfred
A. Knopf, 1981), p. 164.
    3. Julian Carrillo, Sistema General de Escritura Musical
(Mexico City: Ediciones Sonidos 13, 1895), p. 9.
    4. Carrillo, p. 9.
    5. Carrillo, p. 18.
    6. Josiah Warren, Written music remodeled and invested
with the simplicity of an exact science (Boston: J. P. Jewett
& Co., 1860), p. 1.
    7. John Barth, "The Literature of Replenishment," Atlan-
tic Monthly (January, 1980), p. 71.
    8. Joseph Raymondi, Examen critique des notations musi-
cales proposées depuis deux siècles (Paris: Libraire Encyclo-
pédique de Roret, 1856).
    9. Erhard Karkoschka, Notation in New Music (New York:
Praeger Publishers, Inc., 1972).
    10. Hugo Cole, Sounds and Signs (London: Oxford University
Press, 1974).
    11. Karkoschka, p. 15.
    12. N. Collet, La superiorité de la notation usuelle
(Paris: the author).
    13. Quoted in John Cage, Notations (New York: Something
Else Press, 1969), unpaged.
    14. Kurt Stone, Music Notation in the Twentieth Century
(New York: W. W. Norton & Company, 1980).
    15. Alexandre Lavignac, Encyclopédie de la musique et dic-
tionnaire du Conservatoire (Paris: Delagrave, 1913-1930).
    16. Notation article, Grove's Dictionary of Music and Musi-
cians, fifth edition (New York: St. Martin's Press, 1964),
vol. 6, p. 123.

2.
Proposed Staff Reforms

The five-line staff with sharps and flats is utterly
fallacious, inappropriate, inadequate, and unsatis-
factory in recording duodecuple music of either
strictly serial or atonally free compositional procedure.

--Marshall Bailey, Duodecuple Notation, 1962.

Of all the traditional elements of music notation, the five-
line staff is the most basic. All other components -- noteheads, clef signs, time signatures, dynamic indications, and
so on -- must be related to the staff. It is not surprising,
then, that since the late seventeeth century the familiar
pentagram has been modified in guises ranging from an aggre-
gation of sixteen or more lines to its complete abolishment
in certain systems based on numbers, letters, or stenographic
codes. It has even been turned on its head, so to speak, and
drawn vertically in a few unorthodox systems.

In our exposition of staff alterations, we shall not deal
with the various tablature notations, based as they were on
specific instrumental requirements and individual performing
techniques. Rather, our survey is concerned only with notational proposals primarily designed to supplant the general
practice of the period, however unrealistic that expectation
may have been.

We may assume, however, that many reformers of traditional
notation -- especially during the eighteenth and nineteenth
centuries -- were to a degree influenced by knowing various
tablature notations of the past. Martin Agricola's ten-line
staff for the organ (1529), Johann Jakob Froberger's 1649 keyboard Toccata using six lines for the right hand and seven for
the left, Renaissance scores for keyboards, lute, guitar,
harp, or the viol family -- all such unconventional staff ar-
rangements surely had their impact on many proposed novel systems. Some reformers may even have had knowledge of those
thirteenth-century vocal scores that used fifteen-line staves.

Nonetheless, the advocates of unorthodox staff formats,
whatever their inspiration, generally had one paramount objective: to eliminate the accidental signs that are essential

in conventional notation. Having had their genesis in tonal-harmonic music, these symbols -- the sharp, the flat, the natural -- have become all but anachronistic in the twentieth century; in today's atonal and dodecaphonic textures, the double-sharp and double-flat are the ultimate anachronisms. Nearly all the new staff designs, therefore, were intended to circumvent these five ancillary symbols, either by setting each chromatic pitch on its individual staff line or space, or by altering the notehead shape, color, or staff position in order to distinguish one pitch from another. These freshly designated staff relationships, usually functioning unchanged from one octave or register to the next, render obsolete even the standard clef signs and 8va indicators.

In their zeal to transcend the limitations and incongruities of the traditional pentagram, the inventors of unorthodox staff formats quite generally succeeded only in substituting new reading problems for old difficulties. Though most of the reforms managed to overcome the requirement for accidental signs, they either gave the eye a markedly wider area to encompass or, conversely, an excessively narrow field of vision in which to comprehend minute pitch distinctions. Few, if any, of the novel systems focused on the main issue. the creation of another staff as simple in design as the conventional pentagram and as logical in its representation of pitch, duration, intensity, and quality of sound.

Perhaps the greatest -- certainly the most persistent -- fallacy of the staff reforms discussed here is their almost exclusive reliance on the keyboard as the basis for reconstruction. In relating the reading of music to the visual analogy of the keyboard, they bypassed the different viewpoints and reading requirements of the singer and of other instrumentalists. A staff format uniquely designed for the ten fingers of the keyboard player performing on an instrument that cannot vary by so much as a tiny fraction the ratios of its pitch frequencies is obviously of limited use for the vocalist, the string player, or the woodwind/brass performer -- all of whom can indeed vary the pitch vibrations they produce. Furthermore, almost without exception these keyboard-oriented proposals remain rooted in the diatonic-chromatic tonal system of the eighteenth to early twentieth centuries; hence, they cannot operate effectively in music that utilizes microtonal techniques.

To facilitate a consensus on a staff designed expressly for chromatic/atonal and microtonal music, the Chroma Foundation published in 1983 their evaluation of thirty-one recent notational proposals, including thirteen discussed in this source book. The Foundation staff contrasted and analyzed staves from three to six lines in various configurations for their suitability, practicality, and ease of comprehension. In the final analysis they endorsed none of the submitted designs without qualification, concluding that ". . . it cannot be the aim to replace traditional notation with a new one. The aim can only be to replace the chaos of uncountable notations by the interchangeable use of two notations, namely the traditional diatonic notation and one new chromatic notation" (1).

Whether or not it is reasonable or practical to expect

the performing musician -- and the composer -- to master <u>two</u>
notational systems is surely debatable. Far better would be
the continued search for a single, all-encompassing mode of
notation flexible enough for any musical style, harmonic language, or degree of complexity. Perhaps a few of the ninety-
nine system proposals that follow may reveal the potential
for such a new and comprehensive staff format.

1764. Roualle de Boisgelou, [Proposal for a new staff].
   Paris: the author.
Staff: 7-line; for increased range the staff may be expanded
   to ten or more lines.
Clef signs: Not mentioned.
Pitch:

C   C# D   D# E F F# G G# A A# B C
    Db   Eb   Gb   Ab   Bb

ut dé ré ma mi fa fi sol bé la sa si ut

Example 2-1. Chorale, <u>Ein' feste Burg ist unser Gott</u>.

As far as can be determined, Boisgelou's staff proposal was
the first to assign each note of the chromatic scale to its
own line or space, thus eliminating the need for accidental
signs before any altered pitches. This principle was to moti-
vate many later notational reforms.
   A staff of seven lines has the great advantage of accommodating a full octave without recourse to ledger lines, either below or above. One obvious disadvantage of Boisgelou's
system, however, is its lack of register identification. As
it was designed for vocal music, one may assume that either
treble or bass voices would read from the same staff, the
latter sounding at the lower octave.

1811. Karl Christian Friedrich Krause, "Über eine verbesserte
   Tonschriftsprache" (Concerning a notational improvement),
   <u>Allgemeine Musikalische Zeitung 30</u>, pp. 358, 447.

Staff: 13-line for one octave, 25-line for two octaves, 37-line for three octaves, and 49-line for four octaves.

Clef signs: An extended pitch bar on C and shorter bars on E and G for easier orientation within the octave:

Pitch:

C   C#   D   D#   E   F   F#   G   G#   A   A#   B   C
    Db   Eb   Gb   Ab   Bb

Duration: Shown by the proportional lengthening of the pitch bar:

, and so on.

Rests: Indicated by blank space.

Dynamics: The pitch symbols are shaded from light to dark to indicate soft to loud.

Example 2-2. J. S. Bach, <u>Chromatic Fantasy and Fugue</u>.

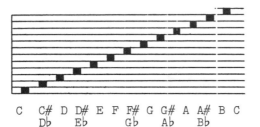

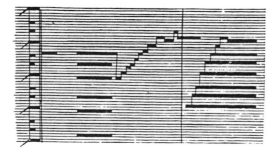

For the year 1811, Krause's was a remarkable proposal for notational reform. A doctor of philosophy and a mathematician,
he devised an unorthodox system that must have stunned his
contemporaries. Krause revealed, however, that although he
had conceived his reform eight years before its publication,
it was only at the insistence of his friends and academic colleagues that he issued his definitive statement in the <u>Allge-
meine Musikalische Zeitung</u>.

A firm believer in the principle that the eye should see
what the ear hears, Krause justified his greatly extended
staff by insisting that each tone in any instrumental or vocal
register should always occupy its own individual position on
a staff, and that the number of staff lines should depend on
the total range of the particular instrument or voice. Furthermore, his system required only one form, instead of twenty-four, for notating the twenty-four major and minor keys.
In consequence, he maintained, sight-reading in any key became "ten times easier" than in traditional notation.

Capping his summation, Krause affirmed that his system
was perfect (the systems are invariably perfect in the inventor's eye!) for music designed for the newly invented chromatic keyboard on which the keys were alternately white and
black. He anticipated criticism of his proposal -- which he
most assuredly received -- but still contended that in time
all the great masterpieces of music would be transcribed into
his <u>verbesserte Tonschriftsprache</u>. Bad music, he could not resist adding, would never be so honored.

Krause's greatly enlarged staff anticipated by more than
a century two similarly constructed staves to be found in
Earle Brown's <u>Synergy</u> for piano of 1956 (50 lines) and the
gargantuan staff of 106 lines in the <u>Five Pieces for David
Tudor</u> (1959) by the Italian avant-gardist Sylvano Bussotti.
Furthermore, Krause's device of outlining duration by extending his pitch symbols proportionately predates the "time-notation" first used by Brown in his <u>Hodograph I</u> of 1959.

1811. Johann Friedrich Christian Werneberg, <u>Allgemeinen neuen
    viel einfacheren Musik-Schule</u> (General plan for simplifying
    the teaching of music). Gotha, Germany: C. Steudel.
Staff: 6-line.
Clef signs: Not discussed.
Pitch:

C   C#   D   D#   E   F   F#   G   G#   A   A#   B   C
    Db   Eb   Gb   Ab   Bb

Example 2-3.

Designed for the teaching of music in the elementary schools
of Germany, Werneberg's staff provides the same advantage as
the seven-line format advocated by Boisgelou (page 11): the
chromatic scale can be confined entirely on the staff, with
no need for ledger lines. One disadvantage is the depiction
of interval size: thirds look like fourths or fifths, to give
one example.

1819. L.D.F. Dumouchel, <u>Notation clavigraphique</u> (Keyboard
    graphic notation). Paris: the author.
Staff: 5-line (3-2).
Clef signs: Not mentioned.
Pitch:

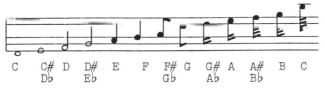

C   C# D   D# E   F   F# G   G# A   A# B   C
     Db   Eb   Gb   Ab   Bb

Example 2-4.

It is not surprising that Dumouchel, as a pupil of the celebrated pianist-composer John Field, should orient his notational innovation toward the keyboard. His proposal, however,
is unique in that it apparently represents the first time that
the staff lines were arranged to parallel the physical layout
of the piano keyboard, the spaces representing the white keys
and the lines the black keys. This organizational principle
would appear again in 1870 in the system proposed by Horton
Wright (U.S. Patent 104,393), in Thomas Howells' <u>Settled Notation Music System which facilitates reading music in all keys
alike for piano</u> (2), and with increasing frequency thereafter.
Each inventor was evidently unaware of comparable previous
attempts to modify the standard five-line staff in this fashion.

1832. Treuille de Beaulieu, "Résumé d'un nouveau mode d'écriture musicale" (Summary of a new musical notation), <u>Revue Musicale de Fétis XII</u>, p. 281.
Staff: 6-line (3-3).
Register symbols:

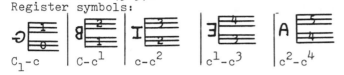

C_1-c   C-c^1 c-c^2 c^1-c^3 c^2-c^4

Pitch:

ré mi fa sol la si ut ré

Duration: Traditionally notated, except that certain beamed note groups are written as follows:

 , for example.

Example 2-5. Chorale, <u>Ein' feste Burg is unser Gott</u>.

The primary advantage of Beaulieu's six-line staff is its accommodation of two full octaves without the use of ledger lines. An eccentric element in the system, however, is that the scale syllables begin with <u>ré</u> rather than with <u>ut</u> (or <u>do</u>), though <u>ut</u> represents the tonic pitch of any key. Also idiosyncratic is the notation of the two-note groupings illustrated above, a departure from the traditional format quite unexpected in this period.

1837. Anonymous, <u>Nouveau système de notation musicale, suivi d'un essai sur la nomenclature des sons musicaux, par un ancien professeur de mathématiques</u> (New system of notation, including an explanation of the naming of musical sounds, by an old mathematics professor). Paris: the author.

Staff: 6-line (2-1-1-2); four staves are used as a keyboard
   system.
Clef signs: None; the upper two staves are for the right hand,
   the lower two for the left hand. Also, the pitch symbols for
   the right hand are darker than those for the left hand.
Pitch:

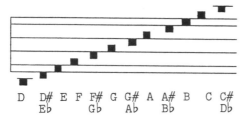

D   D#   E   F   F#   G   G#   A   A#   B   C   C#
     Eb   Gb   Ab   Bb   Db

Duration: Shown proportionately by the length of the pitch
   symbol. Dots are used to mark off the smallest units within
   the barlines.
Rests: Indicated by blank space.
Example 2-6.

This anonymous "old mathematics professor" was evidently an
amateur musician of sorts, hence his interest in music notation. His primary background undoubtedly influenced his approach to musical duration, which is here measured mathemati-
cally. For this experimenter, space equaled time, a basic concept that was to be constantly rediscovered by composers and
theorists throughout the nineteenth century, and into our own
time. It is quite likely that this inventor knew of Karl
Krause's 1811 proposal (see page 12); his own system is a
rational refinement of that earlier reform.

1838. François Ange Alexandre Blein, <u>Principes de mélodie et</u>
<u>d'harmonie déduits de la théorie des vibrations</u> (Melodic and
harmonic principles based on the theory of vibrations).
Paris: Bachelier.
Staff: 6-line.
Clef signs: Standard G-clef, positioned as shown below.
Pitch:

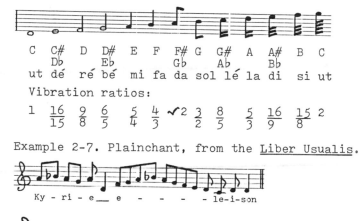

Vibration ratios:

Example 2-7. Plainchant, from the <u>Liber Usualis</u>.

Ky - ri - e__ e - - - - - le-i-son

Undoubtedly influenced by the earlier proposals of Boisgelou
and Werneberg, in which each pitch of the chromatic scale occupied its own line or space, Blein's pioneering treatise
also incorporated his personal research in the field of sound
vibration. He had already published his <u>Théorie des vibrations</u>
<u>et son application à divers phénomènes de physique</u> (3), a no-
table contribution to an area of music that attracted many
nineteenth-century musicians, though few pursued their research with Blein's zeal and perseverance.

Baron Blein designed his six-line staff particularly for
the newly invented chromatic keyboard (<u>mélochrome</u>) of alternating white and black keys, an instrument that had earlier
interested Karl Krause (see page 13). To facilitate reading
music written for this novel keyboard, Blein added a further
refinement: On the top and bottom of the white keys he painted
colored bands -- red for C, violet for D, blue for E, green
for F#/Gb, yellow for G#/Ab, and orange for A#/Bb. This striking visual device was only one of the many <u>mélochrome</u> variations introduced during this period, but none seem to have
inspired the creation of a significant body of literature expressly for the instrument.

1838. Michel Eisenmenger, <u>Traité sur l'art graphique et la</u>
<u>mécanique appliqués à la musique</u> (Treatise on graphic art
and its mechanics applied to music). Paris: Gesselin.

Staff: 6-line (2-3-1); the outer lines are heavy.
Register symbols:

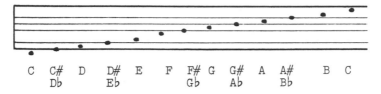

C_1-B_1 |C-B|c-b|c^1-b^1|c^2-b^2|c^3-b^3|c^4-b^4

Pitch:

C	C#	D	D#	E	F	F#	G	G#	A	A#	B	C
	Db		Eb			Gb		Ab		Bb		

Key signatures: Shown by the noteheads that outline the tonic
    triad of the tonality.

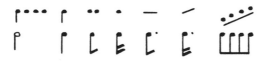

= Eb major;   = B minor, for example.

Duration:

Example 2-8.

Staves with heavily drawn outer lines seem to have intrigued
many a notational reformer of the nineteenth century, Eisenmenger among them. What sets his proposal apart, however, is
the visual analogy with the piano keyboard in its arrangement
of the two- and three-line segments, a format first suggested

by Dumouchel (page 14). Unfortunately, Eisenmenger's solution
for rhythm does not match the rational grasp of his novel
staff and his accurate pitch delineation. His durational distinctions are not logically depicted, and they are certainly
inadequate for all but the most routine and elementary note
values.

1843. Joseph Raymondi, <u>Essai de simplification musicograph-</u>
    <u>ique, avec un précis analytique des principaux systèmes de</u>
    <u>notation musicale proposés depuis le sixième siècle</u> (Attempt
    to simplify musical graphics, with an analytical survey of
    the principal systems of musical notation proposed since the
    sixth century). Paris: Bernard-Latte.
Staff: 2-line, spaced two lines apart.
Clef signs:

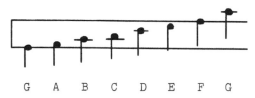

 S = Sol (G).

Pitch:

G   A   B   C   D   E   F   G

This staff system -- the first of several proposals put forward by Raymondi, an indefatigable chronicler of notational
reform -- was designed solely for vocal music of restricted
range. The staff is essentially one of four lines; the middle
two lines appear only as ledger lines when required.

1847. Amadeus Autodidactos (pseud. for Heinrich Friedrich Wil-
    helm Richter), <u>Aphorismen über Musik</u> (Aphorisms on music).
    Leipzig: In commission bei C. A. Klemm.
Staff: 5-line.
Clef signs: Traditional G- and F-clefs.
Pitch:

C   C#   D   D#   E   F   F#   G   G#   A   A#   B   C
    Db   Eb   Gb   Ab   Bb

Example 2-9.

The novelty of the Autodidactus proposal lies not in staff or noteheard modification but in placing each pitch of the chromatic scale on its individual line or space. This simple device for avoiding the use of accidentals became the <u>raison d'être</u> of countless subsequent reforms, whether or not other elements were also altered. Reading intervals so notated, however, can be disconcerting to the traditionally trained musician. Stepwise progressions look like leaps of the third, thirds like fifths, and fifths like octaves -- a visual hazard also present in the reform of Werneberg (see page 13). Thus what is gained in one respect in both proposals is lost in another.

1851. F. A. Adams, <u>The Octave Staff; Diatonic and Chromatic; Reducing the Different Staves to One; Furnishing an Exclusive Place for Each Tone, without Flats or Sharps</u>. New York: Appleton & Co.
Staff: 6-line (1-2-1-2); the lowest line is heavy. Additional full or partial staves are used to extend the range.
Clef signs: None.
Pitch:

| A | A# | B | C | C# | D | D# | E | F | F# | G | G# | A |
| | Bb | | | Db | | Eb | | | Gb | | Ab | |

Meter: A large-sized numerator only, centered on the D-line, as shown below.
Example 2-10.

The premise of Adams' suggested reform -- placing each note
of the chromatic scale on its own line or space -- is admirable, but his solution is inadequate. There is little logic in
using duplicated single and double staff lines separated by
unused space, just to avoid placing notes in the spaces between the two-line segments. Though all the natural pitches
are solely on lines and all sharped or flatted notes occupy
only spaces, to notate a full octave requires inordinate vertical room. For any music with an extended gamut the system
becomes unwieldy to an extreme.

1855. Juan-Nepomuceno Adorno, <u>Mélographie, ou nouvelle nota-
tion musicale</u> (Melograph, a new musical notation). Paris:
Firmin Didot frères.
Staff: 5-line (2-3), drawn vertically.
Register symbols:

1re OCTAVE.	2e OCTAVE.	3e OCTAVE.	4e OCTAVE.	5e OCTAVE.	6e OCTAVE.
C_1-B_1	C-B	c-b	c^1-b^1	c^2-b^2	c^3-b^3

Pitch: Adorno's system is divided into two parts: In the
first, termed <u>Système mélographique relatif</u>, small black
noteheads are used, their stems on the upper side of the
noteheads. To distinguish sharps from flats in a tonal context, the former are written as > and the latter as <.

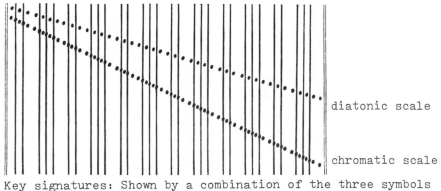

diatonic scale

chromatic scale

Key signatures: Shown by a combination of the three symbols
   demonstrated below. To distinguish a sharp from a flat tonality, the upper two symbols are reversed in position. The
   lowest symbol is borrowed from that used as an accidental
   sign.

Duration: Traditionally expressed.
Example 2-11. Franz Schubert, <u>Sonata in C Minor</u>, op. posth.

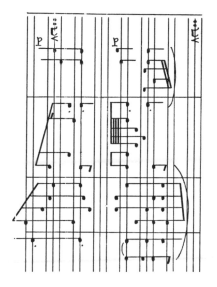

Evidently for the first time in the history of western musical notation, and predating the modern Klavarskribo by almost
a century (see page 74), the staff format advocated by Adorno
is vertically rather than horizontally constructed. Its segments of two and three lines conform, therefore, to the visual
arrangement of the white and black keys of the keyboard instruments, and it is read from top to bottom of the staff.
Thus, from low to high pitch is outlined from left to right,
and durational progress moves from top to bottom of each measure -- the exact reversal of our traditional manner of reading music.

     Once again we have a notational concept that is more suc-
cessful in principle than in practice because it requires a
complete visual reorientation. Furthermore, Adorno's scheme
perpetuates an exclusive keyboard approach, a method of notation that is not conspicuously helpful to other instrumentalists or to vocalists. Daring as Adorno's reform was at the
time of its invention, it was soon forgotten, to be reinvented
only at the end of the nineteenth century by Paternoster (page
42) and by several twentieth-century theorists. Among these
later attempts to construct the staff in a vertical manner,
only Klavarskribo can claim to have achieved a measure of
acceptance.

1856. Eugène Cornier, Traité de l'art musical précédé de
   Echelle Tricolore (Treatise on the art of music based on
   the tricolored staff). Vaugirard, France: A. Choisnet.
Staff: 5-line; lines 1 and 4 are dotted.
Clef signs: None; one staff serves both the treble (black
   notes) and the bass (red notes), the latter sounding one
   octave lower.

Pitch: To create the échelle mobile tricolore the staff lines
   are colored as indicated to point up the half-steps in any
   diatonic scale, ut being the tonic note of any key.

—black
⌐dotted red
⌐black
⌐green
dotted green

ut ré mi fa sol la si ut

Example 2-12. Franz Josef Haydn, Sonatina in F.

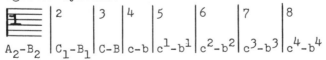

Designed, so its author said, to facilitate transposition and
to eliminate ledger lines, Cornier's novel staff is made to do
double duty in accommodating the notes usually spread between
two staves. Reading music on his single staff is disconcerting,
however, as the bass notes are frequently notated above the
treble pitches, and one must remember to transpose them to the
lower octave. The two colors with which the treble and bass
notes are printed are a welcome, and essential, aid to the eye.
Nonetheless, Cornier's reform made little impact on his contemporaries, and it was quickly forgotten.

1860. Josiah Warren, Written music remodeled and invested with
   the simplicity of an exact science. Boston: J. P. Jewett
   & Co.
Staff: 6-line; two staves constitute a keyboard system.
Register symbols:

A_2-B_2 |C_1-B_1| C-B | c-b |c^1-b^1|c^2-b^2|c^3-b^3|c^4-b^4

Pitch:

C   C# D   D# E   F   F# G   G# A   A# B   C
    Db   Eb   Gb   Ab   Bb

Oddly enough, for the diatonic scale of seven notes, Warren relied on the standard pentagram.

Duration:

= 1 beat, or $\frac{1}{6}$ sec. | = 2 beats, or $\frac{1}{3}$ sec.

= 3 beats, or $\frac{3}{6}$ sec.

or:

Rests: __ = 1 beat; ── = 2 beats; ≡ = 3 beats, and so on.

Meter: Conventionally displayed, each beat equaling 4/6ths of a second.

Dynamics:

pp   p   mp   mf   f   ff

Example 2-13. J. S. Bach, "Bourée II," from English Suite no. 2.

Although this system may be invested with the simplicity of an
exact science, as its inventor maintained, it is debatable
whether this simplicity achieves ready comprehension. Warren's
notation of pitch is clear enough, but to indicate note duration he vacillates between varying stem lengths and horizontal slashes beneath the noteheads. And, because duration here
is related to unspecified measure beats rather than to strict
orthochronic values, it becomes almost impossible to delineate clearly such factors as irregular note-groups. Even so,
Warren's beaming device for note-groups containing rests (see
example under Duration) makes a notable reappearance in countless contemporary scores, in particular those of Elliott Car-
ter and imitators of his notational devices:
Example 2-14.

In addition to certain rhythmic insufficiencies, Warren's
notation sets the visual hurdle of varying the notehead size
to indicate the degree of intensity called for by the composer. Over a hundred years later, the Polish avant gardist Boguslaw Schäffer attempted to incorporate similar notehead distinction in his _Azione a due_ -- and with the same predictable
result: an unreasonable interpretive demand from composer to
performer (see page 258).

1866. John C. Clime, _Musical Staff_. U.S. Patent 52,534.
Staff: 14-line; in essence, thin supplementary lines are inserted between the five lines of a pentagram to provide a
   greatly expanded staff. When required, ledger lines either
   below or above the staff are continuous.
Clef signs: Not mentioned.
Pitch:

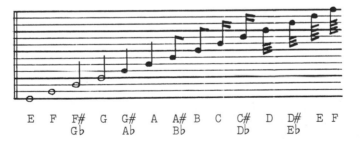

Example 2-15.

"It has been my object," Clime said, "to produce a staff in
which the true position of each note [both] in the scale and
in relation to adjacent notes will be instantly observed, so
that the pupil will not be obliged to pause in order to cal-
culate the effect of signs [accidentals] to which he can only
become accustomed by constant and long continued practice. ...
By the use of a staff thus formed the pupil quickly learns
the position of the semitones on the staff in the various
keys, and is thus enabled, after a short course of study, to
transpose a piece from one key to another."

The purely pedagogical basis of Clime's proposed staff is
evident, but one wonders if his hypothetical student found the
staff easier to master than the familiar pentagram. The principle behind Clime's invention is clear and, in a way, quite
logical, but in practice it becomes unduly cumbersome. Any
staff that makes use only of its lines (or of its spaces) is
extended beyond one's easy reading comprehension. The problem
is even more severe than in the previous proposals of Werneberg and Autodidactus; here, to the eye, intervals of the
third become sevenths, and a sixth assumes the appearance of
two octaves and a fifth, as demonstrated in the illustration
above.

1868. Walter Craig, <u>Octave System of Musical Notation</u>. London:
the author.
Staff: 5-line; the outer lines are black and the three center
lines are red.
Clef signs: The letters are printed in Italian type for the
treble register and in Roman type for the bass register.

Pitch: No notes are ever set in the second staff space.

C   D   E   F   G   A   B   C

Example 2-16. Chorale, <u>Ein' feste Burg ist unser Gott</u>.

The primary virtue of Craig's system lies in the flexibility of his "floating" clef signs, allowing the octave of any scale to be contained on the staff, from bottom to top line. Because these outer lines always bear the tonic pitch of whatever key is in operation, they are differently colored for easy identification. But distinguishing staff lines of contrasting color do pose a practical problem: They add substantially to the cost of printing, which we may assume to be one reason why Craig's Octave System made little impact on the musical notation of his time.

1868. Philetus Phillips, Improvement in Musical Notation. U.S. Patent 75,572.
Staff: 7-line, the basic matrix from which seven different 5-line staves are derived. Each of these seven lines is used as the lowest line of a new staff, the four higher lines alternating the line numbers as indicated below.
Basic staff: Derived staves:

Clef signs: Standard G-clef.
Pitch:

D D# Eb E F F# Gb G G# Ab A A# Bb B C C# Db D

Example 2-17.

Phillips created his seven hybrid staves, he maintained, to
facilitate transposition into any tonality. Through his self-
proclaimed ingenuity, "The position of the notes, both in the
natural and transposed scales, is ascertained at a glance, and
they are read, without any study or perplexity, by the peculiar character of the line on which each particular note is
written."

   Realizing that no printer would take on these "peculiar
characters," the undaunted inventor suggested an alternative
equally impractical -- seven differently constituted barlines
applied to a conventional staff:
Example 2-18.

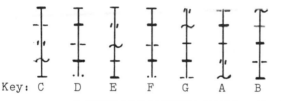

Key: C   D   E   F   G   A   B

1870. Gustave Decher, <u>Rationellen Lehrgebäude der Tonkunst</u>
   (Rational teaching course of music). Munich: the author.
Staff: 6-line (3-3); two staves create a keyboard system.
Register symbols:

C_1-B_1 | C-B | c-b | c^1-b^1 | c^2-b^2 | c^3-b^3 | c^4-b^4

Pitch:

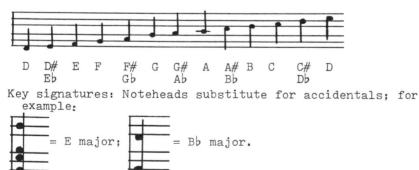

D   D# E   F   F# G   G# A   A# B   C   C# D
    Eb   Gb   Ab   Bb   Db

Key signatures: Noteheads substitute for accidentals; for
   example:

= E major;   = Bb major.

Duration:

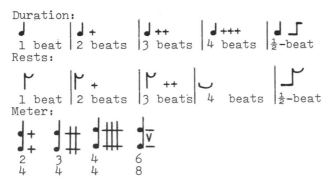

Example 2-19. Ludwig van Beethoven, <u>Sonata in A-flat</u>, op. 110.

Designed to simplify the teaching of music, this proposal does eliminate the need for accidental signs -- a plus; it is inadequate for clearly indicating duration -- a decided minus. Also, far from lightening the students' solfege labors, Decher burdened them by using the lower-case letters <u>a</u> to <u>m</u> (omitting <u>j</u>) for the twelve pitches of the chromatic octave, a procedure basically unessential to the overall effectiveness and validity of his system. Why did he not give pitch reference by number, 1 to 12, a simple and logical plan, and one endorsed by countless theorists of the nineteenth and twentieth centuries?

1875. Adolph Decher, <u>Chromographische Darstellung der Tondichtungen</u> (Graphical chromatic representation of musical sound). Munich: Theodor Ackermann.

Staff: 12-line; lines 1 and 2 are heavily drawn and lines 7
   and 8 are broken.
Register symbols:

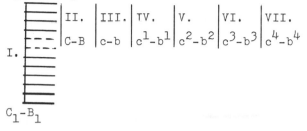

C_1-B_1

Pitch:

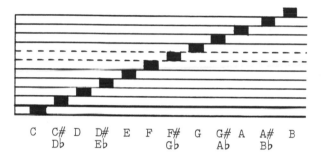

C C# D D# E F F# G G# A A# B
   Db   Eb   Gb   Ab   Bb

Duration: Shown by the proportional length of the pitch symbol between evenly spaced barlines; for example:

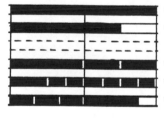

= 2 beats (♩)
= 1½ beats (♩.)
= 1 beat and 2 ½-beats (♩ ♫)
= ½ beat and 6 ¼-beats (♫ ♬)
= 3 ⅓-beats and a ¾-beat (𝅘𝅥𝅘𝅥𝅘𝅥 ♩. 𝄿)
3

Rests: Shown by the proportional length of blank space between the barlines, as illustrated above.
Dynamics: The degrees of intensity, from ff to pp, are indicated by shadings of the pitch symbols:

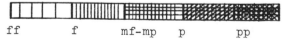

ff   f   mf-mp   p   pp

Example 2-20.

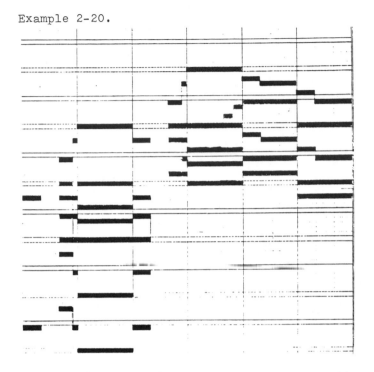

An intriguing extension of Decher's preoccupation with color
and shading, illustrated in his unique proposal, appears in
his suggested notation of orchestral scores, where each instrument has a differently colored or shaded part. Visually,
the notation bears a striking resemblance to certain contemporary scores that subscribe to "time-notation" procedures.
Comparison might also be made with the 1811 reform of Karl
Krause (page 12) and the anonymously proposed system of 1837
(page 16), both of which advocated rectangular pitch bars that
are elongated to show duration.

1877. Gustave Decher, <u>Tonschrift für das gleichstufige Ton-
system in ihrer Anwendung für die chromatische Klaviatur</u>
(Notation for the system of equal tones applied to the chro-
matic keyboard). Munich: Verlag des Vereines Chroma.
Staff: 7-line; the outer lines are heavy.
Register symbols:

I	II	III	IV	V	VI	VII
A_1-G	A-g	a-g^1	a^1-g^2	a^2-g^3	a^3-g^4	a^4-c^5

Pitch:

| A | A#
Bb | B | C | C#
Db | D | D#
Eb | E | F | F#
Gb | G | G#
Ab | A |

(a   b   c   d   e   f   g   h i k   l   m   a)

Duration: Each beat is set off by a thin line, in contrast to the measure barlines, which are heavy. The durational values are calculated according to seconds; each beat equals one second.

Rests: Shown by empty space between the notes or beat lines.

Example 2-21. Chorale, <u>Ermuntre dich, mein schwacher Geist</u>.

This second proposal of Decher was expressly designed for the new chromatic keyboard of alternating white and black keys. Bearing this premise in mind, we can credit the author with inventing a perfectly logical notation for the new instrument, the chromatic scale being fully accommodated on the seven lines of the staff. Duration, however, is not as clearly designated as in Decher's 1870 proposal.

1878. Albert Hahn, <u>Vorstudie zur Notenschrift</u> (Introduction to notation). Place and publisher unknown.

Staff: 11-line; the central line is wavy and lines 3 and 9 are heavy. Two full staves constitute a keyboard system.

Register symbols:

C-B c-b c^1-b^1 c^2-b^2

Pitch:

C C# D D# E F F# G G# A A# B C
  Db   Eb   Gb   Ab   Bb

Duration: As a general rule, Hahn advocated using longer rath-
    er than shorter note-values; thus, sixteenth-notes would be-
    come eighths, quarter-notes would become half-notes, and so
    on. The prime object seems to have been to reduce the num-
    ber of stems, flags, and beams common to conventional nota-
    tion. Because double whole-notes would appear frequently in
    this scheme, Hahn suggested a new format: ♩ instead of ▯ .
Meter: Only the numerator is given; the denominator value is
    implicit in the note-values used. For example:

 = $\frac{4}{2}$

Example 2-22. Ludwig van Beethoven, <u>Sonata in A-flat</u>, op. 110.

In the transcription above, Hahn multiplied all note-values
by a factor of one to four, thus eliminating all flags and
beams except for the single group of thirty-seconds (now
eighths). In so doing, however, Hahn poses a psychological
problem. To modern musicians, long note-values usually suggest very slow tempi. Performing Beethoven's music from Hahn's
notation, a pianist today would very likely not convey the

composer's original concept of a moderate tempo (Moderato can-
tabile molto espressivo).

1878. Gustave Levasseur, <u>Nouvelle portée musicale facilitant
la lecture et l'écriture de la musique</u> (A new musical staff
which facilitates the reading and writing of music). Paris:
the author.
Staff: 3-line; two to four staves are usually combined as a
system.
Clef signs: As shown below. When four staves are used, the
upper three staves carry the G-clef sign.
Pitch:

C   D   E   F   G   A   B

Key signatures: The accidentals are placed on the appropriate
lines or spaces.
Example 2-23. Franz Josef Haydn, <u>Sonatina in F</u>.

Levasseur's is one of the earliest staff proposals to advocate
a reduction rather than an increase in the number of lines.
In actuality, his staff -- for both treble and bass registers
-- is the normal treble staff minus the top two lines. The
bass staff is read like the treble, one or two octaves lower.
Obviously, the system is designed for music of a simple, uncomplicated nature; its principal advantage is that all registers are read alike.

1883. August Wilhelm Ambros, <u>Das System Ambros</u> (The Ambros
system). Vienna: Leuckart.
Staff: 6-line; three lines are solid and three are dotted. Two
to four staves make up a keyboard system.

Register symbols:

A_2-B_2 | II C_1-B_1 | III $C-B$ | IV $c-b$ | V c^1-b^1 | VI c^2-b^2 | VII c^3-b^3 | VIII c^4-b^4

Pitch:

C C# D D# E F F# G G# A A# B C
   Db   Eb   Gb   Ab   Bb

Key signatures: Unstemmed noteheads on the appropriate staff
   lines and spaces substitute for the conventional accidentals. For example:

= Bb major or
  G minor, $\frac{3}{4}$

= A major or
  F# minor, $\frac{4}{4}$

Meter: The numerator only, centered on the three solid lines.

Example 2-24. Franz Schubert, Sonata in C Minor, op. posth.

Composer, musicologist, and music critic, Ambros also attend-
ed law school and became a public prosecutor -- an intriguing
blend of professional endeavors. His major musicological treatise, the Geschichte der Musik, was published in Vienna in
1860.

   Ambros' novel staff has the advantage of placing each half-
step of the octave on its own line or space. It is, however,
unnecessarily confusing to read, especially when it involves
a series of contiguous octaves. Presumably, the division of
the staff into three solid and three broken lines marks the

tritone separation of the two equal halves of the octave, and thus serves as a reading aid. Whether the device accomplishes this objective is something each performer would need to test in practical use.

1885. William Lundie, <u>The Broad Line Staff: A New and Easy Method of Reading Music</u>. Edinburgh: the author.
Staff: 5-line; the heavy outer lines never accommodate note-heads.
Clef signs:

 – C, and  – C.

Pitch:

F   G   A   B   C   D   E   F
Example 2-25.

As the heavy outer lines of Lundie's staff are never used, his staff is actually one of only three lines. Its function is very similar to the three-line staves earlier proposed by Beaulieu (page 15) and Levasseur (page 35). Except as a frame, these distinguishing outer lines seem to serve no useful or compelling purpose.

1886. Kalo Morven, <u>Notation-Morven</u>. Paris: the author.
Staff: 6-line; the outer lines are heavily drawn.
Clef signs: Not mentioned.
Pitch:

C   D   E   F   G   A   B   C
Example 2-26.

Was it purely by coincidence that two musicians -- one living
in France, the other in England -- should in the same year
both propose a musical staff with heavily drawn outer lines?
It does not seem likely that Morven and William Lundie could
have known about each other's invention, yet their innovations
have interesting parallels. Lundie's unused heavy lines frame
what is essentially a three-line staff; Morven's six lines
function as a normal five-line staff, with the first ledger
line below made permanent.

Since the diatonic scale C to C requires only four lines,
not six, we can question the logic of Morven's plan. Nor is
there a compelling reason for his thick outer lines -- a weakness we shall encounter again in the proposal of Müller-Braunau (page 40).

1887. Isaac Jackson Cogswell, The American System of Notation
    for Vocal Music. An Easy, Concise and Comprehensive Method
    of Notation. Fredonia, Kansas: the author.
Staff: 5-line; lines two and four are heavily drawn.
Clef signs: As shown below, and used for all voices.
Pitch:

Example 2-27.

"In presenting the American System . . . I will not descant
upon the defects of other systems, but offer it upon its own
merits, believing that an examination of its principles and
features will convince all of its superiority and completeness. It is <u>simple</u>, <u>concise</u>, comprehensive. Please examine.
(THE INVENTOR.)"

So wrote Cogswell concerning his proposal for new vocal
notation, in words that by now have a thrice-familiar ring.
Simple the system surely is, and concise, too. But comprehensive it most assuredly is not. Admittedly adequate for hymns
and uncomplicated songs, Cogswell's method is too primitive
for music of a more complex texture and sophisticated style.

1889. J. H. Kob, <u>The Note System of Music</u>. Valley Falls, Kan-
   sas: the author.
Staff: 5-line (1-3-1).
Clef signs: None; the upper staff serves the right hand, the
   lower staff, the left hand.
Pitch:

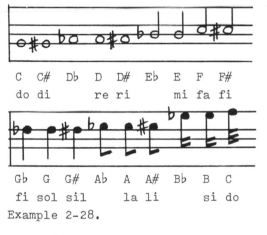

Example 2-28.

A. 4-4.

It is unclear why this inventor bypassed a stepwise progression
between the two pitches in each of the wide staff spaces (A to
B in the C-major scale). From C up to A the diatonic pitches
move from line to space, but from A to B they move from space
to space. Likewise inconsistent is Kob's retention of the standard accidental signs; the primary object of any radical staff
reform is the suppression of these ancillary symbols.

1890, Henry Müller-Braunau, <u>Die Vereinfachung der musikalischen
   Notenschrift</u> (The simplification of musical notation). Ham-
   burg: the author.
Staff: 3-line; the outer lines are thicker.
Clef signs: Not known.
Pitch:

   C   D   E   F   G   A   B   C
Example 2-29.

Müller-Braunau's three-line staff, notating the diatonic
pitches of one octave, duplicates the 1798 proposal of Karl
Horstig (see page 294), except for the use of heavily drawn
outer lines. As with the previously discussed staves of Lundie
and Morven (page 37), the function of these distinguishing
lines is unclear.

1894. Leopold Engelke, <u>Neues System der Musikschrift</u> (New notational system). Bremen: Schweers & Haake.
Staff: 7-line; the central and outer lines are heavy. Two
staves are used as a keyboard system.
Register symbols:

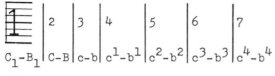

C_1-B_1 | C-B | c-b | c^1-b^1 | c^2-b^2 | c^3-b^3 | c^4-b^4

Pitch:

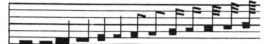

C C# D D# E F F# G G# A A# B C
   Db   Eb   Gb   Ab   Bb

Key signatures: These are designated by syllables derived from
an elaborate solfege terminology:
(Do   Re   Mi Fa   Sol   La   Si)

Da De Ga Ge Ma Me Fa Fe La Le Sa Se

C C# D D# E F F# G G# A A# B
   Db   Eb   Gb   Ab   Bb

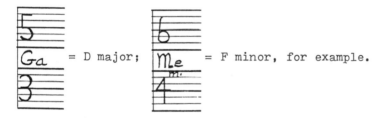

= D major;   = F minor, for example.

Duration: All note symbols are solid oblong or square in
shape, according to their values as illustrated under Pitch.
Rests:

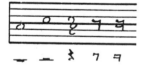

Meter: Conventionally indicated, centered on the staff, but
the time signature is set before the register number rather
than after it.

Example 2-30. Franz Schubert, <u>Sonata in C Minor</u>, op. posth.

Engelke's <u>Neues System</u> could logically be considered under the umbrella of staff modification or of new notehead symbology. Both elements are radically altered in his proposal, following earlier experiments with a three-line staff using conventional noteheads. This plan he discarded in favor of the more exotic system just illustrated.

In his use of meter signatures, Engelke was more orthodox than in his septilinear staff and rectangular note-forms. He was adamantly opposed to using the symbol C to represent 4/4, or common-time, measure, and ¢ for 2/2 meter. All time signatures, he firmly believed, should always display the true values of both numerator and denominator -- a principle with which modern notators would not disagree.

1894. W. Paternoster, <u>Notenblatt zur Benutzung beim Erlernen das Klavierspiele</u> (Examples to be used when learning to play the piano). Gorlitz, Germany: the author.
Staff: 13-line, arranged vertically like a grid beneath a pictogram of the piano keyboard, as shown below. At least five contiguous staves are used as a keyboard system; the central staff segment accommodates the octave of middle C.
Register symbols: None.

Pitch: Each note of the chromatic octave is placed in its appropriate grid square, as shown below. Note-stems are always
   on the lower side of the noteheads.

Duration: Heavy horizontal bars divide each measure into the
   required number of beat subdivisions, each fraction contained in one grid box, plus one empty space before the barline.
   Individual pitch values are notated traditionally, but ori-
   ented vertically, as shown above.
Consciously or unconsciously, Paternoster's staff format
clearly derives from the 1855 proposal by Adorno (see page 22).
The concept in this case is more successful as an abstract
theory than as practical notation, however, for the visual
complexity of Paternoster's grid creates formidable reading
problems. And against the practicality of a separate box for
each chromatic pitch and fractional time-value we must weigh
the unclear delineation of irrational rhythmic groups -- even
a simple triplet. In compound time such groups of three can
be accommodated by the requisite number of grid boxes; in simple time, the present scheme offers no proper solution.

1896. E. Walter, _Notenliniensystem_ (New staff system). Warm-
   brunn, Germany: the author.
Staff: 8-line (3-2-3); two staves used for keyboard music.
Register symbols:

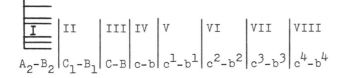

A_2-B_2 | C_1-B_1 | C-B | c-b | c^1-b^1 | c^2-b^2 | c^3-b^3 | c^4-b^4

Pitch:

F   F#   G   G#   A   A#   B   C   C#   D   D#   E   F
     Gb   Ab   Bb   Db   Eb

Rests: The traditional symbols are centered on the 2-line
    staff segment.
Meter: Displayed as a fraction, as shown below.
Example 2-31. German student song, <u>Gaudeamus igitur</u>.

Walter's double eight-line staff is an extended version of
earlier keyboard-oriented designs. The two full staves are
separated by a two-line segment that appears only in the form
of ledger lines when required. The eighteen lines thus provided serve a gamut of three and one-half octaves. Further
range extensions could be accomplished by adding other staff
segments below or above the primary staves.
    Once again, the point must be made that, although this un-
wieldy staff format is logical for the keyboard performer, it
is less than practical for the singer and other instrumentalists.

1896. E. L. Young, <u>The Keyboard System</u>. London: the author.
Staff: 8-line (3-2-3). The two staves of a piano system are
    separated by two ledger lines representing C#/Db and D#/Eb.
Clef signs:

    D#/Eb
    C#/Db

Pitch:

F F# G G# A A# B C C# D D# E F
   Gb   Ab   Bb   Db   Eb
Example 2-32.

This system is but one more manifestation of the keyboard
staff, here arranged as three plus two lines with an added
three-line segment above for extended range.

1897. Walter H. Thelwall, <u>"Note for Note" Musical Notation.
A new notation based on the true relations of sounds used in
music, and representing those sounds by notes only; without
any subsidiary signs -- sharps, flats, naturals, etc., used
in the old notation.</u> London: Chappell & Co., Ltd.
Staff: 7-line; the central line is heavy. When two staves are
used as a keyboard system, they are separated by a broken
line, also heavy, and two thinner broken lines on either
side, which serve as ledger lines.
Register symbols:

C_2 | C_1 | C | c | c^1 | c^2 | c^3 | c^4

Pitch:

F# G G# A A# B C C# D D# E F F#
Gb   Ab   Bb   Db   Eb   Gb
I II III IV V VI VII VIII IX X XI XII I

Individual notes can be identified by the combination of pitch
and register numbers; for example:

X^3 = Eb; IV^7 = a^3; VII^5 = c^1; XII^2 = F_2

Key signatures: ▲ = a sharp key; ▼ = a flat key; for example:

≣≣ = A major or F# minor;   ≣≣ = Db major or Bb minor.

Example 2-33. J. S. Bach, "Fugue in C#," from <u>The Well-Tempered
Clavier</u>, Book II.

In many ways, Thelwall's staff reform is sensible and easy to
comprehend. Two factors are in its favor: A full chromatic octave can be outlined from bottom to top line without ledger
lines, and, as a welcome visual device, the heavy central C-
line provides quick reading orientation. Moreover, the register numerals make good sense, as the same staff arrangement
serves both hands in keyboard music. Thelwall's symbols for
key signatures, it is true, might be considered ambiguous, but
context would quickly inform the player whether the key was
major or minor.

The ease with which a conventional notation liberally be-
sprinkled with sharps and double-sharps can be translated into an unencumbered new scheme is convincingly demonstrated in
the brief excerpt above.

1902. Paul Riesen, <u>Revolte oder Reform? Das schlüssellose No-
ten-System der Zukunft</u> (Revolt or reform? The clefless notation of the future). Dresden: Riesen & Calebow.
Staff: 5-line and 4-line; the outer lines of each are heavily
drawn. The 4-line staff can be expanded to 7 lines to accommodate a two-octave span, to 10 lines for three octaves,
and to 13 lines for four octaves.
Clef signs: None; treble and bass are implied.
Pitch:

Meter: The numerator and denominator are separated by a slash. Example 2-34.

The most unusual feature of Riesen's "clefless staves of the future" is not so much their heavy outer lines as their use of alternating down- and up-stems on the notes of the chromatic scale. This particular notational device, however, was not unique with Riesen; we find it used as early as 1496 in Giorgio Anselmo di Parma's <u>Ars nova musicae</u> (4), as well as in the 1701 reform of Joseph **Sauveur (see page 137).**

The four-line staff proposed by Riesen, which he termed the <u>Viertelsystem</u>, served as the matrix for two enlarged staves: one of seven lines, called the <u>Halbsystem</u>, and one of thirteen lines, which he labeled the <u>Ganzsystem</u>. As indicated, both retained the device of thick outer lines. In effect, the seven-line staff is a juxtaposition of two four-line staves, and the thirteen-line staff is a combination of four four-line staves.

<u>Viertelsystem</u> | <u>Halbsystem</u> | <u>Ganzsystem</u>

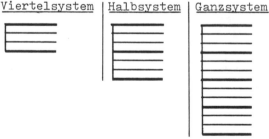

1904. Johann Ailler, [New notation]. Gr. Stettledorf, Germany: the author.
Staff: 8-line (4-4). All ledger lines for the note C are printed in red for easy reference. A keyboard system consists of two 8-line staves, providing for a four-octave gamut.

Clef signs:

Pitch:

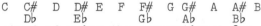

| C | C# | D | D# | E | F | F# | G | G# | A | A# | B |
| | Db | | Eb | | | Gb | | Ab | | Bb | |

Instead of using the conventional 8va indicator above the
treble staff, Ailler inverts the G-clef sign.
Key signatures: D major, F minor, and so on are set above the
upper staff.
Rests: The traditional symbols are centered between the two
staff segments, as shown below.
Example 2-35.

Six years before this proposal appeared, Ailler had experimented with a three-line staff, whose central line (C) was
printed in red, an orienting device he retained in his later
system. Evidently Ailler was dissatisfied with his three-line
staff, for he discarded it in favor of the new format of 4-4
lines. This more recent proposal also included suggested new
symbols for quarter-tones:
Example 2-36.

$b\downarrow = \frac{1}{4}\downarrow$ and $q\downarrow = \frac{1}{4}\uparrow$.

It did not take long for the inverted flat-sign to be adopted
by countless later composers who experimented with microtones;
it is still in use today, though not endorsed universally.

1905. Thorwald Jerichau, "Zur Notenschrift" (Concerning nota-
tion), <u>Zeitschrift der Internationalen Musik-Gesellschaft</u>
VI, p. 330.
Staff: 3-line; up to four staves may be combined as a system.
When four staves are used, the lines of the outer two staves
are dotted.

Register symbols:

Pitch:

    C   D   E   F   G   A   B   C
Example 2-37. Chorale, <u>Ein' feste Burg ist unser Gott</u>.

Like other three-line staff systems previously proposed, Jerichau's version is perfectly suitable for music of a simple
melodic, harmonic, and rhythmic texture. But in common with
similar formats, his staff was too restricted for more complex expression, which may explain why his reform was bypassed
in the continuing process of notational improvment.

1905. Hans Sacher, <u>Volknotenschrift</u> (Elementary notation).
   Vienna: A. Pichlers witwe & sohn.
Staff: 11-line (5-1-5); the central line appears only when
   required.
Register symbols:

		III	IV	V	VI	VII	VIII
		II	III	IV	V	VI	VII
C_1-B_1	C -B	c-b	c^1-b^1	c^2-b^2	c^3-b^3	c^4-b^4
A_2-B_2	C_1-B_1	C-B	c -b	c^1-b^1	c^2-b^2	c^3-b^3

Pitch:

   C C# D   D# E   F F# G G# A A# B C ——— C
      Db   Eb   Gb   Ab   Bb

Example 2-38. Frédéric Chopin, <u>Prelude in B Minor</u>, op. 28, no. 6.

Sacher's format is yet another utilization of the theoretical "Great Staff," its central line relating to either five-line segment and appearing only when required. As a learning aid for the young students for whom the system was devised, Sacher offered this capsule rule: If the tonic note of a key is on a line, the successive notes of the diatonic scale will be on three lines and four spaces. When the tonic note is in a space, the sequent scale will be on four lines and three spaces.

1905. Hans Sacher, <u>Entwurf Drei</u> (Third notational plan). Vienna: A. Pilchers witwe & sohn.
Staff: 11-line (2-2-2-2-2-1); the lines are alternately print-ed in red and black.
Register symbols: The same as in Sacher's <u>Volksnotenschrift</u>.
Pitch:

C C#   D D# E F F# G G# A A# B C ——— C
   Db   Eb   Gb   Ab   Bb
Example 2-39.

Entwurf Drei followed several attempts by Sacher to alter both
staff and notehead designs. Dissatisfied, however, with the
results of utilizing shaped noteheads, he reverted in this experiment to the standard format for the notes, altering instead only the staff -- and in a decidedly radical manner. But
Sacher's new staff is not comfortable to read, and it is questionable whether he actually achieved his stated pedagogical
goal by such an elaborate format and the use of colored lines.
Like his _Volksnotenschrift_, this third notational proposal was
devised for the elementary study of music, principally vocal.
Surely the beginning students of voice must have found the new
staff somewhat puzzling; at any rate, it was never sanctioned
by the musical community of Vienna.

1906. Anna C. Davis, _Musical Notation_. U.S. Patent 828,020.
Staff: 5-line; the outer lines are heavy and the upper two
    lines are drawn closely together. When additional staves
    are joined, either below or above, the central line relates
    to two staves.
Clef signs: Not mentioned in the proposal.
Pitch:

    F   G   A   Bb C   D   E   F
    do re mi fa sol la si do
Key signatures: Designated by pitch letters and _Ma_ for a major
    tonality and _Mi_ for a minor key, as shown below.
Example 2-40.

This inventor's scheme of a flexible staff that can be moved up or down is ingenious but unwieldy. Though Davis insisted that her solution achieved transposition "with little or no mental effort and practically unconsciously," it is patently no more efficient than our traditional method of changing key signatures.

1906. William Emmanuel Naunton, <u>Music Notation</u>. U.S. Patent 832,406.
Staff: 2-line, representing C#/Db and D#/Eb on the piano key-board. 3-line and 2-line segments are added below or above in the manner of ledger lines.
Clef signs: None; the G-clef above and the F-clef below the central 2-line staff are implied.
Pitch:

C C# D D# E F F# G G# A A# B C
   Db   Eb   Gb   Ab   Bb

Duration: Conventionally expressed, except that the added staff lines are broken between measure beats (as shown above); no augmentation dots or ties are used; such durations are designated by the length of the staff lines.
Rests: Indicated by blank space or the absence of any lines.
Dynamics: Heavy staff lines call for loudness; lightly ruled and dotted lines mean progressively softer levels of sound.
For vocal melody writing, Naunton suggests the following modification of his proposal: a 3-line staff consisting of the two heavy lines for C#/Db and D#/Eb, with a thinner line two spaces above. Individual groups of three or two diagonally vertical lines representing the higher black keys of the piano are set in this space, each group representing one measure beat:
Example 2-41.

The author of this reform, an Australian, was head of the Melbourne-based firm, Naunton Music Proprietary, Ltd. His rationale for the proposal is stated as follows: "Various means have been attempted from time to time for the purpose of bringing the art of music within the reach of the masses, without meeting much success, owing partly to the want of simplicity, on the one hand, and the absence of thoroughness and completeness on the other. . . . This invention, being a complete musical system, has been devised in order to render the reading of notes, time, rhythm, light and shade, and accent so simple that any one can thoroughly acquire the art of music in much less time and with much less mental effort."

Whereas Naunton's two-line staff is an easily recognizable version of the 2-3 keyboard format favored by a number of other reformers, his suggested vocal staff is a confusing hybrid, combining as it does two radically different staff concepts -- the horizontal and the vertical. Evidently Naunton was unable to assess the mental effort that would be required from the singer attempting to cope with this peculiar method.

1907. K. M. Bässler, <u>Die neue Deutsche Tonschrift</u> (The new German notation). Zwickau, Germany: Verlag des Herausgebers.
Staff: 5-line, each line consisting of four closely drawn thin lines. Ledger lines are sometimes notated as ⊃ .
Register symbols:

	2	3	4	5	6	7	8
A_2-B_2	C_1-B_1	C-B	c-b	c^1-b^1	c^2-b^2	c^3-b^3	c^4-b^4

Pitch:

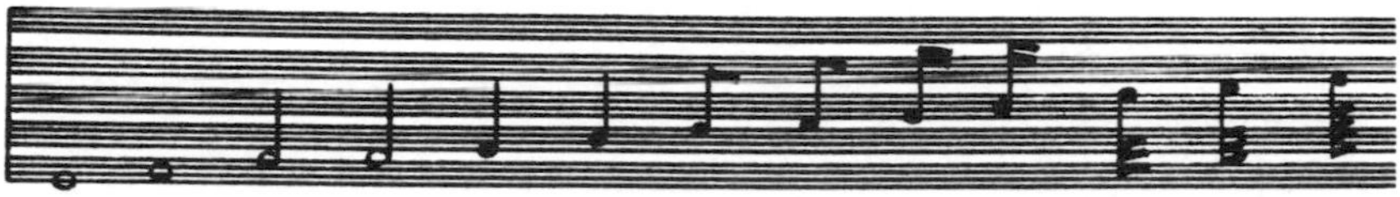

E	F	F# Gb	G	G# Ab	A	A# Bb	B	C	C# Db	D	D# Eb	E

Key signatures: Shown by the initial three pitches of the key to be used, which indicate whether the tonality is major or minor. For example:

C#
B = A major; Ab
A
Ab
G = F minor.
F

Example 2-42. German student song, <u>Gaudeamus igitur</u>.

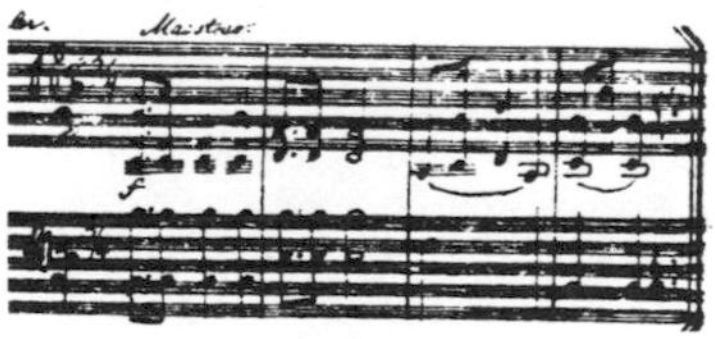

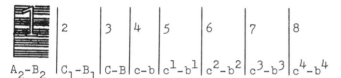

Bässler's key signatures are commendably simple and effective, instantly identifying whether the tonality is major or minor. His register symbols, however, were forced to be visually dramatic so as to dominate the dense concatenation of staff lines used. Why, one wonders, did Bässler consider it necessary or desirable to construct such a complex formulation, with all its attendant reading problems? One is led to believe that this reformer invented this staff merely to prove some hypothetical theory, and not to suggest a viable alternative notation.

A number of earlier reforms proposed by this prolific German theorist focus more on novel notehead designs than on staff formats and will be discussed in another chapter.

1907. Jean Hautstont, <u>Notation musicale Autonome, basée sur la classification des sons d'après le nombre de leurs vibrations et l'état actuel du développement physiologique de l'organe de l'ouïe. Suppriment toutes les difficultés de la notation diatonique et répondant aux besoins de plus en plus complexes de l'art contemporain</u> (Autonomous musical notation, based on the classification of sounds according to their vibration ratios and the current physiological development of the ear. Suppressing all the difficulties of diatonic notation and responding to the ever more complex needs of the contemporary art). Paris: Imprimerie de l'école municipale Estienne.

Staff: 3-line; ledger lines are treated as complete staves.
Register symbols:

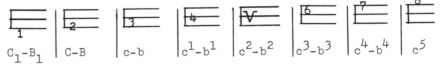

C_1-B_1 | C-B | c-b | c^1-b^1 | c^2-b^2 | c^3-b^3 | c^4-b^4 | c^5

Pitch:

C C# D D# E F F# G G# A A# B C
   Db   Eb   Gb   Ab   Bb

As shown in Example 2-43, note-stems are always to the right of the notehead, up for the right hand and down for the left hand.

Duration:

Rests:

Meter:

, for example.

Example 2-43. Mily Balakirev, <u>Islamey (Oriental Fantasy)</u>.

The <u>Autonomous notation</u> of Hautstont exhibits a number of idiosyncratic and questionable devices. First of these would be
the register symbol identifying the octave above that of middle C, which departs from the Arabic numerals for the other
octaves. Second would be the positioning of all note-stems to
the right of the noteheads, a technique that runs counter to
traditional practice, without any discernable valid reason.
Third is the related practice of reducing the number of flags
or beams for the shorter note values by one factor -- eighths
become quarters, sixteenths become eighths, and so on. This is
a technique we first encountered in the proposed reform of
Albert Hahn (see page 33). Finally, add to these unorthodox
elements the peculiar forms of Hautstont's rest signs and meter signatures, and we are left with a notational plan that is
anything but an indisputable improvement over our traditional
system.

As a measure of the interest generated by Hautstont's system, extracts and illustrations from his proposal were included in the authoritative <u>Encyclopédie de la musique et dictionnaire du Conservatoire</u> (5).

1908. Willard C. Smith, <u>Sheet-Music</u>. U.S. Patent 885,192.
Staff: 5-line; either staff of a piano system may be expanded
  up to a total of 30 lines by the addition of broken ledger
  lines and full staves.

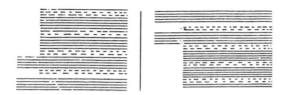

Clef signs:

Pitch: Indicated conventionally, as are all the other elements
   of notation.
"The primary object of the invention," Smith wrote, "is to
provide a musical staff with ledger lines of a distinguishing
character at regular intervals to represent octaves with respect to tone indications to facilitate reading the latter
both above and below the staff and   thus   obviate strain on
the eyes, as well as delay on the part of the performer or
pupil in reading the tone designations. It is the purpose of
the invention . . . to relieve the blurred or confused condition of multiplied, indiscriminate ledger lines, together
with constant strain and monotony incident thereto."
   In Smith's proposal, the same pitch degree is accommodated
by the first ledger line below and the second above either
staff. He provides a logical two-octave increment by the addition of permanent ledger lines and full or partial staves
above and below the G- and F-clefs. Smith is not adamant, however, in his preference for broken ledger lines, and he suggests that they may also be either heavy or wavy unbroken
lines.

———————————————

1909. Erich Moritz von Hornbostel, [A microtonal staff pro-
   posal]. Included in Theory and Method by Bruno Nettl, New
   York, 1964, p. 108.
Staff: 9-line; essentially a pentagram (the heavy lines), with
   an extra thin line inserted within each staff space, which
   accommodate the quarter-tone inflections.
Clef signs: Standard G- and F-clefs, oversized.
Pitch:

G-clef: E F G   A B C   D E F
F-clef: G A B   C D E   F G A

A distinguished authority on tone psychology, Hornbostel was
also a specialist in various ethnic musics. His suggested microtonal staff is both pragmatic and simple in design. It en-

tirely eliminates the need for special quarter-tone symbols,
a welcome boon to the performer who is faced today with an
astonishing number of proposed microtonal signs that are far
from standardized, and often contradictory. Strangely, no one
else seems to have adopted this sensible solution to microtonal notation.

1910. Eugène Louis Bazin, *Écriture et théorie octavinale* (No-
    tation and the octave theory). Nantes: Imprimerie de la
    Loire.
Staff: 3-line.

$$0 \quad\quad |\text{I} \quad |\text{II} \quad |\text{III} \quad |\text{IV} \quad |\text{V} \quad\quad |\text{VI} \quad |\text{VII}$$
$$C_1\text{-}B_1 \quad |\text{C-B}|\text{c-b}|c^1\text{-}b^1|c^2\text{-}b^2|c^3\text{-}b^3|c^4\text{-}b^4|c^5$$

Pitch:

    do   re mi fa sol la si   do
In this scheme Do is the tonic of any key, and the same oc-
tave notation is used for all voices and instruments.
Duration: Shown by double figures, like meter signatures,
    which indicate the number of beats in the measure and the
    number of first-division units, i.e.,

$$\left|\tfrac{3}{6} = \tfrac{3}{4} \text{ (3 beats,} \atop \text{6 divisions)}\right. \quad\quad \left|\tfrac{4}{12} = \tfrac{12}{8} \text{ (4 beats,} \atop \text{12 divisions)}\right.$$

Example 2-44. Chorale, *Ein' feste Burg ist unser Gott.*

Bazin's proposal found an enthusiastic advocate in the critic
Étienne Destranges, who wrote a lengthy and laudatory article
about the reform in *Le Guide Musicale*, No. 48 of 1910. Critics
of the system, however, rightly maintained that although Bazin's theoretical approach seemed simple and easy to understand, it was unworkable for writing chord structures or complex rhythmic formulations. Unique to this system is the use
of double noteheads for the tonic pitch of each key, obviously
an orienting device.

1910. Hans Krenn, "Siebenton- oder Zwölftonschrift" (Seven- or
    twelve-tone notation). *Neue Musikalische Presse* XIV, 10.
Staff: 7-line; the A-line is heavy. Partial staves of only

three lines are added below or above as needed.
Clef signs: Not discussed by the author.
Pitch:

A   A#   B   C   C#   D   D#   E   F   F#   G   G#   A
    Bb   Db   Eb   Gb   Ab
Example 2-45.

The staff proposed by Krenn is so constituted that one whole-
tone scale is outlined on successive lines and another in the
successive spaces. This, of course, is a phenomenon of all
staff constructs in which each note of the chromatic scale occupies its own line or space.

Because of its limited range, even with the addition of
partial staves above and below the primary staff, Krenn's format would appear to be most useful for simple vocal music.

1910. Karl Laker, <u>Vereinfachung der Notenschrift und der Ein-
    führung in die Musiklehre</u> (Simplification of notation and
    its introduction into the teaching of music). Graz, Austria:
    Leuschner & Lubensky.
Staff: 6-line.
Register symbols: Indicated in either of two ways: 1) for a
    series of notes and 2) for individual notes.

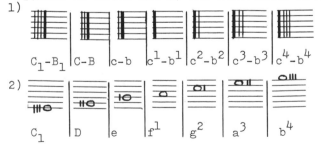

1)

C_1-B_1 C-B   c-b c^1-b^1 c^2-b^2 c^3-b^3 c^4-b^4

2)

C_1 D   e f^1 g^2 a^3 b^4

Pitch:

C C# D D# E F F# G G# A A# B C
   Db   Eb   Gb   Ab   Bb

Example 2-46. Giuseppi Verdi, from Act IV, Il Trovatore.

The author of this system produced numerous treatises on music,
including his Das musikalische sehen (6). Doubly accomplished,
he was also a doctor of medicine, specializing in ear and
throat diseases.

Laker's notation proposal is eminently practical; it en-
sures that any register can be notated without clef signs and
accidentals, retaining the identical pitch positions on the
staff, and obviating the need for either ledger lines or 8va
indicators. It owes its genesis, of course, to the earlier
six-line staff proposals of such theorists as Werneberg, Gambale, and Presbyter. Like these forerunners, Laker's reform
failed to come into general use over the barriers of old habit
and unwillingness to spend on the new. But in the welter of
novel systems discussed in these pages, this proposed method
stands out as one of the most sensible and pragmatic.

Evidently Laker's brief quotation from Verdi's opera,
above, was designed by him for a solo instrument with piano
accompaniment and not for voice as it appears in the score.

1910. Gustav Neuhaus, Neuhaus Notensystem: Naturliches Noten-
system (The natural notational system). Nuremburg: R. Zeil-
ler.
Staff: 5-line (2-3); the first line (C#/Db) is heavily drawn.
Two staves each are used for the left and right hands.
Clef signs:

c-c[1]   c[1]-c[2]

Pitch:

C C# D D# E F F# G G# A A# B C
   Db   Eb   Gb   Ab   Bb

On the left-hand staves, the notes and their stems are written as follows:

, and so on.

Example 2-47. Ludwig van Beethoven, Sonata in G, op. 31, no.1.

As substitutes for the traditional G- and F-clefs, the two unique signs introduced by Neuhaus refer only to the staves on which they are placed; higher and lower octaves are notated on additional staves, above or below these primary staves. Other than these two unorthodox symbols, plus the practice of reversing the note-stems for the left-hand pitches, this system is little different from other proposals based on the white key/black key arrangement of the five staff lines.

1911. D. Emillo Boch, Sistema interzato della musica (Insertion system of music). Rome: the author.
Staff: 7-line; lines two and three are close together.
Clef signs:

, placed on the tonic (do) line or space.

Pitch:

do # re # mi fa # sol # la # si

<u>Do</u> is the tonic pitch of any key. Observe that no note is ever
placed in the narrow second space of the staff.
Example 2-48.

The reason for the close position of lines two and three on
Boch's staff is not evident. Since they do not identify any
special progression of the chromatic scale or contrasting
note-forms, their proximity remains a puzzle. Clearer in intent, while still being novel, are the notehead shapes favored
by Boch -- round rather than the customary ovals.

1911. Annie May Stringfield, <u>Staff and Certain Key-Symbols for
  Musical Notation</u>. U.S. Patent 1,004,215.
Staff: 5-line (1-3-1).
Clef signs:

 and

Pitch:

C   D   E   F   G   A   Bb   C   D   Eb   F   G

"It will be observed," the inventor of this method wrote,
"that the staff has at least two salient features, to wit, the
relatively wide spaces and the center line of each group

[staff] and as these are invariably an interval of a fourth
apart I call the arrangement a 'key meter' since it is in fact
a device by which wide intervals can be at once measured without the necessity of proceeding by [scale] degrees. . . . Additional prominence is obtained by placing correspondingly
larger notes in the larger spaces."

The principal purpose of this system seems to be to aid
the music student in his analysis of scale-degree relationships. This is done by displaying the seven diatonic notes of
the scale in a triangular, or mirror, formation:
Example 2-49.

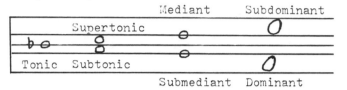

One might reasonably argue that such analysis can be accomplished as easily without a modified pentagram or the utilization of oversized noteheads. But the argument is academic
since Stringfield's system was never adopted by the teachers
of music.

_____

1913. Musikverlag Euphonie, <u>Tastenschrift: ein neuer Weg zur
Hausmusik</u> (A new keyboard method for amateurs). Berlin-
Friedenau: Musikverlag Euphonie.
Staff: 5-line (2-3); two staves as usual are used for piano
music.
Clef signs:

    h = <u>hoch</u>, for the right hand

    t = <u>tiefe</u>, for the left hand

Pitch:

C C# D D# E F F# G G# A A# B
    Db   Eb   Gb   Ab   Bb

Duration: Barlines bisect both staves; beat lines, which are
dotted, are centered between the staves, as shown in Example
2-50. All note values are based on the quarter-note, which
represents one beat.

1 beat | 2 beats | 3 beats | ½-beat

Rests:

1 beat 2 beats 3 beats ½-beat

Meter: The numerator only is given, centered between the staff segments.

Ornamentation: Only the arpeggio is notated unconventionally.

Example 2-50.

Tastenschrift, the collaborative creation of a group of music editors, was designed exclusively for beginners at the piano. It uses the by now familiar "keyboard staff," soon to be endorsed by such eminent theorist-composers as Busoni, Hauer, and Schoenberg, with additional features drawn from other contemporaneous reformers. While it is suitable for rhythmically uncomplicated piano music, Tastenschrift is woefully inadequate for any kind of durational complexity. We have no reports on the popularity of this teaching system, or of its persistence to the present day.

1913. Alicia Anne Scott, Simplex Method of Musical Notation. Spottiswoode, England: the author.

Staff: None; instead, a pictogram of the piano keyboard, in segments, is read down the page.

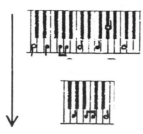

Clef signs: None; a short vertical line above middle C is set
   above the pictogram.
Pitch: Notes are placed on the white or black keys of the pictogram. Stems are up for the right hand and down for the
   left hand.
This is a curious -- and most impractical -- suggestion for
notating piano music. The principal difficulty arises in writing the very small notes on the black keys, and placing their
stems so as not to interfere with the vertical key margins.
Then, too, the necessity to read a horizontal pitch format in
a vertical progress is confusing and illogical. It cannot be
imagined that any beginner at the keyboard was entirely happy
while struggling to learn this author's system. Certainly, her
so-called reform never achieved acceptance in the field of
piano pedagogy, and we may assume it met with acclaim only
among the lady's intimate circle of friends.

1914. Arthur Eaglefield Hull, [Duodecuple Staff] , in his
   Modern Harmony. London: Augener.
Staff: 6-line.
Clef signs:

Pitch:

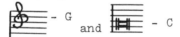

A   A# B   C   C# D   D#   E   F   F# G   G# A
     Bb   Db   Eb   Gb   Ab
Example 2-51.

Hull's choice and positioning of his two clef signs is erratic; the G-clef relates to the fifth instead of the top staff
line, which always carries the note G in his scheme. The alto-
clef sign, though it relates to the space occupied by C, is
unconventionally positioned. Other than the octave scale beginning on A rather than on C, Hull's staff is no different
from the previous formats proposed by Werneberg, Laker, and
Gambale. The same plan was reinvented, so to speak, in 1934 by
Marguerite Roesgen-Champion (see page 78).

1916. Sullivan Conservatorium of Music, Ltd., <u>The Sullivan
    System of Pianoforte Playing</u>. Johannesburg, South Africa.
Staff: 5-line (3-2). A keyboard system consists of three and
    one-half staves.
Clef signs: None; two heavy lines for C#/Db and D#/Eb separate
    the right- and left-hand staves.
Pitch:

F   F#   G   G#   A   A#   B   C   C#   D   D#   E   F
    Gb   Ab   Bb   Db   Eb
Example 2-52.

The idea of dividing the traditional pentagram into two segments to correspond to the physical spacing of the black and
white keys of the piano keyboard seems to have spread quickly
throughout the music world. Although Dumouchel was evidently
the first to advance this format, as early as 1819 (see page
14), it was not until the turn of the century that the concept
attained a certain distinction, largely owing to Ferruccio
Busoni's much publicized "search for an organic notation"
(page 201). Barely fourteen years later we find the novel
staff forming the basis of the piano method devised by this
South African music establishment. One infers that the piano
teachers of Johannesburg must have approved of the system sufficiently to make the publications of the Conservatorium profitable.

1917. José Maria Guervós, <u>Decagrama</u> (10-line staff). Madrid:
    Union Musical Española.
Staff: 10-line.
Clef signs: Standard C-clef, positioned as shown below.
Pitch:

D D# E   F F# G   G# A A# B C C# D —— A
   Eb   Gb   Ab   Bb   Db
Example 2-53.

There seems to be no logical reason for a staff of ten lines
designed only for half-step intervals. A full octave is covered by seven lines and a double octave by thirteen. The greater
reading ease of a seven-line staff is convincingly demonstrated by comparing the example above with those accompanying the
systems of Boisgelou, Blein, Boch, and Feige -- among others.

1920. Frank Taft, Musical Notation. U.S. Patent 1,356,416.
Staff: None; a pictogram of the keyboard is used instead.
Register symbols:

	2nd octave	3rd octave	4th octave	5th octave
C_1-B_1	C-B	c-b	c^1-b^1	c^2-b^2

6th octave | 7th octave

c^3-b^3 c^4-b^4

Pitch:

        C#/Db   D#Eb   F#/Gb   G#/Ab   A#/Bb

    C   D   E   F   G   A   B

Duration: No provision is made by Taft for rhythmic distinc-
    tions, or for meter. One assumes that the separation of each
    piano-key segment indicates one beat and that empty space
    represents silence.
Example 2-54.

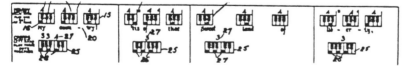

It seems unlikely that Taft could have known about Alicia
Scott's proposal (page 63) made in England seven years prior
to his patent, yet both systems use a piano-keyboard pictogram
in lieu of any kind of staff. Both amateur methods do represent a unique manner of notating music, but both present an
impractical solution to the problem of simplifying traditional
notation for pedagogical purposes. Taft's status as an amateur
is further verified by his complete disregard of symbols for
note duration, an element no effective reform can ignore.

1922. Orlando M. Fee, <u>Musical Notation</u>. U.S. Patent 1,424,718.
Staff: 7-line. The staff is a composite of three 5-line
    staves: the uppermost five lines constitute one staff, the
    central five lines another, and the lowest five lines the
    other. The author suggests that colors may substitute for
    the distinctive marginal lines, as indicated below.
Clef signs:

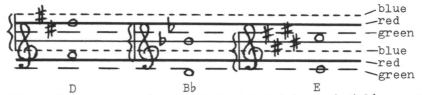

```
        D              Bb             E
```

Pitch: Shown conventionally but related to each 5-line seg-
    ment.
Key signatures: The accidentals are positioned according to
    each segment.
Duration: Depicted traditionally.
Example ?-55.

In the words of its creator, "The object of the invention is
to provide a system or revised method of musical notation
whereby the teaching of music is facilitated and more particularly whereby the transposition of music to vary the pitch
may be attained without difficulty or substantial confusion on
the part of the performer and without an extensive knowledge
of the theory of music. The system contemplates the use of an
augmented staff comprehending a plurality of conventional
staves . . . and it is proposed to distinguishably designate
these several staves represented by different groups of five
lines. . . ."
    After extolling the speculative merits of his staff reform,
Fee went on to say that "the work of the publisher is materi-
ally facilitated in that the composition published in one key
is adapted to cover at least three keys and with no additional
expense other than that which might be incurred in the representation of the augmented staff as compared with the ordinary
or conventional staff."
    Any publisher would be happy to explain that, contrary to
Fee's assertion, the additional expense of reproducing his
staff design would be considerable, with little opportunity to
recoup by way of voluminous sales. It is, therefore, no sur-
prise that Fee's proposal gained little attention and no enthusiastic endorsement by the publishing industry. There are

surely few contemporary composers who would wish to adopt such
a complicated staff design -- a format still rooted in conventional tonality in spite of its radical appearance.

1923. Fred R. Miller, <u>Sheet of Music</u>. U.S. Patent 1,473,495.
Staff: 5-line, arranged vertically. The staff lines terminate
   at the bottom of each page in a keyboard pictogram.
Clef signs: None; a pair of heavy lines representing middle
   C#/Db and D#/Eb separate the staves for the two hands.
Pitch: Stems are angled to the left for notes played by the
   left hand and to the right for those played by the right
   hand. Intervals and chords played by one hand are joined by
   an additional horizontal stem.

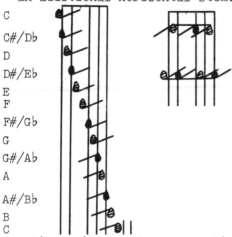

```
C
C#/Db
D
D#/Eb
E
F
F#/Gb
G
G#/Ab
A
A#/Bb
B
C
```

Duration: Miller makes no mention of this element, vital to
   any notation system, but we can deduce the following from
   the illustration that accompanies his proposal: Short beat
   lines between the two central heavy lines set off the measure beats. Half- and quarter-notes have the same written
   form; their durational difference is shown by their position
   relative to the beat lines. The shorter values have flags or
   beams as required.
Example 2-56. Stephen Foster, <u>Way Down Upon the Swanee River</u>.

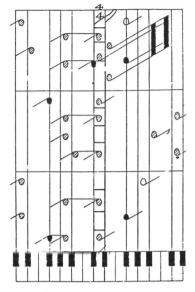

"The primary object of my invention," Miller wrote, "is to provide an improved simplified staff from which pianoforte music may be read by persons unfamiliar with the theory and technique usually required before music can be read and played with any degree of success." How frequently we have heard these sentiments expressed by amateurs hoping to rescue traditional notation from its perceived state of anarchy, while creating systems far more abstruse and impractical.

Miller's amateur status as a musician is further revealed by the glaring rhythmic error in the first measure of the familiar Stephen Foster song he transcribed: The beamed notes in the right hand should be eighths, not sixteenths.

1925. Eugène Hyard, <u>Essai d'une notation chromatique basée sur le tempérament égal, suppression des dièses et des bémols, simplification de la portée, emploi normal d'une clé unique</u> (Attempt at a chromatic notation based on equal temperament, omission of sharps and flats, simplification of the staff, and the exclusive use of a unique clef sign). Paris: B. Roudanez.
Staff: 3-line; two staves are used for the piano, spaced three lines apart.
Register symbols:

Ut 1:	Ut 2:	Ut 3:	Ut 4:	Ut 5:	Ut 6:
C_1-C	C-c	c-c^1	c^1-c^2	c^2-c^3	c^3-c^4

Pitch:

C C# D D# E F F# G G# A A# B C
   Db   Eb   Gb   Ab   Bb

Example 2-57.

Distinctions between the "floating" noteheads in the spaces
of Hyard's staff can be quite difficult to grasp quickly. The
average performer is unaccustomed to seeing three different
pitch levels within one staff space and to distinguishing
widely dispersed ledger lines between the two staves, as demonstrated above.

1926. Josef Matthias Hauer, <u>Zwölftontechnik; die Lehre von der
   Tropen</u> (Twelve-tone notation; the method of tropes). Vienna:
   Universal Edition A.G.
Staff: 8-line (3-2-3).
Clef signs:

 and   and

Pitch:

F F# G G# A A# B C C# D D# E F
   Gb   Ab   Bb   Db   Eb

Example 2-58.

As a noted experimenter with various compositional techniques,
including his then-unique system of <u>tropes</u>, or twelve-tone
patterns, Hauer based most of his theoretical ideas on mathematical constructs. His twelve-tone staff is, of course, only
an extension of the widely propagandized keyboard format of
two plus three lines. An extensive article on Hauer's proposed
notation in the <u>Neue Zeitschrift für Musik</u>, Nr. 9 (1961),
should be of interest to anyone wishing to know more of his
theories in this area.
    It is perhaps foolhardy to question the ideas of such a
professional theorist as Hauer, but one can nevertheless take
issue with his three clef signs, none of which is located in
its customary staff position. As the central line of the
three-line segment is not G, C, or F, some other clef symbol
would surely be more appropriate for Hauer's system.

1927. Marcel Leyat, <u>L'écriture musicale Leyat</u> (Leyat musical
   notation). Paris: Éditions de Musique VITARTIST.
Staff: 5-line (2-3), arranged vertically.
Register symbols: None; an expanded range is covered by addi-
   tional staff segments.
Pitch:

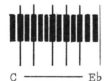

C ————— E♭

Duration: The vertical bars serve to show both pitch and duration; their length designates the rhythmic values.
Example 2-59.

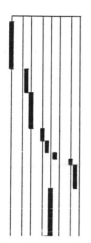

Leyat's notational format is quite obviously indebted to Adorno's earlier proposal (see page 21), but predates <u>Klavarskribo</u>
by some five years. A new element, however, is injected by way
of the unusual note shapes, rather like elongated black piano
keys. It is easy to see that this pitch plan makes the notation of rhythm extremely difficult -- undoubtedly one reason
why Leyat's formulation never gained wide acceptance。

1930. Otto Studer, <u>Neno: Vereinfachtes Klavierspiel</u> (Neno, a
    simplified keyboard notation). Basel: Herausgeber: Neno-
    Verlag.
Staff: 5-line (3-2); the upper pair of lines is heavy. Three
    staves are generally utilized for piano music, but part of
    the center staff appears only as ledger lines when required.
Clef signs: None; treble and bass are implied.
Pitch:

F   F#   G   G#   A   A#   B   C   C#   D   D#   E   F
     Gb   Ab   Bb   Db   Eb

Key signatures: Miniature noteheads of the seven scale de-
    grees are stacked vertically; that for the tonic is full
    size, however。 To distinguish sharps from flats, slashes
    are attached to the noteheads, as shown below.

= D major;   = C minor, and so on.

Duration: Dotted notes are treated as ties, in the manner de-
    picted below。
Meter: Indicated on each staff employed for the two hands, as

illustrated in the example.
Example 2-60. Franz Gruber, <u>Silent Night, Holy Night</u>.

Studer's ingenious solution to the problem of displaying key
signatures on his staff eliminates the need for any accidentals. Although this particular staff construct has greatest
validity for the notation of nontonal music, it can serve conventional tonal composition equally well, including any requirements for key signatures. Neno was devised primarily for
simple music -- hymns, folk melodies, Christmas carols (as illustrated above), and the like, but it is far more logical
than many other elementary systems designed for the amateur
musician.

1931. Cornelis Pot, <u>Klavarskribo</u> (Keyboard notation). Slikker-
    veer, Holland: The Klavarskribo Institute.
Staff: 5-line (2-3); the lines are vertical. Four staves usu-
    ally make up a piano system.
Register symbols:

$\updownarrow$ = c^1

Pitch:

Key signatures: Special symbols distinguish major and minor
    tonalities; for example:

D major   F# minor

Duration: Barlines are unbroken, and "counting," or beat,
lines are dotted; both are uniformly spaced. Note-stems of
the open notes are always above the notehead; for the black
notes, they are below. For the left hand stems point to the
left, and for the right hand they go to the right. Notes
played on the beat have their stems coincide with the barline or interior counting line. Ligatures are used to connect note-groups as in traditional notation. Also, augmentation dots are treated conventionally, but they are placed
below the noteheads.

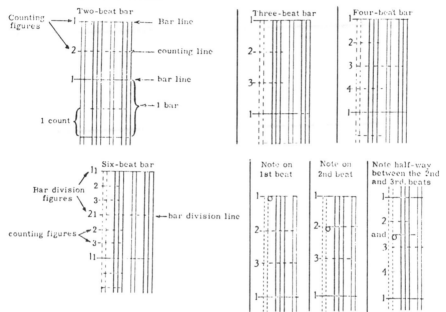

Rests: Silences of all durations are expressed with a single
sign: ᐯ , placed on the measure count where the previous
note ends.

Meter: Time signatures are superfluous in _Klavarskribo_ since
all measure divisions, even including unequal lengths such
as five, seven, eleven, and so on, are graphically indicated
by the counting lines within each measure.

Example 2-61. Ludwig van Beethoven, _Sonata in A-flat_, op. 26.

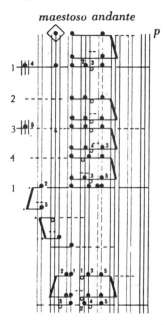

maestoso andante

Esperanto for keyboard notation, <u>Klavarskribo</u> is the invention
not of a theorist or a composer but of a Dutch electrical engineer. Of all the notational reforms discussed in this source
book, it is by far the most successful and the most widely
disseminated. The second edition of "What is Klavarskribo?",
published by the Klavarskribo Institute, cites Busoni, Hindemith, and Schoenberg on the deficiencies of traditional notation; all these, the editors maintain, disappear in their reformed notation:

> Twelve notes per octave (instead of only seven) eliminate
> the need for sharps and flats in any tonality.
> Identical images in all octaves make clefs unnecessary.
> Graphic meter portrayal, with notes appearing at the exact
> point in the measure where they are sounded, is more
> readily grasped than abstract durational symbols that
> must be memorized.
> Measures may be divided as readily into three, five, or
> seven parts as in multiples of two.
> Ledger lines are more quickly comprehended on a vertical
> staff than when added to a horizontal staff.

For many fledgling musicians, young and old, this new system of reading music appeared as a miracle of sorts, and their
enthusiastic letters are quoted in the Institute handbook.
Branch institutes soon flourished in England, Germany, Belgium, France, Switzerland, and Canada -- even in South Africa,
Hong Kong, and New Zealand. As more and more teachers used the
method, the Institute expanded its catalogue to well over
20,000 publications, ranging from the elementary teaching materials of Czerny and Clementi to the sonatas of Haydn, Mozart,

and Beethoven, to the complete works of Bach for organ, and
even to the early tone-poems of Richard Strauss in full score.
    Even so, no single major composer writing music exclusive-
ly in <u>Klavarskribo</u> has emerged, and professional musicians who
wish to range the historic musical landscape must still make
conventional notation their vehicle. As with the previous proposals of Adorno, Paternoster, and Leyat, the reversal of
pitch and duration indications from their traditional positions remains an intellectual hazard. Moreover, <u>Klavarskribo</u>
-- even without accidental signs -- is still rooted in conventional diatonicism and chromaticism, with all their notational limitations. In this scheme, microtonal intervals cannot be easily depicted, and such contemporary compositional
techniques as polymeters become unduly complex to delineate.
    Despite the popularity <u>Klavarskribo</u> enjoys abroad as a
teaching tool, its disadvantages make it an unlikely replacement for conventional practice with advanced performers --
and certainly with composers. As Erhard Karkoschka maintained
in his <u>Notation for New Music</u>, traditional notation, whatever
its imperfections and inadequacies, has always been a rational
vehicle for showing pitch and time. "This is why," he says,
"all the interpreters can realize it equally well -- the pianist with ten fingers, the cellist with five, the violinist
with four, and the singer with none at all" (7).

1933. Constance Virtue, <u>Virtue NotaGraph: Design for a Modern
    Notation</u>. La Mesa, California: Virtue NotaGraph Editions.
Staff: 7-line; the central line is broken. Designed primarily
    for the keyboard, the staff is the same for all seven oc-
    taves of the piano.
Register symbols:

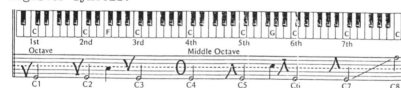

Pitch:

  do di re me mi fa fi so le la te ti do
Key signatures: Although not mandatory, they may be indicated
    by the encircled tonic scale syllable; for example:
    (te) = B♭ major; (fi) = F♯ minor
Rests: The signs are traditional, centered on the broken
    staff line.

Example 2-62. Frédéric Chopin, <u>Etude in G-sharp Minor</u>, op. 25, no. 6.

In her summary of what she perceives to be the advantages of the <u>NotaGraph</u> system (not published until 1974), Virtue stated that "In the forties we did not possess the means of effecting any significant notational reforms. Now, with advanced computer techniques and mass media education, yesterday's impossible becomes today's probable." It is difficult to see what either advanced computer techniques or mass media education can do to overcome the human factor -- the resistance to change and the monetary considerations that any notational reform must overcome. Because of these immutable facts, regardless of <u>NotaGraph's</u> merits, it is not likely that it can achieve the wide acceptance its author desires.

1934. Marguerite Roesgen-Champion, "L'écriture musicale nouvelle" (New musical notation), <u>Le Courrier Musical</u> 7/8.
Staff: 6-line.
Register symbols:

I	II	III	IV	V	VI	VII	VIII
A_2-G_1	A_1-G	A-g	a-g^1	a^1-g^2	a^2-g^3	a^3-g^4	a^4-c^5

Pitch:

A	A#	B	C	C#	D	D#	E	F	F#	G	G#	A
	B♭			D♭		E♭			G♭		A♭	
La	lé	Si	Do	dé	Re	ré	Mi	Fa	fé	Sol	sé	La

Example 2-63.

We have already illustrated several earlier proposals based on
a six-line staff with the pitch A on the bottom line (e.g.,
Eaglefield Hull, page 64); hence, Roesgen-Champion's reform
cannot be considered unique. Neither can her summary statement -- "For twelve pitches, twelve names, and twelve un-
changeable positions" -- claim to be an original deduction;
any number of earlier reformers of notation had previously
arrived at the identical conclusion.

1935. Oewaton Nadjen, [New musical staff]. Kiev: the author.
Staff: 5-line (3-2), arranged vertically.
Clef signs: None.
Pitch: Note-stems are on top of the noteheads, pointing to the
    left for the left hand and to the right for the right hand.

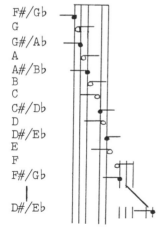

Duration:

Rests:

Example 2-64. Frédéric Chopin, <u>Prelude in A</u>, op. 28, no. 7.

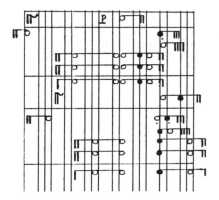

Here we have one more proposal based on the vertical staff first suggested by Adorno in 1855 (see page 22). Unique to Nadjen's scheme, however, is his manner of indicating durational values and rests -- logical in their own way but excessively fussy in appearance. Conventional flags and beams, as well as rest symbols, would function just as effectively here and with less strain on players and potential publishers.

1936. John Leon Acheson, <u>A Douzave System of Music Notation</u>. Pittsburgh: the author.
Staff: 6-line, constituted as shown below. Two or more staves are usually combined as a system.
Register symbols:

C_1-B_1 | $C-B$ | $c-b$ | c^1-b^1 | c^2-b^2 | c^3-b^3 | c^4-b^4

Pitch:

G   G#   A   A#   B   C   C#   D   D#   E   F   F#   G
    Ab   Bb   Db   Eb   Gb

Duration: Two different methods were proposed by Acheson: the
    first utilized conventional open and solid noteheads (as
    illustrated in the example), together with stems, flags, and
    beams as required; his alternative method is a precursor of
    our current "time-notation" symbology, in which durational
    values are shown by extended noteheads. The inventor sug-
    gests that either method can be used with equal effective-
    ness in his new system.
Example 2-65.

Acheson explained the term <u>Douzave</u> as "the range of pitch represented by either ascending or descending the diatonic scale
until the series of single and double subintervals [half-
steps] has been completed." (An unnecessarily complicated manner of describing the chromatic scale, one thinks!)

To his credit, Acheson recognized that his proposal would
never replace traditional notation. He hoped, however, that as
a supplementary system it might challenge and stimulate the
aspiring musician. Since he had previously found conventional
notation cumbersome and illogical, he might have considered
mastering it challenge enough.

1937. J. H. Reuther, <u>Reuther System of Music</u>. New York: the
    author.
Staff: 8-line (3-2-3).
Clef signs: None.
Pitch:

F   F#   G   G#   A   A#   B   C   C#   D   D#   E   F ——— B
    Gb   Ab   Bb   Db   Eb

Meter: The signature is placed before a double left-hand bar-
    line, as indicated following:

Example 2-66.

Here the keyboard staff is once again reinvented. All other
notational elements in Reuther's system, with the sole exception of his meter signatures, are traditionally designated.

1940. Preston Edwards, "A Suggestion for Simplified Musical
    Notation," <u>Journal of the Acoustical Society of America</u>
    11, 3.
Staff: 3-line, with twelve equal, vertical spaces, seven of
    them open and five cross-hatched, analogous to the white and
    black keys of the piano. No note-symbols are set on the
    three staff lines.
Clef signs: None; the G- and F-clefs are implied when two
    staves are combined as a keyboard system.
Pitch:

```
C   C#   D   D#   E   F   F#   G   G#   A   A#   B   C
    Db       Eb               Gb       Ab       Bb
```

Duration: The normal length of the pitch symbol equals one
    beat, whatever the unit of time in operation. Progressively
    longer durations are shown by the proportional lengthening
    of the symbol.
Rests: Not discussed by Edwards; one assumes that empty space
    represents a pause.
Example 2-67. "Resignation," from <u>The Southern Harmony</u>.

One notational reformer's idea of "simplified" notation seldom
corresponds to the norms of other concerned musicians -- this
is a perfect case in point. Edwards' three staff lines merely
enclose, in essence, the two segments of the familiar 2-3-line
keyboard-oriented staff we have seen in a number of previous
proposals, and are therefore addition rather than simplification. His solution of time and individual note duration is
ambiguous at best, for it is difficult to react precisely to
minute extensions of the pitch symbols within regularly recurring barlines. As his system precludes orthochronic notation,
in spite of measure "beats," it can function well only when
durations are to be approximate in the manner of "time-notation."

1940. Bernard L. Bonniwell, "Sixline Music Staff," <u>The Journal
of Musicology</u> 2, 1, pp. 24-26.
Staff: 6-line.
Clef signs:

Pitch:

E   F   G   A   B   C   D   E   F G   A
Example 2-68.

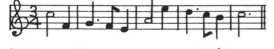

The primary object of Bonniwell's staff format is to add a
permanent ledger line above the treble clef and below the bass
clef, thus making the note positions identical on each staff.
One can mentally transpose the treble part two octaves lower
or the bass part two octaves higher, a notational suggestion
that is not without merit. With the exception of the staff,
all notational factors in this system conform to standard
practice.
    A follow-up article by the author appeared in The Journal
of Musicology 2, 4 (1940), entitled "Historical Note Concerning Clef Conflict."

_____

1946. Mary Bacon Mason, Simplay; music in the modern manner.
    Newton Centre, Massachusetts: the author.
Staff: 7-line for the right hand and 8-line for the left hand,
    constituted as shown below.
Register symbols:

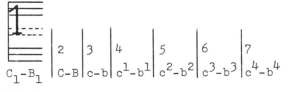

C_1-B_1 | C-B | c-b | c^1-b^1 | c^2-b^2 | c^3-b^3 | c^4-b^4

Pitch:

C   C#   D   D#   E   F   F#   G   G#   A   A#   B   C
    Db   Eb   Gb   Ab   Bb

Duration: Only the half-note is indicated unconventionally, as
    demonstrated below in the example.
Rests: The standard signs are centered on the central dotted
    lines of each staff.
Meter: Displayed as a fraction between the two staves.
Example 2-69. Frédéric Chopin, Prelude in A, op. 28, no. 7.

Designed for the teaching of elementary piano, Mason's system
merely reintroduces in modified format the staff reforms suggested earlier by Mitcherd (page 180), Walter (page 43), and
Hauer (page 71), among others -- all based on the visual analogy with the piano keys. The broken staff lines in Simplay
have validity only as a means of separating the outer pairs of
staff segments for the reader; they are otherwise unnecessary,
as the open and solid noteheads suffice for easy comprehension
of the chromatic scale on this particular staff.

1947. Ernest-Jean Chatillon, <u>Notation musicale bilineaire</u>
   (Bilinear notation). Lyon, France: Musique ERJAC.
Staff: 3-line; the <u>ut</u>-line is heavy. The staff may appear in
   two forms, and additional lines above or below extend the
   range as needed.

Clef signs:

Pitch:

   ut ré mi fa sol la si ut
Chromatic alterations are indicated as follows:

| x | b | bb | ♮ (only in a tonal context)
Key signatures: Indicated by the sharp or flat symbol before
   the Greek phi - φ (the old-style character) on the appropriate line or space, <u>ut</u> representing C. For example:

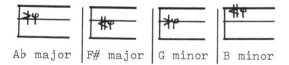

Ab major | F# major | G minor | B minor

Example 2-70. César Franck, <u>Prière</u>.

The explication of Chatillon's proposal in <u>Notation musicale bilineaire</u> was prefaced by a quote from <u>Les jardins de l'intelligence</u> by Lucien Corpechot: "La première des règles imposées à qui prétend à l'intelligibilité, c'est la réduction de toute matière a l'unité" (The primary rule for those who claim intelligibility is the reduction of all matter to an agreement).

There is no doubt that Chatillon's system is intelligently devised and presented; nonetheless, it does not provide an indisputably improved and superior method of notation. Comparison between the author's transcription of Franck's music (above) and the original notation will demonstrate that this inventor's is not the notation of the future.

1948. Velizar Godjevatz, <u>The New Musical Notation</u>. New York: the author.
Staff: 6-line (3-3); an extended staff may be formed by treating the top line of the lower staff as the bottom line of the next higher staff, this central line heavy for visual reference. A keyboard passage that extended over three octaves would be notated on a multiple staff of 3-5-5-3 lines.

Register symbols:

For interval analysis, Godjevatz bases his symbology on the duodecimal number system:

Example 2-71. Frédéric Chopin, <u>Etude in G-flat</u>, op. 25, no. 9.

Few new notational proposals can attract a testimonial from such an eminent public figure as George Bernard Shaw, who described Godjevatz's <u>New Musical Notation</u> as ". . . enormously more readable, writable, logical, graphic and labor saving than any I can remember," which the inventor proudly quoted in his tract. We can agree with Shaw that this system has all the attributes he listed, yet despite the favorable regard of this superlative music critic, the scheme never gathered other supporters or established itself in the mainstream of contemporary notation.

1952. Parry Hiram Moon, "A Proposed Musical Notation," <u>Journal of the Franklin Institute</u> 253, 2, pp. 125-144.
Staff: 6-line (2-2-2).
Register symbols:

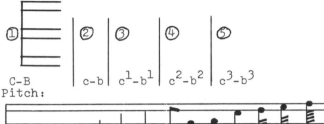

C-B   c-b c^1-b^1 c^2-b^2 c^3-b^3

Pitch:

D   D# E   F   F# G   G# A   A# B   C   C# D
Eb   Gb   Ab   Bb   Db

Meter: Numerator and denominator are set in the staff spaces
Example 2-72.

In addition to the system just illustrated, Moon also advocated a kind of graphic notation in which the linear progress of pitches is shown by a continuous heavy line linking the successive notes. Meter signatures are set above the staff of six lines, and barlines are used as in conventional notation. Because orthochronic noteheads are not utilized, the measure beats are shown by dots beneath the staff. Rhythmic subdivisions of the beat can be outlined solely by visual spacing between these beat indicators. It is evident that Moon's second system is valid only within the context of a very simple rhythmic framework, as, for instance:
Example 2-73.

Moon's second proposal has a remarkable resemblance to Luigi
Russolo's 1914 <u>Noise Music: Awakening of a City</u>, written for
noise-producing instruments alone -- a seminal work in the
Italian Futurist movement during the early decades of this
century:
Example 2-74.

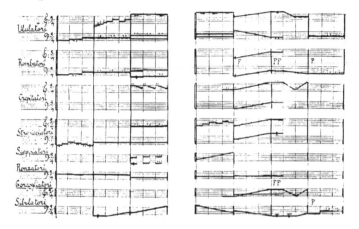

This notation furthermore exhibits a definite kinship with the
graph notation favored by Joseph Schillinger in his 1914
<u>Schillinger System of Musical Composition</u>, published in New
York by Carl Fischer, Inc. Moon, however, relates his grid of
heavy lines to his six-line staff, while Schillinger uses actual graph paper for his complex of continuous lines that delineate pitch, time, and intensity.
    For a welcome change, this inventor was surprisingly prag-
matic about his system: "[It] is not based on a fantastic hope
that the printed music of two centuries will be suddenly
scrapped, to be rewritten in the new notation. Rather, the proposed method is advanced as an aid to [musical] thinking." By
this, Moon evidently meant the musician to be stimulated and
challenged by a new way of looking at the writing down of music, a viewpoint he shared with Arnold Schoenberg (see page
225).

1955. Theodor Feige, "Das Siebenliniensystem: Eine chroma-
    tische Notenschrift" (The seven-line staff system: A chro-
    matic notation), <u>Neue Zeitschrift für Musik</u> 116, 3, pp.
    151-154.

Staff: 7-line.
Clef signs: Not discussed by the author.
Pitch:

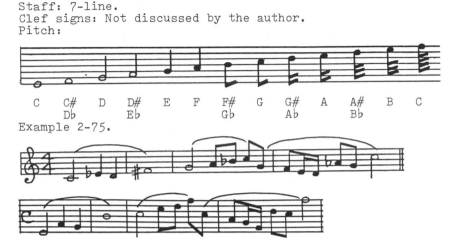

C   C#   D   D#   E   F   F#   G   G#   A   A#   B   C
    Db   Eb   Gb   Ab   Bb

Example 2-75.

Oddly, this author did not address the question of clef or
register symbology as applied to his staff format. It would
seem that numbered octaves, 1 to 7, from the lowest to the
highest C on the piano keyboard, would best suit this particular complex of staff lines, although we cannot know whether
Feige would approve the suggestion. But seven-line staves have
not had the appeal for theorists and composers that other ar-
rangements have had, and Feige's proposal has not been widely
endorsed.

_____

1955. Wilhelm Keller, "Integralnotation" (Integrated notation),
    Neue Zeitschrift für Musik 116, 8/9, pp. 476-481.
Staff: 5-line (2-3).
Clef signs:

c#/db^1

Pitch:

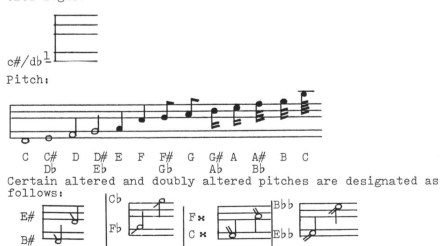

C   C#   D   D#   E   F   F#   G   G#   A   A#   B   C
    Db   Eb   Gb   Ab   Bb

Certain altered and doubly altered pitches are designated as
follows:

E#   B# |Cb Fb |F× C× |Bbb Ebb

Example 2-76.

Essentially, this system is the same as that proposed by Busoni, Hauer, and Schoenberg. Unique to Keller's invention,
however, are the ancillary markings on certain altered and
doubly altered pitches, though these are clearly indebted to
the symbology found in Georg Capellen's 1901 proposal (see
page 201). Keller also advocated the use of various combinations of full or partial staves to provide for an extended
range, e.g., 2-3-3, 2-2-3, or 3-2-3.

1957. James P. Russell, "A Proposed System of Simplified Mu-
    sical Notation," American Music Teacher 6, 3/4, p. 6.
Staff: 3-line; any number of staves may be combined as a sys-
    tem.
Register symbols:

(1)	(2) 110	(3) 220	(4) 440	(5) 880	(6) 1760	(7) 3520
D_1-C	D-c	d-c^1	d^1-c^2	d^2-c^3	d^3-c^4	d^4-c^5

Pitch:

    D   E   F   G   A   B   C   D
Rests:

Example 2-77. Chorale, Ein' feste Burg ist unser Gott.

An unusual feature of this proposal -- one not found in any
other notational reform known to this writer -- is the inclusion of the pitch frequency of A in each of the seven octaves
of register. As Russell's system is geared to the piano keyboard, the necessity for these frequency identifiers is unclear. And since the piano is incapable of producing microtonal intervals, it is surprising, to say the least, that this
conservative inventor also included symbology for quarter-tones
in his proposal; for example:
Example 2-78.

E E¼↑   F F¼↑   F# F#¼↑

1961. Harry Bruce Armstrong, <u>Interval System of Musical Nota-</u>
   <u>tion</u>. n.p., the author.
Staff: 6-line; lines one and four are heavily drawn. The staff
   may be expanded to seven or eight lines as needed.
Register symbols:

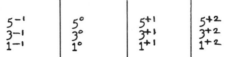

Octave 1 | Octave 2 | Octave 3 | Octave 4 | Octave 5 | Octave 6
Pitch:

    do re mi fa sol la ti do
Key signatures: Appear by key letters, before the time signature.

Example 2-79.

Armstrong's staff comprises basically two sets of three lines;
do is always on the heavy line, which can be duplicated above
or below as required by range. The thinner lines accommodate
mi and sol, the third and fifth degrees of the diatonic scale,
hence the peculiar form of this inventor's register symbols.
The main problem with this format is not the identifying numbers but the inordinate amount of horizontal space they require before the left-hand barline.

1961. Walter Steffens, "Entwurf einer abstrakte-temperierten
    Notenschrift" (Plan for an ideally tempered notation), Neue
    Zeitschrift für Musik 122, 9, pp. 351-355.
Staff: 5-line (3-2); two or more staves may be combined as a
    system.
Register symbols:

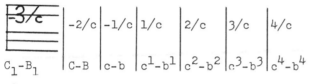

C_1-B_1 C-B   c-b c^1-b^1 c^2-b^2 c^3-b^3 c^4-b^4

Pitch:

F   F#   G   G#   A   A#   B   C   C#   D   D#   E   F
    Gb   Ab   Bb   Db   Eb

Example 2-80.

Only the form of Steffens' register markings sets his scheme
apart from other reforms based on the white key/black key
analogy. Though Steffens reversed the two segments of the
staff (3-2 rather than 2-3), this obviously did not affect
either the note positions of the chromatic octave or the basic
effectiveness of the plan.

1962. Marshall Bailey, "Duodecuple Notation," <u>American Compos-</u>
<u>ers Alliance Bulletin</u> 10, 3, pp. 12-14.
Staff: 6-line. For keyboard instruments two staves are used;
for multiple instruments as many staves as necessary are
used.
Register symbols:

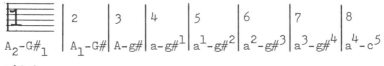

Pitch:

Duration: All noteheads are solid and stemmed, and their individual lengths are shown by the extension of a horizontal
or oblique line on the right side of the stem, rather like a
thin conventional beam (see below). Any number of vertically
stacked notes can be connected to a single stem and beat
line, which always represents one beat. Tied notes designate
various orthochronic rhythmic figures; for example:

If there is no separation between beats, the end of the
first extended beat line touches the stem (but not the beat
line) of the following beat.
Rests: Indicated by note-stems and beat lines unattached to
any noteheads (see measure 1 below).
Meter: Two principal types of meter operate in Bailey's system: <u>unimeter</u> denotes measures (or time spans) of uniform
length, and <u>varimeter</u> refers to segments of irregular
lengths (corresponding to variable meters in orthodox notation). The terms are written over the beginning of the passage to which they apply, followed by a figure representing
the number of beats in the measure. Instead of barlines,
boxed measure numbers are used.

Tempo: A table of seven tempi, or speeds, was worked out by
the inventor, each of which consists of sixty divisions, so
that the whole could total up to 420 beats per minute. Each
of the seven degrees is identified by its World Alphabet

term, its description in modern English, and a series of
figures referring to the number of pulses per minute, from
minimum to maximum. Thus, the tempo called for in the quoted
excerpt above is approximately in the middle range of mid-
speed.

SUPERHGE	— SUPERHIGH SPEED — 361-390-480
HGE	— HIGH SPEED — 301-330-360
MIDHGE	— MIDHIGH SPEED — 241-270-300
MID	— MID SPEED — 181-210-240
MIDLO	— MIDLOW SPEED — 181-150-180
LO	— LOW SPEED — 61- 90-120
SUBLO	— SUBLOW SPEED — 1- 30- 60

Dynamics: A similarly designed table of intensity levels accompanies Bailey's proposal. It ranges from superhigh power
(fff) to sublow power (ppp). The degree desired is indicated
beneath the staff by one or the other of the abbreviations
given in the table below:

SH	—	SH	—	SUPERHIGH POWER
H	—	H	—	HIGH POWER
MH	—	MH	—	MIDHIGH POWER
M	—	M	—	MID POWER
ML	—	ML	—	MIDLOW POWER
L	—	L	—	LOW POWER
SL	—	SL	—	SUBLOW POWER

Bailey's six-line staff, with the pitch of A on its lowest
line, is an exact -- perhaps unknowing -- reincarnation of
Eaglefield Hull's Duodecuple Staff of 1914 (see page 64) and
several sequent reforms. But as one of the most elaborate and
ingeniously worked out systems in our century, Duodecuple Notation deserves serious consideration. Where it falters in
effectiveness is in the depiction of rhythm; the eye is more
distracted than aided by the continuously extended and inter-
linked beat lines. These do not give as precise a representation of duration as one would expect in such an elaborately
conceived method of notation. Especially is this true in the
case of irregular note-groups, where a series of cumbersome
ties must be used.

   This system, its author said, "is not the result of a
brief period of design, but has evolved during a span of many
years. . . . Whether this notation is easier to read than traditional notation is not the principal concern of its development, although it is one of the companion aims. Appropriateness is the major factor under consideration."

   Our principal question is this: Appropriateness for what --
as a replacement for traditional notation? As a suggested alternative? Or does the "appropriateness" refer mainly to con-
sistency within the framework of the author's proposal? Whatever the answer, Bailey's system has not yet gained any appreciable acceptance since its invention, and, like countless
other such reforms, is already becoming only a footnote in the
history of twentieth-century notation.

1964. M. A. Marcelin, "La representation graphique exacte des
    sons et de leurs associations" (The precise graphic repre-
    sentation of tones and their relationships), <u>Acustica</u> 14.
Staff: 7-line, constituted as shown below.
Clef signs: None; the staff accommodates the octave of middle
    C, so higher and lower octaves would be designated by addi-
    tional staves.
Pitch:

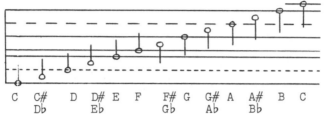

C C# D D# E F F# G G# A A# B C
   Db   Eb   Gb   Ab   Bb

In essence, the black-key notes are on lines that have been
excised so as to avoid the awkwardness of a 12-line staff.
Note also that all stems are centered on the noteheads.
Key signatures: Shown by the noteheads outlining the tonic
    triad of the tonality in operation, for example,

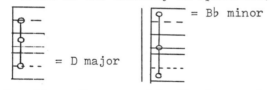

Duration: Shown graphically by precisely measured space. A
    specially constructed typing machine was used by Marcelin
    to measure accurately the distance between notes.
Example 2-81.

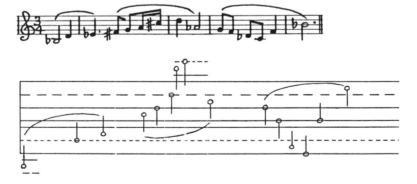

The needless complexity of Marcelin's staff is self-defeating.
One might also question the logic of the dotted and broken
staff lines, as well as the practice of centering the stems on
the open noteheads. Moreover, duration is difficult to gauge
precisely unless time marks are put above the staff. This inventor made the point that timings were to be orthochronic,

yet he did not depict them traditionally, putting a needless strain on the reader of his notation.

1965. Nell Esslinger, <u>Revised Notation</u>. Berea, Ohio: Notation Press.

Staff: 5-line (2-3); extended range is accommodated by adding either full or partial staves above or below. The arrangement of 2-3 lines, called the "C" Staff by the author, may be reversed (3-2) and termed the "F" Staff.

Register symbols:

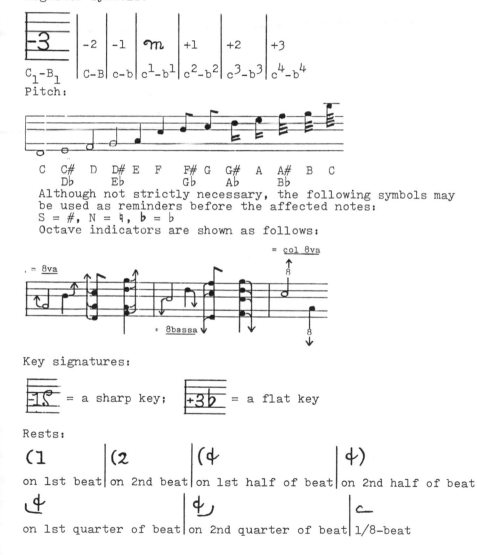

C_1-B_1 | C-B | c-b | c^1-b^1 | c^2-b^2 | c^3-b^3 | c^4-b^4

Pitch:

C C# D D# E F F# G G# A A# B C
   Db   Eb   Gb   Ab   Bb

Although not strictly necessary, the following symbols may be used as reminders before the affected notes:

S = #, N = ♮, ♭ = ♭

Octave indicators are shown as follows:

Key signatures:

= a sharp key; = a flat key

Rests:

(1 | (2 | (4 | 4)
on 1st beat | on 2nd beat | on 1st half of beat | on 2nd half of beat

4 | 4 | c
on 1st quarter of beat | on 2nd quarter of beat | 1/8-beat

Whole-measure rests are shown by the primary and/or secondary beat numbers, as for example:

Example 2-82. Arnold Schoenberg, _Three Piano Pieces_, op. 11.

The keyboard staff is once again reinvented. But whereas this author's pitch symbology applied to that staff, including her new signs for octave transpositions, is clear and noncontroversial, the same cannot be said of her rest signs, which are unnecessarily fussy in appearance and imprecise in meaning.

1966. Carol M. Fuller, "A Notation Based on E and G," _Journal of Research in Music Education_ 14, 3, pp. 193-196.
Staff: 2-line; two staves are commonly combined as a system, 2½ spaces apart.
Clef signs: Treble and bass symbols, as shown below.
Pitch:

E   F   F#   G   G#   A   A#   B   C   C#   D   D#   E
        G♭   A♭   B♭   D♭   E♭

Example 2-83. J. S. Bach, "Chorale," from the <u>Saint Matthew</u>
<u>Passion</u>.

At the conclusion of her proposal summary the author maintained that ". . . a notation has been devised which is based on
the proven values of traditional notation while amending its
inadequacies. The result is a notation which does not run
counter to music theory and is both easier to learn and easier
to read."
     To distinguish sharped and flatted notes from the natural
pitches, Fuller suggested moving their stems to one side of
the noteheads -- a dubious proposition and one that creates
reading hazards, especially for a player some distance from
the music page. Durational factors are unaccountably not discussed, and one can only assume that they are indicated conventionally. An altered whole-note, however, whether a sharp
or a flat, would present a problem in Fuller's notation, there
being no stem to move off the notehead.
     This proposal is a follow-up of sorts to Fuller's 1963
tract, privately published, entitled "Introduction to Speed-
read music; a notation and method designed to make the reading and playing of keyboard music easier and more accurate and
to augment an understanding of fundamentals." A copy of this
tract is presently on file at The Library of Congress.

1966. James Totten, <u>Totten Music Notation</u>. Glasgow: Totten
     Music, Ltd.
Staff: 8-line (3-2-3); partial staves are added above or below
     as needed to increase the range.

Register symbols:

Lowest	Bass	Middle	Treble	Upper
	B	M	T	U
G_1-A	G-a	g-a^1	g^1-a^2	g^2-a^3

Pitch:

| G | G# | A | A# | B | C | C# | D | D# | E | F | F# | G |
| | Ab | | Bb | | | Db | | Eb | | | Gb | |

8va is indicated: | 8bassa is indicated:

Example 2-84. Frédéric Chopin, <u>Polonaise in A</u>, op. 40, no. 1.

LIVELY WITH VIGOUR

Two notational elements set Totten's proposal apart from other
systems based on the keyboard staff of two plus three lines:
his alphabetical register symbols and his note-stem arrows
for octave transpositions. Otherwise, the system adheres to
traditional practice in delineating duration, rests, meters,
and all other required indications.

1968. Thomas S. Reed, Equalized Music Notation. Chillicothe,
   Missouri: the author.
Staff: 6-line, constituted as shown below. Lines three and
   six are called "imaginary lines" by the inventor.
Clef signs:

Pitch: All stems are centered on the noteheads.

C   C# D   D# E F F# G   G# A   A# B   C
    Db   Eb   Gb   Ab   Bb

Duration: Explained by Reed as follows: "To gain proportional
   note spacing accuracy and an improved visual concept of note
   values, a time scale has been added to the equalized staff.
   It is calibrated in approximately 1 centimeter units or multiples thereof, which indicate pulse duration. Noteheads are
   placed on center with the time scale points, in the same
   manner that noteheads are placed on center with the pitch
   scale points. Barlines also fall on center with the time
   scale points, and indicate the exact beginning of each measure." (See Example 2-85.)
Meter: Indicated as illustrated below and combined with the
   symbology for tempo. The metronome markings are related to
   the meter denominator, the numerical scale ranging from 30
   to 200.

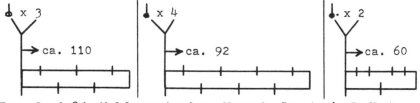

Example 2-85. Wolfgang Amadeus Mozart, Sonata in B-flat,
   K. 333.

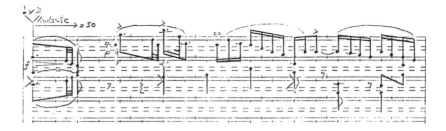

"Equalized notation," Reed wrote, "is intended for the music
reader [student?] and performer. It is a notation for quickly
converting a succession of written symbols into music by a
human being." Does not <u>all</u> notation do precisely this? Reed's
system was obviously designed for elementary piano teaching,
applied as it is to such simple music as an accompaniment to
<u>Mary Had a Little Lamb</u>. The inventor did, however, apply his
method to somewhat more sophisticated music, such as the Mozart
sonata quoted above.
    Reed claimed that clef signs were unnecessary in his sys-
tem as the "reference arrow" identifying middle C is sufficient. In the matter of notehead design, however, he equivo-
cated, saying that traditional open and solid noteheads, together with stems to the right or left as in orthodox practice,
are entirely optional. If that is the choice of the notator,
the time-grid illustrated above becomes superfluous, and we
are left with a visually complex staff for the writing of un-
complex music -- surely not a viable alternative to conventional symbology.

1968. Traugott Rohner, <u>Musica: An Improved Modern System of
    Music Notation</u>. Evanston, Illinois: The Instrumentalist Co.
Staff: 6-line.
Clef signs: Standard G- and F-clefs, positioned as shown below.
Pitch:

| E | F | F# Gb | G | G# Ab | A | A# Bb | B | C | C# Db | D | D# Eb | E |

The author also suggests a new form of the natural sign
(X instead of ♮) and of the double-sharp sign (## instead
of ✗).
Key signatures: Minor tonalities only are indicated by the
    addition of the unstemmed tonic note following the conven-
    tional signature; for example,

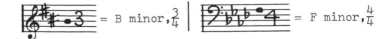

= B minor, $\frac{3}{4}$ | = F minor, $\frac{4}{4}$

Duration: A salient feature of <u>Mūsica</u> is the author's suggestion that the notes be spaced proportionately to show their
time values more clearly, while still retaining the appara-
tus of conventional notation -- open and solid noteheads,
stems, flags, and beams as required.

♪	$\frac{1}{12}$ -note		♪.	$\frac{3}{4}$ -note
♪	$\frac{1}{8}$ -note		♩	1 -note
♪	$\frac{1}{6}$ -note		♩.	$1\frac{1}{2}$ -note
♪	$\frac{1}{4}$ -note		♩	2 -note
♪	$\frac{1}{3}$ -note		♩.	3 -note
♪	$\frac{1}{2}$ -note		o	4 -note
♩	$\frac{2}{3}$ -note		o.	6 -note

Rests:

✗	$\frac{1}{12}$ -rest		૪·	$\frac{3}{4}$ -rest
૪	$\frac{1}{8}$ -rest		/	1 -rest
✗	$\frac{1}{6}$ -rest		/·	$1\frac{1}{2}$ -rest
૪	$\frac{1}{4}$ -rest		//	2 -rest
✓	$\frac{1}{3}$ -rest		///	3 -rest
૪	$\frac{1}{2}$ -rest		▬	4 -rest
✓✓	$\frac{2}{3}$ -rest		▬·	6 -rest

Meter: Only the numerators are given, placed in mid-staff.
Tempo: Metronomic figures only, without the M.M., and omitting
    all terminology, such as Andante or Allegro assai.
Example 2-86.

The most potentially fruitful aspect of Mūsica is not Rohner's six-line staff but his suggested notehead design for the third-note and its multiples. Owing its genesis to Henry Cowell's 1930 proposal (8), a distinctive notehead shape for this particular, and common, value is long overdue in contemporary notation.

Other than this useful suggestion, however, Rohner's system merely duplicates similar staff reforms advanced by any number of other theorists. For those interested in more detailed information on this proposal, the author has written two articles on his experiments in the January and May, 1951, issues of The Instrumentalist. In addition, his Basic Music Notation (also of 1951), on deposit in The Library of Congress, contains essentially the same proposal as was outlined in Mūsica.

1969. Frank R. Denke, New Music Notation System. n. p., the author.
Staff: 5-line (2-3); if a second staff is required, the lines can be dotted, according to the inventor.
Clef signs:

Pitch: As shown, all ledger lines are dotted.

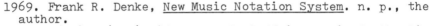

C   C#   D D#   E   F   F#   G G#   A   A#   B   C
     Db   Eb   Gb   Ab   Bb

Example 2-87.

Two minor factors set this proposal slightly apart from other keyboard staff formats previously discussed: the small arrow symbol for middle C and the author's suggestion that a second full or partial staff, whether added above or below, could be written with dotted rather than solid lines. What advantage, if any, would result from this method, Denke does not say.

1973. Richard Bunger, "Notation Format for the Piano: A Multi-
Instrument," Numus-West 3, pp. 22-26.
Staff: Three auxiliary lines added to three standard pentagrams, designed exclusively to notate the novel effects
played on tho keys, the strings, and the piano body, and
the playing of auxiliary instruments by the pianist. Presumably, the author intends his Musiglyph Notation (see page
265) to be used in connection with his proposed staff, although conventional notation could just as effectively be
applied.
Clef signs: Standard forms, as are the indications for all
the remaining notational elements.

Lid
Stick

Strings

Keyboard

Auxiliary

Bunger's suggestion is clear in intent and is eminently pragmatic. Such multiple staff systems are now imperative to record contemporary exploration of new horizons in piano timbre.
When Henry Cowell first experimented with effects produced
directly on the piano strings, he had to notate them on a single or double conventional staff (as in The Banshee), together
with a complicated code for the actions to be taken. Today,
composers require a particularized locale for their key,
string, and piano-frame effects. This proposal offers, then, a
viable format for such specialized notation.

1975. George J. Skapski, PANOT: "Universal Notation." North-
ridge, California: the author.
Staff: 2-line; two or more staves may be combined as a system.
Register symbols:

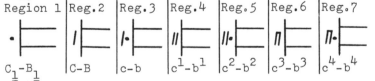

Region 1	Reg. 2	Reg. 3	Reg. 4	Reg. 5	Reg. 6	Reg. 7

C_1-B_1 C-B   c-b c^1-b^1 c^2-b^2 c^3-b^3 c^4-b^4

Pitch:

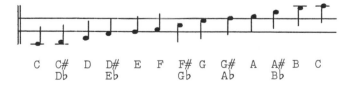

C   C#   D   D#   E   F   F#   G   G#   A   A#   B   C
   Db   Eb   Gb   Ab   Bb

Duration: A stemmed black notehead represents one beat of any
given meter. A single beamed note or group of notes represents two beats, including any component subdivisions. Triple values are indicated by a beamed group with a dot under
or over the beam of the final note. Irregular divisions of
a triplet are distinguished by a longer stem for the longer
note. Noteheads on the first beat of a measure are centered
on the solid barline; if tactus dotted lines are used for
secondary pulses, the noteheads are centered on these lines
as well. All of these conditions are illustrated in the example below.
TRANOT (Traditional notation)

PANOT

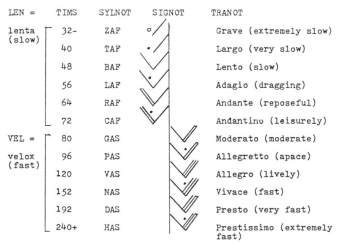

Rests: All values are indicated with a single symbol.

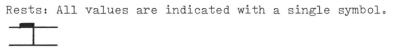

Meter: Indicated by the following special signs which also
denote tempo, qualified by a dot if the meter is triple:

DURTEM = duratio temporalis (transitory duration), or tempo

LEN =	TIMS	SYLNOT	SIGNOT	TRANOT
lenta (slow)	32-	ZAF		Grave (extremely slow)
	40	TAF		Largo (very slow)
	48	BAF		Lento (slow)
	56	LAF		Adagio (dragging)
	64	RAF		Andante (reposeful)
	72	CAF		Andantino (leisurely)
VEL =	80	GAS		Moderato (moderate)
velox (fast)	96	PAS		Allegretto (apace)
	120	VAS		Allegro (lively)
	152	NAS		Vivace (fast)
	192	DAS		Presto (very fast)
	240+	HAS		Prestissimo (extremely fast)

Dynamics: Also designated by special signs that outline a
scale of intensities from quintuple f to quintuple p -- or,
as the inventor expressed it, from "almost inaudible" to
"almost unbearable."

MASKAL = magnitudo scalaris (graduated volume)

MOL = (soft)	DELS	SYLNOT	SIGNOT	TRANOT
	1+	ZYF	o	ppppp (almost inaudible)
	10+	TYF	•	pppp (extremely soft)
	20+	BYF		ppp (radically soft)
	30+	LYF		pp (very soft)
	40+	RYF		p (soft)
	50+	CYF		mp (moderately soft)
FOR =	60+	GYS		mf (moderately loud)
fortis (loud)	70+	PYS		f (loud)
	80+	VYS		ff (very loud)
	90+	NYS		fff (radically loud)
	100+	DYS		ffff (extremely loud)
	110+	HYS		fffff (almost unbearable)

In the words of its inventor, "PANOT is a new system of music
notation which attempts to combine the experience of the past
with the exigencies of the present and the probable demands
of the future." An extremely complex, highly detailed system
of Latin terminology forms the basis for this proposal. Every
parameter of notation -- of pitch, intensity, duration, tempo,
timbre, as well as terms for melodic, harmonic, and formal
components, performance directives, names of instruments,
terminology of all kinds -- is defined by Latin contractions.
A specific note, for instance, is a VINOT, the contraction of
vibrationis nota; a half-step interval would be referred to as
a SEMTON, from semitonus. To request a flutist to employ flut-
ter-tonguing, the term LIVOL, for lingua volubilis, would accompany the passage, while a pianist would be instructed to
use the sostenuto pedal with the term DURPE (duratio pedalis).
These few examples merely demonstrate the scope and the procedures utilized by Skapski in his highly complex and ingenious proposal, a triumph of intellectuality.

1976. Albert Brennink, Die Halbton-Schrift (The Chromatic No-
    tation: a graphical representation of music). Frankfort-am-
    Main: Edition Chroma.
Staff: 4-line; two or more staves may be combined as a system.
Register symbols:

A, ═══════ | A | a | a' | a'' | a''' | a''''
F_1-E | F-e | f-e^1 | f^1-e^2 | f^2-e^3 | f^3-e^4 | f^4-c^5

Pitch: The author advocates using the first twelve letters of
    the Greek alphabet to identify the successive notes of the
    the chromatic scale.

E   F   F# G   G# A   A# B   C   C# D   D# E
        Gb   Ab   Bb   Db   Eb

Duration: After lengthy consideration of the advantages and
   disadvantages of contemporary proportional notation as applied to his new proposal, Brennink settled on traditional
   means of delineating rhythmic values.
Example 2-88.

In summing up the perceived advantages of his notational reform, Brennink was of the opinion that "Some people may be
saddened if the customary calligraphy of printed music appears
no more; but just as we have become familiar with Shakespeare's
works in modern spellings rather than in Elizabethan spellings, so shall we appreciate the disuse of inconvenient traditions in music notation."
   On first glance this seems to be a plausible statement;
on careful consideration it appears simplistic. To equate
Elizabethan spellings with traditional notation is beside the
point; the English language has undergone far more changes in
the centuries since Elizabeth I than has notation since the
consolidation of modern mensural notation in the late eighteenth century. We do "appreciate the disuse of inconvenient
traditions," in English as well as in notation, but that is
no valid argument for embracing Brennink's reform -- or any
other such proposal -- as a consequence and for throwing out
the accumulated practices of notation that we have inherited.
We may well "be saddened if the customary calligraphy of
printed music appears no more," but only if what is offered
in its place is inferior, impractical, and even more anachronistic.

1984. Louis Appell, <u>The Novox Piano Notation</u>. Port Washington,
   New York: Novox, Inc., Publishers.
Staff: 6-line (3-3); a keyboard system comprises a pair of
   6-line staves.
Register symbols:

C_1-B_1 |2 |1 |1 |2 |3 |4
          C-B c-b c^1-b^1 c^2-b^2 c^3-b^3 c^4-b^4

Pitch:

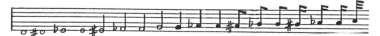

C C# Db D   D# Eb E F F# Gb G G# Ab A A#   Bb B C
Meter: Displayed as a fraction between the staff segments.
Example 2-89. Ludwig van Beethoven, <u>Sonata in C Minor</u>, op. 13.

Grave

This proposal is essentially a repetition of similar and earlier attempts to establish a three-line staff as the norm (see
Appendix A). Appell's system is designed primarily for his re-
arrangement of the piano keys on an instrument he calls a
pianova. On this new keyboard, the keys of C, D, and E are
similar in design and placement to the three familiar black
keys, but are colored white. C#/Db and D#/Eb are flat white
keys; the remaining white keys are unchanged from the standard
layout. These alterations, the inventor rationalized, provide
uniformity in playing all scales and chords on the pianova.
Yet Appell's notation, even with his unorthodox staff design,
still retains the accidental signs that the majority of reformers strive to eliminate.

1985. William Tapley, <u>Gabriel Music Notation</u>. Forestport, New
    York: Gabriel Music.
Staff: 4-line (2-2). The spaces between lines 1-2 and 3-4 ac-
    commodate three pitches each, while the central wider space
    outlines five pitches, with two notes on each of the lines.
Clef signs: Standard G- and F-clefs, positioned as shown in
    Example 2-90.
Pitch:

G Ab A Bb B C Db D Eb E F Gb G
   G#   A#   C#   D#   F#

Duration: Treated traditionally, except that half-notes,wheth-
er black ovals or open diamonds, are stemless. Whole-notes
are somewhat flatter in shape to distinguish them from half-
notes. Tied black noteheads are striped while tied diamond
notes have broken outlines.
Meter: Also designated conventionally, as are all other notational factors such as rests, tempo indications, dynamics,
and so on.
Example 2-90. Frédéric Chopin, <u>Prelude in A</u>, op. 28, no. 7.

This, the most recent proposal to be received, is merely a
refinement of Tapley's earlier ideas, discussed on page 267).
Comparison will show that only the squared noteheads of his
previous plan have been jettisoned in the inventor's modification.

"My Gabriel system," he writes, "is basically a chromatic
notation with all the advantages of such a system. The most
notable advance I have made is to condense the successive
notes in the chromatic scale so that each is separated by a
one-third notehead step rather than the usual one-half step.
This overcomes the only problem of all the other chromatic
proposals that I have seen, namely that other staffs require
seventy percent greater height in order to accommodate twelve
notes instead of the current seven."

Tapley's assertion is not borne out when one compares the
staff heights of the preceding proposals with his own; few of
the earlier designs require up to seventy percent more vertical space than does Tapley's staff. A further question might
be directed toward the logic of employing both shaped and void
noteheads for the sharped and flatted pitches of the chromatic
scale. As the majority of other systems have demonstrated,
either the one or the other is sufficient to distinguish the
altered from the natural notes.

Even as we approach the final decade of the twentieth century, attempts are still being made to devise a new notational
system superior in every aspect to the one we currently use.
In itself this is commendable -- even essential -- yet the

mere reinventing of proposals long ago advanced and quickly
forgotten does not bring us any closer to notational Utopia.
Whether or not we ever attain that elusive goal is an intriguing surmise -- possible, but not probable.

NOTES

1. Anon., Chromatic Notation (Victoria, B.C./Montreux:
Edition Chroma, 1983), p. 4.
2. Thomas Howells, Settled Notation Music System which
facilitates reading music in all keys alike for piano
(Washington, D.C., the author, 1882).
3. François Ange Alexandre Blein, Théorie des vibrations
et son application à divers phénomènes de physique (Paris:
Père et fils, 1831).
4. Giorgio Anselmo di Parma, Ars Nova Musicae, De Musica,
III, "Harmonie cantabalis" (Parma, 1496).
5. Alexandre Lavignac, ed., Encyclopédie de la musique et
Dictionnaire du Conservatoire (Paris: Delagrave, 1913-1930).
6. Karl Laker, Das musikalische ochen; anschauliche darstellung von begriffen und gesetzen der musiklehre. . . .
(Graz: Leuschner & Lubensky, 1913).
7. Karkoschka, p. 12.
8. Henry Cowell, New Musical Resources, Part II (New York:
Something Else Press, Inc., 1969).

3.
Novel Clef and Register Symbology

Even though most proposed reforms were impractical
and were adopted by no-one but their inventors, as a
whole they strikingly illustrate the desire of Western notators for a notation independent of any single musical style.

--"Notation," <u>New Grove Dictionary of Music and Mu-
sicians</u>, 1981.

Called <u>claves signatae</u> by the early music theorists, these
familiar symbols tell performers in what octave to play or
sing the notes written on the staff, whether a traditional
pentagram or a hybrid arrangement of horizontal (or vertical)
lines. Once termed <u>claves</u>, as "the keys by which the secrets
of the staff are unlocked," clef signs are still integral to
music notation if the expression is nonexperimental. Nonetheless, the reformers of common-practice notation have long been
rethinking the shape -- even the presence -- of these signs as
well as reconsidering staves, noteheads, and related symbology.
     Since the late 1600s, notators have variously proposed
altering the appearance of the standard clef symbols (treble,
bass, alto/tenor), consolidating them into a single written
form, or dispensing with them altogether in favor of other designations for instrumental and vocal register, or "pitch re-
gions." The vast majority of these changes have been proposed
in conjunction with unorthodox reforms of the staff to which
any clef signs must relate; hence, many such proposals have
been detailed in the previous chapter. Still others will appear on later pages, in analyses either of reforms of notehead
design or of schemes based on numbers, letters, or stenographic
codings.
     Most of the clef-sign proposals discussed here appear on
the standard pentagram, with traditional noteheads, durational
indications, key signatures, and meter signs. Unless there is
special mention of an exception, these elements may be assumed
to conform to the current practice of the time.
     Historically, this chapter ranges from the proposals of
Athanasius Kircher in 1650 to suggestions made by contemporary
composers. Kircher advocated placing each of the three extant
clef signs (G, C, and F) in five different positions on the

staff (Figure 3-1), a procedure that was adopted in modified form by many subsequent notators.
Figure 3-1. Athanasius Kircher, Proposed Clef-Sign Usage.

The proposals of Bennert, Colet, Gretry, Monteclair, and Saint-Lambert, among the thirty-four illustrated in this chapter, demonstrate similar unusual positioning of clef symbols current in their time. Only with Thomas Salmon's 1672 "casting away the perplexity of different cliffs" was there a significant departure from accepted register forms that initiated a long history of radical alteration of existing clef symbols.

By the middle of the twentieth century, this evolution had arrived at such experimental devices as the "floating clefs" of Luciano Berio's Rounds for Harpsichord, offering the performer a spontaneous choice between two or more registers to which the written notes may be related (see page 260). In John Cage's monumental Concert for Piano and Orchestra (page 133), the pianist's choice of register is indicated by two different clef signs on one staff. Precedence for this device, however, is manifest in a number of seventeenth-century works, such as Frescobaldi's organ compositions (page 133) and Thomas Tomkins' Musica deo sacra (Figure 3-2), published in London in 1668.
Figure 3-2. Thomas Tomkins, Musica deo sacra.

how long will ye love vanity   and

It would be rash, indeed, to suggest that the end of experimentation with clef and register symbology has arrived, but some contemporary composers have already discarded these signs altogether. In Earle Brown's Four Systems for piano, for example, nonconventional pitch symbology refers merely to low, middle, and high space, with no attempt to specify either exact pitch or precise register. Many other modern works dispense with clef signs when they are understood in the context of the medium; in music intended for keyboard instruments, for instance, treble and bass clefs may be assumed. A piece for flute would not be expected to use the bass clef, nor one for trumpet the alto clef; hence, some composers might choose to omit any clef signs where the identity is self-evident.

1672. Reverend Thomas Salmon, An Essay to the Advancement of Musick, by casting away the perplexity of different cliffs.

And uniting all sorts of Musick . . . in one universal char-
acter. London: J. Macock & J. Car.
Staff: 5-line.
Clef signs:
Treble | Mean | Bass

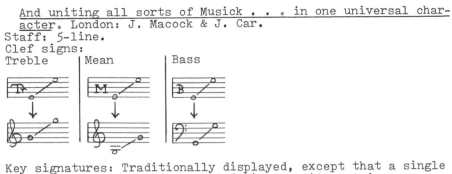

Key signatures: Traditionally displayed, except that a single
   sharp (F#) and a single flat (Bb) are written twice.

Salmon's proposal has the obvious advantage of identical positioning of the octave gamut on all three clefs. Otherwise, his
new symbols are no marked improvement over the conventional
soprano, alto/tenor, and bass clef signs. This reform -- based
on Juan Caramuel de Lobkowitz's 1645 suggestion (1), which required some ninety-two pages of explication and justification
-- was designed to eliminate the excessive changing of C-clef
placement in vocal music. In reality, it did no such thing, inasmuch as his proposal created its own profusion of clef
changes.
   A minor firestorm was ignited by Salmon's idea, and his
proposition was ridiculed in print by his contemporary, Matthew Locke. Locke's blast prompted an angry rebuttal from Salmon, and an extended controversy ensued. Not at all daunted by
Locke's attack on his reform, Salmon published his *A Proposal*
to perform Musick in Perfect and Mathematical Proportions (2).
   The controversy engendered by Salmon's proposal raises an
interesting question: Why have the most recent notational reforms failed to arouse comparable heated discussions, pro and
con, and the same kind of virulent polemics created by many
eighteenth- and nineteenth-century proposals? Lengthy articles
in the musical press of the time, even whole books attacking
or defending various reforms of notation, appeared with regularity. Many eminent musicians joined in the verbal fray, adding their measure of prestige to extolling or denouncing one
or the other of the new systems. Are we now more blasé about
such happenings in the hermetic world of theory and pedagogy,
or are we simply more tolerant of the efforts by our fellow
musicians to improve or to replace standard notation? These
are intriguing, if unanswerable questions.

1702. Michel de Saint-Lambert, *Les principes du clavecin, con-*
   tenent une explication exacte de tout ce qui concerne la
   tablature et le clavier. Avec des remarques nécessaires pour
   l'intelligence de plusieurs difficultées de la musique (The
   rudiments of the harpsichord, including a detailed explana-

tion of everything that concerns keyboard tablature. Also,
necessary comments so as to understand various musical problems). Paris: C. Ballard.
Staff: 5-line.
Clef signs:
G-clef | C-clef | F-clef

Pitch:

, and so on.

  C C# Db D D# Eb E F F# Gb G
Key signatures: Sharps and flats are displayed as shown below.

Meter:

  2   3   4   2   6
  4   4   4   2   8
Example 3-1. J. S. Bach, "Prelude in C-sharp Minor," from
The Well-Tempered Clavier, Book II.

Saint-Lambert based his clef reform on Thomas Salmon's thesis
that each clef sign should appear in only one position on the
staff. What sets this proposal apart is his unique positioning
of the C-clef symbol on the second staff space, there being no
precedent for this practice. Though novel in appearance, Saint-

Lambert's G-clef sign on the first staff line merely duplicates
the so-called "French violin clef." Systematically used by
Lully for the violin and trumpet parts of his orchestral works,
as well as by other composers of the period, this practice was
hardly new with Saint-Lambert.

All the remaining elements of this musician's notation conform to the standard procedures of his time, including the
diamond-shaped noteheads and the double-cross symbol for the
sharp, as well as the duplicated accidentals in the key signatures.

1736. Michel Pignolet de Montéclair, "Nouvelle méthode pour
apprendre la musique par des demonstrations faciles, suivies
d'un grand nombre de leçons à une et à deux voix, avec des
tables qui facilitant l'habitude des transpositions et la
conaissance des differentes mesures" (New method of learning
music by simple examples, including numerous exercises for
one and two voices, and charts which facilitate ease of
transposition and recognition of different cadences), Principes de musique, Partie IV, pp. 101; 110; 127; 131.
Paris: Boivin.
Staff: 5-line.
Clef signs:
Soprano   Alto/Tenor   Bass

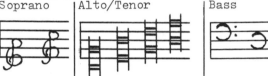

Like Salmon in the previous century, Montéclair based his clef
proposal on one put forward by Caramuel de Lobkowitz in his
1645 Ars nova musicae. At first, Montéclair designated a three-
octave span with the letters D (Dessus), H (Haute-contre), and
T (Taille). He revised his method twice, in 1709 and again in
1736, when his Principes de musique was published. The latter
treatise employs a flexible use of the three familiar clef
signs: the G- and F-clefs are in two positions, and the C-clef
is in four, as shown above.

1766. M. l'abbé Joseph Lacassagne, "Réflexions sur l'usage des
clefs" (Thoughts on the use of clef signs), Traité général
des élémens du chant (General treatise on the elements of
vocal music). Paris: G. Desprez.
Staff: 5-line.
Clef signs: The G-clef only, described by Lacassagne as l'unicléfier musical, in various positions on the staff.
Soprano   Alto/Tenor   Bass

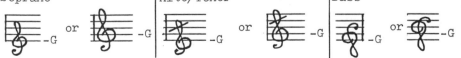

Pitch:

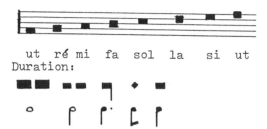

ut ré mi fa sol la   si ut

Duration:

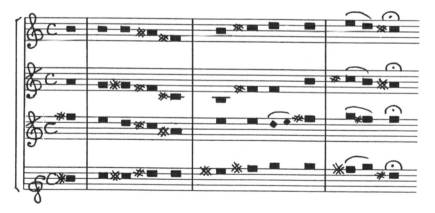

Example 3-2. J. S. Bach, "Chorale," from the Saint Matthew Passion.

Although Lacassagne's unified clef signs were somewhat innovative, his choice of notehead design was more retrogressive than progressive. In their general appearance, his notes were too similar to the Gothic square-note notation of earlier centuries to be considered a useful new manner of denoting pitch.

Written to the editor-in-chief of the monumental Encyclopédie (3), Denis Diderot, Pascal Boyer's Lettre à Monsieur Diderot, sur le projet de l'unité de clef dans la musique . . .

proposée par M. l'abbé Lacassagne (1767) criticized the attempt
of this reformer to reduce all clefs to one symbol. The following year, Lacassagne replied to this attack on his proposal in
his L'unicléfier musical, pour servir de supplément au Traité
général des élémens du chant (4). His defense was to no avail;
his suggestion for a single clef sign never became an accepted
fixture in the notational practice of his time -- nor has it
even today.

1789. André Ernest Modeste Grétry, Mémoires, ou Essai sur la
    musique (An essay on music). Brussels: Academie de musique.
Staff: 5-line.
Clef signs: Although the C-clef symbol has the appearance of
    that used during Grétry's time, it functions as a G-clef an
    octave lower than the treble.

For piccolo | For soprano voice | For alto and tenor voices
            | and high instruments | and instruments

For bass voice and viols | For double bass

Like Joseph Lacassagne before him, Grétry advocated a reduction
of the functional clefs -- in this case, to treble and bass
only. During the latter part of the eighteenth century, the
C-clef was used less and less, but it is curious that Grétry
retained the symbol as a substitute for the G-clef sign. Also
curious, and patently inconsistent, is his dual bass-clef sign;
if the double treble-clef sign indicates an octave higher than
the single symbol, then the double F-clef sign should signify
the octave below the normal symbol. Grétry reverses his symbology here without valid reason.

1840. Hippolyte-Raymond Colet, La panharmonie musicale, ou
    cours complet de composition théorique et pratique . . .
    avec un nouveau système de clés réduites à une seule clé de
    sol et une nouvelle manière de chiffrer plus simple, plus
    logique, à l'usage des artistes, des amateurs, des écoles de
    chant, des pensions, et des collèges (Comprehensive harmony;
    a complete course of theoretical and practical composition
    using a new clef system, reduced to only the G-clef, and a
    new figured bass method, simpler and more logical, for pro-
    fessionals and beginners, singing schools and colleges).
    Paris: Legouix.
Staff: 5-line.

Clef signs:

For soprano and alto voices | For tenor and bass voices, an octave lower

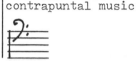

For alto voice in contrapuntal music | For bass voice in contrapuntal music | For viola

Colet's tenor/bass clef sign seems unnecessarily contrived, not to mention his placing of the normal bass-clef symbol on the top rather than on the fourth staff line. It is also unclear what advantage, if any, there might be in using different clef signs for contrapuntal music and for melodic/harmonic textures. As might be expected, Colet's suggested new clef symbols made little impact on the notational practice of the time.

1842. Joseph Lanz, _Das System der Musik-Schlüssel auf die einfachsten Grundsätze, zurückgeführt wodurch die Einheit des Schlüssels und grössere Bestimmtheit Deutlichkeit und Bequemlichkeit in der Tonhöhen bezeichnung erzielt wird_ (System of music clefs reduced to the simplest principles whereby the unity of clefs and the greater distinction and convenience in designating pitch is gained). Vienna: the author?
Staff: 5-line.
Clef signs:

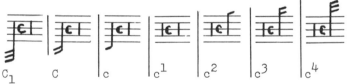

C_1 C   c c^1 c^2 c^3 c^4

Pitch:

F G A BC D E F
Example 3-3.

A simple notational proposal, and one that is eminently logical, yet Lanz's idea never attained wide acceptance. Perhaps
it was little noticed among the welter of reforms that came to
light during this period, else it might have exerted more influence on the development and improvement of notation.

1850. William Striby, <u>Universal System of Music Notation</u>.
   London: A. Burk & Cie.
Staff: 6-line; the fourth line is heavy. Two staves are usu-
   ally combined as a system for the keyboard instruments.
Clef signs: Three different authorities on notational reforms
   rather surprisingly disagree about the symbols used by
   Striby.
   1) David & Lussy, <u>Histoire de la notation musicale depuis
   ses origines</u>:
   Treble Bass

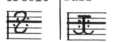

   2) C. F. Abdy Williams, <u>The Story of Notation</u>:
   Treble Bass

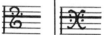

   3) J. Wolf, <u>Handbuch der Notationskunde</u>:
   Descant Baritone/Bass Alto Tenor

The authentic versions, as demonstrated in the full score
given in Example 3-4, are as follows:
Descant or Dessus Barytone or Bass Alto Tenor

Pitch:

C   D   E   F   G   A   B   C

Example 3-4. Ludwig van Beethoven, Symphony no. 3 in E-flat, op. 55.

The most interesting elements of Striby's reform are the novel clef signs he used. His six-line staff, as he conceived it, serves a two-octave span with the addition of only a single ledger line below and above -- a welcome advantage. But in

spite of its pragmatism, Striby's proposal was quickly forgotten by any who were aware of it, and it is now only of historical interest to those concerned with the current improvement
of notation. The republication of the author's proposal in
Paris, 1857, under the title of <u>Système universal de notation
. . . pour le chant et tous les instruments de musique</u> did
nothing to advance his suggested reforms.

1868. Alexis Jacob Azévedo, <u>Sur un nouveau signe proposé pour
   remplacer les trois clefs de la notation musicale</u> (Concerning a new sign intended to replace the three clefs of music
   notation). Paris: L. Escudier.
Staff: 5-line.
Clef signs: One basic symbol ("Une clef générale d'ut") identifying the pitch of C can be referred to any line or space
   of the staff. The specific octave is indicated by ancillary
   markings attached to this symbol.

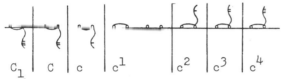

C_1 C   c c^1 c^2 c^3 c^4

Azévedo's novel clef sign was devised primarily to avoid the
use of ledger lines and 8va indicators, thus keeping all the
notes of the music on the staff. Although his basic premise
cannot be faulted, Azévedo's suggested symbol with its ancillary markings is rather too fanciful to be practical. Few composers, one thinks, could have been expected to go to so much
trouble in their notation, and very few publishers would have
cared to take on the expense of adding these symbols to their
store of printing fonts.

1879. A. Gatting, <u>Eine musikalische Reform resp. eine neues
   Notenlinien-System und ein fast durchaus neuer Tonzeichenbau</u>
   (A musical reform for a new staff system and rather new note
   symbols). Strassburg: the author.
Staff: 3-line.
Register symbols:

Grey	Green	Violet	Red	Yellow	Blue	White

C_1-B_1 C-B   c-b c^1-b^1 c^2-b^2 c^3-b^3 c^4-b^4
Pitch:

C   D   E   F   G   A   B   C

Gatting's symbols, shaping one of the most elaborate clef proposals discussed in these pages, are further distinguished by
employing colors in their printing. This appears to be a case
of gilding the lily, as the symbols themselves are sufficiently
individual in design to catch the eye. This inventor's reform,
then, remains an isolated historical curiosity and not a proposition that might have validity for contemporary notational
practice.

1884. Julius Eduard Bennert, <u>Reformen der Notenschrift</u> (Nota-
tional reforms). n.p.
Staff: 5-line.
Clef signs:

For soprano voice and instruments	For alto and tenor voices and instruments	For bass voice and instruments

The unorthodox position of the F-clef sign is the salient feature of Bennert's notation. To use a familiar symbol in unconventional locales on the staff, however, is not the most effective manner to accomplish clef reform. Neither alto and ten-
or voices nor the instruments of parallel range are accustomed
to the F-clef symbol; also, the bass voice and lower instruments would have difficulty adjusting to its placement on other
than the fourth line. What Bennert hoped to gain by his plan
remains unclear; whatever his aim, it is now irrelevant, as
his scheme was never sanctioned.

1890. August Wickström, <u>Die Vereinfachung der Tonbezeichnung</u>
(The simplification of notational symbols). Leipzig: M. P.
Belaieff.
Staff: 5-line.
Clef signs:

Ottavino (for piccolo)	<u>Sopran</u> (for G-clef instruments)	<u>Mezzo</u> (for C-clef instruments)	<u>Bass</u> (for F-clef instruments)

<u>Kontrabass</u>
(for double bass)

This musician was not at fault in using oversized letters to
mark the different clefs, but in concocting an international
language mix for his chosen letters. <u>Ottavino</u> is Italian, <u>Sop-
ran</u> and <u>Kontrabass</u> are German; the other two clef names are
Italian or English. It is odd that Wickström did not rely on

his native language for a consistent nomenclature.

1892. Justizrath Lauff, "Über eine neue Notenschrift" (Concerning a new notation), <u>Klavierlehrer</u> XV, 5.
Staff: 5-line.
Clef signs:
   Discant   Bass

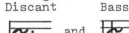 and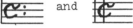

Pitch:

   F   G   A   B   C   D   E   F

Meter: So as not to confuse his two clef signs with the conventional symbols C and ¢, Lauff recommended that these be written as 'i/'i and ?/?.
It would seem that Lauff's two versions of the C-clef sign were intended for vocal music of rather limited range. Because of the confusion that might arise in mistaking these signs for meter signatures, it would have been more sensible for Lauff to have retained the conventional C-clef symbol.

1902. Charles Marie Augustin Meerens, <u>La science musicale à la portée de tous les artistes et amateurs</u> (Musical science within the capability of all professionals and amateurs). Brussels: J. B. Klette.
Staff: 5-line.
Register symbols: Two different proposals were put forward by Meerens, both geared to the piano keyboard.

1) 	II	III	IV	V	VI	VII	VIII	IX-XI
2) 	8	9	10	11	12	13	14	15-17
C_1-B_1	C-B	c-b	c^1-b^1	c^2-b^2	c^3-b^3	c^4-b^4	c^5	?

Pitch:

   C   D   E   F   G   A   B   C

Key signatures: Conventionally displayed, but related to the new disposition of the staff lines; for example,

A major or F# minor | Bb major or G minor

Meter: Instead of a denominator, a figure representing the
metronomic pulse appears in its place; for example,

Example 3-5. Franz Schubert, <u>Sonata in C Minor</u>, op. posth.

In a third proposal concerned with register numbering, Meerens
was a bit more realistic than in the first two plans, illustrated above: The numbers ranged from 6 (for the lowest C)
only to 13 (for the third-octave C). Why two of Meeren's systems should have started with the numbers 6 and 7 identifying
the lowest octave of the keyboard remains a mystery. In his
book on the history of notation (5), Abdy Williams commented
somewhat sarcastically that "the inventor expects future pianos
to extend to eleven octaves." Was it wishful thinking on the
inventor's part to anticipate an enlarged keyboard -- or a momentary mental lapse?

Hardly two years after Meerens put forward his notational
proposals, an institute was established in Brussels to propa-
gandize his novel register systems. Some of the most distinguished musicians of the time lent their support, and every
effort was made to further the widespread adoption of the reform. This unprecedented practical enthusiasm proved to be
fruitless, however, for Meerens' personal method of clef-sign
substitution was soon forgotten. Still, in the decades immediately following these early steps, the idea of using numbers
to mark off vocal and instrumental registers appeared in many
new notational proposals. For purposes of comparison and evaluation, these can be seen side by side in Appendix C.

1905. Thorald Jerichau, "Zur Notenschrift" (Concerning nota-
tion), <u>Zeitschrift der Internationalen Musik-Gesellschaft</u>
VI, pp. 330-336.
Staff: 5-line.

Clef signs: One basic clef sign is used; the octaves above middle C are indicated by the Arabic numerals 2 to 4, and the octaves below middle C by the Roman numerals II to IV.

To utilize the bass-clef symbol as a substitute for the alto-clef sign is illogical. A single clef symbol accompanied by register numbers is in itself perfectly reasonable, but that symbol should be appropriate to its normal position on the staff. It was undoubtedly for this reason that Jerichau's proposal was never accepted by the musical community of his time.

1906. Axel Törnudd, "Uniclef," Säveletär 6.
Staff: 5-line.
Clef signs:

| Piccolo clef | Discant clef | Alto/tenor clef | Bass clef |

From Juan Caramuel de Lobkowitz in 1645 to Andreas Steinfort in 1975 (see page 126), notation reformers have been trying to design a single, acceptable clef sign for all registers. What sets Törnudd's idea apart is that for the three lower octaves he used both the G-clef sign and the letter G, lower case and capital, set on the second staff line. Only a few years earlier, Hermann Stephani had advanced essentially this same idea in his "Einheitspartitur (6)," though Törnudd may well have been unaware of it. The rationale of his choice of clef symbology is obvious, but the last written form of the letter G is rather obscure and not easily read.

1928. A. Saule, Vereinfachtes Notensystem ohne Vorzeichen (Simplified notation without accidentals). n.p., the author.
Staff: 5-line (2-3).
Clef signs:

Pitch:

C   C#   D   D# E   F   F#   G   G#   A   A# B   C
     Db   Eb   Gb   Ab   Bb

This inventor's rather fanciful new clef symbols seem excessively contrived, and they can hardly be considered important
enough to serve as alternatives to the standard G- and F-clef
signs.

1934. André Piaceski, L'écriture et la lecture de toute la
musique avec une seule clef (The notation and study of all
music using a single clef). St.-André près Troyes, France:
Les Editions du chevron.
Staff: 5-line.
Clef signs:

In theory, this single-clef suggestion has considerable merit:
It is simple to write, easy to print, and obvious in intent.
Yet the idea of a single clef for all registers has never been
accepted by the music profession; ingrained habit no doubt explains the reluctance of singers and instrumentalists to read
from an unfamiliar clef, no matter how simple and clear that
sign might be.

1937. Paul Lindorf, Die Notwendigkeit einer Reform unserer
Notenschreibweise und ein Weg dazu (The necessity of reform-
ing our present notation and a suggested method). Görlitz-
Biesnitz, Germany: H. Kretschner.
Staff: 3-line; four staves constitute a system.
Clef signs:

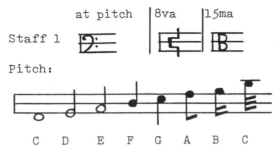

at pitch | 8va | 15ma

Staff 1

Pitch:

C   D   E   F   G   A   B   C

Lindorf's array of novel clef signs is confusingly constructed.
The octave sign for Staff 4 (B) would seem to be the abbrevia-
tion for bass, but the same form is used for Staff 1, the true
bass, but two octaves higher. Also, the F-clef sign used for
Staff 2 two octaves higher is illogical as it represents a
higher tessitura than the G-clef symbol standing for only one
octave higher. All in all, one has the feeling that this inventor did not think through the clef relationships carefully
enough.

1950. Marc Delau, <u>Une position, une clé; principe rationnel
    d'écriture musicale</u> (One position, one clef; a rational prin-
    ciple of musical notation). Paris: Les Editions ouvrières.
Staff: 3-line. Superimposed 3-line segments are used as ledger
    lines.
Clef signs:
<u>clé grave</u> | <u>clé moyenne</u> | <u>clé aiguë</u>

Pitch:

    ut ré mi fa sol la si ut
Example 3-6.

Designed for ease in solfege, according to its inventor, Delau's system introduces three novel clef symbols that approach
a degree of artiness. The one thing that contemporary notation
does _not_ need is one more example of idiosyncratic symbology --
unless it has the potential for clarifying an obscure notational element, which Delau's proposal does not.

1961. Boguslaw Schäffer, _Modell III_. Cracow, Poland: Polskie
   Wydawnictwo Muzycne.
Staff: 5-line.
Clef signs:
G-clef   F-clef

The arrow signs used by Schäffer in his composition, as well
as by Otte and Krauze (see below), are simple yet logical substitutes for the conventional symbols. They must be seen, however, in the context of notational formats that are experimental and nontraditional in every sense, the new symbols for
register being but a part of the whole.

1964. Hans Otte, _Alpha: Omega_. New York: C. F. Peters Corpo-
   ration.
Staff: 5-line.
Clef signs:
G-clef   F-clef

1966. Zygmunt Krauze, _Triptych_. Cracow, Poland: Polskie Wy-
   dawnictwo Muzycne.
Staff: 5-line.
Clef signs:
G-clef   F-clef

1968 Franz Herf, "Das Chromatische Tonsystem" (The chromatic
   notation system), _Muzikerziehung_ 21, 5, pp. 219-220.
Staff: 6-line.

Register symbols:

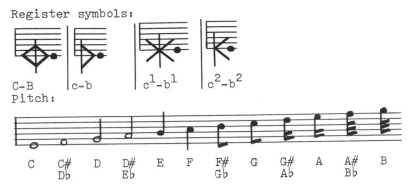

C-B   c-b c^1-b^1 c^2-b^2

Pitch:

C   C#/Db   D   D#/Eb   E   F   F#/Gb   G   G#/Ab   A   A#/Bb   B

Example 3-7.

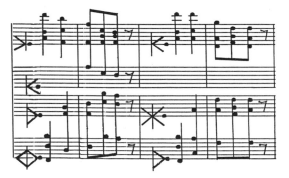

Herf's reform is sufficiently up-to-date to propose a pitch notation that avoids the necessity for accidentals, yet unaccountably provides a register symbology for designating only four out of a possible seven octaves. Comparable clef signs derived from Herf's basic format could easily be devised for the missing octaves, for instance:

Example 3-8.

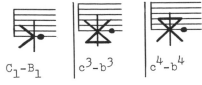

C_1-B_1 c^3-b^3 c^4-b^4

1969. Barry Brosch, <u>Prolations for Solo Cello</u>. Urbana: Media
   Press.
Staff: 5-line.
Clef signs:
G-clef | F-clef

1969. George Cacioppo, <u>Holy Ghost Vacuum or America Faints</u>.
   Don Mills, Ontario: B.M.I. Canada.
Staff: 5-line.
Clef signs:
G-clef | F-clef

Brosch and Cacioppo neatly illustrate the avant-gardist's tote-
bag of diverse notational techniques, both past and present,
available for their creative innovations. Oversize letters, for
instance, served as clef signs long before their metamorphosis
into the familiar symbols, yet these two composers reverted to
the antique practice in these works. As with the arrow signs
in the scores of Schäffer, Otte, and Krauze, this reversion
does not necessarily constitute an improvement, but must be
regarded in the context of unorthodox notational schemes.

———————————————————————

1973. Andras Szenkiralyi, "An Attempt to Modernize Notation,"
   <u>The Music Review</u> 34, 2, pp. 100-123.
Staff: 5-line.
Clef signs:
G-clef | F-clef

New symbols also substitute for octave transpositions:

⇓	⇓	↓	↑	⇑	⇑
22b	15b	8b	8va	15ma	22ma

Pitch:

E	F	F#	G	G#	A	A#	B	C	C#	D	D#	E
		Gb		Ab		Bb			Db		Eb	

Duration: Shown proportionately within evenly spaced barlines
   that represent 1-second intervals of time. Notes which are
   held to sequent pitches are extended by a thin line.

Rests: Designated by blank space within the barlines, as il-
    lustrated above.
By virtue of incorporating the technique of proportional duration, this proposal is very much in the mainstream of contemporary notational practice. The two letter-A clef signs are
perfectly logical in that no existing clef symbol relates to
the pitch A on the central staff line. Yet apparently no other
composer has adopted this particular staff layout or the inventor's suggestion for a new clef identifier.

1975. Andreas Steinfort, <u>Reform in der Musik-Schrift, oder die</u>
    <u>Unterdrückung der Schlussel</u> (Reform of music notation, or
    the suppression of clef signs). Santiago, Chile: the author.
Staff: 5-line.
Register symbols:

![Oct. -2]	I	II	III	IV	V	VI
Oct. -2	Oct. -1	Oct. 1	Oct. 2	Oct. 3	Oct. 4	Oct. 5

VI	VI
Oct. 6	Oct. 7

Pitch: Indicated traditionally, except that any single note
    may be notated in three different ways, as for example,

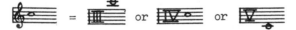

Without apparent rhyme or reason, Steinfort uses the same
Roman numeral to identify more than one register in his nine-
octave compass. Why not the numbers I to IX, so that each octave has its own number? And why, we might ask, <u>nine</u> octaves?
Steinfort thus joins with Charles Meerens (page 124) in providing for a nonexistent total compass, one that is not even
attainable in the modern orchestra. Even if it were obtainable,
its extremes would be inaudible to the human ear.

1975. Andrew Stiller, [<u>Clef sign proposal</u>]. Buffalo, New York:
    the author.
Staff: 5-line.
Clef signs:

and

Stiller's suggestions for double-octave transpositions in
treble and bass clefs are somewhat "arty" and tricky to draw.
Composers and copyists would surely find it much easier and
more convenient to use the 15ma sign in either instance.

The notational technique of relating two different clef signs to one staff first appeared in such early seventeenth-century works as Frescobaldi's organ compositions. In our own time, the device has been appropriated by a number of composers, a few of whom are cited below. Multiple clef signs offer the twentieth-century performer several options as to choice of instrumental or vocal register, thus introducing the element of controlled chance into the interpretation of the composer's notation.

ca. 1616. Giralamo Frescobaldi, various organ works.

1958. John Cage, <u>Concert for Piano and Orchestra</u>. New York: C. F. Peters Corporation.

1959. Karlheinz Stockhausen, <u>Zyklus</u>. Vienna: Universal Edition A.G.

1962. Boguslaw Schäffer, <u>Course "J"</u>. Cracow: Polskie Wydawnic-two Muzycne.

    and

1967. Sidney Hodkinson, <u>The Dissolution of the Serial</u>. Ann Arbor: manuscript.

NOTES

1. Juan Caramuel de Lobkowitz, Arte nueva de musica (Rome: Pedro de Talco, 1669).

2. Thomas Salmon, A Proposal to perform Musick in Perfect and Mathematical Proportions (London: the author, 1688).

3. Encyclopédie, ou Dictionnaire raisonné des sciences, arts et métiers (Paris: 1751-65).

4. Joseph Lacassagne, L'unicléfier musical, pour servir de supplement au Traité general des élémens du chant (Paris: G. Desprez, 1769).

5. Charles Francis Abdy Williams, The Story of Notation (London: The Walter Scott Publishing Co., Ltd., 1903).

6. International Musical Society Zeitschrift, vol. 2, 1900, pp. 313-315.

4.
Proposed Notehead Designs

If we sum up all the notes, as they lie scatter'd in
the several Compositions of Music, we shall find just
twelve of them, no fewer nor more. The unlearned will
stand amazed at this doctrine. What! They'll cry, Is
there not an infinite number of notes in one opera
only? Is there not four or five times Twelve Notes
upon such little instruments as Violins or Spinets?
Is there not more even in one little tune? Again, the
learned will perhaps look upon this position with
scorn, and call it a ridiculous innovation. But I
hope I shall easily make the unlearned leave wonder-
ing, and the learned cease to despise.

--John Francis LaFond, <u>A New System of Music both</u>
<u>Theoretical and Practical, and yet not Mathematical</u>,
1725.

Next to reforms concentrated on the traditional five-line
staff, the most frequently altered notational component has
been the notehead -- the standard symbol in Western music for
delineating pitch. This basic character has been altered in
shape or color and has been relocated in unexpected positions
on the staff to accomplish one of two missions: To distinguish
one pitch from another without using accidental signs or to
clarify rhythmic constructs that cannot be expressed succinctly in conventional notation. (Henry Cowell's 1917 experiments
constitute the paradigm of the latter schema -- see page 277).
   Most inventors of unorthodox notational systems retained
common-practice methods in depicting rhythmic and durational
values, concentrating their reform efforts on pitch clarify-
cation. Only when the procedure that individualized pitch made
time values unclear did the reformers search for new approaches
to indicating duration.
   Likewise, many proposals illustrated in this chapter retained the traditional pentagram as the locale for their experimental noteheads. In certain instances, the lines were more
widely spaced than was customary, so as to accommodate more
than one notehead position on the lines or in the spaces. Proposals by K. M. Bässler, Hugo Riemann, and Hans Sacher, among
others, are typical of this procedure. Other systems, however,

even when they stressed distinctive note shapes or colors also
employed novel staff designs. A number of these have already
been illustrated in a previous chapter, and they will be combined with notehead proposals included in this chapter in Appendix D, a comparative table of proposed notehead designs.

Noteheads of varying design and color are, of course, no
recent innovation, for they were integral to notational systems widely practiced during the Middle Ages and the Renaissance. In manuscripts of both periods, we find a variety of
note and stem designs contrived by the composer-theorists or
by copyists dissatisfied with the existing state of notation
and ambitious to place their personal stamp on its improvement.

Figure 4-1. Early notehead and stem designs.

Figure 4-2. Excerpt from a medieval manuscript.

But these fanciful designs were not devised to individual-
ize pitches or to make infallible durational distinctions.
These are, however, the precise aspirations of the notehead
reforms to be outlined here, fallible though their products
may have been. As fanciful and inventive as the designs just
illustrated, many of the altered noteheads are so complex that
they defeat their very purpose; the intricate characters of
Hermann Schroeder (page 184) and of Edith Faunt (page 136) are
prime candidates for this dubious honor. Certain other proposals alter the notehead so minutely that the eye has extreme
difficulty in perceiving the variations (as in Joseph Raymondi's system, page 155, or in Ludwig Latte's, page 186).

Concomitant alterations to note-stems, flags, or ligatures
sometimes accompany novel notehead designs; occasionally only
these ancillary symbols are altered. In such a case, the
changes affect pitch relationships rather than duration (as,
for instance, in Joseph Sauveur's proposal, page 137).

Other systems, such as the so-called Wiener Notenschrift
of the late 1800s, based their pitch symbology on recurring
patterns of contrasted note shapes (Figure 4-3). Still others
relied on alternating note shapes or colors to outline the
twelve pitches of the chromatic scale. Any number of related
schemes of notehead design will be evident in the 156 reforms
to follow.

Figure 4-3. Wiener Notenschrift.

NOTEHEAD DESIGNS FOR PITCH

1701. Joseph Sauveur, <u>Principes d'acoustique et de musique, ou
système général des intervalles des sons et son application
à tous les systèmes et à tous les instruments de musique</u>
(Principles of acoustics and music; a general system of the
intervals of sound and its application to all musical systems and all instruments). Paris: Histoire de l'Academie
Royale des Sciences.
Staff: 1-line.
Register symbols:

C-B   c-b   c^1-b^1 c^2-b^2 c^3-b^3

Pitch:

C   C#   Db   D   D#   Eb   E   E#   Fb   F   F#

Gb   G   G#   Ab   A   A#   Bb   B   B#   Cb   C

Duration:

Rests:

Example 4-1. Chorale, <u>Ein' feste Burg ist unser Gott.</u>

Born a deaf-mute, Sauveur was phenomenal in devising his notational reform and in being the first theorist to apply the
term acoustics to the science of sound. He was also one of the
first musicians to propose the use of different note forms for
each pitch of the octave scale, a technique that was to enjoy
wide currency in the nineteenth century in the hands of vari-

ous "shaped-note" advocates, such as Galin and Chevé (see pages
296 and 307).

Influenced to a considerable degree by the system of Giorgio Anselmo di Parma (1), Sauveur applied his acoustical research to the division of the octave into 43 mérides, or microtonal intervals -- surely the progenitor of Harry Partch's 43-tone scale devised 250 years later. Each méride was divided further into seven eptamérides, each of which contained ten decamérides. A full octave, therefore, comprised 43 mérides, or 301 eptamérides, or 430 decamérides. The chart below shows the note forms for the 43 mérides of ut; each scale syllable has its own individualized note forms.
Example 4-2.

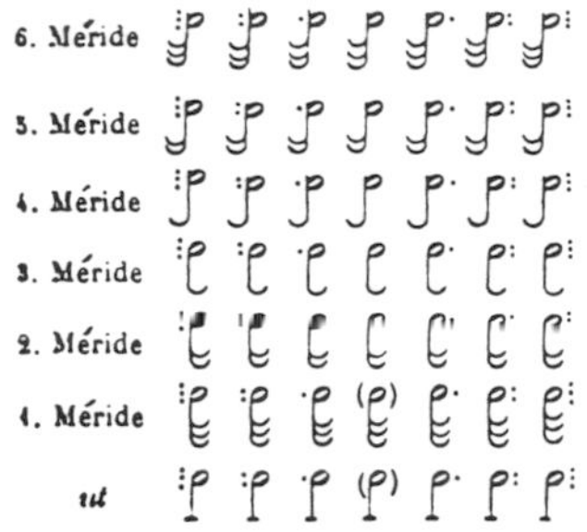

Instead of numbering the diatonic scale with Arabic numbers, Sauveur used Roman numerals except for the fourth degree. He also substituted his own invented scale syllables for the customary ut, re, mi. . . . A diatonic scale, therefore, was indicated as follows:

I	II	III	4	V	VI	VII
pa	ra	ga	so	bo	lo	do

Sauveur's system is one of the most elaborate and detailed of all the notehead reforms proposed during the eighteenth and nineteenth centuries. It is a system, however, more theoretical than practical; no notator or performer could be expected to master the intricacies of Sauveur's notehead and stem designs -- and perhaps Sauveur was realistic enough not to think they could. The proposal remains, then, a historical curiosity, pointing the way to intense future experimentation with all the elements of notation, notehead design being only a part of the search for improved notation.

1728. Démotz de la Salle, Méthode de musique selon un nouveau système très-court, très-facile et très-sûr, approuvé par messieurs de l'Academie royale des sciences, et par les plus habiles musiciens de Paris (A music method according to a new system, very brief, easy and sure, approved by the members of the Royal Academy of Sciences and by the most accomplished musicians of Paris). Paris: Chez Pierre Simon.
Staff: None.

Register symbols:

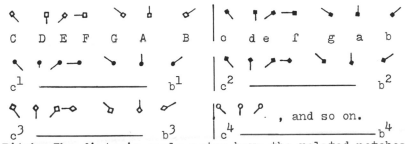

Pitch: The diatonic scale notes have the related notehead formats shown above. Altered notes are accompanied by the traditional flat sign and the double-cross symbol for a sharp.
The note-stem angles derive from a matrix arranged like the
spokes of a wheel; the stems of ascending pitches proceed in
a clockwise direction.

Duration:

Rests:

$$\mathsf{T} \quad \bot \quad \curlyvee \quad 7 \quad \overline{7}$$, and so on.

Meter:

⊂ ¢ 2 3· 2· , for example.

$\frac{4}{4}$ $\frac{2}{2}$ $\frac{2}{4}$ $\frac{3}{4}$ $\frac{6}{8}$

Example 4-3. French folk song.

While this elaborate proposal of Démotz was published anonymously, two years after he had put forth his ideas in a maga-
zine article, this did not prevent its incurring a storm of
virulent criticism. The complexity of the reform was evidently
too much for the theorists and composers of the time to accept, and it was dismissed as unworkable. Adding to its negative appraisal was the fact that it largely duplicated the suggestions made in 1601 by Joachim Burmeister in his <u>Musicae
practicae sive artis canendi ratio</u> (Rostock). Today, with the
advantage of hindsight, we have to agree with Démotz's critics;
the system is, indeed, too complicated to be a reasonable method of notating music.

1734. Johann Mattheson, <u>Kleinen Generalbassschule</u> (Brief thor-
  ough-bass method). Hamburg: Joh. Christoph Kissner.
Staff: 4-line.
Clef signs: None; the staff accommodates the vocal range from
  c to c above middle C.
Pitch:

C   C#   D   D#   E   F   F#   G   G#   A   A#   B   C ——— C
    Db   Eb   Gb   Ab   Bb

Duration: Indicated by the size of the note symbols.

Example 4-4.

Although Mattheson was both a composer and a theorist, it is
his theoretical writings that are most important in his extensive catalogue. Modern scholars assert that the historical information they contain is as significant as his forward-looking
views on the art and science of music, notation being but a
part of his larger interests. Especially significant is Mattheson's concept of note-symbol size to denote duration, a concept that was to reappear in many subsequent notation reforms,
culminating in the current technique of proportional, or "time"
notation.

1785. François Henri Stanislaus de l'Aulnaye, Mémoire sur un
   nouveau système de notation musicale, système par lequel,
   sans le secours des portées ni d'aucune espèce de clef, on
   peut exprimer tous les sons appréciables renfermés dans
   l'étendue du clavier, en représentant chacun de ces sons
   (Treatise on a new system of musical notation, a method by
   which -- without the assistance of staves or any kind of
   clef -- one can express all the perceptible sounds of the
   keyboard by depicting each one of those sounds). Paris: Musée
   de Paris, 1.
Staff: None.
Register symbols:

A_2-B_2 | C_1-B_1 | C-B | c-b | c^1-b^1 | c^2-b^2 | c^3-b^3 | c^4-b^4 | c^5

Pitch:

C   C#   Db   D   D#   Eb   E   F   F#   Gb   G   G#   Ab   A   A#   Bb   B   C

Duration: Successive beats are indicated by / between noteheads.

Rests: All values = s; the precise duration is determined by
   context.
Example 4-5. Chorale, Ein' feste Burg ist unser Gott.

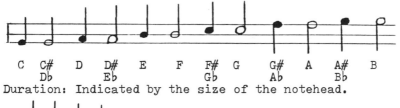

The system of l'Aulnaye in all likelihood represents the first
attempt to distinguish the natural and altered pitches of the
scale by notehead color, though here unrelated to a staff. It
is a procedure that was to inform innumerable subsequent reforms of notation, especially those based on physical analogy
with the piano keyboard. But the inventor of this system complicated his symbology by varying stem positions and lengths
and by attaching further markings to denote register. Reading
difficulty is still further compounded by the durational signs
placed over the noteheads, adding one more complication to the
performer's task.

A number of composers in our own time have availed themselves of the "white-note/black-note" principle in their notation, though disagreeing about which color should apply to
which function of the notehead. Larry Austin, Mauricio Kagel,
Roland Kayn, and Toru Takemitsu, among others, prefer solid
noteheads for the natural pitches and open noteheads for the
sharps or flats -- these to be placed on the standard pentagram.
Certain other composers, however, such as Hans Otte, Henri
Pousseur, and Bernd Alois Zimmermann, resort to the opposite
procedure -- confusing, one may be sure, to the performer of
contemporary keyboard music.

1792. Johannes Rohleder, Chromatischen Notenschrift für chroma-
    tische Klaviatur (Chromatic notation for the chromatic key-
    board). Friedland, Germany: In commission F. Nicolovius.
Staff: 3-line.
Clef signs: As shown in Example 4-6.
Pitch:

| C | C# Db | D | D# Eb | E | F | F# Gb | G | G# Ab | A | A# Bb | B |

Duration: Indicated by the size of the notehead.

Example 4-6. Hymn, "Resignation," from The Southern Harmony.

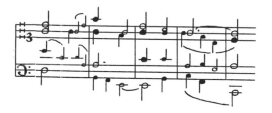

Rohleder's system was designed to serve his newly invented chromatic keyboard, with alternating white and black keys on the same level. It is also one of the first notation reforms based on the alternation of open and solid noteheads. Rohleder's rationale was to divide the twelve chromatic tones of the octave into two groups of six half-steps each, rather than into seven diatonic and five altered pitches. The second, fourth, and sixth tone of each group was thought of as the raising of notes one, three, and five.

The obvious flaw in Rohleder's concept is that the method cannot work on the conventional keyboard, thus making it unusable for anyone not having access to his chromatic keyboard. It cannot work for the simple reason that the first three natural pitches (C, D, and E in the C-major scale) are solid noteheads in Rohleder's system, while the next four (F, G, A, and B) are open noteheads. Such switching of symbological horses in midstream, as it were, is disconcerting to theorist and performer alike. Only after some fifty years did a notational reform recognize this conceptual flaw and solve the problem by using the same color of notehead, whether open or solid, for the half-step intervals (E-F, B-C; see page 159).

Another imperfection in Rohleder's proposal is his reliance on notehead size to delineate duration. Quick perception of minute differences in the size of successive notes is extremely difficult -- unreasonable for the player or singer and taxing for the notator/composer.

1801. William Little & William Smith, The Easy Instructor; or A New Method of Teaching Sacred Harmony. Albany: Websters & Skinners & Daniel Steele.
Staff: 5-line, used for vocal music only.
Clef signs:
  Treble and Tenor | Alto | Bass

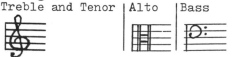

Pitch:

Key signatures: The accidentals are smaller than normal and are stacked vertically, as, for instance:

Duration: Traditional; according to the custom of the period, whole-notes are centered between two barlines.
Rests: The conventional symbols are retained, with two exceptions:

The Easy Instructor was the first of a long line of solfege texts published in the United States and based on the premise of shaped notes. Designed exclusively for the student and amateur, the purpose of these methods was to simplify the process of learning to read music. Thus Little and Smith's system was not meant either to improve standard notation or to supplant it, but only to serve as a foundation for further study and musical development.

Shaped notes have definite advantages over either numerical or alphabetical notation systems. For one thing, retaining the five-line staff enables the notator to show graphically the rise and fall of pitch, which cannot be done as easily by the use of numbers and letters. Furthermore, other traditional elements of notation -- clef signs, key signatures, and specific durational values -- can be retained, making it much easier for the amateur than a wholly new method.

The success of The Easy Instructor can be appreciated by the fact that the book went through many printings; the final edition appeared in 1831. For a fascinating historical account of Little and Smith's pioneering book, one should consult an article entitled "A History and Bibliography of the First Shape Note Tune Book," written by Irving Lowens and Allen P. Britton, which appeared in the Journal of Research in Music Education, No. 1 (1953), pp. 31-55.

For purposes of comparison, we list in Example 4-7 a number of the shaped-note (also called "buckwheat note") textbooks, together with their authors and date and place of publication. Like the proverbial tip of the iceberg, these works represent only a fraction of those printed and disseminated throughout the United States during the nineteenth century. Indeed, many are still being used today, eloquent testimony of their staying power.

Example 4-7.
    1803. Andrew Adgate, Philadelphia Harmony (Philadelphia).

1809. Charles Woodward, <u>Ecclesias Harmonia</u> (Philadelphia).

1810. N. Chapin & J. Dickerson, <u>The Musical Instructor</u>
(Philadelphia)

1832. David Sower, <u>Norristown New & Improved Music Teacher</u>
(Norristown, Pennsylvania).

1844. B. F. White & E. King, <u>The Sacred Harp</u> (Philadelphia).

1846. Jesse Bowman Aiken, <u>The Christian Minstrel</u> (Philadelphia).

1847. Alexander Auld, <u>Ohio Harmonist</u> (Cincinnati).

1848. M. L. Swan, <u>New Harp of Columbia</u> (Nashville)

1853. Andrew W. Johnson, <u>Western Psalmodist</u> (Nashville).

1854. J. J. Fast, <u>Die Cantica Sacra</u> (Hudson, Ohio).

1854. William B. Gillham, <u>Aeolian Lyricist</u> (Columbia, Tennessee).

1854. S. Wakefield, <u>The Sacred Choral</u> (Cincinnati).

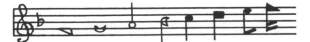

1856. E. D. M'Cauley, <u>The Harmonia Unio</u> (Fredericksburg, Pennsylvania).

1866. William Walker, <u>Christian Harmony</u> (Spartansburg, South Carolina).

1869. Joseph Funk, <u>The Harmonia Sacra</u> (Singer's Glen, Virginia).

Example 4-8.
  1938. Annabel Morris Buchanan, <u>Folk-Hymns of America</u> (Abingdon, Virginia)

1810. Charles Guillaume Riebesthal, <u>Nouvelle méthode pour noter</u>
  <u>la musique et pour l'imprimer avec des caractères mobiles</u>
  (New notational method and printing music with movable type).
  Strassburg: Levrault.
Staff: None.
Register symbols: Various alterations of the pitch symbols
  designate an eight-octave span:

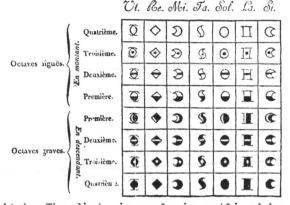

Pitch: The diatonic scale is outlined by the symbols shown
  above, and sharps, flats, and naturals are used as required.
  Chord structures and intervals are designated as in traditional notation; the note symbols are stacked vertically.

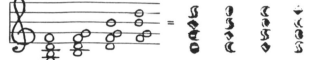

Key signatures: Identified by the keynote as an oversize capital letter.
Duration: Using the note symbol for the sixth scale degree as
  prototype, note values are designated as follows:

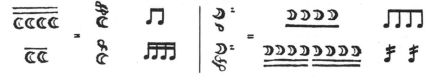

Barlines are indicated as /. Tied notes over a barline are shown as ⌐.

Rests:

⊞ (2)	= ⊏⊐	⊤̣	= 7
⊞ (•)	= ▬.	⊎	= ꓘ
⊞	= ▬	⊎	= ꓱ
⊖	= ▬	⌒	= ꓱ
⊢⊣	= ⸝		

Meter:

¢	C	2/4, 3/4, 3/8 , and so on.
2/2	4/4	2/4 3/4 3/8

Miscellaneous directives: The signs are placed on the same level as the note symbols.

▬ / = the notes at the end of a measure are repeated at the beginning of the next measure

▬ = unison

←⬛ = repetition of a figure

)—◇ = change of key and tempo

℧ = Da capo

∞ = end of movement or work

Example 4-9. <u>Air de Philippe et Georgette</u>.

This, the first of two proposals made by Riebesthal (see page 345 for his alphabetical system), is eccentric to the point of being utterly useless to those concerned with the improvement of notation. The over-elaborate note symbols and duration and rest signs, and the sundry performance directives, evidently precluded the system from being taken very seriously by the inventor's contemporaries; certainly, it has little to commend itself to today's composers.

1829. Charles Lemme, Nouveau système. Nouvelle méthode de musique et gamme chromatique qui abrégé le travail et l'étude de
la musique de onze douzièmes, ou la reduit à un douzième
(New system; a new musical method and the chromatic scale
which reduces the labor and study of music by eleven-
twelfths). Paris: Firmin Didot frères.
Staff: 5-line.
Register symbols:

(Contre)	(Grosse)	(Petite)				
C_1-B_1	G C-B	P c-b	1 c^1-b^1	2 c^2-b^2	3 c^3-b^3	4 c^4-b^4

Pitch:

C C# D D# E F F# G G# A A# B
   Db   Eb   Gb   Ab   Bb

Unaccountably, Lemme did not address the question of duration in his system, although this element would certainly require a nonorthochronic solution.

Lemme's method is the first in our survey of alternating notehead color to begin the chromatic scale with an open notehead. The prior proposals of Mattheson and Rohleder had commenced with a solid notehead for the first pitch of the scale. As earlier pointed out, either procedure breaks down halfway through the scale, the white noteheads not always representing the natural pitches nor the black notes the altered pitches.

1830. Henri Barthélemy Aigre, Réforme à faire dans la manière
d'écrire la musique, au moyen de laquelle les commençants
n'éprouveront plus de difficultés, soit dans la lecture, soit

même dans l'exécution; par un ignorant, qui frissonne au seul nom de Bémol (Suggested reform in the manner of notating music by means of which beginners are not intimidated by an overabundance of difficulties, either in reading or in performance; for the ignoramus who shivers at the very word flat). Paris: Ladvocat.
Staff: 5-line.
Clef signs: Standard G- and F-clefs.
Pitch:

| C | C# | D | D# | E | F | F# | G | G# | A | A# | B | C |
| | Db | | Eb | | | Gb | | Ab | | Bb | | |

ut da ré bo mi fa di sol fi la ri si ut

Example 4-10.

The squared noteheads in Aigre's system primarily designate flatted pitches, as they are set at the same level as the notes they alter, yet they also serve the enharmonically sharped pitches. On the whole, Aigre's proposal is logically worked out and has the advantage of keeping the notes in their traditional positions on the staff, without recourse to additional staff lines or to ancillary markings on the noteheads or on their stems.

1840. Emmanuele Gambale, La riforma musicale riguardante un nuovo stabilimento di segni e di regole per apprendere la musica (The musical reform concerning a recent consolidation of the symbols and rules for learning music). Milan: Coi tipi di P. A. Molino.
Staff: 6-line for instrumental music; 3-line for vocal music.
Clef signs: None.
Pitch:

| C | C# | D | D# | E | F | F# | G | G# | A | A# | B | C |
| | Db | | Eb | | | Gb | | Ab | | Bb | | |

Ba Ca Da Fa La Ma Na Pa Ra Sa Ta Va Ba

Duration: A single note without stem represents one full measure; two stemless notes occupy a half-measure each, and

three such notes one-third of a measure each。 Whole-, half-,
quarter-, and eighth-notes are all notated as eighths, a single beam connecting the notestems. For note-groups containing
mixed values, additional beams are used, as for example,

Dotted-note values are indicated:

All notestems are on the right, and there are no barlines.
Rests:

1 beat │ 2 beats │ 3 beats, and so on.
Example 4-11. Franz Liszt, Grand Galop Chromatique.

"Reasonable, but not practical," was Joseph Raymondi's judgment
of Gambale's proposal (2), and we must concur with his assessment. This inventor's alternating white and black noteheads
cannot function logically when outlining the chromatic scale,
as the pitches they represent are not concomitantly white and
black。 A second and more serious flaw is the author's treatment
of rhythm and duration; to reduce all values to eighth-notes
and shorter note lengths is both psychologically false and
technically dubious. Moreover, the absence of all barlines dis-
orients the performer when the music itself is based on strict
orthochronic principles.
    Two years after Gambale's reform appeared, the Italian
writer on music, Giuseppe Borio, published his appraisal of the
system (3). From our perspective, one advantage of his assessment is a clearer illustration of Gambale's notation, which we
give below for comparison.

Example 4-12.

1840. Edouard Jue de Berneval, <u>Music simplified, or A new</u>
  <u>method to propagate the study of music.</u> London: the author.
Staff: 5-line.
Clef signs: Standard G- and F-clefs.
Pitch:

    do   re   mi   fa   sol   la   si   do

All scales are reduced to a single written form, similar
to the shaped-note systems earlier illustrated; the example
above arbitrarily outlines the diatonic scale of C major.
Example 4-13. Southern hymn, <u>Oh! for the Blood that We Shed</u>.

"And here let me again and again impress on the mind of my Pupils this important truth," wrote Jue de Berneval in the course of his proposal, "that by proceeding from the <u>known</u> to the <u>unknown</u>, there is no difficulty than [sic] an attentive intelligence may not surmount. The knowledge of music would be much sooner acquired, if there were only <u>one</u> Alphabet, just as there exists in reality but <u>one</u> Gamut. But in the absence of this simplicity not to be met with in the System extant, we must seek a remedy in embarrassing cases, by <u>transposing</u> or translating into the <u>known</u> Scale of UT."

One would naturally assume that Jue, as a pupil of Pierre Galin (page 295), would continue the tradition of his mentor's numerical notation -- with the hope of sparing his pupils still another "Alphabet" or the encounter with "embarrassing cases." His system, however, was a reaction against the use of numbers as substitutes for noteheads. He was convinced that shaped notes represented a clearer approach to solfege teaching, with which Galin and Jue, in turn, were concerned. Whether his particular choice of notehead design was more effective than the use of numbers is perhaps academic; systems based on shaped notes certainly were very successful in the United States (pages 143-146) as well as in England and Europe.

1842. Friedrich Johann von Drieberg, "Vorschlag zu einer Vereinfachung unseres Notensystem" (Suggestion for a simplification of our notation), <u>Allgemeine musikalische Zeitung</u> 46,
   pp. 914-915.
Staff: 5-line.
Clef signs: Traditional G- and F-clefs.
Pitch:

The pitches Cb, E#, Fb, Fx, Bbb, B# are shown enharmonically.
Duration:

, and so on.

Example 4-14.

Drieberg was known to his contemporaries as a writer on Greek music, although his theories have now been largely discredited. His notational reform has also vanished _post obitum_, despite his airy comment: "If anybody should believe that my suggested notation is only applicable for keyboard instruments, I have nothing to fear." Its failure notwithstanding, Drieberg's system was the first that used contrasting notehead colors for the natural and altered pitches that took into consideration the half-step intervals between notes three and four and seven and eight of the diatonic major scale, making them the same color.

1842. V. D. de Stains, "Reformed Characters, or Musicography," Phonography; or, The Writing of Sounds. London: the author.
Staff: 5-line.
Clef signs: Standard G- and F-clefs.
Pitch:

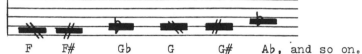

F   F#   Gb   G   G#   Ab, and so on.

Duration: Shown by the length of the pitch symbol.

Example 4-15.

Reformed Characters was the first of two notational methods proposed by de Stains in his Phonography . . . ; the second, stenographic in nature, is discussed in a later chapter.

While the elongated pitch symbols shown here were advocated earlier by Karl Krause (see page 12) and several other reformers, including T. Van Tassel in his The Phonographic Harmonist (Syracuse, New York, 1846), de Stains was the originator of the slashed lines crossing the note bars to distinguish naturals, flats, and sharps. His flat signs, however, are almost obscured by the heavy pitch bar. A more sensible solution would be to leave the natural symbol without any ancillary marks and to transfer the slanting double lines to the flatted-note bars.

1843. Joseph Raymondi, <u>Essai de simplification musicographique</u>,
   avec un précis analytique des principaux systèmes de notation
   musicale proposés depuis le sixième siècle (Attempt at notational simplification, with an analytical summary of the
   principal systems of music notation proposed since the sixth
   century). Paris: Bernard-Latte.
Staff: 5-line.
Clef signs: Traditional G- and F-clefs.
Pitch:

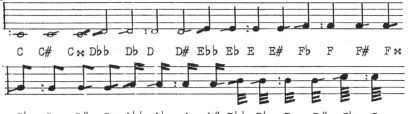

It is strange that Raymondi -- author of two critical surveys
of new notational proposals made up to his time -- should himself devise a complicated system based on minute notehead ap-
pendages that are difficult to perceive. "Bizarre, and impractical" might have been his own assessment of the plan if he had
applied the same criteria to his proposal as he had to the
other systems he analyzed. Surely he could not have maintained
that his notehead formats were easier to notate or to decipher
than notes in traditional practice. In modified forms, however,
Raymondi's suggestions were taken up by several twentieth-century composers, among them Georg Capellen and Henri Pousseur
(see pages 201 and 257). They, in turn, like Raymondi before
them, were unsuccessful in establishing their supposed innovations.

1844. Bartolomeo Montanello, "Di un modo facile ed economico
   per istampare la musica," <u>Lettera a Giovanni Ricordi</u> (Con-
   cerning an easy and economical method of printing music).
   Milan: G. Ricordi & C.
Staff: 5-line.
Clef signs: Standard G- and F-clefs.
Pitch: Traditionally indicated, except for double-flatted and
   double-sharped pitches.

Ebb Eb E E# Fb F F# F✕ , and so on.

Montanello's letter to the publisher Ricordi is full of ideas
for simplifying the printing of music, but one might question
whether his plan for the doubly altered pitches is either easier to write or more economical to print than the traditional
symbols: bb and ✕. If any accidental sign is to be changed, why
not all? By dispensing with all such symbols, as proposed by
reform after reform, the labor of writing music is made easier
and the cost of printing music more economical.

1844. Arthur Wallbridge (pseud. for William Arthur Brown Lunn),
    The Sequential System of Musical Notation: A Proposed New
    Method of Writing Music in Strict Conformity with Nature.
    London: Simpkin, Marshall & Co.
Staff: 9-line; two staves make up a piano system.
Clef signs: As indicated in Example 4-17. The specific register
    is indicated by the shape and color of the note symbol and
    the direction and angle of the stem:

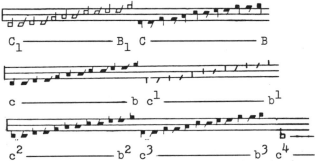

The chromatic scale of any tonality is outlined from its
keynote on the space below the staff to its octave on the
space above the staff. The example above gives the chromatic pitches of the scale of C.
Key signatures: The numeral is calculated by the number of
    half-steps from the pitch of C. ⌒ indicates a major tonal-
    ity; ⌣ represents a minor key, as, for example:

⌐5⌐ = F major | ⌐10⌐ = Bb minor

Duration:

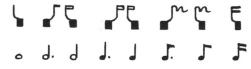

Rests:

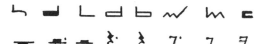

Meter:

Double rhythm | Triple rhythm

$\frac{4}{4}$, $\frac{2}{4}$ | $\frac{6}{4}$, $\frac{6}{8}$ | $\frac{12}{4}$, $\frac{12}{8}$ | $\frac{3}{2}$, $\frac{3}{4}$ | $\frac{3}{8}$ | $\frac{9}{4}$, $\frac{9}{8}$

Each measure is divided into equal "partments"; in double
rhythm there are two partments per measure, and in triple
rhythm,   there are three. Each partment contains one integer,
or division, consisting of either two or three subunits.
Example 4-17.

What Arthur Wallbridge (or his alter ego, William Lunn) had in
mind when he characterized his new system as operating "in
strict conformity with Nature" remains, to quote Winston
Churchill, "a riddle wrapped in a mystery inside an enigma."
Nature can indeed be fanciful, but not, one thinks, as fanciful as this notation. Idiosyncratic to the ultimate degree,
his sequential system could have lured few composers or performers away from conventional notation to agonize over these
visual intricacies.

Chord structures, as can be seen, are not aligned as in
traditional writing but have their component notes staggered,
illustrated in the right-hand part of measures 16 and 17 in
Example 4-17. Beams zigzag erratically and are extended beyond
the final note of a group whose noteheads they connect. All in
all, Wallbridge's notation possesses more interest and validity as a visual phenomenon than as a vehicle for setting down

a musical idea. It might be considered a precursor, perhaps, of some of the more eccentric graphic notations of the twentieth-century avant-garde.

1846. Joseph Raymondi, *Nouveau système de notation musicale. Suivi du rapport fait au congrès scientifique de France sur le premier essai de simplification musicographique* (New system of musical notation following the report of the French Scientific Congress on the first attempt at simplifying musical graphics). Paris: E. Brière.

Staff: 2-line, spaced three lines apart -- the equivalent of the standard pentagram minus the three central lines.

Clef signs: S (Sol), combined with register numbers.

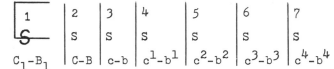

Pitch: No pitch is placed on the central ledger line.

Key signatures: The tonic note with stem and five flags, as, for instance:

Duration:

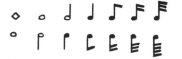

Rests:

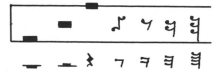

Meter:

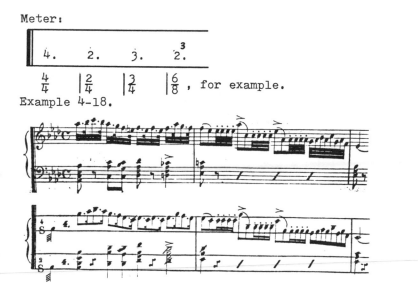

$\frac{4}{4}$ $\bigg|\frac{2}{4}$ $\bigg|\frac{3}{4}$ $\bigg|\frac{6}{8}$, for example.

Example 4-18.

This second proposal of Raymondi (the first is discussed on page 155) bears a striking resemblance to the method known as Equitone, invented 112 years later (see page 252). Both systems rely on two-line staves; the lines are separated by a wide space in which are arranged six pitch levels. Raymondi's staff, however, was designed primarily for simple, essentially diatonic music, usually vocal, whereas Equitone is meant to serve keyboard and other instrumental writing of a more complex texture.

1849. Ernst von Heeringen, Von Heeringen's Celebrated Instruc-
tion Book for the Pianoforte, Containing the Principles of
His Newly Invented Notation by the Name Chromatic, or Presi-
dential System. Washington, D.C., the author.
Staff: 5-line.
Clef signs:

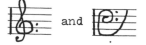 and

Pitch:

C	C# Db	D	D# Eb	E	F	F# Gb	G	G# Ab	A	A# Bb	B	C

The author uses a personalized series of pitch syllables:
  doe dee ray ree me fa fee sole see la lee pa doe
Duration: Whole- and half-notes are slightly larger and more elongated than the shorter values.

Rests: Traditionally expressed, except that the half-rest is
   set below the third staff line, and the quarter-rest is
   written Ⲣ .
Meter: Displayed as a fraction, as illustrated below.
Example 4-19.

In his published proposal, von Heeringen wrote that "New methods [of notation] have been produced by Gambale, Rousseau,
etc., but although each has presented some individual points
of excellence, none have hitherto been found generally prac-
ticable. Gambale invented a method which dispenses with the
sharps and flats, but unfortunately in other particulars it
proved three-fold more difficult than that which it was intended to simplify. I trust that I may say, with all due modesty, that in constructing the system which is now presented to
the public . . . I have profited by the failures as well as
the successes of my predecessors in musical reform."
   To this inventor must be accorded the distinction of being
the first to suggest using open noteheads for the natural
pitches and solid noteheads for the altered notes, while still
utilizing the traditional five-line staff. This method thus
corresponds to the visual analogy of the white and black piano
keys, a concept that was unaccountably slow in being formulated.
(Refer to Chapter 2 for discussions of similarly designed proposals.) Von Heeringen also neatly solved the problem of distinguishing the half-note from the quarter-note by its larger
size, as notehead color could no longer achieve this durational
distinction.
   A few years after the appearance of the Celebrated Instruction Book, the author published his Youth's Song Book, for
Schools, Classes, and the Social Circle according to the new
system of musical notation (Philadelphia, 1854), which further
detailed and illustrated his reform proposal. Evidently both
publications enjoyed a certain popularity with the amateur
musicians of the period.

1853. Maurice Delcamp, Notation musicale, pouvant remplacer les
   signes usuels sur le plain-chant . . . (A musical notation
   able to replace the customary signs for plainchant). Paris:
   Chez Chaillot, éd.
Staff: 3-line.
Register symbols:

II ⊟	III	IV	V	VI	VII	VIII
1st octave	2nd	3rd	4th	5th	6th	7th

Pitch:

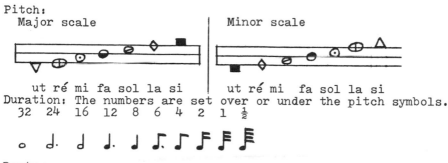

Major scale | Minor scale

     ut ré mi fa sol la si | ut ré mi fa sol la si

Duration: The numbers are set over or under the pitch symbols.
32   24   16   12   8   6   4   2   1   ½

Rests:
32   24   16   12   ∅   ∅   4   2   1   ½

Meter: The numerator only is placed in the first space. Normal
   barlines mark off the measures; short note-values are written
   close together while longer notes are more separated.

Example 4-20. Plainchant, from the Liber Usualis.

Ky - ri - e__ e - - - - - le-i-son

Delcamp's shaped-note system was formulated as a reaction
against the numerical methods of Rousseau and the Galin-Paris-
Chevé triumvirate (see pages 292 and 295). It did not succeed,
however, in its objective; Delcamp's proposal was soon forgotten, while the rival numerical systems prospered for many
years. Patently, his so-called reform did not prevail because
of the extreme difficulty of deciphering his odd note shapes,
while at the same time, reacting to the durational figures
above each note. Far from simplifying the reading of music,
or offering a viable alternative to numerical notation, Delcamp only compounded the difficulties inherent in other notational methods.

_____

1859. Karl Bernhard Schumann, Vorschläge zu einer gründlichen
   Reform in der Musik durch Einführung eines höchst einfachen
   und naturgemässen Ton- und Noten-systems nebst Beschreibung
   einer nach dieses System construirten Tastatur für das Forte-
   piano (Proposals for a thorough musical reform by introducing
   a very simple and natural notation and a description of this
   system applied to the piano keyboard). Berlin: Gullius.
Staff: 11-line (the theoretical "Great Staff"); the central
   line is omitted when not required. Two staves are combined
   as the customary keyboard system.

Clef signs:

 and

Pitch:

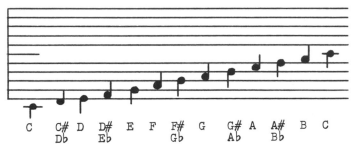

Duration: Not discussed in the proposal.

Example 4-21.

Like Schumann, other innovative notators used the principle of the "Great Staff"; still others placed each chromatic note of the scale on its own line or space. Unique with Schumann, however, were his miniature stems attached to solid noteheads. These stems -- up for one series of six notes and down for the other -- visually confirmed the outline of two whole-tone scales, one on the lines and one in the spaces.

Schumann's system was designed to be applied to his recently invented version of the chromatic keyboard, the first of five such constructions devised during the second half of the nineteenth century. Eleven years after Schumann's keyboard (Neue Tastenfolge) appeared, Gustave Decher brought out his Chromatische Klaviatur, followed by the Neueklaviatur of Leo Kuncze in 1877, the Chromatik of the firm Vereines "Chroma" (Munich, 1877), and Paul von Jankó's 1882 Jankó-Klaviatur. All of these keyboards were based on the principle of alternating white and black keys, a concept that first appeared in Johann Rohleder's chromatic keyboard of 1792 (see page 143).

Both the staff design favored by Schumann and his accompanying pitch symbols are logical, but one of the primary elements in any notational system is unaccountably overlooked -- that of individual note duration. No mention is made by the author as to how rhythmic differences are to be indicated, a

special problem when all the noteheads are solid and have
stems too short to bear flags or beams.

1860. Valentino Arnò, <u>Nuovo sistema di tastiera e musico-
grafia</u> (New keyboard system and its notation). Turin: the
author.
Staff: 3-line. Four staves are used as a piano system.
Register symbols:

L.H.   R.H.

F_1-E | F-e | f-e^1 | f^1-e^2 | f^2-e^3 | f^3-e^4.

Pitch:

F F# Gb G G# Ab A A# Bb B

C C# Db D D# Eb E

Duration: All values are written as quarter-notes. The noteheads are placed directly on the barlines, which are extra
long, on the shorter beat lines, and on the dotted subdivision lines; in effect, all these lines become note stems.
The stems of slurred notes are joined by a curved line:

꙾ or ꙫ

Rests: A single symbol, ꙾ , serves all values and is in effect
until the next written note.
Example 4-22.

Half of Arno's proposal is logically devised: the upward- and
downward-pointing triangular noteheads for sharped and flatted
pitches. The same, however, cannot be said of his depiction of
rhythm. It does not make sense to reduce all durations to a
single written form so that half-, quarter-, eighth-, and six-
teenth-notes appearing simultaneously have the same written
form.

1862. Heinrich Joseph Vincent, "Der Doppelstiel in Fünflinien-
    system" (The double-stem in the 5-line staff system), Die
    Einheit in der Tonwelt (The Unity of Music). Leipzig: H.
    Matthes.
Staff: 5-line.
Register symbols:

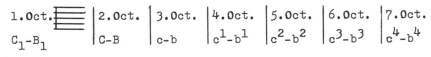

1.Oct. | 2.Oct. | 3.Oct. | 4.Oct. | 5.Oct. | 6.Oct. | 7.Oct.

C_1-B_1 | C-B | c-b | c^1-b^1 | c^2-b^2 | c^3-b^3 | c^4-b^4

Pitch:

C   C# D   D# E   F   F# G   G# A   A# B   C
    Db   Eb   Gb   Ab   Bb

Meter: Written in the form of a fraction and placed before
the left-hand barline.

Example 4-23.

The staff and note placements in this system exactly duplicate
the scheme the musician known as Autodidactus had published
twenty-nine years earlier (see page 19). Vincent was, however,
notably forward-looking as an advocate of a twelve-tone compositional system several decades before its endorsement by
Schoenberg and Hauer.
    In addition to his proposal just illustrated, Vincent pub-
lished several other works concerned with notation, culminating in Eine neue Tonschrift (1900). As early as 1862 he had
written his Neues musikalisches System. Ein kurzgefasstes Lehr-

buch für Musiker und Dilettanten, which made use of the numerical notation schemes of Galin and Chevé. Since Vincent was primarily concerned with harmonic relationships, his system was
intended more for analysis than as a new method of notation.

Vincent also authored a number of articles on the newly
invented chromatic keyboards of Decher, Kuncze, von Jankó,
and others; these appeared in leading German musical journals
and in his book Die Neuklaviatur of 1900. Many other authorities, such as Hans Weimar, Melchior Sachs, and Albert Hahn,
also published articles on the chromatic keyboard in important
German and French periodicals of the time.

1865. Cesare Paganini, Et fiat lux in caos! Nuova teoria musicale vera normale, ossia radicale riforma ortografica-gram-
maticale degli elementi della musica (And let there be light
in darkness! Musical theory will be standardized: A radical
and accurate grammatical reform of the elements of music).
Florence: Tipografia italiana F. Martini.
Staff: 5-line (2-3). Ledger lines are incomplete staff segments.
Register symbols:

C_1-B_1 | C-B | c-b | c^1-b^1 | c^2-b^2 | c^3-b^3 | c^4-b^4

Pitch:

C   C#   D   D#   E   F   F#   G   G#   A   A#   B   C
     Db   Eb   Gb   Ab   Bb

Example 4-24. Ludwig van Beethoven, String Quartet in E-flat,
op. 74 (first movement).

This Italian theorist's "light in darkness" is well-intentioned,
but somewhat late in the ongoing search for notational improvement. Paganini's proposal, other than its rather fanciful clef
sign, is little more than a repeat of several earlier suggestions by other reformers to arrange the five staff lines to
conform to the physical spacing of the white and black keys of
the piano keyboard. Someone once said that if little fishes
could speak, they would sound like whales -- an apt description of Paganini's self-proclaimed "new musical theory."

1868. George S. Dwyer, Dwyer's Phonographic Music. New York:
   the author.
Staff: 5-line.
Clef signs: Standard G-clef and reversed F-clef sign.
Pitch: The natural notes are indicated by light-faced type
   and the altered notes by dark-faced type. No stems are used.

	E	F	F#/Gb	G	G#/Ab	A	A#/Bb	B	C	C#/Db	D	D#/Eb	E

Duration:

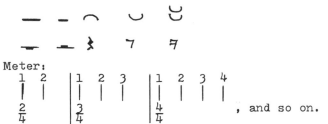

Rests:

Meter:
1 2   1 2 3   1 2 3 4
| | | | | | | | |
2   3   4
4   4   4   , and so on.

Miscellaneous directives:

Example 4-25.

Dwyer's notational proposal combines elements of traditional notation with stenographic markings and pictorial signs. Although the latter are logically devised, writing them presents problems to the notator. Quarter-moon shaped symbols are always difficult to draw freehand, especially when their positions are altered in four ways. The author suggests substitutes in manuscript preparation -- O, (| , (,),)),))),)))), which are certainly easier to draw, but are more space consuming. For these various reasons, this <u>Phonographic Music</u> system is less than satisfactory as a viable method for simplifying traditional notation.

1871. Fielding Wallace Acee, <u>Improvement in Musical Notation</u>.
  U.S. Patent 122,096.
Staff: None; the notes are set in space roughly equivalent to
  their normal position on a staff.
Clef signs:
  G-clef   F-clef

Pitch:

green	yellow	red	brown	blue	black	pink
C	D	E	F	G	A	B
do	ra	me	fa	sol	la	se

Duration: Indicated conventionally.
Example 4-26.

This proposal, which all can agree is <u>no</u> improvement in music notation, was designed solely for vocal music. Evidently its author had in mind only simple diatonic melodies, as he makes no mention of altered notes or how they would be notated. The amateur character of Acee's plan can be fully appreciated from his accompanying statement that "the application of color to the notes of the scale in music brings the heretofore difficult and beautiful art of singing by note, which is the only correct method, within the reach of everyone." Further comment seems superfluous.

1875. Johannes Baumann, "Musikalische Stenographie" (Musical
    shorthand), <u>Harmonie</u> 22, p. 175.
Staff: 5-line (2-3); as many as seven staves are combined as
    a keyboard system.
Clef signs: None; the fourth staff from the bottom would ac-
    commodate the octave of middle C.
Pitch:

C   C#   D   D#   E   F   F#   G   G#   A   A#   B
     Db   Eb   Gb   Ab   Bb

Duration: Shown by the relative length of the pitch symbol.
Rests: Indicated by blank space.
Example 4-27.

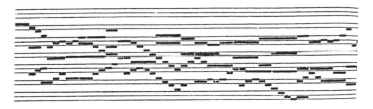

The notation of Baumann is nearly identical to the format that
Adolph Decher devised for his new chromatic keyboard during
the same year (see page 30). Both systems are indebted to the
1811 proposal of Karl Krause (page 12), who introduced elongated bars as substitutes for conventional noteheads. In systems utilizing this format, the delineation of pitch is relatively unproblematical, but the representation of rhythm and
duration is considerably less clear. The relative note values
of Baumann's notation (as illustrated in Example 4-26) are
fairly evident, an improvement over similar formats (such as
Krause's) where the depiction of note lengths is vague.

1877. Melchiore Balbi, <u>Nuovo sistema armonico fundato sulla
divisione dell'ottava in dodici semitoni equali</u> (New harmonic
system based on the division of the octave into twelve equal
semitones). Padua: V. Crescini.
Staff: 5-line (2-3).
Clef signs: Not discussed by the author.
Pitch:

C   C#   D   D#   E   F   F#   G   G#   A   A#   B   C
    Db   Eb   Gb   Ab   Bb
Example 4-28. J. S. Bach, <u>Chromatic Fantasy and Fugue</u>.

Balbi's proposal was based in part on his 1872 treatise, <u>Nuova scuola basata sul sistema semitonato equabile</u> (New method based on the system of equal semitones). His 1877 publication appears to be the first instance of the keyboard-oriented staff distinguishing the white-key from the black-key notes by their corresponding color.

Of all the methods employed by various notational reformers who favored the keyboard staff, this is certainly the most logical. It is odd indeed that the idea did not attain significant endorsement by other musicians until well into the twentieth century, when such eminent composer-theorists as Busoni, Hauer, and Schoenberg attempted to establish the principle as a pragmatic procedure. Yet even today, this particular staff format and notehead design have not gained universal acceptance.

1880. Bartolomeo Grassi-Landi, <u>Descrizione della nuova tastiera cromatica ed esposizione del nuovo sistema di scrittura musicale</u> (Description of the new chromatic keyboard and explanation of the new notational system). Rome: Tipografia di Roma.
Staff: 5-line.
Clef signs: None; the treble and bass are implied.
Pitch:

C	C# Db	D	D# Eb	E	F	F# Gb	G	G# Ab	A	A# Bb	B	C
ba	be	bi	bo	da	de	di	do	la	le	li	lo	ba
(do		re		mi	fa		sol		la		si	do)

Example 4-29. Franz Schubert, <u>Sonata in C Minor</u>, op. posth.

Grassi-Landi was evidently the first musician in Italy to publish a description of the new chromatic keyboard and to es-

pouse a notation based on its alternating white and black keys.
This notation, however, was not unique with Grassi-Landi but
was borrowed almost intact from Johann Rohleder's 1792 proposal
(see page 142). The two systems differ only in the German's
favoring a three-line staff, while the Italian retained the
standard pentagram.

   The visual appearance of intervals in this present method,
as demonstrated in the transcription above, is disturbing to
those trained to read traditional notation. Octaves look like
sevenths, and fifths resemble fourths, for instance. And the
vertical stacking of open and solid noteheads together is likewise disconcerting to the musician accustomed to complementary
note values.

1882. Hugo Riemann, "Die zwölfstufige Notenschrift" (Twelve-
   tone notation), <u>Musikalischen Wochenblatt</u> XIII, 52, pp. 617-
   619.
Staff: 5-line; the lines are more widely spaced than usual to
   accommodate three different notehead positions in each space.
Register symbols:

E_1-E | E-e | e-e^1 | e^1-e^2 | e^2-e^3

Pitch:

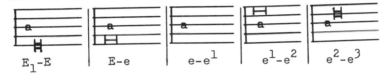

E   F   F#   G   G#   A   A#   B   C   C#   D   D#   E
          Gb   Ab   Bb   Db   Eb

Example 4-30.

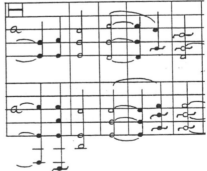

As a noted theorist and writer on musical topics, Riemann here
anticipated the later experiments carried on by his compatriots
Hauer and Schoenberg. All were designed to create a simplified
notation of the twelve pitches of the octave by dispensing with
accidentals, and in this goal Riemann obviously succeeded. But
his proposed staff is illogical in that the chromatic octave
in his plan can be outlined on only four lines, there being no
need for a fifth line, unless to extend the range by a few
notes.

   Also questionable is Riemann's clef symbology; the letter
a on the C-line of each octave does not make sense. In addition, the ancillary symbols (H and H) are inconsistently positioned -- two on the E-line and two in the F#-space. Also,
the smaller than normal noteheads undoubtedly caused difficulties for some performers reading this notation. Riemann's plan
is therefore less effective than those of other reformers who
placed each chromatic pitch on a separate line or space of the
staff, whether this had fewer or more lines than the standard
pentagram.

1885. Paul Bonnard, <u>Notation musicale à l'aide de traits sur</u>
   <u>le clavier</u> (Musical notation based on the characteristics
   of the keyboard). Paris: Typographie Charles Unsinger.
Staff: A pictogram of the standard keyboard with the black
   keys colored light gray.
Register symbols: None.
Pitch: Solid vertical bars are used in place of noteheads,
   set directly on the key diagrams.

Duration: Shown by the extension of the pitch symbols.

As will be immediately obvious, this is a highly impractical
plan of notation. The pitch bars are especially difficult to
discern when set on the shaded black keys. Furthermore, Bonnard's solution of duration is ambiguous at best and would
require an inordinate amount of vertical space for long-held
notes.

1885. J. Stott, <u>Improved Staff Notation</u>. London: the author.
Staff: 5-line.
Clef signs:
   Soprano clef | Alto clef | Tenor clef | Bass clef

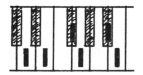

Pitch: Sharps and flats are used as required, but not the natural sign. The note G is on the lowest line for all clefs.

G AB C   D   E F G

Duration:

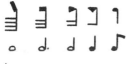

Meter:

3 4 6
P P P

Example 4-31. J. S. Bach, "Chorale," from the <u>Saint Matthew Passion</u>.

A comparatively late essay in shaped-note music writing, Stott's designs are no more or less effective than earlier attempts in this area. His symbology for duration, however, is limited in range and illogically devised. If the series of straight flags

on the note-stems were reversed, the number of flags increasing
as the values became shorter rather than longer, there would
be less confusion with the principle of orthochronic notation.

1888. Paul Austman, <u>Musical Notation</u>. U.S. Patent 393,054.
Staff: 4-line (2-2); a heavy line divides the pairs of lines.
Register symbols:

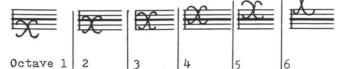

Octave 1 | 2 | 3 | 4 | 5 | 6
Pitch:

C C# Db   D D# Eb   E   F F#

Gb G G#   Ab A A# Bb B C

Key signatures: A notehead representing middle-C is set in
front of the register symbol, its relationship to the tonic
note on the bottom line identifying the new tonality, as,
for example:

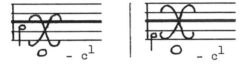

Tempo:

I	II	III	IV	V	VI	VII
Grave	Largo	Lento	Moderato	Allegretto	Allegro	Presto

Example 4-32.

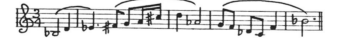

Paul Austman's system provides a perfect example of a notational proposal that could logically be considered under each
of three categories: novel staff format, unusual clef signs,

and unorthodox notehead designs. In our final analysis, the
last category won out; his reform seemed more remarkable for
its unusual notehead symbology than for the changes in the
other two elements.

"This invention," its author explained, "aims at facilitating the art of playing keyboard instruments, and enables
singers to sing at sight quickly. It removes nine-tenths of
the difficulties found in reading, writing, thinking, and
playing or singing music, and is easily mastered by both performer and vocalist." One can certainly question Austman's
naive assumption of ease in mastering his system, though at
the same time we might concur with his stated conviction "That
all music be written in one standard key (4) is very desirable,
since every octave is capable of two hundred and sixty-four
transpositions in the major and minor keys, the same being so
many and so complex that by the old method all keys are mastered only by experts." Be that as it may, Austman's proposal
met the same inevitable fate as countless other notation reforms that if they did not actually hinder the progress of
written music, neither did they advance it a whit.

1888. Christian A. B. Huth, <u>Farbige noten. Vorschlag eines
neuen vereinfachten Notensystems. Analogie zwischen Farben
und Tönen</u> (Colored notes. Proposal for a new simplified
notation. Analogies between color and sound). Hamburg/Leip-
zig: Verlagsanstalt und druckerei actiengesellschaft.
Staff: 5-line.
Register symbols: The spaces are numbered, 1-6 for the left
hand and 3-8 for the right hand.

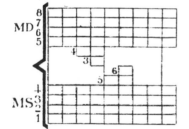

Pitch: All noteheads are in the form of a curved ribbon, and
each pitch of the chromatic scale is a different color.

1	2	3	4	5
C	C#/Db	D	D#/Eb	E
dark blue	blue-green	dark green	yellow-green	yellow

6	7	8	9	10
F	F#/Gb	G	G#/Ab	A
yellow-orange	dark orange	dark brown	carmine	lavender

11	12
A#/Bb	B
violet	indigo blue

Duration: Shown by the length of the curved pitch symbols.
  Each measure, which is set off by heavy barlines, is divided
  into grids representing the smallest beat unit of the measure.
Rests: Indicated by empty grids.
Meter: Designated by the number of grids in each measure.
Example 4-33. Ludwig van Beethoven, <u>Sonata in A-flat</u>, op. 26.

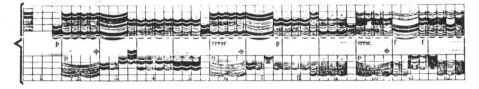

In previous commentary it has sometimes been tempting to in-
dulge in superlatives -- the most unusual, the most ingenious,
the most bizarre, the most unrealistic. But surely Huth's
colored-notes proposal merits the ultimate in descriptive ad-
jectives. This notation is so far removed from standard practice, so idiosyncratic in symbology, and so elaborately fanciful in construction that it defies professionally objective
assessment. The analyst may be awed by the detail and extent
of Huth's schema, but mystified by his Jovian disregard of
reality.
  It is a matter of deep regret that economic considerations
preclude reproducing Huth's notation in its entire color gamut;
it is a system that truly must be seen in its original form to
be believed. For the year 1888, the publication of <u>Farbige no-
ten</u> must be seen as a miracle of sorts in its extraordinary
range of true color and high standard of printing. Either the
printer was a man willing to gamble on an unprecedented project, or -- more likely -- the inventor was a person of sufficient means to subsidize the propagation of his personal
vision. It stands here, then, as a monument of one musician's
overriding ego and an exemplar of what music notation could
never become.
  Huth's proposal is accompanied by a technically detailed
argument on the relation of color to sound, according to the
theory of vibrations applied to both phenomena. Each pitch and
each tonality is related to a specific color, in scientifically
measured proportions. For example, the tonalities of C major
and C minor are based on the following proportions of certain
basic colors:

C major

C minor

9 parts blue
8 parts orange
7 parts yellow

7 parts green
6 parts orange
5 parts blue

The inventor further divides his color palette into "warm tones" (yellow, orange, red, and brown) and "cold tones" (green, blue, grey, and violet).

A year after <u>Farbige noten</u> appeared, Huth published his <u>Weiterer verfolg der neuen Theorie auf das Tonsystem. Grund-züge einer naturgemässen Harmonie- und Compositionslehre</u> (Further progress in the new theoretical tone-system. Features of a basic harmony and composition method). Here, the author developed further his obsession with color and sound relationships, an obsession shared by several other late nineteenth-century musicians, most notably by the Russian composer, Alexander Scriabin. While musicians in particular have been affected by the relationship of color to pitch, synesthesia -- the physiological transference of sensation -- has for millenia intrigued painters and poets as well. Huth was by no means, then, unique in his single-minded pursuit of this phenomenon.

1888. Hans Wagner, <u>Vereinfachte Musiknotenschrift</u> (Simplified musical notation). Vienna: the author?
Staff: 5-line.
Clef signs: Standard G- and F-clefs.
Pitch: The noteheads slant to the left for a scale with flats and to the right for a scale with sharps.

C   Db D   Eb E   F   Gb G   Ab A   Bb B   C

C   C# D   D# E   F   F# G   G# A   A# B   C

Enharmonic pitches have a dot placed before the notehead.

Fb = E   Fx = G

Duration: As no individual note values are designated, approximate duration is shown optically by the spacing of the notes. Irrational note-groups are identified with Roman rather than Arabic numbers.

III | V

Rests: One symbol only is used for all rest durations.

Meter: As the system is nonmensural, there are no time signa-
    tures. The quarter-note is the basic beat of the measure;
    progressively heavier tactus lines indicate primary and sec-
    ondary beats in the measure. There are never more than four
    notes between any two tactus lines.
Tempo: Indicated by the German term that equals the number of
    measures playable in 10 seconds.
Example 4-34.

In the opinion of Diettrich-Kalkhoff (5), this system is easily
comprehended and can be used in conjunction with traditional
notation. On careful scrutiny, however, Wagner's method seems
more readily accessible in theory than in practice. The slanted
noteheads take extra time to write precisely, and one must con-
tinually remember in which direction to slant them. In addition, Wagner only sketchily addressed the whole question of
duration and rhythm, though some may find in his system the
seeds of twentieth-century proportional notation, especially
in those scores where barlines are measured in inches or centi-
meters to represent seconds of time.

1888. Ernest Weigand, <u>Anschauungssystem für Klanghöhe und
    Klangdauer</u> (Graphic system for pitch and duration). Mainz:
    Kern.
Staff: 5-line.
Clef signs: Traditional G- and F-clefs.
Pitch:

C   C# D D#   E F   F# G   G# A A# B
    Db   Eb   Gb   Ab   Bb
Duration:

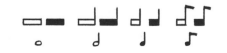

Tied notes are indicated in the following manner:

Rests:

, and so on.

Meter:

$\frac{4}{4}$ $\frac{3}{4}$ $\frac{2}{2}$ $\frac{6}{8}$

Example 4-35.

This is the first of two slightly different proposals advanced by Weigand (the second is discussed on page 185). It was intended to act as a transition between the processes of traditional notation and Weigand's later expansion of the new elements. In many ways his initial concept is simpler to notate than the subsequent development, in which the squared noteheads appear in three different forms. One welcome feature of both systems is Weigand's keeping the notes on their customary staff lines and spaces. Both methods also make use of the principle of open symbols for the natural pitches and closed forms for the altered notes, a logical premise that is at the heart of many notational reforms.

1889. Hans Sacher, _Entwurf einer Vereinfachung der Tonschrift_ (Plan for the simplification of notation). Vienna: A. Pichlers witwe & sohn.
Staff: 5-line; the lines are more widely spaced than usual to accommodate three different notehead positions in each space.
Register symbols:

I	II	III	IV	V	VI	VII
C_1-B_1	C-B	c-b	c^1-b^1	c^2-b^2	c^3-b^3	c^4-b^4

Pitch:

C C# D D# E F F# G G# A A# B C
   Db   Eb   Gb   Ab   Bb

Example 4-36.

In his survey of notational reform (6), Diettrich-Kalkhoff
contends that Sacher's system has the special advantage of
providing the notator with three note positions in each space,
in effect adding more spaces to the staff. We find this plan
in several other proposals, notably those of Ernest Weigand
(page 178) and Hugo Riemann (page 171). The primary objection
to this device is that either the staff must be greatly enlarged, to provide extra space, or the noteheads made much
smaller than normal, creating a writing and reading hazard.

1890. J. Walter Mitcherd, Mitcherd's Easy System of Music.
  Music revolutionized. No flats or sharps. Portmadoc, Wales:
  the author.
Staff: 7-line, constituted as shown below.
Clef signs: Standard G-clef, positioned between lines 1 and 5.
  Although the treble-clef symbol is used, it relates to the
  second staff line, which is D#/Eb rather than G.
Pitch:

C C# D D# E F F# G G# A A# B C
   Db   Eb   Gb   Ab   Bb

Example 4-37. Chorale, <u>Ein' feste Burg ist unser Gott</u>.

Basically, this staff is patterned after the 2-3 arrangement
of lines devised for keyboard music, but with broken lines inserted between the two segments. These extra lines are really
not essential to the function of the staff as they do not bear
noteheads; perhaps Mitcherd included them only as a kind of
guidepost for the player. Not at all logical is this inventor's
use of the G-clef symbol, as it does not represent the pitch
of G. It would have been better if he had devised a new symbol
for his particular staff or else had resorted to register numerals.

1891. Josef Brisgaloff, <u>Vereinfachung der Tonschrift</u> (Simpli-
    fication of musical notation). Moscow: the author.
Staff: 5-line.
Clef signs: Traditional G- and F-clefs.
Pitch:

Brisgaloff's is an impractical proposal inasmuch as the question of duration is left unanswered. By using only solid noteheads, some without stems that could otherwise bear flags and
beams, the author severely limits his options in delineating
rhythm and duration.

1891. Giuseppi Napoleone Carozzi, <u>Ballads and Songs, written</u>
    <u>according to an aesthetic and monotonic system and more sim-</u>
    <u>ple notation, doing away with the incongruous signs of nat-</u>
    <u>ural, sharp and flat</u>. Chicago: the author.
Staff: 5-line; the fourth line is heavy.
Clef signs:

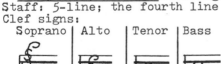

Pitch:

Ebb Eb E Fb F F# F✕Gb G, and so on.
Duration: According to standard practice, except for tied
notes, which are notated as follows:

$\circ \; \textcircled{\scriptsize ✕} = \; \epsilon\!\!\downarrow \quad | \quad \downarrow\,\textcircled{\scriptsize ⑪} = \downarrow\!\!\downarrow\,^{\mkern-8mu\smallint} \quad | \quad \downarrow\,\textcircled{\scriptsize ⑧} = \downarrow\!\!\downarrow^{\smallint}$

Rests: The eighth-rest has a new form: ꓶǀ
Meter:

$\dfrac{2}{✕} = \dfrac{2}{4} \quad \Big| \quad \dfrac{6}{ꓶǀ} = \dfrac{6}{8}$, for example.

Example 4-38.

<u>Carozzi's Synthetic Notation: A Complete Theoretical, Practi-</u>
<u>cal and Historical Method</u> (7), which appeared a year after the
<u>Ballads and Songs . . .</u> ,consolidated and modified his origi-
nal ideas. Example 4-38 illustrates the changes he made in the
clef signs and notehead shapes. Puzzling to the modern reader,
however, are the staggered barlines, plus the fact that the
bass part -- here put above the tenor -- uses a five-line
staff, while the other voice parts are written on four-line
staves.
      "It is not an easy task to introduce a system which shall
supercede one already universally received, and many have
therefore concluded that the object can never be effected.
. . . I know that the following improvements regarding a more
consistent mnemonic system of notation will oft encounter the
opposition with which all startling innovations are met." We
may safely assume that Carozzi's proposal did indeed oft encounter opposition; nearly every parameter of conventional
notation is drastically altered in this strange system, which
is anything but "more simple." Not only do his clef signs bear
no resemblance to those commonly used, but his noteheads, rest
symbols, and time signatures are also similarly transformed,

so that one must approach this so-called reform as though
learning a completely new language.

One can persuasively contend, of course, that the novelty
alone of any proposed new system of notation does not by itself
preclude its being ultimately proven superior to traditional
means. It is entirely possible -- though not probable -- that
a system could now be invented, one bearing little or no resemblance to conventional notation, that would so improve upon
and simplify common practice that musicians the world over
would -- and should -- master it by choice and personal conviction. Yet it is surely moot that Carozzi's proposal meets
such an elementary criterion as the unequivocal improvement
of a long-established method of writing down musical ideas.
No single proposal discussed in these pages has succeeded in
displacing our standard notation, which continues to serve the
contemporary composer, the performer, and the pedagogue in
spite of its many deficiencies and anachronisms.

1891. F. Howard Miller, <u>Crystal Music. A Natural and Easy System of Music which thoroughly Simplifies that Science, and
without any Mystery or Complications</u>. Philadelphia: the
author.
Staff: 5-line.
Clef signs: Standard G- and F-clefs.
Pitch:

do   re   mi   fa   sol   la   si   do

As an aid in solfege singing, the author proposed the following series of syllables for the chromatic scale; the
scale here begins on C, chosen arbitrarily.

C   C#   Db   D   D#   Eb   E   F   F#

doe dee raw ray ree may mee faw fee

Gb   G   G#   Ab   A   A#   Bb   B   C

say sole see lay law lee say see doe

Duration:

Example 4-39. Traditional hymn, <u>Lead, Kindly Light</u>.

A relatively late entry in the shaped-note vocal notation of
the nineteenth century, Miller's pitch symbols are as serviceable as those proposed by his predecessors. Only his choice of
the quarter-moon sign for the second scale degree is open to
question, as it is awkward to draw.

1891. Hermann Schroeder, <u>System der neuen verbesserten und
vereinfachten Tonschrift</u> (System of new, improved and simplified musical notation). Berlin: Breitkopf & Härtel.
Staff: 5-line.
Register symbols:

C-B   c-b c^1-b^1 c^2-b^2 c^3-b^3

Pitch:

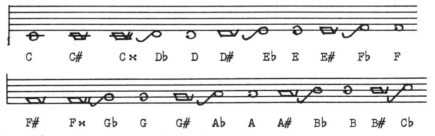

C   C#   C×   Db   D   D#   Eb   E   E#   Fb   F

F#   F×   Gb   G   G#   Ab   A   A#   Bb   B   B#   Cb

Duration: Not discussed by the author.

In addition to his career as a violinist and composer, Schroeder was a writer on theoretical subjects. Like Christian Huth
(see page 175), he was especially interested in the relationships of color and musical sound, and in 1906 he published his
<u>Ton und Farbe</u> (Sound and Color), in which he outlined his per-
sonal theories on the subject.

    Evidently, this musician was more successful in music

theory than in notational reform. His novel noteheads are unfortunately too idiosyncratic to offer any viable alternative
to conventional designs. Furthermore, they almost defy adaptation to durational symbology, which may possibly explain why
Schroeder's proposal contains no mention of this vital element.

1891. Ernest Weigand, <u>Die unhaltbarkeit der bisherigen Ton-
schrift und Theorie</u> (The inadequacy of conventional notation
and theory). Frankfurt am Main: the author.
Staff: 5-line.
Clef signs: Stsndard G- and F-clefs.
Pitch:

C C# Db D D# Eb E F F# Gb G G# Ab A A# Bb B Cb C

Duration: The same as in Weigand's earlier proposal (page 178),
as are the designations for rests and meter.
Example 4-40.

Weigand's second proposal -- a modest modification of his earlier scheme -- is logically constructed, although it is not
as simple to write, especially in dealing with the longer note-
values.

1892. F. W. Hoeftmann, "Neuen Notenschrift" (New notation),
<u>Klavier-Lehrer</u> XV, 5.
Staff: 5-line.
Clef signs: Conventional G- and F-clefs.
Pitch:

C   C# Db D D# Eb E F F#

Gb G G# Ab A A# Bb B C

Example 4-41.

Hoeftmann's system of notehead delineation was designed for piano music. A major limitation to the effectiveness of his proposal is the direction in which the chromatic noteheads are slanted; logically, they should slant to the right for raised pitches and to the left for lowered tones, instead of the reverse as the inventor wrote them.

1892. Ludwig Latte, <u>Neuen Notensystem</u> (New notation). n.p. Staff: 5-line.
Clef signs: Standard G- and F-clefs.
Pitch:

Duration: Designated traditionally, except for modifications to the noteheads of whole- and half-notes, as shown below.

$\odot = b\,o \quad \Big|\; \mathrm{d} = b\mathrm{d} \quad \Big|\; o = \#o \quad \Big|\; \mathrm{d} = \#\mathrm{d}$

Example 4-42.

This inventor's half-filled-in noteheads for the chromatic inflections are -- in theory -- effective indicators; they are,

however, time-consuming to write cleanly, a fact that would
surely inhibit many notators. In addition, minuscule curved
marks within the whole- and half-note symbols are apt to be
overlooked by a performer reading his part from any distance.

1892. John W. Robberson, <u>Musical Notation</u>. U.S. Patent 482,442.
Staff: 4-line, differently constituted for each of the three
   clefs in operation.
Clef signs: G-, C-, and F-clefs, positioned as shown below.
Pitch: The chromatic tones are set on the dotted lines in the
   three staff spaces.

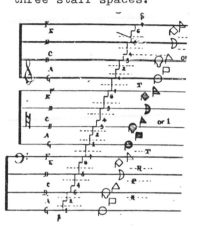

Duration: Not discussed by the proposer.

This system is a prime example of an eccentric notation that
completely ignores the indispensable element of meter, rhythm,
and duration, thus removing Robberson's proposal from any
serious consideration.

1893. Howard Orsmond Anderton, [A notational proposal].
   London: the author.
Staff: 5-line.
Clef signs: Traditional G- and F-clefs.
Pitch:

Example 4-43.

There is something quite positive to be said for Anderton's using a slash through a notehead to designate a sharp or a flat. It occupies little space on the staff, it is easy to write and is equally uncomplicated to print, and it is logical in design. Furthermore, the use of a slash does not affect mensural differences; open and solid noteheads can continue their traditional distinctions of duration -- a decided plus in any proposed new system of notation.

1893. Levi Orser, The Natural Method of Writing Music. Boston: Eastern Publishing Co.
Staff: 5-line (2-3); the customary two staves are used for piano music.
Clef signs:
    G-clef | F-clef

Pitch: Do is the tonic note of any key, major or minor.

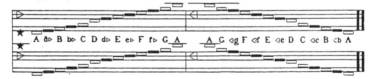

    do

Octave transpositions are indicated:
8va |15ma |22ma |loco |8b |15b |22b |col 8

Key signatures:

    = a sharp key | = a flat key

Duration:

When there is any durational ambiguity, the author suggests
using the following symbols:

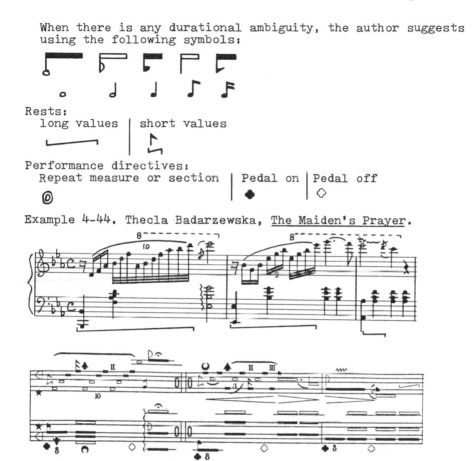

Rests:
  long values │ short values

Performance directives:
  Repeat measure or section │ Pedal on │ Pedal off

Example 4-44. Thecla Badarzewska, <u>The Maiden's Prayer</u>.

"Is it necessary to say that this extraordinary notation went
to the tomb at the same time as its author?" This rhetorical
question in David and Lussy's <u>Histoire de la notation musicale</u>
(8), following their analysis of Maurice Delcamp's proposal
(see page 160), could well be applied to Orser's equally extraordinary concoction. The young ladies who were wont to render <u>The Maiden's Prayer</u> (Example 4-44) on their parlor pianos
could not possibly have read Orser's version of that Victorian
favorite. Who, then, did ever use it -- other than Orser himself? Our music historians, unfortunately, have not enlight-
ened us on this subject.

———————————————

1896. K. M. Mayrhofers, <u>Klavierschlüssel</u> (Keyboard clef).
  Vienna: the author.
Staff: 4-line; two staves constitute a keyboard system, en-
  closed by single lines that serve as permanent ledger lines.
Clef signs: None; treble and bass are implied.

Pitch:

```
C C# D D# E  F F# G G# A A# B C——B
  Db   Eb       Gb   Ab   Bb
```

Key signatures: Combined with meter signatures in the following manner:

Duration: Conventionally expressed, except for the curved
stems for half-notes to distinguish them from quarter-notes.
Example 4-45. "Resignation" from The Southern Harmony.

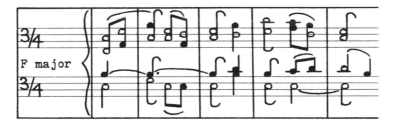

The curved half-note stems favored by Mayrhofers should be
compared with the stem designs devised by Joseph Sauveur (see
page 137). Mayrhofer's solution for distinguishing half- from
quarter-notes is neatly accomplished, simple to write, and
immediately comprehensible. But this commendable aspect of
the system is offset by the irrationality of the notehead colors and by the over-elaborate staff format. Every one of the
reformers who chose to alternate black and white noteheads for
the chromatic octave failed to realize that these color distinctions reverse halfway through the scale. Only by assigning
the open noteheads to the natural pitches (the white keys) and
the solid noteheads to the black keys exclusively can such a
method operate logically.

1896. Robert Stehle, <u>Rational System of Musical Notation</u>.
   London?: the author.
Staff: 5-line.
Clef signs: Standard G- and F-clefs.
Pitch:

To use an x as a substitute for the conventional sharp sign is
to beg the question, unless the x itself takes the place of
the notehead. This more sensible technique was incorporated
into several later proposals, in particular those of Nicholas
Obouhov (page 214) and Ernst Toch (page 229). Stehle's system,
therefore, cannot be considered a contribution to improved
notation.

1897. Edition Heinrich, <u>Lettern-Notation</u>. Vienna.
Staff: 5-line.
Clef signs: Usual G- and F-clefs.
Pitch:

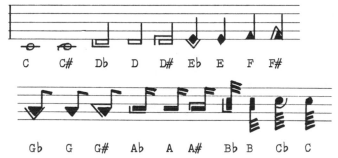

Example 4-46.

<u>Lettern-Notation</u> is the first proposal surveyed here to be the
effort of a publishing firm rather than an individual. Ostensibly, the method was reached by editorial consensus, but one
wonders, to what use was this notation put? The note symbols

are highly fanciful and, whereas their printing might not cause
problems, their hand copying by composers, arrangers, and or-
chestrators would surely present calligraphical difficulties.
It is obvious that this odd notational system was not destined
to have a long life.

1897. Walter Hampton Thelwall, <u>Note for Note Musical Notation</u>.
    London: Chappell & Co., Ltd.
Staff: 7-line; the central line is heavy. When two staves are
    present as a keyboard system, they are spaced five lines
    apart. To provide a two-octave span on one staff, five bro-
    ken lines are utilized as ledger lines.
Register symbols:

$A_2\text{-}E_1$ | $F_1\text{-}E$ | F-e | f-e^1 | f^1-e^2 | f^2-e^3 | f^3-e^4 | f^4-c^5

Pitch:

F   F#   G   G#   A   A#   B   C   C#   D   D#   E   F
     Gb   Ab   Bb   Db   Eb

Example 4-47. Frédéric Chopin, <u>Prelude in C-sharp Minor</u>,
    op. 28, no. 25.

The welcome absence of the clutter of accidental signs in Example 4-47 is counterbalanced by the clutter of ledger lines
between the two staves. The question of which version of the
passage is easier to read is one that can be answered only
subjectively by the pianist. We have no information about the
success of Thelwall's system, but it cannot have been extensive or long lasting.

1900-1907. K. M. Bässler, [Notation proposals]. Zwickau, Ger-
    many: the author.

In the eight-year period between 1900 and 1907, the German
theorist K. M. Bässler invented fourteen different notation
systems, which he published at his own expense. Inasmuch as
one of his proposals also involved a significant staff reform,
it was discussed in an earlier chapter (page 135). In eleven
of the remaining reforms, the standard pentagram is retained,
but not other notational elements, notably the pitch indicators, the clef signs, and the method of displaying key signatures, including various combinations of these factors. Certain of the proposals are closely allied, their differences
more a question of degree than of substance.

The first seven reforms discussed retain the unaltered
five-line staff; the next four employ a pentagram more widely
spaced than customary to enable each staff space to accommodate
more than one notehead form; the final two utilize three-line
staves as well as unorthodox notehead designs.

1. _Das Fünflinige Non-plus-ultra Notensystem_ (The five-line
"Non-plus-ultra" notation).
Staff: 5-line.
Clef signs: Standard G-clef and a modified F-clef, as shown
under _Key signatures_.
Pitch:

C   C#   D   D#   E   F   F#   G   G#   A   A#   B   C
     Db   Eb   Gb   Ab   Bb
Key signatures:

= 3 sharps | = 2 flats, for example.

Example 4-48.

2. _Das Chromatische Notensystem_ (The chromatic notation).
Staff: 5-line.
Clef signs: Modified G- and F-clefs, as shown below.
Pitch:

C   C#   D   D#   E   F   F#   G   G#   A   A#   B   C
     Db   Eb   Gb   Ab   Bb

Key signatures:

Duration: The noteheads for half-notes are elongated to distinguish them from quarter-notes.
Example 4-49.

3. Das Diatonische Notensystem mit halbgefüllen Schalt-
  noten (The diatonic notation with half-solid noteheads).
Staff: 5-line.
Clef signs: Normal G- and F-clefs, although neither functions
  conventionally.
Pitch:

C   C#   D   D#   E   F   F#   G   G#   A   A#   B   C
     Db   Eb   Gb   Ab   Bb

Key signatures:

Example 4-50.

4. Das Fünfliniensystem mit Zwischennoten (The five-line
  staff system with half-step symbols).
Staff: 5-line.
Clef signs: Standard G- and F-clefs.
Pitch: Stems are always on the right for the natural pitches
  and on the left for the sharps and flats.

C   C#   Db   D D#   Eb   E   F   F#

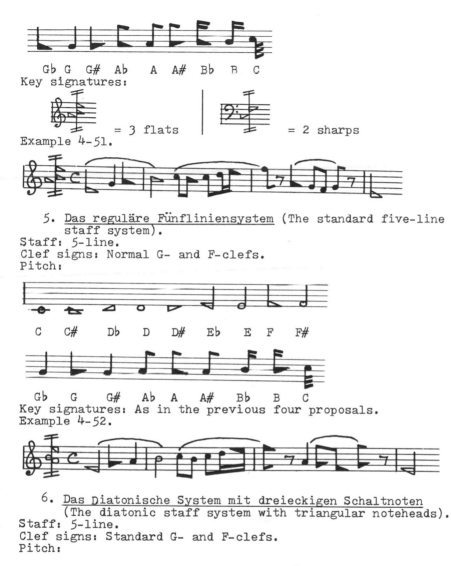

Gb G G# Ab   A A# Bb B C
Key signatures:

= 3 flats | = 2 sharps
Example 4-51.

5. Das reguläre Fünfliniensystem (The standard five-line staff system).
Staff: 5-line.
Clef signs: Normal G- and F-clefs.
Pitch:

C   C#   Db   D   D#   Eb   E   F   F#

Gb   G   G#   Ab A A#   Bb   B   C
Key signatures: As in the previous four proposals.
Example 4-52.

6. Das Diatonische System mit dreieckigen Schaltnoten
(The diatonic staff system with triangular noteheads).
Staff: 5-line.
Clef signs: Standard G- and F-clefs.
Pitch:

C C# D D# E F F# G G# A A# B C
   Db   Eb   Gb   Ab   Bb

Key signatures: As in the previous five proposals.

Example 4-53.

7. <u>Das Chromatische System mit Punkt und Dreiecknoten</u> (The chromatic staff system with round and triangular notes).
Staff: 5-line.
Clef signs: Modified G-clef, as shown below.
Pitch:

C   C#   D   D# E   F   F#   G G# A   A# B   C
     Db   Eb   Gb   Ab   Bb

Key signatures: As in the previous six proposals.
Example 4-54.

8. <u>Das Ideal-Punktnoten-System</u> (The ideal round notehead system).
Staff: 5-line; the lines are widely spaced.
Clef signs: Oversized G-clef and modified F-clef.
Pitch:

C   C#   D   D# E   F   F#   G   G# A   A#   B   C

As is evident, each staff space accommodates three noteheads.
Note also the alternating stem positions, to the left and to
the right of the notehead. The principle is retained when a
common stem links the notes of intervals and chords.

 and ____ , for example.

Key signatures: As in the previous seven proposals.
Example 4-55.

9. <u>Das Diatonische-Chromatische Notensystem</u> (The diatonic-chromatic notation).
Staff: 5-line; the lines are widely spaced.
Clef signs: Oversized G- and F-clefs.
Pitch:

Stems for the natural pitches are always on the left and on the right for the chromatic alterations. In chords containing both solid and open noteheads, the common stem adheres to the same principle.

and ⎓⎓⎓ , for example.

Key signatures: As in the previous eight proposals.
Duration: Whole- and half-notes are larger than the other values.
Example 4-56.

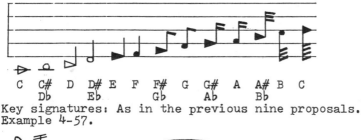

10. <u>Das reguläre Zweinotensystem</u> (The regular dual-notehead system).
Staff: 5-line; the lines are widely spaced.
Clef signs: Oversized G- and F-clefs.
Pitch:

C C# D D# E F F# G G# A A# B C
   Db   Eb   Gb   Ab   Bb

Key signatures: As in the previous nine proposals.
Example 4-57.

11. <u>Zwölfstufen-Tonschrift</u> (Twelve-tone notation).
Staff: 5-line; each line is double.
Register symbols:

Pitch: The open noteheads have thick lower and upper rims.

C C# D D# E F F# G G# A A# B C
   Db   Eb   Gb   Ab   Bb

Duration:

, and so on.

Example 4-58.

12. <u>Das reguläre Dreiliniensystem</u> (The regular three-line
    staff system).
Staff: 3-line.
Clef signs: Modified G- and F-clefs as shown in Example 4-59.
Pitch:

C C# D D# E F F# G G# A A# B C
   Db   Eb   Gb   Ab   Bb

Key signatures:

= 2 sharps   = 3 flats, for example.

Example 4-59. Franz Schubert, <u>Sonata in C Minor</u>, op. posth.

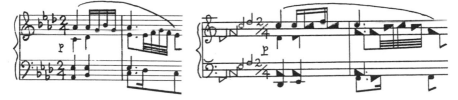

13. <u>Das Octavensystem</u> (The octave staff system).
Staff: 3-line.
Clef signs: Identical to those in the previous proposal.
Pitch:

C C# D D#E E F F# G G# A A# B C
   Db   Eb   Gb   Ab   Bb
Key signatures:

Example 4-60. Ibid.

As mentioned on page 54, Bässler's many novel systems appear
to have been invented for theoretical demonstration rather
than for providing the practicing musician with a viable alternative to orthodox notation. His numerous and essentially
minute permutations of one or two basic plans merely present
modified versions of an unconventional approach to staff and
notehead design. To assess the merits of the one over the other is really an exercise in futility, for none is in any way
superior to our traditional means of placing lozenge-shaped
notes on a staff of five equidistant lines.

1901. Johann Peter H. Adams, <u>Musical Notation</u>. U.S. Patent
    682,015.
Staff: 3-line.

Register symbols:

C_1-B_1 C-B   c-b c^1-b^1 c^2-b^2 c^3-b^3

Pitch:

C   C#   D   D#   E   F   F#   G   G#   A   A#   B   C
    Db   Eb   Gb   Ab   Bb

Example 4-61.

This proposal of Adams has the advantage of retaining the same staff position for the scale in all six octaves. Register symbols are simple in design and logical in their modifications for the various octaves. The alternating slashed and standard noteheads, however, are not as logical, owing to the two "white-key" half-steps (E-F, B-C). Because the slashed notes represent three natural pitches and the normal notes represent three altered pitches, the reverse characterizing the unslashed notes, the arrangement violates a cardinal principle of notation: A single symbol should not represent two diametrically opposed elements.

1901. Georg Capellen, "Vorschlag zur vereinfachung des Systems der Versetzungszeichen und Tonartvorzeichen" (Suggestion for the simplification of the system of accidentals and key signatures), <u>Zeitschrift der Internationalen Musik-Gesellschaft</u> II, pp. 193; 273.
Staff: 5-line.
Register symbols:

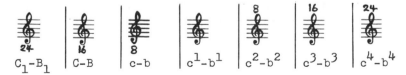

C_1-B_1 C-B   c-b c^1-b^1 c^2-b^2 c^3-b^3 c^4-b^4

Pitch:

C   C#   C✕ Db   D D# Ebb Eb E   E# Fb F F# F✕

Gb   G G#   Ab A A# Bbb Bb B   Cb C

Example 4-62.

Georg Capellen was a prolific writer on theoretical subjects,
whose articles appeared in many of the scholarly German music
journals of the period. Although his proposal demonstrates a
lively imagination in its unique manner of designating sharps
and flats, the system is actually no more pragmatic than various other methods invented by many of his peers. In theory,
the small angled slashes attached to the noteheads are reasonable devices, yet they can easily be overlooked in reading
Capellen's notation from any distance -- a hazard, of course,
that is present in any number of other notational reforms.

1902. Ferruccio Busoni, <u>Versuch einer organischen Klaviernoten-
schrift</u> (Search for an organic keyboard notation). Leipzig:
Breitkopf & Härtel.
Staff: 5-line (2-3); up to four staves make up a keyboard
system.
Clef signs: The Old German capital letters S, A, T, and B,
correspond to Soprano, Alto, Tenor, and Bass registers.

Pitch:

C C# D D# E F F# G G# A A# B C
    Db   Eb   Gb   Ab   Bb

Duration: Conventionally expressed, except that whole- and
    half-notes are squared.

Example 4-63. J. S. Bach, <u>Chromatic Fantasy and Fugue</u>.

To demonstrate the practicality of his proposal, Busoni published in 1910 his transcription of Bach's keyboard work, using
the new staff and notehead formats. In his foreword, Busoni
declared, "I believe in the practical application of this idea
and its effective simplicity and clarity. I will, however,
willingly listen to any well-intentioned criticism which seems
to me a means of offering eventual improvement. This idea by
itself is only an improvement of an old and unrefined organ-
ism."

Busoni also discussed his search for an organic notation
in his <u>Sketch of a New Esthetic in Music</u> (9), also published
in 1910. For those especially interested, a critical analysis
of Busoni's system may be found in the January, 1968, issue of
<u>The Music Review</u>, in an article by Larry Sitsky (pp. 27-33).

Feasible principally for keyboard works, Busoni's reform
is less successful for vocal and other instrumental music, as
were all the previous keyboard-oriented proposals. Apparently
his format was never applied to printed compositions other than

the Bach quoted above; other composers, including Schoenberg
and Hauer, utilized Busoni's staff format from time to time,
but not consistently.

1902. Meta Römer-Neubner, <u>Quadratnoten. Ein neues vereinfach-</u>
<u>tes Notensystem ohne schlüssel, ohne pausen- und versetzungs-</u>
<u>zeichen mit nur 12 verschiedenen, periodisch wiederkehrenden</u>
<u>notenbildern</u> (A new simplified notation system without clefs,
rests, and accidentals, with only 12 note-symbols recurring
periodically). Kronstadt, Hungary: Wilhelm Hiemesch.
Staff: 7-line; the outer lines are heavy, and the third space
is crosshatched in red. Vertical lines define the rhythmic
units, as explained below. Additional staves are superimposed to extend the range.
Register symbols:

a	b	c	d	e	f	g	h
C_1-B_1	C-B	c-b	c^1-b^1	c^2-b^2	c^3-b^3	c^4-b^4	c^5

Pitch:

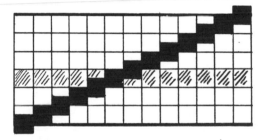

-- cross-hatched in red

F	F♯	G	G♯	A	A♯	B		C	C♯	D	D♯	E	F
	G♭		A♭		B♭				D♭		E♭		

Key signatures: Indicated by a number calculated from the note
C as number 1. Therefore, Eb major/minor would be number 4,
A major/minor would be number 10, and so on.
Duration: Each vertical segment of the staff equals one eighth-
note; shorter values occupy a proportional fraction of the
space, and longer values require more segments. Each measure
contains as many vertical lines as there are eighth-notes
belonging in the meter.
Example 4-64. Ludwig van Beethoven, <u>Sonata in F Minor</u>, op. 2,
no. 1.

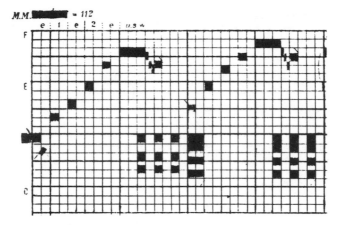

Although Römer-Neubner's system has the virtue of requiring
relatively few symbols, it is difficult to decipher, especially in relation to durational values. The longer note lengths
take up an inordinate amount of horizontal space, whereas very
short values, such as sixteenths and thirty-seconds, would require such minuscule marks as to be nearly invisible. A precursor of mid-century "time-notation," the system does have a
certain historical interest, but it is not the ultimate solution to the insufficiencies of traditional notation.

1903. Hans Sacher, "Die Wiener Notenschrift" (The Viennese
    Notation), Unsere Tonschrift, kurzer Rückblick auf deren
    Werdegang sowie auf die Vorschläge zu deren Verbesserung,
    ferner ein neuer Vorschlag für Tonbennung und Notenschrift
    (Our notation: A brief glance at its development and sug-
    gestions for its improvement; also a new proposal for
    naming and notating tones). Vienna: A. Pichlers witwe & sohn.
Staff: 5-line.
Register symbols:

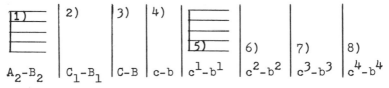

Pitch: Each set of three similarly shaped noteheads outlines
    an augmented triad.

Key signatures: Designated by the tonic pitch symbol, placed
   on the upper of two staves.
Meter: Expressed as a fraction and centered on the staff.
Example 4-65. Johann Strauss, Jr., <u>On the Beautiful Blue
   Danube</u>.

Before choosing the four notehead designs used in his so-called
Viennese notation, Sacher had experimented with various other
note formats. Ultimately he felt that the present forms were
easier to write and to print, and even went so far as to stipulate their precise measurements in millimeters. Anyone who
takes the time to practice drawing Sacher's four notehead
shapes quickly discovers that it is quite difficult to make
them all the same size, in length and in height -- a human
limitation, of course, that a printing press could overcome.
Still, Sacher's method does not offer the contemporary notator the ultimate choice among the various proposed systems.

1903. Hans Wagner, <u>Primavista Schrift</u> (Sight-reading notation).
   Vienna: the author?
Staff: 5-line.
Clef signs: Standard G- and F-clefs.
Pitch: The oval noteheads tilt to the left for tonalities in
   flats and to the right for those in sharps. No stems are
   placed on the noteheads.

Duration: Indicated by primary and secondary barlines; the former are drawn through all the staves of a system, and the
latter bisect each staff individually. Notes on the beat are
set next to all barlines, actually touching them as though
they were note-stems. A tied note is indicated by a secondary barline, or barlines, standing alone.
Rests: All durations are indicated by a single symbol:

Meter: Displayed in the following manner:

Example 4-66.

One would think that the primary objective of any sight-reading
notation would be to simplify that reading as much as possible.
By using an imprecise method of showing duration, Wagner weak-
ened his proposed system and made it much more difficult for
the sight-reader, whether amateur or professional.

1904. Angel Menchaca, <u>Nuevo sistema teórico-gráfico de la
   música. Breve, claro, científico y preciso en la representa-
   ción del sonido, igual para todas las voces y todos los in-
   strumentos</u> (New theoretical and graphic system of music:
   brief, clear, scientific, and precise in the representation
   of sound for all voices and instruments). La Plata, Argen-
   tina: Taller de publicaciones.
Staff: 1-line.
Register symbols: Indicated by note-stem placement and length,
   as follows.

A_2 | A_1 | A | a | a^1 | a^2 | a^3 | a^4

Pitch:

A	A♯	B	C	C♯	D	D♯	E	F	F♯	G	G♯
	B♭			D♭		E♭			G♭		A♭
la	se	si	do	du	re	ro	mi	fa	fe	sol	nu

Duration:

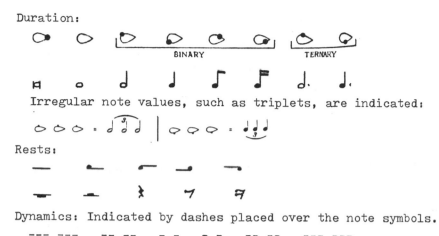

Irregular note values, such as triplets, are indicated:

Rests:

Dynamics: Indicated by dashes placed over the note symbols.

```
---  ---      --  --      -  -      .  .      --  --      ---  ---
 pp           p          mp        mf        f          ff
```

Performance directives: An elaborate system of symbols, too extensive and detailed to include here, indicates such factors as accents, slurs, chords, tremoli, arpeggios, and so on.

Example 4-67.

A native Paraguayan, Menchaca was active as a theorist-composer and teacher of music history and literature at the National College of Buenos Aires. He toured extensively in both Europe and the United States propagandizing his new system of notation, and for a time it enjoyed a certain popularity in our country. By now, of course, his reform has receded into musicological history. Nonetheless, for those interested in a fuller exposition of Menchaca's proposal, an English translation appears in the <u>Report of the 4th Congress of the International Musicological Society</u> (1911).

Like other notational reformers, Menchaca was the target of conservative critics who found his methods unacceptable. One of them, the writer Emile Ergo, penned a particularly savage attack in his fancifully titled <u>L'acte final de la tragicomédie musicale les "aveugles-réformateurs" de la notation musicale actuelle et les belles (!) perspectives du système à dix-neuf sons dans l'octave</u> (The final act of the musical tragic-comic "deluded reformers" of our present notation, and the happy (!) prospects of a system of 19 tones to the octave (10). But Menchaca was not the only notational reformer to be

castigated by Ergo -- Mattheson, Rousseau, Busoni, and Hautstont, all received equally contemptuous treatment. Setting
aside the virulent tone of Ergo's remarks, however, we must
agree that Menchaca's system is too idiosyncratic and impractical to warrant the serious consideration of today's notators.

1907. Franz Diettrich-Kalkhoff, "Eine neue, vereinfachte Noten-
    schrift" (A new, simplified notation), Geschichte der Noten-
    schrift. Jauer, Germany: Verlag von Oskar Hellmann.
Staff: 5-line.
Register symbols:

A_2-B_2 | C_1-B_1 | C-B | c-b | c^1-b^1 | c^2-b^2 | c^3-b^3 | c^4-b^4

Pitch:

C   C#   Db   D   D#   Eb   E   F   F#   F

Gb   G   G#   Ab   A   A#   Bbb   Bb   B   C

Key signatures: By the German term, written over the upper
    staff.
Duration: Half-notes are distinguished from quarter-notes by
    the tiny zero signs on their stems, as shown above.
Meter: Indicated as fractions (for example, 3/4, 6/8).
Example 4-68. Franz Schubert, Sonata in C Minor, op. posth.

As the author of an important treatise on notational reforms,
Diettrich-Kalkhoff inevitably attempted a reform of his own.
His notehead distinctions are based on three simple designs:
an enlarged dot for natural pitches, an open ring for flatted
notes, and an x for sharped scale degrees. It would seem more
logical, however, were his flat and natural noteheads reversed.
Furthermore, a single zero-sign on the stem of a half-note
would be sufficient to distinguish it from a quarter-note.

1911. August Unbereit, "Ein neues Notensystem von August Un-
   bereit" (August Unbereit's new notation system) by Heinrich
   Bohl, <u>Blätter für Haus- und Kirchenmusik</u> XVI, 1.
Staff: 6-line (3-3); two staves constitute a piano system.
Clef signs:
   V (<u>Violinschlüssel</u>), sounding at pitch.

   B (<u>Bassschlüssel</u>), sounding two octaves lower.
Pitch:

C C# Db   D D# Eb E F F#   Gb G   G# Ab A A# Bb B C
Doubly-altered pitches are indicated:

   F♯✕   B♭♭, for example.
Example 4-69.

Example 4-70.

Except for a favorable assessment of Unbereit's proposal made by the German theorist Heinrich Bohl, this system did not succeed in being accepted by the influential theorists of the period. Although the note forms for the sharped pitches are easy to draw, and present no problems in printing, Unbereit's choice of symbol for the flatted notes is open to question; his sign is more difficult to notate and is not as easily read as the traditional flat sign.

1912. [?] Perbandt, [A new notational proposal]. n.p.
Staff: 3-line (2-1).
Clef signs: Mono.
Pitch:

F F# G G# A A# B C C# D D# E
   Gb   Ab   Bb   Db   Eb

Duration:

, and so on.

Rests:

, and so on.

Example 4-71.

The parallelograms of Perbandt's notation are questionable;
if the object is merely to distinguish natural pitches from
their chromatic inflections, a simple rectangle or normal
square would serve -- and would be easier to draw. Then, too,
the diamond-shaped noteheads seem a curious regression to the
note forms of earlier centuries, and not very appropriate to
a twentieth-century proposal for notehead reform.

1913. W. Fleischhauer, <u>Siebentonschrift-Klavierschule</u> (Seven-
tone keyboard method). Berlin: Friedenau.
Staff: 1-line.
Clef signs: None.
Pitch:

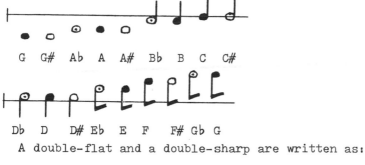

G   G#   Ab   A   A#   Bb   B   C   C#

Db   D   D#   Eb   E   F   F#   Gb   G

A double-flat and a double-sharp are written as:

Bbb   F×

Duration: Stemmed notes receive one beat (usually a quarter-
note); unstemmed notes receive two or more beats. Stemmed
notes with flags receive a half-beat.
Rests: All values are indicated with a single symbol: -o-.
Example 4-72. Wolfgang Amadeus Mozart, <u>Menuetto in D</u>, K. 355.

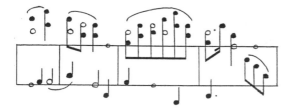

Optically, Fleischhauer's notational method is something of a disaster. The complete absence of ledger lines makes it extremely difficult to relate the pitches suspended in space, unless the notes progress scalewise. Intervals of the third, for instance, look like fifths, while an octave leap appears to be twice that distance in visual terms, as demonstrated in the Mozart excerpt above. It is little wonder that this so-called reform was quickly relegated to a deserved obscurity.

1913. Erman Gaudard, _La musique espérantiste_ (Esperanto music). Besançon, France: Imprimerie de l'est.
Staff: 3-line.
Clef signs:

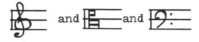

Pitch:

Rests:

Example 4-73.

Gaudard's ancillary signs for sharps and flats are completely
gratuitous. To substitute one symbol for another is pointless
unless something positive is gained by the substitution, either
in readability or in space savings. As is evident, this inventor's new signs do neither.

1913. Joseph Graaff, <u>Einzeichen-Tonschrift, eine vereinfachte</u>
   <u>verbesserte Notenschrift, mit beispielen</u> (A one-symbol nota-
   tion; a simplified and improved notation, with examples).
   Cologne: Verlag von Heinrich Z. Gonski.
Staff: 5-line.
Clef signs: Traditional G- and F-clefs.
Pitch:

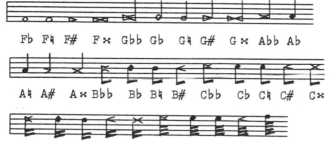

Duration: The basic form of each shaped notehead is modified
   to distinguish the various rhythmic values, as, for example:

Example 4-74. J. S. Bach, "Fugue in C-sharp Minor", from <u>The</u>
   <u>Well-Tempered Clavier</u>, Book I.

As is evident, four basic symbols make up Graaff's scheme of
shaped noteheads, of which two are modified to provide rhyth
mic distinctions. Logical enough in their construction and
sequence, these notehead designs are fussy in appearance, time
consuming to write, and hard to perceive in their minute differences.

1915. Nicolas Obouhov, [Proposal for notating sharped notes].
   Moscow: the author.
Staff: 5-line.
Clef signs: Standard G- and F-clefs.
Pitch:

Duration: Obouhov's solution for notating whole- and half-notes
   that are sharped was to encircle the x-symbol; all other
   values are notated traditionally.
Example 4-75.

Nicolas Obouhov, along with his compatriot Alexander Scriabin,
was a confirmed mystic. Obsessed with the symbol for the cross,
he insisted that only an x-shaped notehead should serve for the
chromatic pitches of the scale. His religious obsession also
extended to his writing the performance directives in his
scores in red ink, signifying Christ's blood on the cross.
   This mystic's notational proposals were most notably in-

corporated in his monumental, 2000-page score entitled <u>Le livre</u>
<u>de vie</u> (The Book of Life). Only a mere handful of other com-
posers of the period were sufficiently intrigued by his reform
to emulate it. One momentary convert was Arthur Honegger, whose
<u>Deux Esquisses</u> for piano (1944) utilizes x-shaped noteheads
for the chromatic inflections. Other musicians who briefly experimented with Obouhov's notation include Herbert Eimert,
Ernst Toch, and Jacques Chailley.

1919. Josef Achtélik, <u>Vereinfachte Notenschrift</u> (Simplified
   notation). Leipzig: Druck von C. G. Roder.
Staff: 5-line.
Clef signs: Standard G- and F-clefs.
Pitch: Traditionally expressed, except that sharped notes are
   printed in red and flatted notes are in green. For whole-
   and half-notes, the notehead rims are colored. Enharmonic
   pitches are notated with black diamond-shaped noteheads,

 , for example.

Doubly-altered pitches are also diamond-shaped, colored red
or green, and placed on the line or space of the actual
sounding pitch,

Key signatures: Shown by open noteheads, red for sharp tonalities and green for flat keys.

The use of noteheads of different colors (other than black and
white) to distinguish sharps from flats is a concept that has
intrigued several notation reformers. We have already witnessed
the remarkable color spectrum of Christian Huth's <u>Farbige noten</u>
(page 175); in Achtélik's proposal we find a more modest utilization of color. In addition to the solid and void noteheads
for natural pitches, only red and green are used for the raised
and lowered notes. Eye-catching though the printed page may be,
we might question the necessity for a four-color format. A
music publisher might well feel that the dubious potential of
Achtélik's concept hardly justifies its excessive cost.

1919. Sidney Armor Reeve, <u>Musical Notation</u>. U.S. Patent
   1,313,015.
Staff: 11-line (2-3-1-2-3), encompassing three octaves.

Register symbols:

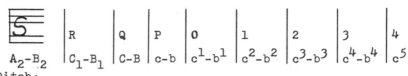

R	Q	P	0	1	2	3	4
A_2-B_2	C_1-B_1	$C-B$	$c-b$	c^1-b^1	c^2-b^2	c^3-b^3	c^4-b^4	c^5

Pitch:

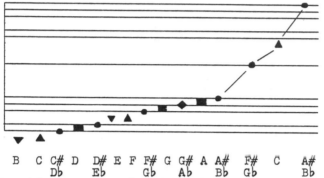

B C C# D D# E F F# G G# A A# F# C A#
     Db   Eb   Gb   Ab Bb Gb   Bb

Duration: Not mentioned by the author.

In the lengthy and detailed explication of his system, Reeve stated, "My invention consists not alone of a staff which of itself is useful, from its graphic and clear representation of the spacing of the piano-keyboard, but in the combination therewith of as few different forms of notehead as may be consistent with having a distinct form to correspond to each of the different and contrasted sorts of location upon the staff or keyboard. These sorts are four in number, namely: (1) a white key with a black key contiguous upon either side [C#-D-Eb], which I prefer to represent by a rectangular notehead, which form best fits a space between two lines. (2) A white key having a black key contiguous on one side and a white key on the other [E-F-Gb], which I prefer to represent by a triangular notehead, with its apex pointing toward the line representing the contiguous black key. (3) A black key having a pair of white keys as its neighbors on one side [A#-B-C], which I prefer to represent by a circular notehead. (4) A black key in the middle of a group of three black keys [Gb-Ab-Bb], which I prefer to represent by a diamond-shaped notehead, or oblique square, with its apexes pointing vertically in both directions."

In purpose and rationale, Reeve's proposal cannot be faulted, but like so many earnest reformers both before and after, he did not achieve a valid solution. Especially is this true in his entirely bypassing the question of duration in all its aspects -- note values, rests, barlines, meters, and so on -- without which his system cannot possibly operate.

Hoping for wider acceptance of his 1919 proposal, Reeve in 1924 issued a second pamphlet entitled The Threshold. The Reeve rational system of musical notation. This did nothing, however, to advance his notational ideas among the professional musicians of the time.

1920. Mlle R. Frémond, <u>Nouvel exposé de la "Musique Frémond,"</u>
<u>extra simplifiée</u> (New explanation of "Music Frémond," fur-
ther simplified). Paris: L'Institut de musique Frémond.
Staff: 3-line; the range is extended either by ledger lines
or by a change of notehead form on the staff (see below).
Register symbols: The complete range of the piano keyboard is
designated by a different notehead form for each octave.

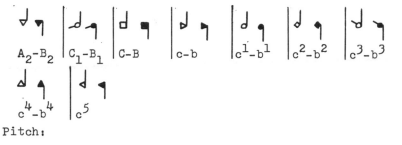

A_2-B_2 | C_1-B_1 | C-B | c-b | c^1-b^1 | c^2-b^2 | c^3-b^3

c^4-b^4 | c^5

Pitch:

C	C#	D	D#	E	F	F#	G	G#	A	A#	B	C
	Db		Eb			Gb		Ab		Bb		
do	ta	ro	pa	mo	fa	co	sa	vo	la	bo	ga	do

Key signatures: Indicated by the scale syllable representing
the tonic note of the key, placed over the first measure.
<u>Ton de Pa</u> = Eb <u>Ton de La</u> = A <u>Ton de Co</u> = F# or Gb
Duration:

𝅗𝅥... 𝅗𝅥.. 𝅗𝅥. 𝅘𝅥 𝅘𝅥𝅮 𝅘𝅥𝅯

𝅝 𝅗𝅥. 𝅘𝅥 𝅘𝅥 𝅘𝅥𝅮 𝅘𝅥𝅯

Triplets are indicated:

Rests: A single symbol, 乙 , placed on each beat of the measure.
Meter:

3/4 | 4/4 | 6/8 , for example.

Example 4-76. Vincent d'Indy, <u>Fervaal</u>.

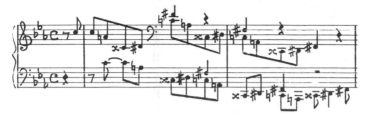

Musique Frémond consists of three different proposals for
changes in notation: the first, discussed here, is based on
a three-line staff and ordinary and differently shaped noteheads; the second uses numbers for the pitches; and the third
is stenographic in its symbology. Both the second and third
proposals are staffless and are analyzed in later chapters.

   In summarizing the efficacy of her first proposal, which
she demonstrated in the example above, the author emphasized
that she had eliminated three clef signs, twenty-three accidentals, and twelve ledger lines that would have been required
in conventional notation. Furthermore, she claimed that octave
relationships could be immediately perceived and noted that
all ancillary signs had been abolished. All true, but her system fell into the same trap that ensnared many another reform
proposal: Alternating open and solid noteheads cannot accurately depict the half-step intervals in any diatonic scale, so
that the notehead colors cannot represent the same relationships throughout.

1920. Edward V. Huntington, "A Simplified Musical Notation,"
   <u>Scientific Monthly</u> 11, pp. 278-283.
Staff: 5-line; four staves are suggested by the inventor as a
   piano system.
Register symbols:

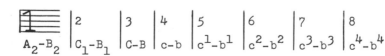

Pitch:

C   C#   D   D#   E   F   F#   G   G#   A   A#   B   C
    Db   Eb   Gb   Ab   Bb

Example 4-77. Johannes Brahms, Sonata in F Minor, op. 5.

This inventor's proposal depends not on differently colored or
shaped notes for the chromatic scale, but on placing each
half-step on a successive line or space. This is a perfectly
sensible suggestion; at the same time, however, it is regret-
table that Huntington retained the conventional 8va sign with
its accompanying, far-ranging dotted lines. A simple change of
register number would accomplish the identical transposition
with considerably less visual clutter.

1922. Edith A. Faunt, Music Notation. U.S. Patent 1,539,308.
Staff: 5-line, as shown below. When two staves are combined as
  a piano system, they are spaced one line apart.
Clef signs:

= G-clef | = F-clef

Pitch:

Cbb   Cb   C   C#   C×   Dbb   Db   D   D#   D×   Ebb   Eb   E   E#   E×

Fbb Fb F F# F✕ Gbb Gb G G# G✕ Abb Ab A A# A✕

Bbb Bb B   B# B✕

Key signatures: Designated by the tonic keynote substituting
for the customary sharps or flats.

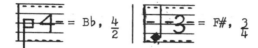 = Bb, $\frac{4}{2}$ | = F#, $\frac{3}{4}$

Rests:

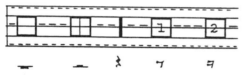

Meter: Only the numerator is given; the denominator is implicit in the note value used for the key signature (as shown
above).
Example 4-78.

Ostensibly, the dotted lines that parallel the solid lines of
Faunt's staff are meant to pinpoint the half-step relationships in the diatonic scale (E-F and B-C in the C-major scale).
But these modifications to the staff are minor when compared
to the elaborate system of shaped noteheads she devised, including those for enharmonic pitches that do not exist. Many
are theoretical only, as it is doubtful that one could find
in printed literature such pitches as Cbb, D✕, Fbb, E✕, Abb,
A✕, or B✕. The whole system is too eccentric to warrant serious consideration, and surely this accounts for its speedy
demise.

1924. George Antheil, <u>Antheilcized Notation, or Instantaneous System of Reading Music</u>. New York: the author.
Staff: 5-line (2-3), displayed vertically.
Clef signs: A wavy line separates the left and right hands.

LH ⟩   RH

Pitch:

Duration: Indicated by the relative length of the pitch symbol, as demonstrated above. The measures are marked off by heavy barlines and divided by thin beat-lines.
Rests: Shown by empty space.
Example 4-79. Ernst Krenek, <u>Toccata</u>.

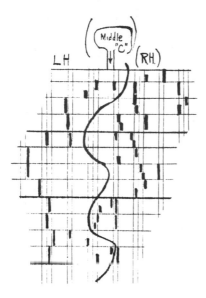

Who would have thought that George Antheil, the celebrated
"bad boy of music" in the 1920s, would be interested in elementary piano teaching? But he designed his Antheilcized Notation, so he claimed, for "everybody who can tell one from two,
and two from three," so that "without previous experience, anyone can now read music at sight."
     On the inefficiencies of traditional notation he was rele-
gating to the dustbin, Antheil's little pamphlet pontificated:
"Is there any wonder that so few people become musicians!!!!
. . . with such an imbecile [sic] and relic of medieval monks
by whom it was invented . . . system in existence. One of the
greatest benevolences to mankind would be the establishment of
such a system [as Antheil's] , and the substitution of the en-
harmonic-pianoforte system for all instruments."
     In the face of such unquestioning belief in his creation,
what can a mere chronicler say? Point out to Antheil's ghost
that the vertical staff had long ago been invented? That extended pitch symbols, a la twentieth-century "time-notation,"
had appeared in notational reforms of the early nineteenth
century? No need -- in his autobiography, Antheil wrote the
obituary: His notation system (later called by him "See note")
"had gotten nowhere, eaten up a good Braque and Picasso [paint-
ings owned by the Antheils] , and finally completely emptied
our bank account."

1924. Herbert Eimert, <u>Atonale Musiklehre</u> (Atonal music method).
   Leipzig: Breitkopf & Härtel.
Staff: 5-line.
Clef signs: Traditional G- and F-clefs.

Pitch:

F   F#   G   G#   A   A#   B   C   C#   D   D#   E   F
    Gb   Ab   Bb   Db   Eb

Example 4-80. Franz Schubert, Sonata in C Minor, op. posth.

Eimert's method of distinguishing sharped notes (and enharmonic flats) is based in part on Nicolas Obouhov's proposal (see page 214). He proposed two modifications to the earlier reform: first, all the x's are to be encircled, and second, the rims of these noteheads are to be thick for whole- and half-notes, in contrast to thinner rims for quarter-notes and the shorter values. This 1924 proposal by Eimert should be compared with his much later suggestion (page 248), which uses ancillary markings attached to normal noteheads instead of x-shaped notes.

1925. Arnold Schoenberg, "Eine neue Zwölftonschrift" (A new twelve-tone notation), Musikblätter des Anbruch 7, 1, pp. 1-7.
Staff: 3-line. Any number of staves may be combined to extend the range; a piano system usually consists of a pair of 6-line staves (each a combination of two 3-line staves), separated by a space equal to three lines. Schoenberg also suggested several alternative formats for combining two 3-line staves.

1)   2)

3)   4)

Clef signs: A dual-clef symbol serves two octaves on one staff. All three clefs (G, C, and F) are related to different staff lines depending upon the instrument or voice using them.

Pitch: Each trio of similarly designed noteheads outlines an augmented triad, a notational device that is also incorporated in the proposal of Hans Sacher (see page 204).

C   C#   D D#   E   F   F#   G   G#   A   A#   B   C
    Db   Eb   Gb   Ab   Bb

Example 4-81. Arnold Schoenberg, "Der Mondfleck," from <u>Pierrot Lunaire</u>. (© 1914 by Universal Edition A.G.)

Schoenberg commands our respect, if not our unanimous agreement, in his practical approach to new notation as a second
language, not a replacement. "I am not of the opinion that all
music so far printed and written will have to be reprinted and
rewritten, any more than every single book has been rendered
into shorthand. But just as any schoolchild can read and write
cursive and italic script . . . so the ability to master two
different musical notations equally well will have to be acquired."

In his personal innovations, Schoenberg embodied standards
many fanciful notators ignore: "The only possible task of any
pictorial notation is to make its effect purely through the
picture, without using abstractions of any kind." Certainly
he practiced what he preached in his twelve-tone notation,
which accurately conveys the composer's ideas by its fastidi-
ous written language.

In addition to its description in the cited music-journal
article, Schoenberg's notational proposal is included in the
revised edition (1950) of his Style and Idea, published in
London.

1926. Dora C. Burgess, Musical Notation. U.S. Patent 1,594,
194.
Staff: 5-line.
Clef signs: Usual G- and F-clefs.
Pitch:

C   C#   C×   Db   D   D# Eb   E   F   F#   F×Gb   G

G#   G×   Ab   A   A# Bbb Bb   B   Cb   C

Note that the symbols for double-sharps and double-flats
point to the line or space of the actual sounding pitch.
Key signatures: The letters R (for Right-raise) and L (for
Left-lower) substitute for the conventional accidentals.

= D major or   = Eb major or
B minor   C minor

Example 4-82.

This inventor ended her proposal description with the statement: "This invention . . . provides a comprehensive means of
quickly learning to read the representation of musical sounds,
thereby shortening the time [and] lowering the expense of a
musical education." Perhaps. To this compiler of notational
proposals, only the author's simple key signatures offer spec-
ulative potential for future notators.

1926. Willy Neumann, Notensystem "Rapid." Rostock, Germany:
    Musikverlag Rapid.
Staff: 5-line (2-3); a keyboard system comprises two and a
    half staves, as illustrated in Example 4-83.
Clef signs: None; the central pair of staff lines accommodates
    the pitches of middle C#/Db and D#/Eb.
Pitch: All notes for the left hand are void; notes for the
    right hand are solid. Stems are centered on the noteheads;
    when they are used to connect intervals and chord structures,
    the stems do not extend beyond the outer noteheads.

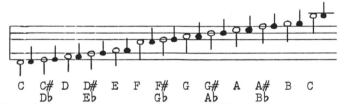

C C# D D# E F F# G G# A A# B C
   Db   Eb   Gb   Ab   Bb

Duration: Measure beats are indicated by dotted vertical lines
    which divide the upper and lower five lines; notes on the
    beat are placed directly on these tactus lines. Dotted notes
    are represented by a short, thin line after the notehead.
    Beat subdivisions are calculated according to their visual
    relationships to the beat lines. Triplets, quintuplets, and
    all other irregular rhythmic groups are identified with a
    Roman numeral, as illustrated below.
Rests: All durations are expressed as follows:

Left hand | Right hand

Meter: Only the numerator is given, positioned in the staff
    center.

Example 4-83. Frédéric Chopin, <u>Polonaise in A</u>, op. 40, no. 1.

The discerning reader will surely have noticed several discrepancies in Neumann's transcription of the above-quoted passage from Chopin's "Military" Polonaise: the single notes rather than octaves in the left hand, and the truncated chords in the right hand. Evidently, Neumann used a simplified version for young piano students. But the easing of technical requirements is at odds with the author's notational demands, which are rather too eccentric to be helpful to the embryonic pianist.

The most perplexing aspect of "Rapid" is its utilizing open or solid noteheads to designate which hand plays the notes, rather than to distinguish rhythmic values or chromatic pitch differences. Neumann's procedure can be disconcerting to the musician habituated to orthochronic notation, especially when all durational values are expressed by the same note form, without any flags or beams to identify rhythmical differences.

1926. Dom John Stéphan, O. S. B., <u>The Isotonic Notation</u>.
  Exeter, England: S. Lee, Ltd.
Staff: 5-line.
Clef signs: G- and F-clefs, as shown in Example 4-85.
Pitch:

Gb   G   G#   Ab   A   A#   Bbb   Bb   B   C

Key signatures: The requisite noteheads are placed on the
appropriate lines or spaces, as demonstrated below.
Example 4-84. Ludwig van Beethoven, <u>Sonata in A-flat</u>, op. 26.

Example 4-85.

"Certain it is that much time and valuable energy are wasted
on needless efforts to unravel the intricacies of musical notation," wrote Dom Stéphan in explication of his proposal. If we
wished to be uncharitable, we might paraphrase by saying that
much time and valuable energy are wasted on needless efforts

to unravel the intricacies of many a notational reform proposal,
Dom Stéphan's system among them.

Derived from the Greek (<u>iso</u>, equal, and <u>tonos</u>, tone), this
reformer's "isotonic" is only another way of saying "twelve-
tone notation."

1926. Ernst Toch, "Vorschläge zur Vereinfachung der Noten-
   schrift" (Proposals for the simplification of notation),
   <u>Musikblatter des Anbruch</u> 8, 7, pp. 308-312.
Staff: 5-line.
Clef signs: Standard G- and F-clefs.
Pitch:

Duration: Conventionally expressed, except that a note having
   the value of a full measure is notated as: ◊ , ◈ .
Rests: All durations are expressed as R (<u>Rest des Taktes</u>).
Example 4-86.

Toch's system of chromatic noteheads is little more than an
endorsement of Obouhov's earlier proposal (page 214). Only his
suggestion of a special notehead to represent a full measure,
regardless of the meter involved, and a new symbol to replace
the standard rest signs, qualify as personal contributions.

1929. Paul Koch, <u>Type specimen of a new system of notation</u>.
   Offenbach am Main, Germany: the author.
Staff: 5-line.
Clef signs: G- and F-clefs, as letters, shown in Example 4-87.
Pitch:

Gb   G   G#   Ab   A   A#   Bb   B   C

Duration:

Note-stems are placed on the noteheads of the outer parts
only; the inner voices are unstemmed. Tied notes are indicated:

Example 4-87. J. S. Bach, "Bourée II," from English Suite
no. 2.

The square and oblong noteheads of Koch's reform are a reversion to the notational convention of the Middle Ages, when
Gothic square-notes were the prevalent form of notehead design.
Archaic, too, is Koch's positioning accidental signs above the
notes, a practice characteristic of various tablature notations. Neither revival has proved useful enough to be copied
by other notators.

1930. Pierre Hans, La notation musicale "continue." (Music
    notation progresses). Brussels?
Staff: 20-line, comprising four standard pentagrams, separated
    from each other by three spaces that accommodate two ledger
    lines each.

Register symbols:

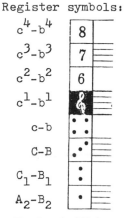

Each staff is read as the G-clef. Note that the G-clef sign is white against a black background.

Pitch:

| Natural pitches | Flat pitches | Sharp pitches |

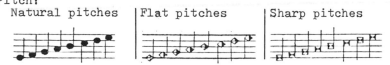

Key signatures: Indicated by a special symbol placed on the appropriate line or space of the uppermost staff, following the register sign, as shown below.

Example 4-88. Maurice Ravel, "Ondine," from Gaspard de la nuit. (© 1908, Durand et Cie.)

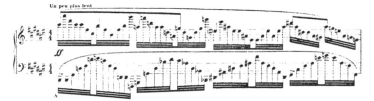

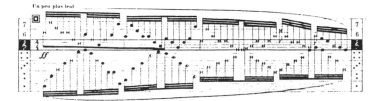

This system (11) is geared to Hans' invention of a two-keyboard piano (Clavier Hans) with the lower keyboard pitched a half-step higher than the upper keyboard. Each black key on the lower keyboard corresponds in position to a white key on the higher keyboard, thus permitting the same fingering to be used on either.

The musical excerpts shown in Example 4-88 vividly illustrate the immense reading difficulties in both the traditionally notated version and in the transcription into Hans' method of notation. Only the experienced performer can decide which
version offers fewer complications to the reader's eye.

1931. L. H. Hora, <u>Simplified Musical Notation</u>. London: the
    author.
Staff: 5-line.
Clef signs: Standard G- and F-clefs.
Pitch:

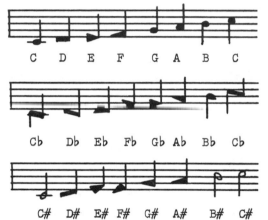

C   D   E   F   G   A   B   C

C♭   D♭   E♭   F♭   G♭ A♭   B♭   C♭

C#   D#   E#   F#   G#   A#   B#   C#

Duration: Indicated conventionally.
Example 4-89.

Three different notehead series form the basis for Hora's system: one for the diatonic scale, and the other two for the
flatted and sharped alterations of the scale. Designed exclusively for vocal music, this was a late entry in the long list
of Tonic Sol-fa solfege methods so popular in the nineteenth
century. It is, however, no improvement over the earlier proposals in this area of notation.

1931. Felix Peyrallo, "Reforma del sistema Pentagramel" (Re-
    form of the pentagram system), <u>La Pluma</u> IV, 18.
Staff: 5-line (1-2-2).

Clef signs: Not discussed.
Pitch:

C   C#   Db   D   D#   Eb   E   F   F#

Gb   G   G#   Ab   A   A#   Bb   B   C

It should be noted that the stems of flatted pitches are always on the left of the noteheads, and on the right for sharps.

Rests: Indicated by diagonal lines and special symbols relating to dotted beat-lines in each measure.

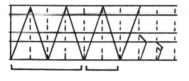

Example 4-90.

In this notational proposal the novel staff and notehead design are of equal significance. Especially eccentric, however, are the elongated note shapes favored by Peyrallo. The basic point of his chromatic distinctions could just as well have been made with ordinary noteheads; their position on the staff and the placement of their stems are more crucial than their actual form. But compromise seems not to have been in this inventor's mind; hence, the alteration of staff, noteheads, and rest symbols are key factors in his reform.

1933. Otto Marcus, <u>Die chromatische Notenschrift</u> (The chromatic notation). St. Gallen, Switzerland: Drei farben-musik

verlag, O. Marcus.
Staff: 5-line.
Clef signs: Traditional G- and F-clefs.
Pitch:

Example 4-91.

Like Christian Huth and Nicolas Obouhov before him, Marcus was intrigued by the relationship between color and sound. "Den tönen entsprechen die noten. Durch rot und grün erhöhe und erniedrige ich sie, -- taten und leiden des lichts!" ran his prefatory remarks. (Tones correspond to notes. By means of red and green I show them as higher or lower -- actions and sufferings of light!)

Marcus' dissertation was buttressed with passages from Schopenhauer, Goethe, Riemann, and Brahms, and it ended with a pertinent quotation from Heinrich Schenker: "Man gewöhne sich endlich, den tönen wie kreaturen ins auge zu sehen" (One should ultimately get used to looking at tones as if they were living beings).

Even in the face of this scholarly array, we must ask Marcus: If color is used to distinguish sharped from flatted pitches, why is it necessary to alter notehead shapes as well? Color alone or contrasting note forms would have provided sufficient distinction.

1935. Henk Beunk, <u>Notenschrift</u> (Notation). Zwolle, Holland: the author.
Staff: 4-line (2-2); usually six lines are utilized as a keyboard system.
Clef signs: None; treble and bass are implied.

Pitch:

E   F   F#   F✕ Gb   G   G#   Ab   A   A#   Bbb

Bb   B   Cb   C   C#   C✕ Db   D   D#   Ebb   Eb   E

Duration:

, and so on.

Rests:

, and so on.

Example 4-92.

Possibly realizing that his notehead forms presented writing
problems for the composer and copyist, Beunk made a second
suggestion based on the standard pentagram and using open
noteheads for the naturals and solid ones for the sharps (no
flats). A double-sharp was written ♩. For his durational
scheme, Beunk increased the value of the whole- and half-notes
by a factor of one.

1935. Charles Stewart Middlemiss, <u>A New Graphic Notation for Keyboard</u>. London: the author.
Staff: 3-line, vertical; the central line is broken.
Clef signs: None; treble and bass are implied.
Pitch:

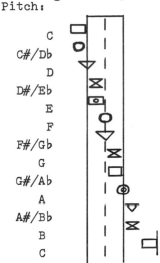

Harmonic intervals of the 2nd are written as a combination of the two note symbols, for example,

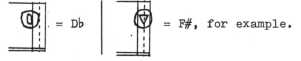

Key signatures: The tonic note symbol is circled.

Duration: According to the following scheme, using the symbol for C as a model:

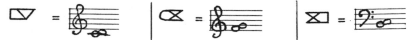

Rests:

▬   ▬   ⸀   ꓶ
⸝   ⸝
▬   ▬   ⸯ   ꓶ   , and so on.

Example 4-93. Franz Schubert, <u>Impromptu in A-flat</u>, op. 142, no. 2.

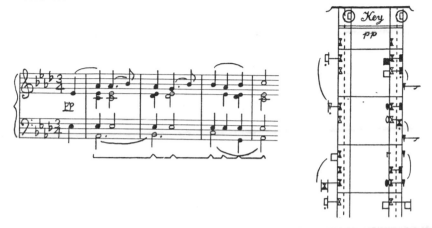

There can be no doubt that this is indeed a "graphic nota-tion," but eccentricity is no substitute for practicality. Certainly the proposal of Middlemiss is neither a simplifica-tion nor an improvement of our traditional system -- only an expression of one man's misguided ego. Visually amusing though it may be, this notation cannot be regarded as pointing the way to the future.

1941. Luis Arellano, <u>The Arellano Musical Notation</u>. Philadel-phia: the author.
Staff: 5-line.
Register symbols:

E_1-E   E-e   e-e^1 e^1-e^2

The 8va sign is used to extend the upper range. Notes in the lower staff are read like those in the upper staff, but they are played two octaves lower.

Pitch:

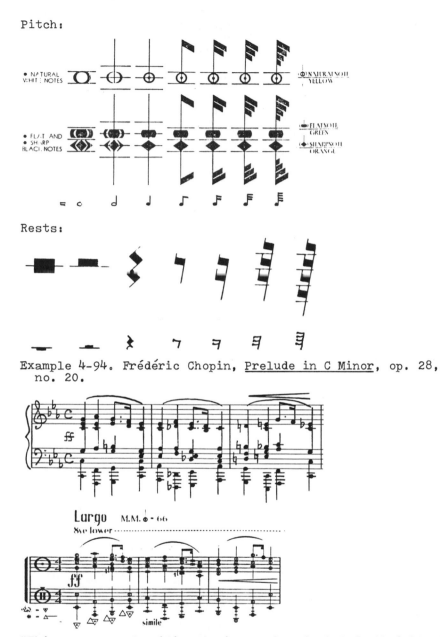

Rests:

Example 4-94. Frédéric Chopin, <u>Prelude in C Minor</u>, op. 28, no. 20.

"This new way of writing music can be adopted forthright without disturbing the equanimity of the music world," Arellano
stated. Time and time again we have read similar statements
by reformers convinced of the simplicity of their ideas and
their potential for immediate recognition by the world of

music. Why, we may ask, were these proposers of new systems
blind to the defects of their reforms? Although Arellano's
notation may be no more fanciful or impractical than many another method already illustrated in these pages, it has joined
countless other well-meaning notational proposals in obscurity
-- mainly because of its eccentrically shaped noteheads, difficult both to write and to read.

1941. Otto Studer, <u>Neues Notensystem</u> (New notation). Basel,
    Switzerland: Herausgeber: Neno-Verlag.
Staff: 5-line.
Clef signs: Traditional G- and F-clefs.
Pitch:

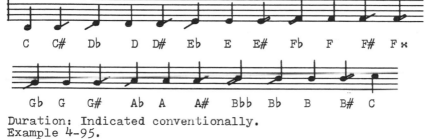

Duration: Indicated conventionally.
Example 4-95.

Studer's depiction of chromatic inflections of the scale uses
essentially the same method used by Capellen before him (see
page 201) and Arthur Hartmann sometime later (page 251). Only
Studer's slight modification of the slash mark to identify
certain enharmonic alterations (such as B# = C, or Fb = E) is
unique in his system. Later we will see that other contemporary composers -- Henri Pousseur, for one -- sometimes adopted
the same technique.

1942. Henry-Louis Sarlit, [New notational proposal]. Paris?
    the author.
Staff: 5-line.
Clef signs: Standard G- and F-clefs. The following symbols
    indicate octave transpositions:

= 8va | = 8bassa

Pitch:

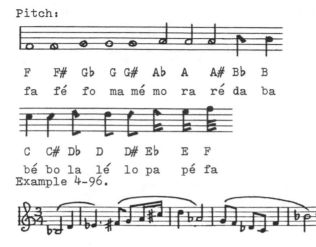

F	F#	Gb	G	G#	Ab	A	A#	Bb	B
fa	fé	fo	ma	mé	mo	ra	ré	da	ba

C	C#	Db	D	D#	Eb	E	F
bé	bo	la	lé	lo	pa	pé	fa

Example 4-96.

Sarlit's device for indicating octave transpositions is simple and sensible. The same cannot be said, however, of his suggested notehead forms; in particular, the slanted oblong symbols, though logically differentiated, are not easy to draw. Furthermore, the symbological differences between the altered forms of the whole- and half-notes and the quarter-notes and smaller values are too extreme.

1944. Frank Wilson Adsit, <u>Modrn Music</u>. n.p., Modrn Music Publication.
Staff: 4-line (1-2-1).
Clef signs: Normal G- and F-clefs.
Pitch: Two different systems were proposed; in the first, the noteheads of each octave are differently colored, and in the second they are shaped differently for each octave.

1) A_2-G_1 | A_1-G | A-g | a-g^1 | a^1-g^2 | a^2-g^3 | a^3-g^4 | a^4-c^5

    black | brown | green | red | blue | orange | violet | tan

2)

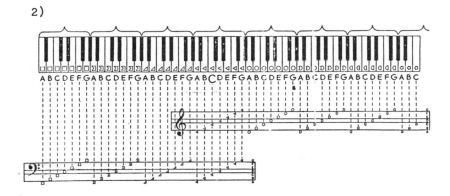

Duration:

Example 4-97. Frédéric Chopin, <u>Prelude in A</u>, op. 28, no. 7.

It would be impossible for the notator to utilize and prohibi-
tively expensive for any publisher to print eight differently
colored or eight differently shaped noteheads. Adsit's staff,
of course, is only a truncated version of the white-key/black-
key staff devised by many reformers for keyboard music.

1947. Alchanan Cohen, <u>Pictorial Codes of Music of the Future</u>.
London: the author.
Staff: 4-line. Two staves are used for Code "A," one for regis-
ter and one for pitch. Code "B" employs two staves for pitch
only.
Register symbols:
Code "A"

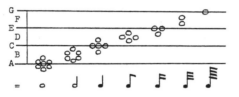

Code "B"

	Octave 1	Octave 2	Octave 3	Octave 4	Octave 5
	A_2-G_1	A_1-G	A-g	a-g^1	a^1-g^2

Octave 6	Octave 7
a^2-g^3	a^3 g^4

Pitch and Duration:
Code "A"

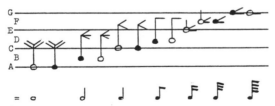

Code "B"

Cohen also suggested a 1-line staff, using the following
pitch format:

A   B   C   D   E   F   G

Example 4-98.

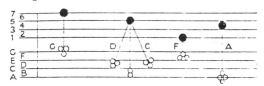

"It is the task of a musical code to prescribe a graphic as-
signment," Cohen wrote, "whereby the notes are individually
configurated, permanently discerned and located, with regard
to octave, note, and time value allotment." His system, the
author continued, "opens a new field for cinema-music projec-
tion. You can project on the screen dancers on a marked-out
platform of octaves or notes stepping in accordance with rhythmic wave form of song [melody] and time values indicated by
a clock. . . . Here is an appealing entertainment and instruction potential for home and export, ready for fertile minds to
turn to good profitable account." Cohen was obviously thinking
in terms of mixed media in conjunction with his notational
codes -- a fanciful concept, and one we must admit was ahead
of his time. Whether or not contemporary dancers or musicians
would endorse Cohen's unique symbology cannot be definitely
stated, but in the arts today everything is grist for the mill.
Cohen's Pictorial Codes of Music for the Future might very
well become a part of that art.

1947. Herbert Rand, The Trilinear System of Musical Notation.
    London: the author.
Staff: 6-line (3-3).
Register symbols:

C_1-B_1 | II $C-B$ | III $c-b$ | IV c^1-b^1 | V c^2-b^2 | VI c^3-b^3

Pitch:

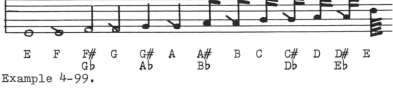

E   F   F#   G   G#   A   A#   B   C   C#   D   D#   E
          Gb   Ab   Bb   Db   Eb

Example 4-99.

Noteheads with attached slashes have appeared in several previous reforms of pitch notation. Rand's alternation of normal
and altered noteheads has validity only if each slashed note
is considered as the raised version of the antecedent note;
even so, the concept does not correspond to the white key/
black key relationships of the piano keyboard, for which this
system was devised.

1948. Floyd A. Firestone, <u>Firestone Hand-Shape Notation</u>.
   Washington, D.C., the author.
Staff: 5-line.
Clef signs: None; treble and bass are implied.
Pitch: The triangular noteheads for the black keys relate to
   flatted notes only.

C   Db   D   Eb   E   F   Gb   G   Ab   A   Bb   B   C

Duration: The author favors unorthodox beaming formats, even
   though the note values are conventionally designated.

Grace notes are written as normal-sized noteheads but without stems. To eliminate double stems for dual values played
by the same hand, open and closed noteheads share a common
stem, as illustrated above.
Rests:

, and so on.

Example 4-100. Frédéric Chopin, <u>Prelude in A</u>, op. 28, no. 7.

Hand-Shape Notation was designed to be used in elementary piano teaching. Firestone's use of triangular noteheads to designate flatted pitches should be compared with Robert Whitford's similar proposal made in the same year (page 246). It is difficult to see how either system makes piano study easier for young pupils by demanding that they learn still another set of symbols. And Firestone's odd beaming formats add one more stumbling block in the path of the elementary piano student.

1948. Friedrich Weisshappel, <u>Die Frage der Notenschriftreform</u>
  (The question of notation reform). Vienna: the author.
Staff: 3-line.
Clef signs: None.
Pitch:

Example 4-101.

One unusual feature of Weisshappel's proposal is his inclusion of symbols for certain enharmonic pitches -- Ebb, Fb, B#, E#, for example -- not often included in other notehead reforms. Carrying his idea one step further, Bbb can also represent G×; Fb is also D×; and B# is the same as Dbb. Granted that these enharmonics are rarely if ever encountered, even in the superchromatic writing of Wagner, Richard Strauss, or Schoenberg in his early works, they could be accommodated by Weisshappel's method of pitch notation.

1948. Robert H. Whitford, <u>Whitfordized Music Notation</u>. Erie,
    Pennsylvania: the author.
Staff: 5-line.
Clef signs: Standard G- and F-clefs.
Pitch: Sharps are written enharmonically as flats.

          C B Bb A Ab G Gb F E Eb D Db C
Duration: Indicated traditionally.
Example 4-102.

"Here is the musical discovery the music world has been wait-
ing for -- a more logical and practical way to read and write
music." So wrote the author of this proposal, and so have written countless other earnest but uninformed reformers of common-practice notation. Whitford's "musical discovery" was,
alas, long ago advanced by others who proclaimed the same sentiments for their supposed innovations.

1949. Edgar T. Haines, <u>Haines Keyboard Notation (Advancement
    of Music)</u>. Tenbury Wells, England: the author.
Staff: 4-line.
Clef signs: None; the boxed pitches on the right of the verti-
    cal staff lines shown below are for the pianist's right hand
    and those on the left are for the left hand an octave lower.
Pitch:

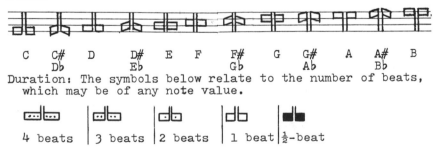

   C   C#   D   D#   E   F   F#   G   G#   A   A#   B
       Db   Eb   Gb   Ab   Bb
Duration: The symbols below relate to the number of beats,
    which may be of any note value.

  4 beats │ 3 beats │ 2 beats │ 1 beat │½-beat

Example 4-103. Hymn, <u>St. Anne</u>.

"[This is] a simplified notation designed to facilitate the teaching of music. This notation dispenses with the usual signs of sharp, flat, natural, clef, key signatures, and bar-line, and it is based upon a single staff of only four lines of the C-clef upon which four or more parts can be written. . . . Now you say, why hasn't this system been adopted or at least more widely publicized? The answer is, quite simply, the powers that be give it the description of being 'very ingenious' but dismiss it as being 'too revolutionary,' which of course is rubbish!"

Haines' self-justification continues: "The plain facts are that it is revolutionary in the sense that what is now complicated becomes simple even to school children. It would appear that they [the powers that be] fear that any alteration in the structure of notation would be damaging to their profession, which makes them stumbling blocks to thousands -- thus depriving most people of the pleasure of understanding music."

From our admittedly professional standpoint, it is not the opinions of "the powers that be" that are rubbish, but the sanctimonious protestations of the inventor of this system. Nowhere can we find evidence that Haines' method has accomplished what it so loudly trumpets -- an improved conventional notation that can open up the world of music to untold thousands.

1950. Jacques Chailley, <u>Les notations musicales nouvelles</u> (The new musical notations). Paris: Librairie Larousse.
Staff: 5-line.
Clef signs: Usual G- and F-clefs.
Pitch:

Meter: Numerator and denominator are reversed in position; the
   latter is expressed with a notehead instead of a numeral.
Example 4-104. Frédéric Chopin, Prelude in A, op. 28, no. 7.

Chailley's proposal, which he included in his book on the notational reforms of other theorists and composers, was developed from several earlier experiments patterned after the
ideas of both Joseph Raymondi (see page 155) and Franz Diettrich-Kalkhoff (page 208). The small angled slashes attached
to the flatted pitches are devices found in several other systems, notably those of Georg Capellen (page 201), Otto Studer
(page 239), and Herbert Rand (page 243). Chailley's solutions
for sharped whole- and half-notes should also be compared with
those present in the reforms of Obouhov (page 214), Toch (page
229), and Eimert (see below). Chailley's proposal, then, is an
amalgam of the ideas of several previous reformers.

1950. Herbert Eimert, Lehrbuch der Zwölftonmusik (Text on
   twelve-tone music). Wiesbaden, Germany: the author.
Staff: 5-line.
Clef signs: Standard G- and F-clefs.
Pitch:

Example 4-105.

Two years after Eimert published his proposal, Siegfried Koh-
ler advanced the same idea in the April, 1952, issue of <u>Musica</u>
("Was ist Zwölftonmusik?"). Both men were disenchanted with
the various notations that espoused the x-shaped notehead, although their solution, in effect, was to attach half of the
x-symbol to the notehead itself. It is difficult to see what
this accomplishes, as the substitution of one ancillary sign
for another (x = #) hardly qualifies as a simplification. At
any rate, we do not find this particular technique in any other notation proposals of the mid-twentieth century.

1950. Manuel Godoy, <u>Nueva escritura musical grafo-analítica</u>
    (New graphic-analytical notation). Santiago, Chile: the
    author.
Staff: 5-line.
Clef signs: None.
Pitch:

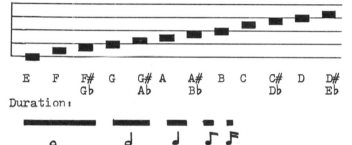

E   F   F#   G   G#   A   A#   B   C   C#   D   D#
          Gb   Ab   Bb   Db   Eb

Duration:

Rests: Indicated by blank space.
Example 4-106. Franz Schubert, "Ständchen," from <u>Schwanen-
    gesang</u>.

Once again we have a reincarnation of the Gothic square-note
format of the thirteenth and fourteenth centuries, here applied
to the five-line staff, and with three different notes occupy-
ing certain staff spaces. Durationally, Godoy's method is modern enough to utilize the time-notation concept of mathemati-
cally calculated extensions of the note symbols; in addition,
beat-lines are placed within each pair of barlines, which aid
the performer in assessing the briefer durations. The system
is thus a curious fusion of the old (the note symbols) and the
new (the depiction of time and duration).

   We must assume that the curious transcription of Schubert's
well-known song, shown above, is the effort of this proposer;
it does not, of course, correspond completely to the original.

1952. Tadeusz Wójcik, "Zagodnienie racjonalizacji systemów
   znakowania muzycznego" (The problem of rationalizing notation systems), Muzyka 1, 2, pp. 71-124.
Staff: 7-line (3-1-3); two staves, widely separated, constitute a keyboard system.
Register symbols:

Pitch:

Key signatures: The following signs indicate whether the music
   is in a sharp or a flat key:

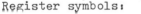

Duration: Primary barlines and secondary beat lines are heavy
   vertical bars set above the staff; beat subdivisions are indicated by broken vertical lines centered on the staff. Notes
   on a beat or a beat division are centered on these vertical
   lines. Tied notes are shown by dots following the notehead,
   as illustrated below.
Rests: A single symbol, >, which serves all values, is related
   to the line or space of the preceding notehead.
Meter: Indicated by the secondary beat-lines and dotted subdivisions within each pair of longer barlines; for example:

Example 4-107.

A curious feature of this Polish theorist's system is the use
of non-mensural beamings, as illustrated above. Wójcik's method
of displaying barlines and measure beat-lines is also unorthodox, as is the manner in which he indicates tied notes. Also
noteworthy is the arrangement of the two staves in a piano system: 3-1-3 for the left hand, a central ledger line for the
middle-octave d, relating to either staff, and 3-1-3 for the
right hand.

An informative and reasoned critique by Erhard Karkoschka
of Wójcik's proposal, as well as those of Rodney Fawcett (Equitone), J. M. Hauer, and Cornelis Pot (Klavarskribo), may be
found in Melos 38 (1971), pages 230-234. The pros and cons of
each new system are presented with Karkoschka's expected authority and special insight into their potential for assimila-
tion into late twentieth-century practice.

1956. Arthur Hartmann, "Anregungen zur einer Reform der Noten-
schrift" (Suggestion for a reform of musical notation), Neue
Zeitschrift für Musik 117, 1/2, pp. 50-51; 118-119.
Staff: 5-line.
Clef signs:
G-clef   F-clef

Pitch: Hartmann makes two different proposals:

1)

C   C#   Db   D   D#   Eb   E   F   F#

Gb G G# Ab A A# Bb B C

2)

C   C#   Db   D   D#   Eb   E   F   F#

Gb   G   G#   Ab   A   A#   Bb   B   C

Key signatures: Although they are not necessary in Hartmann's
two proposals, he says they may be included, enclosed within
parentheses as a reminder.
Example 4-108.

The first of Hartmann's two suggestions is the simpler; it
essentially duplicates the reform of Georg Capellen (see page
201) and several other advocates of new notehead notation. His
second proposal is akin to previous systems that relied on
x-shaped noteheads for sharps and flats. One awkward feature
of Hartmann's second method is the need to use two symbols to
express the value of a whole-note, not a very sensible solution to indicating durational difference.

1958. Rodney Fawcett, Equitone. Zurich: the author.
Staff: 2-line; a piano system may require up to seven lines.
Register symbols:

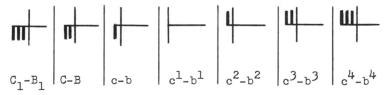

C_1-B_1 | C-B | c-b | c^1-b^1 | c^2-b^2 | c^3-b^3 | c^4-b^4

Pitch:

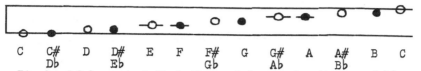

C   C#   D   D#   E   F   F#   G   G#   A   A#   B   C
    Db   Eb   Gb   Ab   Bb

It should be noted that the noteheads for E, F, G#/Ab, and
A are <u>not</u> on ledger lines; the bisecting slash is part of
the notehead itself.
Chord structures usually require two staff lines. Certain
minor seconds, which are contained in a vertical sonority,
are treated as altered unisons (C/C# rather than C/Db, for
instance) and are represented by a half-open notehead.

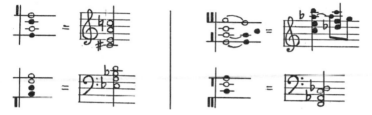

Duration: Notes are placed proportionately between measure
   barlines and any beat subdivisions, shown by dotted vertical
   lines. Generally speaking, a note is prolonged until the
   appearance of the following note or a pause sign. Or extended duration lines can also be used to show the progress
   of one pitch to another. Or, as Karkoschka suggests, the
   noteheads can be stemmed and beamed together for the same
   purpose.
Example 4-109.

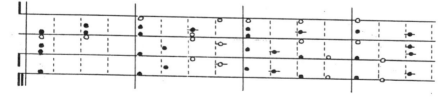

It is significant that Erhard Karkoschka felt that <u>Equitone</u>
had more interest and potential for the contemporary composer
than <u>Klavarskribo</u> -- and this though the latter system has enjoyed far more success and is more widely disseminated than
Fawcett's proposal. Yet there are patent drawbacks to this

reform. One of the most serious is the identical visual representation of meters having the same numerators but completely different denominators. For example, 3/16, 3/8, 3/4, and 3/2 are notated precisely alike, with no possibility of demonstrating the psychological distinctions inherent in the four meters. Certainly, composers have their own valid reasons for choosing one meter over another, just as their choice of tonality -- or its negation -- is subjective. That the symbology in <u>Equitone</u> cannot portray these subtle distinctions may be a powerful reason today's composers have not accepted the system as a viable means for notating their creative output.

1958. Antal Maldacker, <u>Chromakott: The New Musical Notation</u>. Toronto: Chromakott Music Publishing Co.
Staff: 1-line; a keyboard system requires four or more lines.
Register symbols: None; G- and F-clefs are implied.
Pitch:

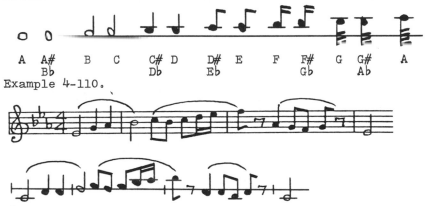

Example 4-110.

It is not evident why Maldacker settled on a one-line rather than a three-line staff for his system. Using ledger lines for every note following the four initial pitches makes no sense, when two additional staff lines would carry the complete chromatic scale without the need for ledger lines. In addition, the backward-slanting noteheads are awkward to write, a minus factor for any experienced notator.

1959. Thomas H. Stix, <u>Proposal for a New System of Music Notation</u>. Princeton, New Jersey: the author.
Staff: 4-line (2-2).
Clef signs:

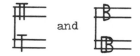

and

Pitch:

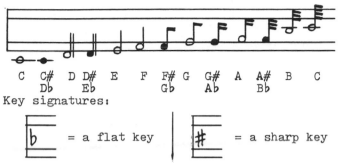

```
C  C#  D  D#  E  F  F#  G  G#  A  A#  B  C
   Db     Eb        Gb     Ab     Bb
```

Key signatures:

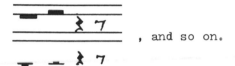

= a flat key   = a sharp key

Rests:

, and so on.

Example 4-111.

By means of this reform, Stix promised "to speed the learning process not by increasing the instrumentalist's 'vocabulary' but by reducing the size of the 'dictionary'." The reduction in notational elements is not immediately evident; compared to the leanness of certain other reforms, Stix's elimination of accidentals constitutes a minimal weight loss. Noteheads, clef signs, staff lines, and rest symbols persist to outweigh one minor advantage.

1961. Carl Johannis, <u>Notenschriftreform</u> (Notation reform). Stuttgart: Schuler Verlagsgesellschaft.
Staff: 2-line; additional staves, below and above, extend the range as necessary. A keyboard work normally requires four staves, an ensemble work, six or more.

Register symbols:

C_1-B_1 | C-B | c-b | c^1-b^1 | c^2-b^2 | c^3-b^3

Pitch:

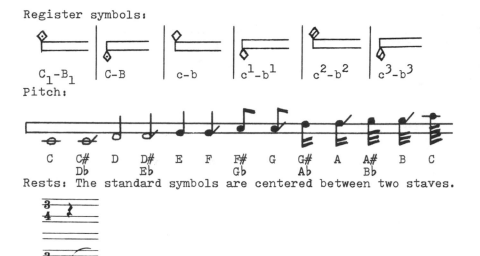

C   C#   D   D#   E   F   F#   G   G#   A   A#   B   C
    Db   Eb   Gb   Ab   Bb

Rests: The standard symbols are centered between two staves.

Example 4-112. Arnold Schoenberg, "Heimweh," from <u>Pierrot Lunaire</u> (© 1914, Universal Edition A.G.).

Like Julian Carrillo's notational reform of 1895, <u>Notenschrift-reform</u> garnered impressive testimonials from contemporary conductors -- Antal Dorati, Herbert von Karajan, Rafael Kubelik, and Dmitri Mitropoulos among them. Conspicuously absent from this list, however, are the names of today's composers. Other notehead reforms have also advocated the use of angled slashes attached to the noteheads to designate chromatic inflections, but they too were unable to win the approval of composers in general, in spite of one or two half-hearted attempts to test the proposition.

1961. Henri Pousseur, <u>Ode pour quatuor à cordes</u>. Vienna: Universal Edition A.G.

Staff: 5-line.
Clef signs: Standard G- and F-clefs.
Pitch: The upper symbol is used when two or more pitches are
  superimposed.

C   C#   Db   D   D#   Eb   E   F   F#

Gb   G   G#   Ab   A   A#   Bb   B   C

Duration: Shown proportionately within variable dotted barlines, the notes linked by extended stems, as shown below.
Example 4-113.

Pousseur applied this experiment in notehead symbology to only
one of his compositions, which is experimental in every aspect.
As shown in the pitch illustration above, he offered two forms
of the thick slashes attached to the noteheads; when vertical
structures are involved, as they are in the quoted excerpt from
Pousseur's score, the upper of the two forms becomes imperative.
Neither form is invariably clear to the eye, however, and the
tiny marks can be easily overlooked.

1963. Boguslaw Schäffer, <u>Azione a due</u>. Berlin: Ahn & Simrock.
Staff: 5-line.
Clef signs:

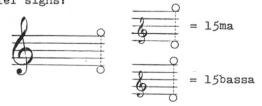

= 15ma

= 15bassa

Pitch:

C   C#   Db   D   D#   Eb   E   F   F#

Gb   G   G#   Ab   A   A#   Bb   B   C

Duration: Shown by an extended horizontal bar from the notehead. Short notes are successively linked together by thin
lines. Vertical structures are joined by dotted stems to the
right of the noteheads.

Rests: Designated by blank space.

Dynamics: A scale of intensity is indicated by the open notehead being progressively filled in, in a clockwise direction,
as follows:

ppp   *pp*   *p*   *mp*   *mf*   *f*   *ff*   *fff*

Example 4-114.

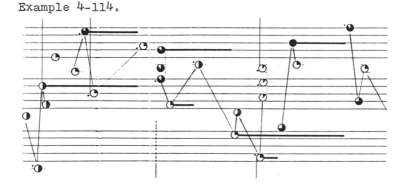

This Polish avant-gardist's notation, like that of Henri Pousseur before him, was not devised as a new system for all music,
but only as an isolated experiment in one composition. Inter-
estingly, his method of designating sharps and flats by placing
dots before the noteheads reverts to an early practice in the
evolution of mensural notation.

   Less obvious in its genesis and more dubious in effectiveness is Schäffer's system of graded intensities. From any distance, it is very difficult to perceive the minute alterations
within the noteheads and to react precisely to their message.
It is undoubtedly for these reasons that other composers familiar with Schäffer's experiment did not borrow from it in their
own works of similar nature.

1964. Hilbert Howe, <u>Howe-Way 6-3-3 Notation System</u>. Phoenix,
   Arizona: Howe-Way Music Method.
Staff: 6-line, comprising two 3-line segments called septums.
   The fourth staff-line is heavy.
Register symbols:

Pitch: The solid notes are always a half-step higher than the
   preceding pitch; the author does not explain how flatted
   notes are to be notated.

C   C# D   D# E F F# G G# A A# B C
1   1½ 2   2½ 3 3½ 4   4½ 5   5½ 6   6½ 1
Key signatures: Designated by the tonic notehead, minus stem,
   placed on the appropriate line or space preceding the register numeral.

, for example.

Meter: Numerator and denominator are separated by a dash and
   set above the heavy fourth line, as shown above.
Example 4-115. "Resignation," from <u>The Southern Harmony</u>.

Each three-line segment of Howe's staff accommodates seven
notehead positions; the heavy central line is intended to aid
the eye in relating the two septums that share the staff. An
unusual feature of Howe's proposal is the numbering of the
staff lines and spaces as shown in Example 4-116. The system
was designed to correlate with the author's invention of the
so-called "6-3-3 keyboard" on which six white keys alternate
with three black and three red keys, which are raised like the
black keys on the standard keyboard.

Example 4-116.

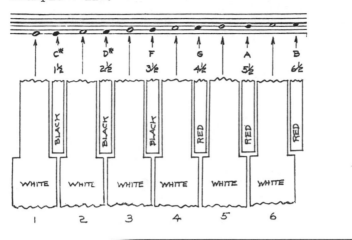

1966. Luciano Berio, <u>Rounds for Harpsichord</u>. Vienna: Universal
    Edition A.G.
Staff: 5-line; the usual two staves for the keyboard instru-
    ment.
Clef signs: None; treble and bass are implied.
Pitch:

    C   C# D D# E   F F# G G# A A# B   C
Duration: The note lengths are proportionately notated, in-
    dicated by extended beams.
Example 4-117.

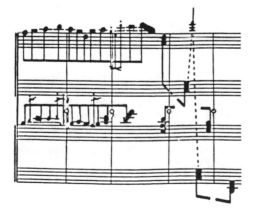

Berio's device of using square noteheads for sharped pitches
is more sensible than the x-shaped notes favored by a number
of other notators. He does not use flats in this harpsichord
piece, so we cannot know how he would have solved this notational problem. Another musician who used square noteheads for
the black-key pitches was Herman Nieland, a music editor living
in Amsterdam, who published an arrangement of the opus 39
Waltzes of Johannes Brahms incorporating this device.

1967. Helen Gregg Glenn, Musical Notation. U.S. Patent 3,331,
271.
Staff: 1-line; additional lines may be added, below or above,
as needed.
Register symbols: The pitch letter of whichever note is on
the staff line (shown here as C) is set before the line.

C_3	C_2	C_1	C_0	C^1	C^2	C^3
C_1	C	c	c^1	c^2	c^3	c^4

Pitch:

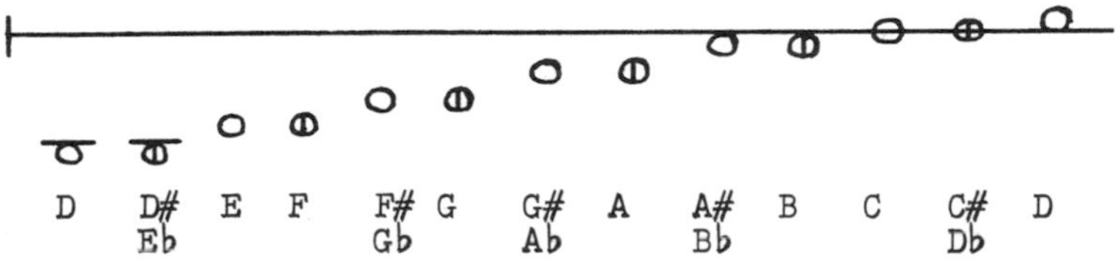

D	D♯	E	F	F♯	G	G♯	A	A♯	B	C	C♯	D
	E♭			G♭		A♭		B♭			D♭	

Duration: Not discussed by the author.
This proposal was designed to apply either to conventional
seven-white-key, five-black-key piano keyboards, or to a suggested six-white-key, six-black-key layout -- a variant of the
chromatic keyboards invented by Rohleder (see page 143) and
other later musicians.

With no false modesty, Glenn promised her readers that
"[This] novel notation system is of substantially universal
utilization and is simple and efficient in both the writing
and reading of music." The words and the conviction behind
them are by now thrice familiar. But one is immediately aware
of a serious lacuna in her proposal: No mention whatsoever is
made of the crucial element of duration, including rests and
meter. As all twelve notes of the chromatic scale are open in
form, the traditional orthochronic method of delineating note
values cannot be applied, making the system unusable as presented.

1967. Benke Lajos, "Javaslat a tizenkétfokú hangrendszer új
írásmodjára" (Recommendation for a New Way of Notating the
Twelve-Tone System), Magyar zene VIII, 4, pp. 401-407.
Staff: 5-line.
Clef signs: Conventional G- and F-clefs.

Pitch:

C	C# Db	D	D# Eb	E	F	F# Gb	G	G# Ab	A	A# Bb	B	C
do	vu	re	po	mi	fa	ne	so	cu	la	be	ti	do

Duration: Conventionally expressed, except for the whole-note, as shown above.

Rests: Standard forms, except for the quarter-note sign: ⅄ .

Example 4-118.

For Lajos, the "twelve-tone system" meant the tonal chromatic scale and not the compositional system promulgated by Schoenberg and his disciples. Of the three different proposals advanced in his <u>Magyar zene</u> article (the second and third are discussed in Chapter 6, page 366), the first is the closest to our traditional notation. Here Lajos' solution for avoiding all accidental signs by positioning note stems to the left for the natural pitches and to the right for chromatic alterations, is both clever and pragmatic.

1972. Donald P. Barra, <u>Analog System of Music Notation</u>. U.S. Patent 3,698,277.

Staff: 5-line; two staves are used for a keyboard system, a common ledger line between them (for middle C, as on the theoretical "Great Staff").

Clef signs: Standard G- and F-clefs.

Pitch: Represented by variously shaded bands whose width equals one staff degree and whose length signifies duration. The bands for articulated notes are slightly separated; those for slurred notes are joined together.

Duration: As explained by the author, "Duration is represented by the proportional length of the tone band. . . . Fractions of a whole-note are represented by lengths directly proportioned thereto, not in incremental terms by symbols."

Rests: Shown by blank space between the tone bands.

Meter: A figure indicating the number of beats per measure is
centered between the two staves.

 2 , 3 = simple time | ⬡ , ⬡ = compound time

Dynamics: In the words of the proposer, "Dynamics are represented analogously by the proportional intensity of the tonal band. These are colored, hence changes in the intensity
will not be in gradation of gray from white to black but in
changes in color intensity or temperature, from a light to
dark hue. Thus a light tone band indicates a soft sound, and
a dark tone band a loud sound, intermediate values being
represented by gradations in color intensity."
Example 4-119.

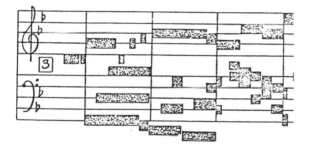

According to Barra, "It is the main object of this invention
to provide a novel system of musical notation, which is based
on analog representations for the characteristics of sound."
Even for 1972 the system could hardly be termed "novel," since
Barra's tonal bands are but a slightly modified version of current time-notation techniques. His system runs into considerable difficulties for both notator and performer in deciphering tonal intensity; the subtle shadings of the tonal bands
required to show minute gradations of volume are neither easy
to draw nor quickly perceived.

1973. Ralph G. Cromleigh, <u>Musical Notation and Actuator Sys-
tem</u>. U.S. Patent 3,741,066.
Staff: 3-line; two staves are combined as a piano system,
spaced slightly less than one line apart.

Register symbols:

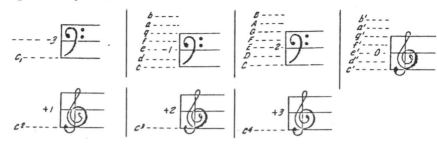

Pitch:

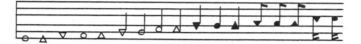

G G# Db D D# Eb E   F F# Gb G G# Ab A A# Bb B

Key signatures: The requisite pitch symbols are placed on the appropriate lines or spaces; in addition, a "tuning mark," or notehead representing the tonic pitch, is set on the staff before the clef sign.

 = 2 sharps    = 2 flats, for example.

Example 4-120. Robert Schumann, from _Traumerei_.

This proposal is geared to Cromleigh's invention of a modified keyboard, called the "Correlated Keyboard," on which the keys are marked in various ways to correspond to the staff degrees. Designed solely for teaching elementary piano, the system is too limited to work effectively for music of any complexity, in spite of its efficient symbology for sharps and flats.

1973. Jean-Etienne Marie, "Sur quelques problèmes de notation" (Concerning certain problems of notation), _Musique en jeu_ 13, pp. 36-48.
Staff: 3-line.

Clef signs:
  Treble register | Bass register
  low   high | low   high

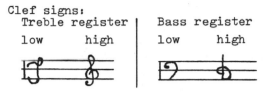

Pitch:

  C   C#   D   D#   E   F   F#   G   G#   A   A#   B
       Db   Eb   Gb   Ab   Bb

Example 4-121.

Essentially, Marie's proposal is the same as those of Obouhov,
Toch, and a few other notation reformers, here transferred to
a three-line staff. The sole novel feature is the author's
designation of two levels for the treble and bass registers,
low and high. The exact boundaries, however, are not specified;
presumably they change when too many ledger lines are required
for either staff.

1974. Richard Bunger, "A Musiglyph Primer," <u>Numus-West</u> 5,
  pp. 16-32.
Staff: 5-line.
Register symbols:

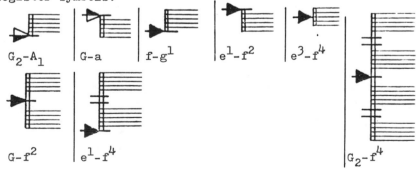

G_2-A_1 $G-a$ $f-g^1$ e^1-f^2 e^3-f^4

$G-f^2$ e^1-f^4 G_2-f^4

Pitch: Sharped pitches are notated enharmonically as flats.

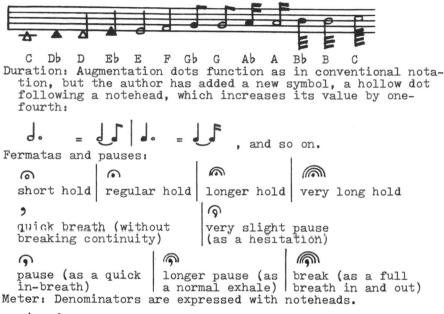

C Db D Eb E F Gb G Ab A Bb B C

Duration: Augmentation dots function as in conventional notation, but the author has added a new symbol, a hollow dot following a notehead, which increases its value by one-fourth:

 , and so on.

Fermatas and pauses:

 short hold |  regular hold |  longer hold |  very long hold

 quick breath (without breaking continuity) |  very slight pause (as a hesitation)

 pause (as a quick in-breath) |  longer pause (as a normal exhale) |  break (as a full breath in and out)

Meter: Denominators are expressed with noteheads.

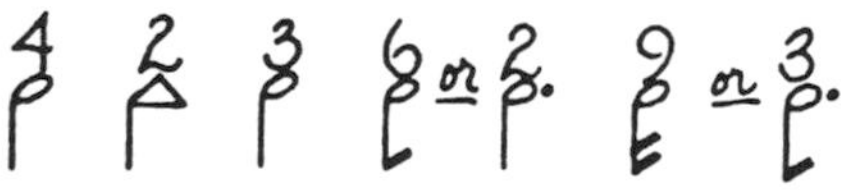

Dynamics: Four modified levels of intensity are added to the standard scale of dynamics:

ppp mpppp pp mpp p mp mf mff ff mfff fff

Example 4-122. Arnold Schoenberg, "Valse de Chopin," from Pierrot Lunaire (© 1914, Universal Edition A.G.).

"Musiglyph is a comprehensive notational system and theory that incorporates theories of communication and language, principles of graphic design, and the historical basis of Western European musical notation. Musiglyph reconciles standard notation with recent advances such as musical graphics, degrees of indeterminacy, action notation, and new instrumental techniques." So wrote the author concerning the purpose and scope of his reform.

In addition to the modifications of the notational elements just cited, Bunger suggested new symbology for approximate and indeterminate pitch, approximate rhythm and duration, randomly variable dynamics, complex articulative effects, and individualized instrumental devices. All of these schemata are too detailed and extensive for inclusion and discussion here, and should be consulted in the author's published article.

Bunger has devised an extremely pragmatic system -- unusual for its time inasmuch as the avant-garde is not noted for its concern with practicality. Whether one agrees with this or that individual suggestion is beside the point; Musiglyph warrants close study and serious consideration by today's composers and performers.

1974. William Tapley, [An improved system of musical notation].
Forestport, New York: the author.
Staff: 4-line (2-2).
Clef signs: Treble and bass, positioned as shown below.
Pitch:

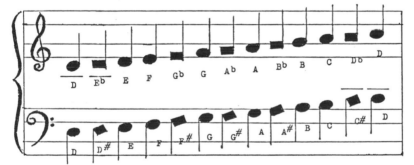

1975. _____, "Notation Reform: Proposal for a New System,"
Contemporary Keyboard 1/2, pp. 14-15.
Staff: 4-line, as before.
Clef signs: Same as before.
Pitch:

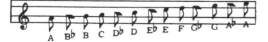

Doubly-altered pitches are notated:

Duration: Traditionally expressed in both proposals.
Example 4-123. Franz Schubert, <u>Sonata in C Minor</u>, op. posth.

An art teacher, draftsman, and freelance artist, Tapley also
devised this proposal for a new notational system. He lists
the following advantages "which make it considerably simpler
and more accurate than our conventional system: 1) One chromatic 'key' replaces the present fifteen separate sharp and
flat signatures as well as all accidentals. 2) Each octave
shows a repetitive staff pattern, and both clefs are analogous.
3) Contrasting note formations and unequal staff degrees provide greater clarity and distinction for the entire scale. 4)
Visual presentation of tone relationships no longer lacks uniformity or precision."

Tapley's system may be all that he claims, yet it is not
so superior to traditional notation that it offers an acceptable alternative. The slanted oblong noteheads for the altered
pitches are particularly troublesome to draw, a minus factor
in any unorthodox notational system.

1976. Georg Pum, <u>Dreilinien-Notensystem</u> (Three-line notation
    system). Modling, Germany: the author.
Staff: 3-line; an added line below the staff extends the range.
Register symbols:

Duration:

, and so on.

Example 4-124.

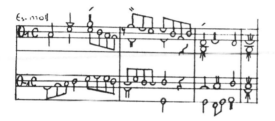

Pum's rationale for his proposal is based on the figure 12 and its prime factors, which a five-line staff and the five black and seven white keys of the piano keyboard cannot justify. "From the mathematical point of view," he writes, "the twelve tones must be treated according to the numerical system. The number 12 has the prime factors 2x2x3. The number 5 is not a prime factor of 12. For that reason, the five lines used for notation do not create a proper sequence and order. Five is a prime factor of 10 and belongs to that system. This is also true of the 5 black keys of the piano. One can certainly use traditional instruments for my new way of notation; however, concerning notes and instruments, one should operate as far as possible with numbers through which the number 12 can be divided, namely 2, 3, 4, and 6."

Its mathematical justification notwithstanding, Pum's is an eccentric proposal, more decorative than serviceable, and one not likely to gain many adherents.

1980. Nachum Schoffman, "A Shorthand for Atonal Music," The Music Review 41, 4, pp. 297-301.
Staff: 5-line.
Clef signs: Standard G- and F-clefs.

Pitch:

C   C# D   D# E F   F# G   G# A A# B   C
    Db   Eb   Gb   Ab   Bb

As Schoffman's proposal title indicates, his suggested notation
is meant solely for atonal or twelve-tone music. In spite of
its being called a shorthand method, its only timesaving feature lies in dispensing with accidental signs. Since all other
elements of traditional notation are retained, using this method does not save the copyist an appreciable amount of labor or
time.

NOTEHEAD DESIGNS FOR RHYTHM AND DURATION

It is curious indeed that the purpose of most notehead reforms
has been to distinguish pitch levels rather than to define
rhythmic values. Yet our present mensural notation is notably,
if not notoriously, inadequate in expressing complex and irregular rhythmic schemes. Why were theorists and composers not
motivated to eradicate this notational ineptitude, long before they addressed the question of inherited pitch symbology?
Given the intense experimentation with new staves, clef signs,
and pitch factors, it is hard to believe that from 1657 --
when Joannes Van der Elst suggested radical changes in rhythmic note forms -- until Henry Cowell's 1917 exploration of new
rhythmic notation (see page 277), few significant systems that
dealt with this vital aspect of notation were proposed. Furthermore, despite the undeniable virtues of Cowell's proposal as
well as Bruno Bartolozzi's subsequent schema (page 279), no
single reform of durational notation has been universally
adopted by composers.
    The one durational innovation now embraced by musicians
the world over is non-mensural, which does not depend on notehead color, size, or form to make its point. Modern proportional notation, in which space is equivalent to time, is firmly
embedded in the writing technique of composers of every na-
tionality and stylistic persuasion. They have thus eradicated
the inadequate manner of designating unconventional note values by ignoring notehead distinction altogether.

1657. Joannes Van der Elst, <u>Notae Augustinianae, sive musices</u>
    <u>figurae seu notae novae concinendis modulis faciliores tabu-</u>
    <u>latoris organicis exhibendis aptiores</u> (Augustinian note-sym-
    bols, whether old or new notations, made easier for group
    singing and better adapted to clear instrumental tablatures).
    Ghent:
Staff: 5-line.

Clef signs:

and

Pitch:

C C#   Db D D# Eb E F F# Gb G G# Ab A A# Bb B C

Duration:

Old note names:	Longa	Brevis	Semibrevis	Minima
Old note symbols:				
New note names:	Maxima	Longa	Brevis	Semibrevis
Elst's note symbols (printed):				
The same (written):				
Modern note symbols:				

Old note names:	Semiminima	Fusa	Semifusa	
Old note symbols:				
New note names:	Minima	Semiminima	Fusa	Semifusa
Elst's note symbols (printed):				
The same (written):				
Modern note symbols:				

Example 4- 125.

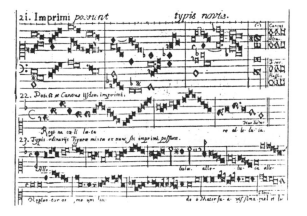

A noted Flemish theorist, Van der Elst was a brother in the
Ghent monastary of Augustinian monks. Because of his association with the order he named his notational proposal in their
honor. Contending that stems, flags, and beams on notes were
confusing and often difficult to read, Elst devised a series
of new note symbols for the common durational values found in
the plainchants of the church. He was not, however, successful
in establishing his reform as a permanent factor in the notational practice of his century, perhaps because it was one of
the very first attempts to alter radically the noteheads then
in common usage.

1684. Joannes Balthasar Friderici, *Cryptographie, oder Geheime
schrift- mund- und würkliche Correspondentz, welche lehr-
mässig vorstellet eine hochschätzbare Kunst verborgene
Schriften zu machen und auffzulösen* (Cryptology, indicating
secret messages to solve hidden meanings in a highly es-
teemed art). Hamburg: Georg Rebenlein.
Staff: None.
Clef signs: None.
Pitch:

◇ ————————————————————→

ut   re   mi   fa   sol   la   si   ut
Duration: The capital letters A to Z, but omitting J and V,
designate 24 rhythmic patterns; a few examples are given
below to illustrate the system.

A = ◇ ◆ ◇   B = ◇ ◇ ♀   C = ◇ ◇ ♦

K = ♀ ◇ ◇   L = ♀ ◇ ♀   M = ♀ ◇ ♀

This musician's suggested system of rhythmic notation, which
was but one part of his extensive treatise on cryptology in
all its varied aspects, was not offered as a new method per se,
to supplant the standard notation of his period, but only as
one unique permutation of his subject.

1842. Gaspare Romano, *Notazione stenografica musicale* (Shorthand musical notation). Milan: the author.
Staff: 1-line.
Clef signs: None; a three-octave gamut is specified by the
position of the note-symbol below, on, or above the staff
line.
Pitch: The note-symbols incorporate both pitch and duration.

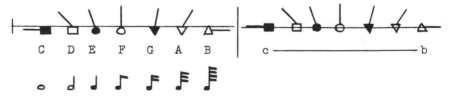

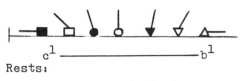

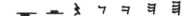

Rests:

Example 4-126.

Although Romano's system is called stenographic, it is included
here because of its reliance on notehead and stem differences
to outline pitch and duration. Romano was obviously indebted
to the reform of Démotz de la Salle (see page 139) for the device of varying stem angles on the noteheads. Dissatisfied
with the limitations of the exclusively diatonic format of his
proposal, Romano later expanded his symbology to include all
twelve pitches of the chromatic scale.

1898. Ludwig Groll, Neuen Noten. Ein Fünfminutensystem (New
   notation: a five-minute system). Berlin: Commissious-verlag:
   M. Gottfurcht.
Staff: 3-line; the central line is printed either red or green.
Register symbols:

3 Minus-Septave	2 Minus-Septave	1 Minus-Septave
C_1-B_1	C-B	c-b

Null-Septave	1 Plus-Septave	2 Plus-Septave	3 Plus-Septave
c^1-b^1	c^2-b^2	c^3-b^3	c^4-b^4

Pitch:

C   D   E   F   G   A   B

Duration:

Example 4-127.

Groll termed each octave of seven diatonic pitches a septave.
Sharps, flats, and naturals are used as required. The elaborate
system of stem design to designate each of the seven septaves
might be compared with the somewhat similar procedures of Sauveur (page 137) and Aulnaye (page 141). As long as registers
do not change too frequently or rapidly, Groll's method of
register identification works reasonably well.

1903. Laura H. Beswick, <u>Musical Notation</u>. U.S. Patent 733,351.
Staff: 5-line.
Clef signs: Normal G-clef only.
Pitch: Indicated traditionally.
Duration: In addition to the conventional subdivision of the
    whole-note into halves, quarters, eighths, and so on, the
    author has provided a system based on the tripartite divi-
    sion of the whole-note, indicated as follows:
    3rd-note |6th-note |12th-note |24th-note |48th-note

Rests:

or

Antedating Henry Cowell's experiments with unorthodox rhythmic
values by fourteen years (see page 277), this proposal has the
advantage of being able to meld nonstandard note lengths with
conventional durations. Triplets, for instance, may be divided
up within the measure so that each third is separated by an
orthodox note-value, a rhythmic construct that would be impossible to delineate clearly in conventional notation.

Example 4-128.

1915. Anne Marie Eugène d'Harcourt, Abréviation rationelle de la notation musicale actuelle (Rational condensation of standard musical notation). Paris: F. Durdilly & C. Hayet.
Staff: 5-line.
Clef signs: Standard G- and F-clefs.
Pitch: Indicated conventionally.
Key signatures: Expressed by the number of sharps or flats pertinent to the tonality.

5# = | 6b =   , for example.

Duration: The examples shown indicate typical condensations of standard rhythmic patterns.

Rests:

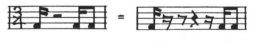

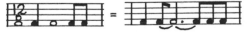

Example 4-129.

This is not a new notational system as such, but a suggestion for reducing certain traditional notational elements -- key signatures, duration, and rest symbols -- to their simplest written forms. The examples shown above are prototypes for similar reductions possible in each category.

The author's reductions accomplish what they were intended to do, but the economy is gained at a price. No self-respecting theorist or composer would so distort metrical and rhythmical values if his notation were based on strict orthochronic principles. Admittedly, the orthodox versions of the rhythmic constructs illustrated are space consuming and rather cluttered in appearance, yet they clearly designate the primary measure beats and correct beat subdivisions, which the compressed versions do not. These rhythmic condensations are really a lazy man's way of notating, which only an untrained student or a sloppy copyist would try to emulate.

1921. Charles Morrell, <u>A System of Shorthand Notation</u>. Chicago: the author.
Staff: 5-line.
Clef signs: Standard G- and F-clefs.
Pitch: Traditionally expressed.
Duration:

о ∩ ⊃ ∪ ⊂ \ ╱

о   ♩   ♩   ♩   ♪   ♪

Example 4-130. George Frederick Handel, <u>Concerto Grosso in D</u>, op. 6, no. 5.

"The music notation now in vogue is very slow to write. It would consequently be a great advantage to music composers and copyists if some brief and legible method could be had to take the place of the old one for manuscript writing -- a music shorthand, so to speak," Morrell contended. "Many a bright passage would then be saved by the composer that is now lost owing to the slow and cumbrous forms of the printed system. The latter, however, need not be changed."

Whether or not Morrell's method is useful to composers and copyists is something each must determine for himself. But it is doubtful, indeed, if "many a bright passage" has ever been lost to the world because the composer found it awkward to write down his inspiration. Most composers practice their own brand of shorthand when making sketches and find writing out their final copy a rewarding task. Well-intentioned as they are, Morrell's suggestions will not, one thinks, greatly assist the composer in putting down on manuscript paper his imperishable tonal visions.

1930. Henry Cowell, "Rhythm," in New Musical Resources. New
    York: Something Else Press (1969).
Staff: 5-line.
Clef signs: Traditional G- and F-clefs.
Pitch: Indicated conventionally.
Duration: In addition to the usual subdivisions of the whole-
    note, Cowell proposed an elaborate system of note shapes to
    delineate numerical increments of unorthodox rhythmic values.

Example 4-131. Henry Cowell, _Fabric_ (© 1950, Breitkopf Publications, Inc.).

It was in 1917, in this experimental piano piece, that Cowell first used his proposed system of unorthodox noteheads to delineate certain rhythms not obtainable with a single symbol in traditional notation. His proposal, however, was not put into final form until 1930, when he published his pioneering book, New Musical Resources.

One outstanding advantage of Cowell's system is that highly unorthodox rhythmic groupings, which are virtually impossible to notate conventionally, become simple to delineate. Taking the same two-measure design cited in a similar reform discussed previously (page 275), we can see that its complications are easily notated using Cowell's suggested plan. Example 4-132.

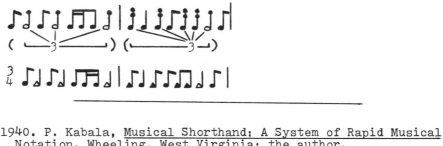

1940. P. Kabala, Musical Shorthand; A System of Rapid Musical Notation. Wheeling, West Virginia; the author.
Staff; 5-line.
Clef signs; Standard G- and F-clefs.
Pitch; Indicated by the symbols shown under Duration below.
Duration;

For simple diatonic scale figures, the author suggests the following shorthand notation;

"In view of the sanctity of present notation," Kabala said,
"I would rather that <u>Musical Shorthand</u> be known of more as an
addition to present notation and not as an improvement over
it." It is, we think, an addition that modern notation can
easily dispense with, each composer or copyist being free to
devise a personal shorthand when it seems preferable to conventional symbols.

1945. Reginald T. Tarrant, <u>Tarrant's Dual-Notation</u>. Hudders-
field, England: the author.
Staff: 5-line.
Clef signs: Standard G- and F-clefs.
Pitch:

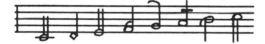

    C   D   E   F   G   A   B   C

Duration: Individual notehead designs distinguish whole- and
half-note values; the former are illustrated above and the
latter are shown below. The shorter values have solid noteheads, together with stems and pertinent flags.

Example 4-133.

This inventor's rhythmic notation is anything but a simplified
or improved method of distinguishing note-values. Overcompli-
cated in design and time-consuming to write carefully, the
note shapes devised by Tarrant are too impractical to be considered seriously.

1961. Bruno Bartolozzi, "Proposal for Changes in Musical Notation," <u>Journal of Music Theory</u> 5, 2, pp. 297-301.
Staff: 5-line.
Clef signs: Conventional G- and F-clefs.
Pitch: Indicated traditionally.
Duration: Like Henry Cowell (page 277), Bartolozzi proposed a
system for delineating irrational rhythmic values, not by
different note shapes, however, but by a combination of
stems and augmentation dots, as shown below.

In his article in the _Journal of Music Theory_, Bartolozzi
stated his basic premise (somewhat loosely translated from the
Italian) as follows: "To obtain those values not attainable
with the present system of notation, one augments the value
necessary for completion of the note by adding, above or below
the note, the tail [flag] or dot corresponding to the deficient value." What Bartolozzi actually does is to add an extra
stem to a traditional note-value, with or without a flag, which
adds its value to that of the given notehead. Augmentation dots
are included in the composite symbol when necessary.

The primary advantage of this procedure is that irrational
rhythmic values can now be expressed with a single symbol rather than several. There are, however, visual complications that
lessen the practicality of Bartolozzi's ideas. It is all too
easy to confuse an 11/8th-note (♪) with a 14/8th-note (♪),
for instance, or a 5/4th-note with a 10/8th-note (which are
not identical in metrical terms). Evidently, these visual
problems helped to dampen the enthusiasm of other composers
for incorporating the suggested reform in their own notation.

1966. Leslie A. Osburn, "Notation Should Be Metric and Repre-
sentational," _Journal of Research in Music Education_ 14, 2,
pp. 67-83.
Staff: 5-line.
Clef signs: Standard G- and F-clefs.
Pitch: Indicated conventionally with unstemmed black noteheads.
Duration: Non-metrical; the noteheads are extended by a thin

line to show length of duration.
Rests: All durations are depicted by the excision of the middle three staff lines.

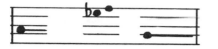

In the words of its author, this proposal " . . . is a new form of notation calling for equidistant spacing of barlines, proportionate placement of notes, and the use of striae to visualize beats." The proposal is not "new" as its procedures parallel current time-notation techniques in which both note and rest values are expressed optically rather than metrically. The excision of staff lines to show rests may present no problems in printing but can be time-consuming for the composer when copying.

NOTES

1. Giorgio Anselmo di Parma, <u>Ars nova musicae</u> (Parma, 1496).
2. Joseph Raymondi, <u>Examen critique des notations musicales proposées depuis deux siècles</u> (Paris: Libraire Encyclopédique de Roret, 1856).
3. Giuseppe Borio, <u>Sulla opportunità di una nuevo segnatura musicale</u> (Rome: A. Ubicini, 1842).
4. Austman surely means one standard staff position rather than a transcription of all music into a single key, such as C major.
5. Franz Diettrich-Kalkhoff, <u>Geschichte der Notenschrift</u> (Jauer in Schlesien: Verlag von Oskar Hellann, 1907).
6. Ibid.
7. Giuseppi Napoleone Carozzi, <u>Carozzi's Synthetic Notation: A Complete Theoretical, Practical and Historical Method</u> (Chicago: the author, 1892).
8. Ernest David and Mathis Lussy, <u>Histoire de la notation musicale depuis ses origines</u> (Paris: Imprimerie nationale, Heugel et fils, 1882). One may take a certain perverse pleasure in the coincidence of the early demise of Orser's system and that of the youthful composer of "The Maiden's Prayer," whose obituary by an unnamed German writer alleged that her "early death saved the musical world from a veritable innundation of intolerable lachrymosity" (quoted by Nicolas Slonimsky in the seventh edition of <u>Baker's Biographical Dictionary of Musicians</u>, page 124. New York: Schirmer Books, 1984).
9. English translation by Dr. Theodore Baker (New York: Dover Publications, 1962).
10. Emile Ergo, <u>L'acte final de la tragi-comédie musicale les "aveugles-réformateurs" de la notation actuelle et les belles (?) perspectives du système à dix-neuf sons dans l'octave</u> (Anvers, Belgium: Libraire néerlandaise, 1911).
11. Pierre Hans' proposal is discussed in <u>De Gregorie le Grand à Stockhausen</u>, Bernard Huys, editor (Brussels: Bibliotheque royale de Belgique, 1966), pp. 149-150.

5.
Numerical Systems

Staff notation is too efficient and too flexible to
be allowed to fossilize, and it is too deeply rooted
and too widely used to be easily swept away in favor
of any new system, however satisfactory this might
eventually prove to be.

-- Thurston Dart, Grove's Dictionary of Music and
Musicians, 1964.

Music notation, one of the most versatile of semiotic mani-
festations, is also an exceedingly hybrid system of communication. To form a unified whole, it combines a wide range of
visual elements -- geometric designs (staff, clef signs,
braces, and brackets); letters (dynamic markings); words (tempo and expressive designations and instrumental nomenclature);
abstract symbols (noteheads, stems, flags, and beams); and
numerals (meter signatures, octave transpositions, and metronome marks). Of these varied elements, numbers most readily
designate a scale of values in pitch, duration, pace, or intensity. Numerical scales can be virtually infinite, whereas
letter scales are necessarily limited in potential resources.
Yet the use of numbers to identify pitch and duration in Western musical notation appeared only in the nineteenth century;
to show degrees of intensity, in the mid-twentieth century.
Numerals, of course, were basic in early tablature notation,
but their only function was to identify strings, keys, or fingering on such instruments as the viols, lute, guitar, or
organ.
    The first truly significant use of numbers as substitutes
for conventional noteheads appeared in Pierre Galin's 1818
Exposition d'une nouvelle méthode pour l'enseignement de la
musique (see page 296). This pioneering treatise signaled the
beginning of a long history of numerical notation, a concept
that is still evident in many current proposals for improved
or simplified notation. But just as no single alphabetical or
stenographic method has ever succeeded in displacing traditional staff notation, so no numerical system has proved superior
to our standard way of notating music. It does not seem likely
that alternative methods -- numerical, alphabetical, or steno-

graphic -- will ever become the universally accepted modus
operandi for composers and theorists working in the mainstream
of twentieth-century musical expression.

1560. Pierre Davantes, <u>Nouvelle et facile méthode pour chanter
chacun couplet des Psaumes sans recours au première</u> (New and
easy method of singing each verse of the Psalms without reference to the first verse). Lyons, France: the author.
Staff: 5-line.
Clef signs:

Pitch: Indicated by nine numbers and two letters, based upon
the arrangement of the three hexachords as follows:

hexachordum molle					
f	g	a	bb	c^1	d^1
ut	re	mi	fa	sol	la

hexachordum durum											
G	A	B	c	d	e	g	a	b♮	c^1	d^1	e^1
ut	re	mi	fa	sol	la	ut	re	mi	fa	sol	la

hexachordum naturale						
c	d	e	f	g	a	c^1 ——————
ut	re	mi	fa	sol	la	ut ————————

| 1 | 2 | 3 | 4 | 5 | 6 | 7 | 8 | 9 | A | B | 1 —————— |

A dot before a numeral or letter indicates a flat; after a
numeral or letter, a natural.
Duration:

1'!, 2'!, A'! | 3', 4', B' | 5   6   A | !7, !8, !B

Rests: All durations indicated by ! .

Example 5-1. Psalm XXVIII, <u>Ad te, Domine, clamave</u>.

Davantes -- referred to by his compatriots as the "Inventeur de la musique chiffrée" -- devised his pioneering notation for teaching solfege to untrained singers. At the time, only the notes of the first verse of psalm tunes were printed. Davantes and his theorist-pedagogue successors considered the substitute numerals and letters easier for the amateur to grasp and so space-saving that they could appear above every word without creating a ponderous volume, too heavy to be portable.

According to the English musicologist-composer, John Stainer, Davantes' numerical system "far from simplifying musical notation, creates an alternative which is tolerably difficult even for an expert musician to master, and would certainly be most confusing and puzzling to any untrained person (1)." Though Davantes' original system was not conspicuously successful, the principle of numerical and alphabetical notation ultimately was firmly established and flourished during later centuries.

1636. Padre Marin Mersenne, "Expliquer une autre méthode pour apprendre à chanter et à composer sans les notes ordinaires par le moyen des seules lettres" (Explanation of a different way of learning to sing and compose without the customary notes, by means of characters alone), <u>Harmonie universelle contenant la théorie et la pratique de la musique</u>. Paris:

Pierre Ballard.
Staff: None.
Clef signs:

Superior	Kontratenor	Tenor	Bassus
S = 𝄞	K = 𝄡	T = 𝄡	B = 𝄢

Pitch:

1	2	3	4	5	6	7	8
ut	ré	mi	fa	sol	la	za	ut

A four-octave span is indicated by the following sequence
of numbers:

S	1800	1620	1440	1350	1200	1080	960
	c^2	d^2	e^2	f^2	g^2	a^2	b^2
K	3600	3200	2880	2700	2400	2160	1920
	c^1	d^1	e^1	f^1	g^1	a^1	b^1
T	7200	6480	5760	5400	4800	4320	3840
	c	d	e	f	g	a	b
B	14400	12960	11520	10800	9600	8640	7680
	C	D	E	F	G	A	B

Duration: Implied; the pitch numbers follow the rhythm of the
plainchant, which was known to the singers.
Example 5-2.

S	1800	1920	1800	2160	2400	1620	1800	1920
K	2400	2400	2400	2700	2880	2700	2880	2880
T	2880	3200	3600	3600	3600	1320	4320	4608
B	7200	4800	5760	5400	7200	6480	8640	5760

Ve — xil — la   re — gis   prod — e — unt

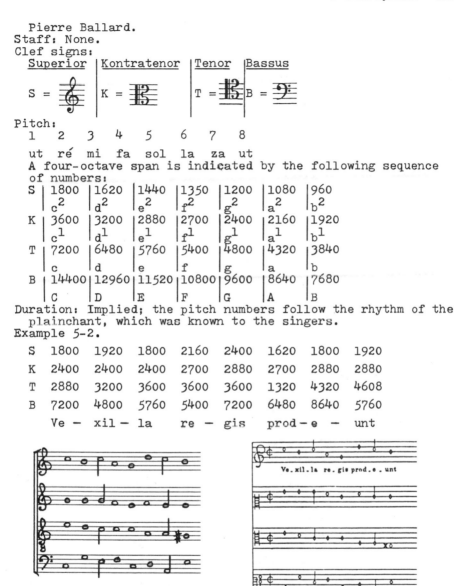

A noted philosopher and musical scientist as well as a theorist, Mersenne was the author of a huge reference work in seven
volumes, the Universal Harmony Containing the Theory and the
Practice of Music (title in English translation). This primary
source of information on seventeenth-century music, especially
on the instruments of the period, must have been known to such
future authors of instrumentation texts as Hector Berlioz,
François Gevaert, and Nikolay Rimsky-Korsakov.

Mersenne's numerical method of notation, a far cry from the one proposed by Davantes, must have intimidated many a singer of plainchant. No less complex is his alphabetical system of designating pitch, which is discussed in Chapter 6. It is ironic that of Mersenne's many theoretical proposals, only his suggestion for counting the intervals of the scale from the tonic note (1) ever became an accepted analytical procedure.

1638. William Braithwait, "Scala musica cantus regularis" (Musical scale for ecclesiastical music), <u>Siren coelestis</u>. London: Johann Norton.
Staff: None.
Register symbols: Different designs of the seven pitch numbers specify low, medium, and high register, as shown below.
Pitch:

1	2	3	4	5	6	7	1
ut	ré	mi	fa	sol	la	si	ut

Duration: The specific design of each numeral determines not only its pitch but also its rhythmic value.

SCALA MVSICA CANTVS REGVLARIS.

SCALA CANTVS TRANSPOSITI..

Rests: The seven different symbols representing seven degrees of pause are shown in the right-hand column above.

Example 5-3.

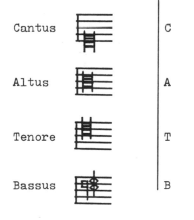

In theory, Braithwait's numerical system of notation is highly ingenious, to say the very least; in practice, it presents formidable obstacles to immediate and easy comprehension, since there are 231 different number forms to memorize. The degree of reading difficulty may be judged by Example 5-3, a sample of Braithwait's unique notation.

1650. Athanasius Kircher, <u>Musurgia universalis sive Ars magna consoni et dissoni in X. libros digesta</u> (Universal music system, the great art of consonance and dissonance, divided into ten volumes). Rome: Extypographia haeredum Francisci Corbelletti.

Staff: 5-line for Kircher's staff notation of the first verse of the plainchant, but no staff for the sequent verses in numerical notation.

Clef signs:

For staff notation:	For numerical notation:
Cantus	C
Altus	A
Tenore	T
Bassus	B

Pitch:

1	2	3	4	5	6	7	8
ut	ré	mi	fa	sol	la	si	ut

Duration: On the staff, the note-values conformed to the common practice of Kircher's time; for the numerical notation, the note durations are implied, based as they were on the

known rhythms of the plainchant.
Example 5-4.

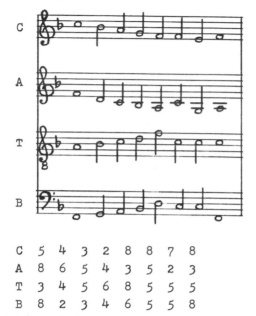

```
C  5  4  3  2  8  8  7  8
A  8  6  5  4  3  5  2  3
T  3  4  5  6  8  5  5  5
B  8  2  3  4  6  5  5  8
```

This musician's numbered notation was not offered as a replacement for the system in common use, but merely as a musical
shorthand. It was only one of many theoretical explorations,
which also included a fascination with hieroglyphic notation,
treated in his Oedipus aegiptiacus (2). Kircher's parallel
interest in musical cryptology appears in the second volume
of his Musurgia universalis under the heading Parsu Cryptologia musurgica sive Ars Steganographica.
    With decided reservations about Kircher's diversification,
the eminent François-Joseph Fétis held that "This learned man
shows in his writings a bizarre conjunction of deep knowledge
in mathematics, physics, natural history, philology, and a
credulous mind, greedy of the marvelous, and devoid of judgment. In his immense works the false and the true are mixed
together pell-mell, but there are plenty of good and interesting things for those who take the trouble to seek them (3)."
Nonetheless, we must admire Kircher's wide-ranging interest
in musical curiosa as well as his early advocation of numerical notation.

1657. Giovanni d'Avella, Rêgole di musica, divisi in cinque
    trattati, con le quali s'insegna il canto fermo, e figurato,
    per vere, e facile rêgole. Il modo fare il contrapunto. Di
    comporre l'uno e l'altro canto. Di cantare alcuni canti dif-
    ficili, e molte cose nuòve e curiose (Rules of music, divid-
    ed into five parts, with the same symbols for the cantus
    firmus and figured bass -- in truth, an easy rule. Also the

manner of writing counterpoint, of composing various songs,
and of singing difficult melodies and many other new and
curious things). Rome: Stampa di Francesco Moneta.
Staff: None.
Clef signs:

Canto	Alto	Tenor	Bass
C	A	T	B
c^1-c^2	g-g^1	c-c^1	G-g

Pitch:

Canto and Tenor	Alto and Bass
1 2 3 4 5 6 7 8	1 2 3 4 5 6 7 8
C D E F G A B C	G A B C D E F G

Canto and Tenor are based on the natural hexachord; Alto
and Bass on the hard hexachord. An altered pitch, whether a
sharp or a flat, is indicated by ✳ set beneath the number.
Duration: All pitch numbers have the same rhythmic value.
Example 5-5.

C   7-6-5-4-5-8-6-5

A   5-4-5-5-5-6-6-5

T   5-3-5-6-7-6-6-7

B   1-2-3-5-1-2-4-1

Avella's wide-ranging treatise on the rules of music differs
from earlier expositions of numerical notation in that the
same scale of numbers, 1 to 8, refers to different pitches
for the canto (soprano) and tenor, and for the alto and bass.
But, as in the method favored by Davantes (page 283), the numbers are related to the hexachordal system of Guido d'Arezzo.

1660. Johannes Andreas Bontempi, <u>Nova quatuor vocibus compon-
    endi methodus, qua musicae artis plane nescius ad composi-
    tionem accedere potest</u> (A new method of notation for four
    voices by which one ignorant of the art of music can clearly
    approach the composer's idea). Dresden: Typis Seiffertinis.
Staff: None.
Clef signs:

Cantus	Altus	Tenore	Bassus
C	A	T	B

Pitch:

1	1#	2b	2	2#	3b	3	4	4#	5b	5	5#	6b	6	7	7#	8b	8	-	15-	22
G	G#	Ab	A	A#	Bb	B	c	c#	db	d	d#	eb	e	f	f#	gb	g	-	g^1-	g^2

Duration: The notehead values are set beneath the bass part.
Example 5-6.

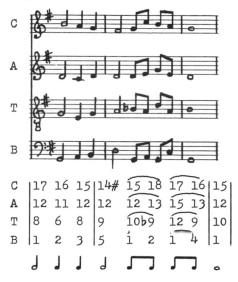

Bontempi's compendium was considered to be one of the preeminent treatises on counterpoint written during the Baroque period. By extending his system of numbers to cover the complete vocal range from G to two-line g, Bontempi made contrapuntal notation much more practical than was possible in the earlier, more limited numerical systems of Mersenne or Avella, for instance. Also, his depiction of rhythm, indebted as it was to tablature notation, made varying durations absolutely clear to the performer of vocal music.

1679. Jean-Jacques Souhaitty, <u>Essai du chant de l'Eglise par</u>
   <u>la nouvelle méthode des nombres</u> (Treatise on the new numerical notation for church music). Paris: Pierre le Petit.
Staff: None.
Register symbols:

1, 2,	3 4	5. 6.	7; 1;	2* 3*
C-B	c-b	c^1-b^1	c^2-b^2	c^3-b^3

Pitch:

1	⫽	2	t3	3	4	ⱬ	5	ⱷ	6	t7	7	1
C	Db	D	Eb	E	F	Gb	G	Ab	A	Bb	B	C

As the numerals 3 and 7, with diagonal slashes, were not available in type, Souhaitty substituted a lowercase t for the slash.
Duration: The letters and syllables are set beneath the pitch numbers.

   f   e   di   d   ci   c   bi   b   a

Rests:

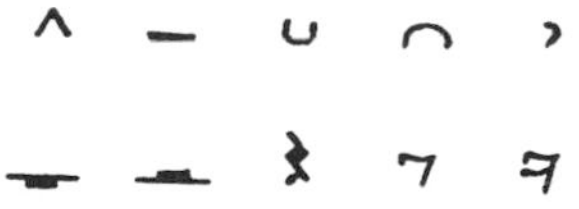

Example 5-7.

t3. 5. ∅. t7. 1; t7. 1; 2; t3; 4;⌒ ∅. 5. 4. 5.⌒ t3.
d c c ci b b ———— b c b b b d

In addition to his Essai du chant de l'Eglise, just summarized, Souhaitty wrote several other treatises that dealt with numerical notation: In their English translations, they are A New Method for Learning Plainchant and Music (4) and New Elements of Song, or an Attempt at a New Discovery Applied to the Art of Singing (5). As a Franciscan monk, Souhaitty designed his numerical system exclusively for the singing of plainchant. His system was not popular with his contemporaries, however, and it was not widely used. Not until Jean-Jacques Rousseau's experiments some eighty years later (see page 292) did notation with numbers flourish once again.

Both Souhaitty and Rousseau were denigrated in Oscar Commetant's Les musiciens, les philosophes et les gaîtes de la musique en chiffres (Musicians, philosophers, and the merriment of numerical notation), published in Paris in 1870. At least the author gave Souhaitty credit for being among the first to propose this method of notation. In his opinion, however, Rousseau had lost many years devising a system "very ingenious and very useless." But for Gioacchino Rossini (who had nothing to do with numerical notation) Commetant reserved the ultimate sarcasm -- that on leaving his estate to the Milan Conservatory of Music, Rossini "forgot to stipulate in his will the establishment of a special chair for the teaching of number notation."

1691. Johann Christoph Stierlein, Trifolium musicae consistens in musica theoretica practica et poetica (A three-octave plan based on theoretical, practical, and poetical music). Stuttgart: the author.

Staff: None.

Register symbols: None.

Pitch:

1 2 3 4 5 6 7 8 — 15 — 21

F G A B c d e f — f^1 — e^2

The same procedure advocated by Stierlein was later utilized by the theorist known as Jacob; his 1769 proposal, entitled Méthode de musique sur un nouveau plan (privately printed in Paris), identified the pitches c to two-line b with the numbers 1 to 21. Both proposals were designed solely for vocal music, hence their restricted ranges.

1742. Jean-Jacques Rousseau, "Projet concernant de nouveaux
signes pour la musique" (A plan concerning new musical symbols), Ecrits sur la musique (Writings on music), Tome XIII,
pp. 7-22. Paris: Lefevre, 1819.
Staff: 1-line for the first of Rousseau's two proposals. Additional lines are used below and above as needed.
Register symbols: A seven-octave gamut is specified by the relation of the pitch numbers to the primary and secondary
staff lines, as shown below.
Pitch:

							1 - 7	1 - 7	1 - 7
1	2	3	4	5	6	7	1 - 7	1 - 7	
C_1						B_1	C - B	c - b	c^1 - b^1

1 - 7	1 - 7	1 - 7
c^2 - b^2	c^3 - b^3	c^4 - b^4

This first proposal was designed for full-scale instrumental
works. Rousseau's second plan was intended for simple vocal
melodies.
Staff: None.
Register symbols:

x	a	b	c	d	e
below C	C-B	c-b	c^1-b^1	c^2-b^2	above b^2

In addition to these specific vocal register-symbols, dots
are placed under or over the numbers to show a change of
register relative to those numbers without such dots. The
absence of a dot indicates that the pitch remains in the
same range as that of the preceding note, not changing register until the next dotted numeral appears. Two dots indicate a two-octave transposition.
Pitch:

1 𝄈 𝄈 2 𝄈 𝄈 3 4 𝄈 𝄈 5 𝄈 𝄈 6 𝄈 𝄈 7
C C# Db D D# Eb E F F# Gb G G# Ab A A# Bb B

Key signatures: For other than the tonality of C, the identifying tonic syllable is set before the meter numeral and the
series of pitch numbers.
Fa 2 = F major, 2/2; Ré 4 = D major, 4/4, for example.
Duration: Each pitch number receives one beat, set off by commas. A period following a number indicates two beats; a tie
over a barline is shown by a slur mark. Horizontal lines
placed over or under groups of pitch numbers function as do
beams in mensural notation.
Rests: Shown by the symbol 0.
Meter: Only the numerator is given, indicating the number of
beats per measure.

Example 5-8. Ludwig van Beethoven, <u>Septet in E-flat</u>, op. 20.

Example 5-9. "Air to sing with a Bass."

As France's most celebrated philosopher-theoretician, Rousseau
applied his intellect to every facet of music, and numerical
notation was one of his most engrossing projects. "Ce projet
tend à rendre la musique plus commode à noter, plus aisée à
apprendre et beaucoup moins diffuse" (This project makes music
more convenient to notate, easier to learn, and much less pro-

lix), he maintained in his <u>Dissertation sur la musique moderne</u>
(6). Rousseau was certainly familiar with the earlier attempts
at numerical notation made by Mersenne and others, and his
system was mainly a search for improvement or simplification
of their innovations.

Rousseau's compatriot Rameau was extremely critical of
Rousseau's notational ideas, and he attacked his project on
more than one occasion. Condemned by Rameau and other theorists as being unoriginal and too greatly indebted to Souhaitty's prior reform (see page 290), Rousseau's several projects
never achieved the success that he so fervently desired. It is
not hard to see why. Perfectly adequate for simple vocal or
instrumental melodies, his method is almost useless for complex harmonic and rhythmic expression.

"La notation par chiffres," complained the critic Etienne
Destranges, "est lourde, anti-esthétique, ennuyeuse" (Numerical
notation is awkward, non-aesthetic, and tedious)(7). He concluded his critique (which was specifically on the system of
Eugène Bazin -- see page 57) by declaring that no number system can ever replace traditional notation, any more than our
present alphabet will ever be superseded by another.

1798. Karl Gottlieb Horstig, "Vorschläge zu besseren Einrich-
    tung der Singschulen in Deutschland" (Proposals to better
    regulate the German ecclesiastical singing schools); and
    "Chiffern für Choralbucher" (Number notation for hymnals),
    <u>Allgemeine musikalische Zeitung</u> I, 11, pp. 166-174; IV (12),
    pp. 183-189; 13, pp. 197-201; 1799, I, 14, pp. 214-220.
Staff: 3-line.
Clef signs:

$$G$$

pitches c^2-b^2

pitches c^1-d^2

pitches C-d^1

Pitch:
    1 #1 b2 2 #2 b3 3 4 #4 b5 5 #5 b6 6 #6 b7 7   8   9

    ut   re   mi fa   sol   la   si ut re
    Ut (1) is always the tonic pitch of a major key and the
    mediant (3) of its relative minor.
Duration: Each pitch number represents one beat; for two beats,
    the numbers are farther apart. Two half-beats are shown by
    a horizontal line over the numbers, and two quarter-beats
    by a second line.
Example 5-10.

In our survey of the numerical modes of notation, this system is the first to retain the conventional sharp and flat signs, which were placed before the affected numerals. Horstig utilized some of the elements proposed by Rousseau, but he was more pedagogically motivated than his French counterpart because he hoped that his proposal could be used to reform the teaching of music in the numerous German singing schools. To him, numerical notation seemed the most effective means of achieving this improvement, and his series of articles in the Allgemeine musikalische Zeitung provided a forum for his arguments.

1815. Albrecht Ludwig Richter, Musikalisches Schulgesangbuch (Song book for schools). Berlin: the author?
Staff: None.
Register symbols:

```
 1   2   3   4   5   6   7  |1-7  |1-7  |1-7
 o   o   o   o   o   o   o  |     |     |
 C   D   E   F   G   A   B  |c-b  |c¹-b¹|c²-b²
```

Pitch:

```
 1   2   3   4   5   6   7   1
 C   D   E   F   G   A   B   C
```

Key signatures: Calculated by the number of diatonic intervals from C.
    1 = 3, E major   1 = 5, G major, for example.
Duration:

```
 1      2 2     3 3 3     4 4 4 4
 ♩      ♩       ♩.        o
```

Example 5-11.

It is interesting to compare Richter's ancillary markings over the pitch numbers to denote register (o) with those of Pierre Galin (-) and Carl von Ziwet (.). These marks were necessary when there was no staff to which the pitch numbers could be related, as they were in Horstig's proposal (page 294). From the standpoint of its limited numerical scale and total possible register, Richter's method was effective only when applied to rather simple vocal writing.

1818. Pierre Galin, Exposition d'une nouvelle méthode pour l'enseignement de la musique (Explanation of a new way of teaching music). Paris: the author.
Staff: None.

Register symbols:

$\underline{1}$ $\underline{2}$ $\underline{3}$ $\underline{4}$ $\underline{5}$ $\underline{6}$ $\underline{7}$ | 1 -7 | $\overline{1}$ -$\overline{7}$
c   d   e   f   g   a   b | c^1-b^1 | c^2-b^2

Pitch:

1   2   3   4   5   6   7   1

ut   ré   mi   fa   sol   la   si   ut

Key signatures: Indicated by pitch syllable.
  Fa = 1, La = 1, Sol = 1, for example.

Duration:

1 | 1. | 1.. | 1...

1 beat | 2 beats | 3 beats | 4 beats

Pitch numbers between two commas (,3 5,) are of equal duration. Horizontal lines over or under two or more numbers
serve the same function as do beams in mensural notation.

Rests:

0 | 00 | 000 | 0000

1 beat | 2 beats | 3 beats | 4 beats

Example 5-12. Chorale, <u>Ein' feste Burg ist unser Gott</u>.

Ré = 1: ,$\overline{1}$ | $\overline{1}$ $\overline{1}$, $\underline{56}$ 7 | $\overline{17}$,6 5 $\overline{1}$ | 7 6 5, $\underline{65}$ | $\underline{43}$,2 1, |

Galin was among the first of the nineteenth-century pedagogues
to understand the importance and feasibility of numerical
notation for teaching singing to musical illiterates. He was
so intrigued by its potential that he gave up a successful
career in medicine to devote all his time to developing and
perfecting Rousseau's basic premise. In this, he was supported
by his pupils Emile and Nanine Chevé. Later expanded by the
Chevés, together with Mme. Chevé's brother, Aimé Paris, the
system came to be known as the Galin-Paris-Chevé Method. It
exerted considerable influence on the teaching of voice during
the mid-1800s, and revised editions of the method were published in 1824 and 1831. Naturally, Galin's radical changes
engendered controversy; attacks on and defenses of the method
fill several good-sized volumes. There were seemingly endless
letters to and from Galin in the Paris press, letters violently
castigating his system and eliciting further stubborn justifi-
cations by the inventor.

      According to the historian Fétis (8), Galin was "an honest
man, but a mediocre musician, and was full of illusions as to
the apparent success of his method." For all Fétis's reservations, however, Galin's proposal enjoyed considerably more
success during his lifetime than did comparable systems advanced by a number of his contemporaries. Foremost in its favor was the fact that numerical notation was simple to print
and economical of space, potent factors in the publishing industry.

      It is significant that disciples of Galin's method estab-
lished singing schools in Germany, Holland, Denmark, Switzerland, and even Russia -- an eloquent testimony of its wide

appeal and pragmatism.

1819. Friedrich Dammas, <u>Ziffernchoralbuch zu allen Melodien</u>
<u>des alten und neuen Stralsundischen Gesangbuchs</u> (Number
notation for all melodies in the old and new Stralsund
hymnals). Stralsund, Germany.
Staff: None.
Register symbols: None.
Pitch:
    1 ♪ b2 2 ♪ b3 3 4 ♯ b5 5 ♪ b6 6 ♪ b7 7 1
    C C# Db D D# Eb E F F# Gb G G# Ab A A# Bb B C
Duration:

1̲1̲1̲1̲   2̲2̲2̲   3̲3̲   4   ♩/5   ♩/6

    o   ♩.   ♩   ♪   ♫   ♫

Example 5-13. Chorale, <u>Ein' feste Burg ist unser Gott</u>.

    2 | 2 2 6 7 ♪|2 ♪ 7 6 2 |♪ 7 6   7 6 | 5 4 ♯ 3 2 |

Although the numerical system of Dammas was designed for a
specific hymnal, it could well have been used by congregations
other than those of the city of Stralsund. The notation is
simplicity itself and should have caused no puzzlement among
the untrained choir members of the local churches.

1821. Johann Friedrich Wilhelm Koch, <u>Einstimmigen Choralbuch</u>
<u>in Ziffern für Volksschulen</u> (Unison choral book in number
notation for primary schools). Magdeburg, Germany: W. Hein-
richshofen.
Staff: 1-line.
Register symbols:

		1 - 7
	1 - 7	
1-7		
c-b	c¹-b¹	c²-b²

Pitch:
    1 *1 +2 2 *2 +3 3 4 *4 +5 5 *5 +6 6 *6 +7 7 1
    C C# Db D D# Eb E F F# Gb G G# Ab A A# Bb B C
Key signatures: Indicated by the pitch letter as the tonic (1).
    E1 = E major,   Ab1 = Ab major,   F#1 = F# major
Duration:

    1̲:̲ : 2: 3   4. 5   ♩/6   ♪/7

    o·   o   ♩   ♩.   ♩   ♫   ♫

Rests:

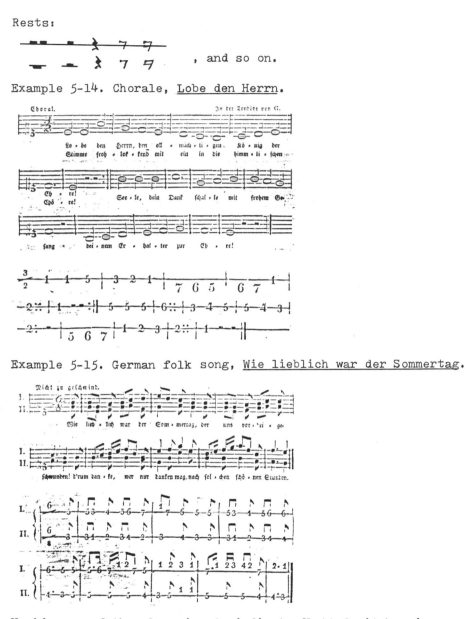

, and so on.

Example 5-14. Chorale, <u>Lobe den Herrn</u>.

Example 5-15. German folk song, <u>Wie lieblich war der Sommertag</u>.

Koch's use of the plus sign to indicate flatted pitches is questionable; a minus sign, or even the reversing of the two signs for sharp and flat (* and +), would have been more appropriate symbology. Other than this, however, the proposal is simple and concise, and it should have been easily comprehended by the primary school pupils for whom the method was devised.

1824. Jens Andreas Bramsen, <u>Lieder für das frühere und reifere</u>
<u>Alter mit Melodien</u> (Songs for both younger and older child-
ren). Copenhagen: the author?
Staff: None.
Register symbols:

$_{**}1$-$_{**}7$ | $_*1$-$_*7$ | 1 - 7 | $_*1$-$_*7$
C-B | c-b | c^1-b^1 | c^2-b^2

Pitch: Only flats are used, not sharps.
 1 $\underline{2}$ 2 $\underline{3}$ 3 4 $\underline{5}$ 5 $\underline{6}$ 6 $\underline{7}$ 7 1

 C Db D Eb E F Gb G Ab A Bb B C

Duration: Measure beats are indicated by a comma; beat subdivisions by an apostrophe. Longer notes are shown by wider
spacing between the numbers.
Example 5-16.

|$\underline{3}$, ,5,$\underline{6}$ |$\underline{7}$,$_*1$,$\underline{7}$'$_*1$,$_*2$'$_*\underline{3}$ |$_*4$,$\underline{6}$,5'4,5 |$\underline{3}$, ,

Compared to the contemporaneous numerical systems just discussed, Bramsen's is cluttered with ancillary markings and is,
consequently, not as simple to read. In addition, it is curious
that this Danish musician restricted his chromatic alterations
to flats only; surely the young singers for whom the notation
was devised must have encountered songs in a sharp key from
time to time. How, then, would Bramsen have solved the problem? Transposition into a flat tonality would seem to be the
only reasonable answer.

1824. Bernhard Christoph Ludwig Natorp, <u>Anleitung zur Unter-</u>
<u>weisung im Singen für Lehrer in Volksschulen</u> (Suggestion
for teaching singing in the primary schools). Essen, Germany: Bädeker.
Staff: 1-line.
Register symbols:

$\overline{1-7}$ | 1 - 7 | 1 - 7
c-b | c^1-b^1 | c^2-b^2

Pitch:
 1 #1 b2 2 #2 b3 3 4 #4 b5 5 #5 b6 6 #6 b7 7 1

 C C# Db D D# Eb E F F# Gb G G# Ab A A# Bb B C

 ut   re   mi   sol   la   si
                fa   ut

Duration:

1: : 2: 3· 4 $_5$· 6 $_7$⌐· $_8$⌐ $_9$⌐F

o· o $\downarrow$· $\downarrow$ $\downarrow$· $\downarrow$ $\intercal$· $\intercal$ $\intercal F$

Tied notes are indicated, for example, as

Rests: Traditional, except for the quarter-rest: ↴ .
Meter:
$$\frac{4}{4} \quad \frac{3}{8} \quad \frac{2}{2}, \text{ for example.}$$

Example 5-17. Plainchant, from the Liber Usualis.

Ky - ri - e__ e - - - - le-i-son

Natorp was the author of several other books and articles on
the teaching of vocal music, most notably his Anleitung der
Singekunst in zwei Kursen (Guide to the art of singing in two
courses), published in 1816. Obviously indebted to Rousseau's
1742 proposal and to Koch's reform of 1821, the method just
cited was successful enough to go through five editions -- and
this in spite of severe criticism by Natorp's fellow theorists
and singing teachers.

1827. M. C. A. Klett, Beiträge zur Volksnote (Contributions to
    "Volksnote"). Stuttgart, Germany.
Staff: 4-line.
Register symbols:

| | II | I |

    lower octave middle octave higher octave
Pitch:
    1   2   3   4   5   6   7   8

    ut   re   mi   fa   sol la   si   ut
Duration: Tactus lines through the middle space set off the
    beats within each measure. A dot between two tactus lines
    indicates a tied note of the same value. Slurs under a group
    of pitch numbers serve the same purpose as beams in mensural
    notation.
Rests: All values are indicated by 0.
Example 5-18.

1830. Carl von Ziwet, <u>System zur Verbesserung der Musik und
zur leichteren Erlernung der selben ohne die jetzt gebräuch-
lichen italienischen Noten</u> (System concerning the improvement of music and its easier learning without using Italian
symbology). Berlin: the author?
Staff: None.
Register symbols:
 1-7 |1-7 |1-7
lower octave |middle octave |higher octave
Pitch:
 1 2 3 4 5 6 7 1
 C D E F G A B C
Duration:

 (1) (2 3 4 or 4 5 or 5 6 or 6

Example 5-19.

This notation, like many others, was based on Rousseau's second numerical system (see page 292). The early decades of the
nineteenth century were obviously a time of intense preoccupation with number codes of notation among both theorist-composers and vocal pedagogues. With such a surfeit of systems,
it is no wonder that no single method of numerical notation
became the undisputed paradigm for all to emulate.

1835. Jacques Claude Adolphe Miné, <u>Méthode d'orgue</u> (Organ
method). Paris: Libraire encyclopédique de Roret.
Staff: None.
Register symbols:
 1 2 3 4 5 6 7 |8-15 |a - q
 C D E F G A B |c-c^1 |d^1-f^3
Pitch:
 1 1̸ 2 2̸ 3 4 4̸ 5 5̸ 6 6̸ 7 8-15
and: a a̸ b c c̸ d d̸ e e̸ f g-q
 C C# D D# E F F# G G# A A# B C-F
    Db   Eb   Gb   Ab   Bb

Duration: Equal values are shown by the close positioning of
the pitch numbers and letters, and long notes by more space.
Tied notes are indicated by a horizontal line between the
symbols.

Example 5-20. "Resignation," from The Southern Harmony.

Suggested alternative notation:

Miné's system of combined numbers and letters was devised to
correspond to the total compass of the organ keyboard (C to
three-line f) at that time. The combination, however, is confusing to read, especially when a melodic line or a harmonic
component veers back and forth between the two symbols. It
would seem that either a system using only numbers (1 to 32),
or letters that correspond to register (C, d, one-line e, two-
line f, and three-line f), would have proved a more practical
method of showing pitch. An alternative version of the example
above (by this writer), using only numbers, was included for
the sake of comparison.

Miné's hybrid system is discussed critically by Wilhelm
Tappert in two issues of the Musikalischen Wochenblatt XV
(1884): No. 1, pages 1-2, and No.2, pages 17-18. Tappert also
comments in his articles on the earlier numerical proposals
by Louis Danel (see page 302), finding much to disagree with
in both notational suggestions.

1839. Thomas Harrison, Music simplified: or A new system of
music, founded on natural principles; designed either for
seperate [sic] use, or as an introduction to the old system,
and intended chiefly for educational and religious purposes;
to which is added A collection of Christian melodies. Spring-
field, Ohio: the author.
Staff: 2-line.

Clef signs:
  <u>Counter</u> (high part) | <u>Double</u> (second Air) | <u>Air</u> (leading part)

  C̄ | D̄ | Ā

  <u>Base</u> [sic] (low part)

  B̄

Pitch:
  1 1s. s.2 2 2s. s.3 3 4 4s. s.5 5   5s. s.6 6 6s.
  do #   ♭ re #   ♭ mi fa #   ♭ sol #   ♭ la #

  s.7 7 8
  ♭   ti do

Duration:

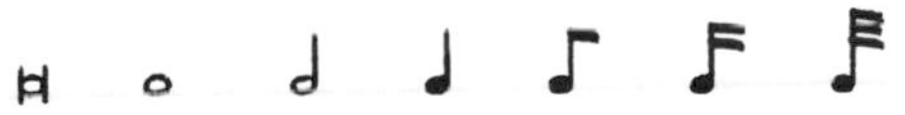

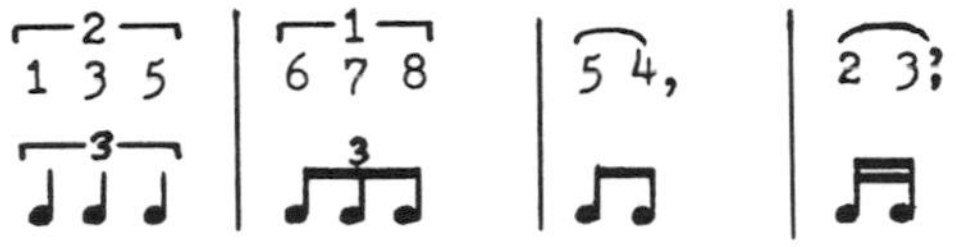

Rests:
  :R   .R   R   R,   R;
                              , and so on.

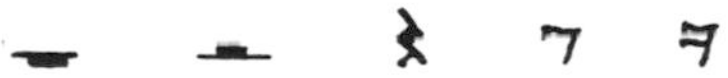

Example 5-21. Hymn, <u>Bedford</u>.

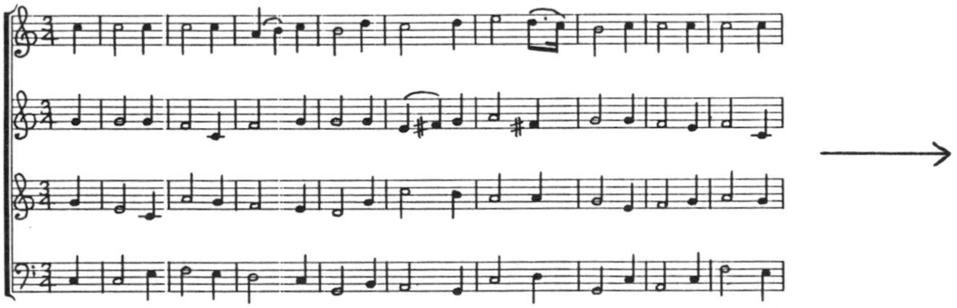

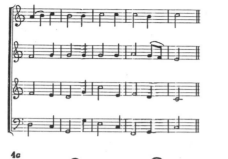

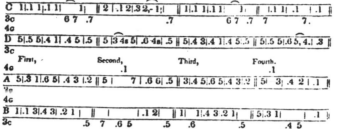

Unique to this numerical notation are the chromatic pitch symbols (s.2, 4s., for instance), as well as the durational markings, including rests. Additionally, it should be pointed out
to the critical reader that the lowest part in Harrison's vocal score is not misspelled; "base" appears in many early
nineteenth-century anthems to identify the lowest voice line.
Also according to one practice of the time, the hymn tune is
given to the tenor rather than to the soprano.

1841. Joseph Waldmann, <u>Gesanglehre für Volksschulen</u> (Singing
   method for primary schools). Karlsruhe, Germany: Herder.
Staff: 1-line.
Register symbols:

```
                    |1-7           |1-7
1-7                 |1-7           |1-7
 lower octave |middle octave |higher octave
```

Pitch:
  1   #1 b2 2   #2 b3 3   #3 b4 4   #4 b5 5   #5 b6 6   #6 b7 7

  ut   re   mi   fa   sol   la   si
When a modulation occurs, the new scale interval number is
  enclosed in parentheses: 3 (4), meaning mi = fa.
Key signatures: The tonic number is calculated from C, as
  shown in Example 5-22.
Duration:

$$\overset{o}{1} \quad \overset{\smile}{2}. \quad \overset{\smile}{3} \quad 4. \quad 5 \quad \overline{6} \quad \overline{\overline{7}}$$

Rests: Indicated conventionally, with the exception of the
   quarter-rest: ⌒ .
Meter: The numerator only is given, centered on the staff line.
Example 5-22.

As were most of the numerical systems of notation proposed
during the nineteenth century, Waldmann's was designed exclusively for vocal music. It formed the basis of Heinrich Joseph
Vincent's 1862 proposal, which was published in Leipzig as
Neues musikalisches System. Ein kurzgefasstes Lehrbuch fur
Musiker und Dilettanten (A new musical system: a condensed
textbook for professionals and amateurs), not discussed in
this chapter as it largely duplicates Waldmann's method. Like
Karl Horstig before him (see page 294), Waldmann retained the
conventional sharp and flat signs to designate chromatic pitch
alterations. But unlike the later method known as Klavierspiel
Helvetia (page 321), Waldmann's depiction of rhythm and duration is clear and relatively unambiguous.

1842. J. E. Miquel, Arithmographie musicale; méthode de musique simplifiée par l'emploi des chiffres, composée et dé-
   diée aux artistes (Musical numerology; a simplified way of
   notating with numbers, devised for and dedicated to professionals). Paris: A. Catelin et cie.
Staff: 1-line.
Register symbols:

C_1-B_1	C-B	c-b	c^1-b^1	c^2-b^2	c^3-b^3	c^4-b^4

Pitch:
   1 #1 b2 2 #2 b3 3 4 #4 b5 5 #5 b6 6 #6 b7 7 1
   ut   re   mi fa   sol   la   si ut
Duration:
   1 1   2·   3   4°   5   6   7

   o   ♩·   ♩   ♪·   ♪   ♪   ♪

Rests: All values are shown as 0.
Meter:

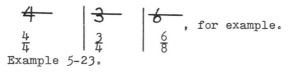

, for example.

Example 5-23.

Miquel's methodology owes its overall format to Rousseau, Horstig, and Natorp, among other inventors of systems of number
notation. His refinements, neither extensive nor substantive
in nature, can be considered just as serviceable as those of
his predecessors. As is evident, this method of notation works
best with simple melodic lines whose rhythmic structure is
equally uncomplicated.

1842. Jules Charles Teule, <u>Exposition du système de l'écriture
   musicale chiffrée suivie d'une note sur le comparateur des
   tons</u> (Explanation of the system of number notation and an
   observation on the comparison of tones). Paris: the author?
Staff: 1-line.
Register symbols:

3 |4 |5 |6
C-c |c-c^1 |c^1-c^2 |c^2-c^3

Pitch:

1 2 3 4 5 6 7 8

C D E F G A B C

The register numerals and the pitch numbers are combined
to form Teule's notation: 31, 42, 53, 64, for example.
Duration: Measure beats are shown by short tactus lines set
   above the single staff line. Two or more beats are indicated
   as ▬▬ following a pair of numbers; half-beats are designated by the number 1 above the staff line, and a beat and
   a half by the number 3.
Example 5-24.

Two different proposals were put forward by Teule in his 1842
publication; this numerical system was the second. (Refer to
page 378 for his stenographic method.) The primary handicap in
reading Teule's number system is having to mentally separate
the register and pitch numbers, which are always written as
pairs. It would seem to be more logical to set the two figures
on different levels -- the pitch above and the register below,
for instance.

1844. Emile Joseph-Maurice Chevé, Nanine Paris (Mme. Chevé),
   and Aimé Paris, Méthode élémentaire de la musique vocale
   (Elementary vocal method). Paris: the authors.
Staff: None.
Register symbols:

1-7	1-7	1-7
lower octave	middle octave	higher octave

Pitch:

   1 1♮♭ 2 2♭♮ 3 4 4♯♭♮ 5 ♭♮ 6 ♭♮♮ 7 1

   ut # b ré # b mi fa # b sol # b la # b si ut

To distinguish upward from downward melodic leaps, Chevé
placed a small arrow sign after the initial number, as shown
in Example 5-25.
Duration:

1	2.	3..	4...	, and so on.
1 beat	2 beats	3 beats	4 beats	

Rests:

0	00	000	0000	, and so on.
1 beat	2 beats	3 beats	4 beats	

Example 5-25.

As Pierre Galin's most noted pupil, Chevé naturally continued
to modify and expand his mentor's system of numerical vocal
notation. Although the Galin-Paris-Chevé method was very popular with the amateur musicians and vocal teachers of France,
it drew the scorn of some professionals, particularly the pro-
fessors at the Paris Conservatory where Chevé taught. To quote
Nicolas Slonimsky: "Acrimonious polemics raged for years and
numerous pamphlets were issued by adherents and foes of the
Chevé method (9)."
    An interesting by-product of the controversy generated by
Chevé's system was the support he received from the operatic
composer, Jacques Halévy, teacher of Gounod and Bizet. Halévy
not only used Chevé's method of indicating chromatic pitches
with diagonal slashes through the numbers, but also expanded
the device by using double slashes to indicate doubly altered

notes, such as F𝄪 and B♭♭♭.

In England, the Galin-Paris-Chevé method was slightly modified by a Miss Busby in her quaintly titled <u>Exposition of a
new method of writing music, scientifically and stenographic
railway for composition, the pianoforte and organ</u> (London,
1850). This music educator kept the diagonal slashes through
the pitch numbers for sharps but preferred horizontal slashes
for flats; otherwise, her method was little different from
that of Chevé.

The French pedagogue Jean Baptiste Clavière also utilized
Chevé's ideas in his <u>Méthode élémentaire, ou principes méthod-
iques de la musique en chiffres arabes, à l'usage du chant
populaire</u> (Elementary method of music, its principles expressed
with Arabic numerals for the use of popular song), a treatise
published in Paris in 1848. Thus it can be seen that Chevé
exerted an immediate and widespread influence among other notational reformers in spite of the negative assessment of his
method in some quarters.

1856. Albert Gereon Stein, <u>Kölnisches Gesang- und Andachts-
buch</u> (Hymnal and prayerbook for Cologne). Cologne.
Staff: None.
Register symbols:

   1-7 |1-7, 1-7 |1̄-7̄
   lower octave|middle octaves|higher octave
The numbers for the lowest two octaves are printed in large
type; those for the highest two octaves, in small type.
Pitch:
1 2 3 4 5 6 7 1

C D E F G A B C
Duration:
1... 2.. 3. 4

o   d.   d   d
Example 5-26.

|5... 6.7. |1̄... 5... |6.5.4. 3 4 |5... 2...|3.2.1.5.|
1̄... 1̄...‖

Stein's hymnbook notation is clear and concise, and it should
have caused no problems for the Cologne congregations for whom
the system was devised.

1877. H. Hohmann, <u>Chromatische Notenschrift nach einem Vor-
schläge</u> (A proposed chromatic notation). Munich: the author.
Staff: None.

Register symbols:

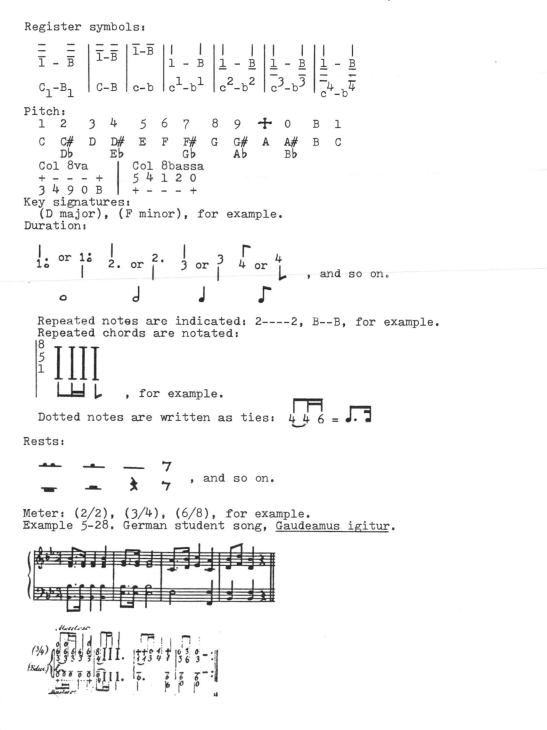

Pitch:

1	2	3	4	5	6	7	8	9	✝	0	B	1
C	C#	D	D#	E	F	F#	G	G#	A	A#	B	C
	Db		Eb			Gb		Ab		Bb		

Col 8va | Col 8bassa
+ - - - + | 5 4 1 2 0
3 4 9 0 B | + - - - +

Key signatures:
(D major), (F minor), for example.

Duration:

1. or 1:   2. or 2.   3 or 3   4 or 4   , and so on.

Repeated notes are indicated: 2----2, B--B, for example.
Repeated chords are notated:

8
5
1

, for example.

Dotted notes are written as ties: 4 4 6 =

Rests:

7
7   , and so on.

Meter: (2/2), (3/4), (6/8), for example.
Example 5-28. German student song, Gaudeamus igitur.

This rather elaborate system is the first of the numerical
proposals surveyed to mix letters, abstract symbols, and Arabic numbers in outlining the chromatic scale. There seems to
be no valid reason for this symbological mixture, other than
novelty for novelty's sake. It is interesting to note, however,
that Hohmann's method for repeated chord structures is one
that has reappeared in several mid-twentieth century avant-
garde scores -- a simple and eminently practical solution of
this particular problem of notation.

1877. Leo Kuncze, B⊥D: Tonziffer-Notation fur die Neuklavia-
tur (Numerical notation for the new keyboard). Martinsburg,
Hungary: Raab - Sziget.
Staff: 2-line; the lines are widely spaced apart.
Register symbols:

Pitch:
1 2   3   4   5   6   7   8   9   0   Ⴑ   Ⴈ   1

C C# D D# E F F# G G# A A# B C

Duration: Time values other than the meter denominator are indicated in small notes just above the upper, "time," line,
somewhat in the manner of lute tablature.
Rests: Represented by blank space.
Meter: The denominator, depicted as a notehead, follows the
numerator, as shown below.
Example 5-27. Franz Schubert, Impromptu in A-flat, op. 142, no. 2.

The influence of tablature notation is quite in evidence here
-- a surprising retrogression for the final quarter of the
nineteenth century. Moreover, the reversed numerals for the
last two pitches of the chromatic scale are difficult both to
read and to write. Why not 10, 11, and 12 for the final three
notes, as would be the logical sequence? An academic question,
to be sure, as there is no possibility that Kuncze's system
would ever be adopted by twentieth-century notators.

1884. Pater Pagi, <u>Number notation: or, singing made easy. A
simple system for the use of vocalists, with a scheme of
abbreviated long-hand writing, designed to save space when
writing words under the number-notes</u>. London: W. S. Sonnen-
schein.
Staff: None.
Register symbols:

$\underline{1}$-$\underline{7}$	1-7	$\overline{1}$-$\overline{7}$
lower octave	middle octave	higher octave

Pitch:

		#	b		#	b			#	b			#	b			#	b			
1	1	2	2	2	3	3	4	4	5	5	5	6	6	6	7	7	8
C	C#	Db	D	D#	Eb	E	F	F#	Gb	G	G#	Ab	A	A#	Bb	B	C

Duration:

$\overset{\bullet\bullet}{1}$	$\overset{\bullet}{2}$	$\overline{3}$	$\overset{x}{4}$	$\overset{x-}{5}$	$\overset{xx}{6}$
¼-beat	½-beat	1 beat	2 beats	3 beats	4 beats

Rests:

$1\overset{\bullet\bullet}{\_}$	$2\overset{\bullet}{\_}$	3-	4x	5x-	6xx
¼-beat	½-beat	1 beat	2 beats	3 beats	4 beats

Example 5-29.

One confusing aspect of Pagi's system is the use of the dash
over a pitch numeral to mean both register and duration. This
practice violates a cardinal principle of notation, namely,
that a single symbol should never represent two meanings. In
general, it must be added that this inventor's durational
signs are clumsy and not notably logical in either form or
sequence.
     This proposer's name, incidentally, is a pseudonym, but
his true name has not been revealed.

1890. Charles Clements-Kropp, <u>Musical Notation</u>. U.S. Patent
429,841.
Staff: 2-line; the lower line is double.
Register symbols:

56 7̅	0̲2̲3̲7̅5̲6̲7̅	0̲2̲3̲7̅5̲6̲7̅	0̲̅2̲3̲7̅5̲6̲7̅
Octave 1	Octave 2	Octave 3	Octave 4

0̲̅2̲3̲7̅5̅

Octave 5
Pitch:

□	2	3	4	5	6	7	1
do	re	mi	fa	sol	la	si	do

Duration:

4 beats   (o) = □ — — —

3 beats   (d.) = □ — —   , and so on.

2 beats   (d) = □ —

1 beat   (♩) = **0̲2̲3̲7̅5̲6̲7̅0̲**

½-beat   (♪) = **0̲ 2̲ 3̲ 7̅ 5̲ 6̲ 7̅ 0̲**

¼-beat   (♬) = **0̲ 2̲ 3̲ 7̅ 5̲ 6̲ 7̅ 0̲**

¾-beat   (♪.) = **0̲2̲3̲7̅5̲6̲7̅0̲**

Example 5-30. John Stafford Smith, <u>The Star-Spangled Banner</u>.

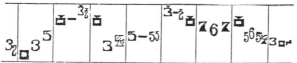

"The object of my invention," said the author of this proposal,
"is to write and print a more perfect and less complicated
notation than heretofore used by introducing and using newly-
invented indications for such important elements in music,
which have never before received a directly visible indication
within any notation known to me." A great many notational indications were apparently unknown to this amateur musician,
whose transcription of our national anthem (above) is both
melodically and rhythmically inauthentic.

Even a cursory glance at this system will demonstrate that
it was impractical to read and to write. While there is a certain logic in varying the size of the pitch numbers to indicate
their duration, the overwrought character of the numbers themselves minimizes their effectiveness. Further, as in so many
"improved" methods of notation, there is no provision for
chromatic alterations of notes, or for the most rudimentary
irregular rhythmic constructs.

1892. Johann Karlowicz, <u>Entwurf einer neuen Notenschrift</u> (Plan
for a new notation). Warsaw: the author.
Staff: None.
Register symbols:

$$+ \quad\quad | - \quad\quad | / \quad\quad | \backslash \quad\quad | ^\wedge \quad\quad | \bullet \quad\quad | ^{\bullet\bullet} \quad\quad | ^{\bullet\,\bullet\,\bullet}$$
$$A_2\text{-}B_2 \quad | C_1\text{-}B_1 \quad | C\text{-}B \quad | c\text{-}b \quad | c^1\text{-}b^1 \quad | c^2\text{-}b^2 \quad | c^3\text{-}b^3 \quad | c^4\text{-}b^4$$

Pitch:

V	D	2	R	3	4	F	5	A	6	H	7	V

| C | C# | D | D# | E | F | F# | G | G# | A | A# | B | C |
| | Db | | Eb | | | Gb | | Ab | | Bb | | |

Duration: Individual beats are indicated by the pitch symbols
laid on their sides, as shown below. Longer values are expressed by more space between the symbols.
Example 5-31.

^   ·^·   ^
R   ᴧ∢ᴋ V꞊V ᴓR ⁺   ∢ᴓ4ᴓ   R

This is not the first instance of a numerical system of notation that uses letters for certain pitch indications. Both J.
C.A. Miné (see page 301) and J. B. Clavière also combined the
two modes in their proposals, but in a more logical fashion
than did Karlowicz. It is unclear why the pitch C should be
expressed by a letter when all the other natural tones are
represented by numerals, the letters being reserved for the
"black-key" pitches. This becomes a minor impediment, however,
when compared to the awkwardness of having to read (and write)
both numbers and letters on their sides.

1892. Hans Schmitt, <u>Eine neue Notenschrift</u> (A new notation).
Brünn, Czechoslovakia: Rudolf M. Rohrer verlag.
Staff: 1-line.
Register symbols:

$$| \underline{2} \quad\quad | \underline{\quad} \quad\quad |^2 \underline{\quad}$$
$$\text{c-b} \quad\quad c^1\text{-}b^1 \quad\quad c^2\text{-}b^2$$

Pitch:

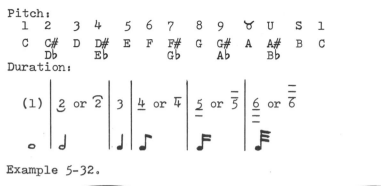

Duration:

Example 5-32.

Again, we have a system that mixes numbers, letters, and abstract symbols to outline the chromatic scale. In so doing, Schmitt's method is neither better nor worse than those of his predecessors who favored the same device. Also, like them, Schmitt devised a limited gamut suitable only for vocal music, which correspondingly limits its usefulness.

1895. Julian Carrillo, _Sistema General de Escritura Musical_ (General system of music notation). Mexico City: Ediciones Sonido 13 (1957).
Staff: 1-line.
Register symbols:

$\overline{9}$ - $\overline{11}$	θ - 11	$\overline{0\text{-}11}$	$\overline{0\text{-}11}$
A_2-B_2	C_1-B_1	C-B	c-b

θ - 11	0 - 11	$\overline{0}$ - $\overline{11}$	θ - 11
c^1-b^1	c^2-b^2	c^3-b^3	c^4-b^4

Pitch:

0	1	2	3	4	5	6	7	8	9	10	11	0
C	C#	D	D#	E	F	F#	G	G#	A	A#	B	C
	Db		Eb			Gb		Ab		Bb		

Duration: Short stems, flagged or beamed as required, are set above or below the pitch numerals. The vertical economy of Carrillo's system is conclusively demonstrated below:

Example 5-33. Julian Carrillo, <u>Balbuceos</u>.

After extensive theoretical research, Carrillo concluded that
to notate a single pitch the composer must chose only two out
of seventy-eight potential symbols and staff positions. Not
only are there three ways to write any single pitch, for example, G×, A♮, B♭♭, but there are also eight octaves on the
piano keyboard and in the total range of the orchestra in
which to write that pitch, as well as thirteen possible clefs
for those octaves. Carrillo did overstate this last problem
somewhat, as we no longer use the obsolete "French violin"
clef, the baritone clef, or the mezzo-soprano clef, for example. His calculation was also based on including such unlikely
note forms as B×, C♭♭, E×, and similarly irregular pitch

spellings. Nevertheless, Carrillo's aim was to reduce the number of symbols necessary for notating the twelve pitches of the
octave in all registers, and a numerical scale seemed to him
the simplest and most logical solution to the problem.

Carrillo carried his proposal much farther by advocating
numbers in series for microtonal scales. In the excerpt from
his string quartet above, the octave is divided into ninety-
seven intervals, numbered 0 to 96. Theoretically, this proposal is beyond reproach; pragmatically, it becomes almost unusable as few performers can be expected to react quickly and
accurately to such rapid fluctuations as 56 - 16, or 40 - 64,
or 4 - 40, to pick out but three such instances from the composer's microtonal score. At any rate, Carrillo's procedure
has had a direct influence on the notation of other composers
of microtonal music, such as Harry Partch and his 43-tone scale
devised for his unique collection of unorthodox instruments.

1897. Charles C. Guilford, "Guilford Musical Shorthand": Graph-
ic Music. Boston: Guilford Music Publishing Co.
Staff: None.
Register symbols:

I	II	III	IV	V	VI	VII	VIII
A_2-B_2	C_1-B_1	C-B	c-b	c^1-b^1	c^2-b^2	c^3-b^3	c^4-b^4

Individual or isolated notes are indicated as follows:

-	$\stackrel{=}{~}$	$\stackrel{3}{-}$	$\stackrel{4}{=}$
1 = 8va	2 = 15ma	= 8bassa	= 15bassa

Pitch:

1	2	3	4	5	6	7	8	9	10	11	12	1
C	C#	D	D#	E	F	F#	G	G#	A	A#	B	C
	Db		Eb			Gb		Ab		Bb		

Duration:

-5	:,4	:3	.2
$\frac{1}{16}$-beat (♬)	$\frac{1}{8}$-beat (♪)	$\frac{1}{4}$-beat (♪)	$\frac{1}{2}$-beat (♩)

9	|8| |	|7|||	|6||||
1 beat (♩)	2 beats (♩)	3 beats (♩·)	4 beats (o)

Irregular rhythmic figures are notated, for example:

1.2.3.   2----

Rests: All values are designated by the symbol * .
Meter: Indicated by thin beat-lines within a pair of heavy
  barlines.
Two examples of Guilford's notation are given here: one, a
single melodic line; the other, a few measures for keyboard.

Example 5-34.

Example 5-35. Wolfgang Amadeus Mozart, from Act I, The Magic Flute.

This inventor's amateur status is manifest by his misnotating the meter of Mozart's music, to say nothing of his offering the excerpt in the wrong tonality. Perhaps anticipating eventual martyrdom as the proposer of a new notational system, Guilford prefaced his presentation by quoting an anonymous writer in the Boston Home Journal for 20 March 1897: "Any new system of musical notation is bound to encounter just such bitter, persistent, and universal prejudice as ages ago placed the Arabic figures on trial for more than half a century before they were accepted as substitutes for Roman numerals."

In his own voice, Guilford continued: "The present notation is just as defective in its means for expressing time as it is in its means for expressing pitch. Thus while the real unit of time is the measure, the present notation attempts to make the note the unit. . . . The modern conception of musical time is that of accent or stress rather than of duration or meter. The present system of notation does not express this idea with certainty and precision."

Guilford did not explain why he considered the measure, not the beat, to be the true unit of time. In any event, he had to devise a scheme to indicate individual note duration, but in this he fell short, largely on the basis of readability. He also failed to explain why he transposed the Mozart excerpt, above, and changed the meter from 6/8 to 3/4.

1902. Johann Martin Schleyer, <u>Vereinfachung und Erleichtering der musikalischen Notenschreibung</u> (Simplification and facilitation of musical notation). Konstanz a.B., Germany: Welt-sprache-zentralbüro.

Staff: 5-line; the lines are widely spaced and the central line is heavy.

Clef signs: None; the heavy central line divides the left-hand and right-hand registers.

Pitch: The wide spaces between the staff lines accommodate four levels of pitch numerals (see Example 5-36).

1	2	3	4	5	6	7	8	9	10	11	12	1
C	C#	D	D#	E	F	F#	G	G#	A	A#	B	C
	Db		Eb			Gb		Ab		Bb		

Key signatures: Indicated by Roman numerals according to the sequence of pitches, such as,

II. = C# or Db, VIII. = G, XI. = Bb.

Duration:

, and so on.

Chord structures are notated:

Rests:

, and so on.

Example 5-36.

This notational system is designed exclusively for keyboard music; as such, it is sensibly worked out and clear in intent, though passages that exploited the extreme registers of the keyboard would undoubtedly create reading complexities. The method devised by Schleyer would work best in fairly simple music that is concentrated in the central section of the piano.

1907. Christian Peder Vilhelm Geisler, "Neue Notation für
   Gesangsmusik" (New notation for vocal music), *International
   Musical Society 2nd Congress Proceedings*, pp. 48-55.
Staff: 1-line.
Register symbols: None; the system is designed solely for
   single-line vocal music.
Pitch:

1 1̄ 2 2 2̄ 3 3 4 4̄ 5 5 5̄ 6 6 6̄ 7 7 1

C C# Db D D# Eb E F F# Gb G G# Ab A A# Bb B C

Duration: Designated by small noteheads set above the pitch
   numerals. For brief modulations, the numbers are placed
   beneath the staff line.
Example 5-37.

Geisler's early proposal was further developed in his 1948
publication, *Die verschiedenen Gesang-Schriftsprachen und
ihre Beziehungen zu den Naturtönen* (The various speech patterns and their relation to natural sounds). His system at
hand owes its depiction of register to Rousseau and his fol-
lowers and its delineation of rhythm to tablature notation.

1924. Howard Parsons, "A New System of Musical Notation,"
   The Musical Times 980, 65, pp. 900-904.
Staff: 4-line.

Register symbols:

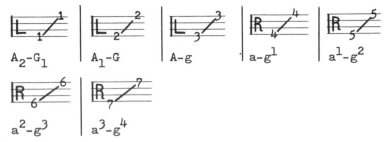

A_2-G_1 | A_1-G | A-g | a-g^1 | a^1-g^2

a^2-g^3 | a^3-g^4

Pitch:

A A# B♭ B C C# D♭ D D# E♭ E F F# G♭ G G#

Duration:

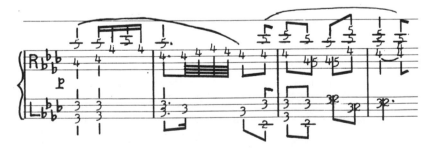

3   5   6 or 6   7 or 7

Example 5-38. Franz Schubert, <u>Sonata in C Minor</u>, op. posth.

"The objects of this system," said its author, "are to provide
that music be taught 'without tears' on the part of the pupil,
or despair on the part of the master, and to facilitate the
reading of music by musicians, even those of the highest skill;
in short, to supersede the present system of musical notation

by something far more scientific." Scientific this system may
be, in the mind of its inventor, but capable of facilitating
the reading of music it is not. Nor will it ever supersede
traditional notation, one can be sure.

What does set this method apart from others based on numerals is that the numbers refer not to specific pitches of the
octave but to their register positions. Because of the two substitute clef symbols employed (R for the right hand and L for
the left hand), the system is obviously designed for piano
music. It could function for other instruments and for voices
merely by eliminating these two signs and using only the register numbers.

Duration is only sketchily addressed in Parsons' proposal;
he makes no provision for whole-notes or for dotted values,
though he does distinguish half-notes from quarter-notes by
making the former heavier in the printing. The inclusion of
augmentation dots in Example 5-38 is a liberty exercised by
this writer.

1936. Walter Kobelt, <u>Klavierspiel Helvetia</u> (Swiss Piano Meth-
    od). Basel: Helvetia-verlag.
Staff: 2-line; a keyboard system consists of two widely sepa-
    rated staves.
Clef signs: None; register is indicated by the position of
    the pitch numbers relative to the staff lines.
Pitch:

Duration: Measure beats are marked by dotted vertical lines;
    beat subdivisions are indicated by the spatial relationship
    of the pitch numbers to the beat-lines.
Rests: Indicated by the symbol * on each beat involved.
Meter: The numerator only, boxed below the key signature, as
    shown below.
Example 5-39. Franz Schubert, <u>Sonata in C Minor</u>, op. posth.

Kobelt's is still another system designed for elementary piano teaching. It is difficult to see how this method of reading music is superior to our traditional notation, especially in the area of note duration. Obviously, only the simplest of rhythmic constructs can be clearly shown in <u>Klavierspiel Helvetia</u>.

1947. William Alexander Mathews, <u>Mathews' Melodic Notation System</u>. El Cajon, California: the author.
Staff: None.
Register symbols:

1-7 |1-7 |1-7
lower octave |middle octave |higher octave

Pitch:

1	V	2	W	3	4	X	5	Y	6	Z	7	1
C	C#	D	D#	E	F	F#	G	G#	A	A#	B	C
	Db		Eb			Gb		Ab		Bb		

Duration:

1   V   2   W   3   4   X
                    —   =

: o   d.   d   d   ♪   ♬   ♬

Certain common rhythmic figures and grace notes are written:

2 X   1W5   76
· — = ♪.♪   3   = ♪♪♪   ◠Y = ♫

Rests:

□   o   ∧   _   =   ≡

▬   ▬   ↧   ↥   ↥   ↧

From Mathews' list of brief melodic excerpts from thirteen well-known compositions, this compiler has selected three for comparative illustration. The titles of all the works in Mathews' table are given just as they appear.
Example 5-40.
    Line 1. Wolfgang Amadeus Mozart, from Act II, <u>Don Giovanni</u>.

Line 12. Victor Antoine Edouard Lalo, "Rondo," from <u>Symphon-
ie Espagnole</u>.

Line 13. César Auguste Franck, <u>Symphonic Variations</u>.

1.	-|- ‖1̣2̣1̣7̣6̣7̣|123̣-|0∧|4531|6̣ 7̣‖	Mozart: Don Giovanni, Act 2. Il Mio Tesoro
2.	1̣|Ṿ|2̣4̣3̣|2̣6̣5̣|5444 4333|3222	Mozart: Don Juan Overture.
3.	1̣2̣4̣3̣2̣1̣|5 6̣3̣6̣ 5-5̣|67 1̣-∧763̣|	Bizet: Carmen-Entr'acte (2-3).
4.	1̣|3 1̣-1̣|3 1̣-1̣|5-∧4̣2̣|7̣--5̣4̣|	Mendelssohn: Symphony No. 4, 1st Movt.
5.	1̣-4̣=3̣|2̣6̣5̣1̣|4321|32-|	Tchaikovsky: Nut Cracker Suite (Ovt.).
6.	1̣ 5̣1̣|231 2̣2̣ 5-∧--|3 1̣6̣|	Gunod [sic] : Faust, Act 1.
7.	1̣6̣1̣6̣|77-5̣|6̣3̣6̣3̣|55∧|	Puccini: Madame Butterfly, Act 2. Un Bel Di Vedremo.
8.	-1̣7̣1̣ v222|443w w3|-3w3	Rubenstein: Romance.
9.	-2- ²1̣ 1̣2̣ 1̣7̣|²3²3|²1̣1̣2̣ 1̣3̣|³6³6|	Schubert: Moment Musicale.
10.	2̣2̣3̣ 5̣4̣3̣2̣|3̣3̣4̣ 6̣5̣4̣3̣|2̣2̣3̣	Beethoven: Symphony No. 7, 4th Mov.
11.	2|3212|3233̣2̣|3233̣4̣|4̣4̣,	Beethoven: Piano Concerto No. 5, 1st Movt.
12.	-2̣4̣|3̣5̣3̣ 2̣4̣2̣|13̣5̣ -2̣4̣|3̣5̣3̣	Lalo: Symphonie Espagnole, Rondo (V).
13.	-W- W|3∧1|5∧3|2̣1̣?̇|1∧3|543|	Franck: Symphonic Variations.

Even the most casual perusal of the transcribed versions of
Mathews' shorthand notation will reveal several curious results: None of the originals was in the tonality of C major,
and rhythmic distortions are present. Possibly these technical
lapses did not unduly disturb the inventor, as his sole purpose was merely to identify as briefly as possible certain
frequently performed compositions of his day.
"The long-felt need for a system of identification of
tunes is at last afforded in the <u>Melodic</u> filing system," maintained the author of this proposal. Mathews' plan is designed
not for composers to use or performers to read but for librar-
ians, cataloguers, and researchers to codify melodies for easy
reference. He suggests that only a measure or two is suffi-

cient for the filing, and the melodies can be catalogued by
their initial note symbol, similar to the alphabetical list-
ings in a dictionary. To illustrate his ideas, the author provided a sample page, reproduced above.

1965. Andrew J. Lotz, <u>The death of the alphabet; musical notation for standard typewriters (and rapid longhand) and how
to dictate the notation</u>. New York: Carlton Press.

Staff: None; the system is designed solely for typewriter
characters, and no conventional notational elements are used.

Register symbols:

$1''-7''$	$1'-7'$	$1-7$	$1-7$	$1'-7'$	$1''-7''$	$1'''-7'''$
C_1-B_1	$C-B$	$c-b$	c^1-b^1	c^2-b^2	c^3-b^3	c^4-b^4

Pitch: Sharps are either B (black key) or s (sharp); flats are
either b (black key) or f (flat).
  1 B1 b2 2 B2 b3 3 4 B4 b5 5 B5 b6 6 B6 b7 7 1
    s1 f2 ⋅ s2 f3   s4 f5   s5 f6   s6 f7

  C C# Db D D# Eb E F F# Gb G G# Ab A A# Bb B C
  A repeated accidental is indicated as r; for example:
  3 s4 s4 5 = 3 s4 r 5, or 1 f6 f6 f6 4 = 1 f6 r r 4.

Key signatures: The pitch number is preceded by K (key) for a
major tonality and by mK (minor key) for a minor tonality;
for example:
K4 = F major, Kf7 = Bb major, mK2 = D minor, mK6 = A minor.

Duration:

1	1-	1--	2.	2-.
1 beat	2 beats	3 beats, etc.	1½ beats	2½ beats

2--.	(3	((3	(((3
3½ beats, etc.	½-beat	¼-beat	⅛-beat

(4s5), (6f7), etc.	/	//
same rhythmic value	barline	double-bar

Rests:

0	0.	0-	0--
1 beat	1½ beats	2 beats	3 beats, and so on.

Meter: t (time) precedes the numerator.

t2	t4	t3	t6
$\frac{2}{2}$ or $\frac{2}{4}$	$\frac{4}{4}$ or $\frac{4}{8}$	$\frac{3}{4}$ or $\frac{3}{8}$	$\frac{6}{4}$ or $\frac{6}{8}$
duple time		triple time	compound duple time

t9

$\frac{9}{4}$ or $\frac{9}{8}$

compound triple time

Surely any observant reader can quickly identify the following
familiar Christmas carol transcribed into Lotz's typewriter
notation.

Example 5-41.

mk3 t4 //3/3776/5432/3456/7--3/3776/5432/3456/7-07/8678/
2'3'76/5345/6-56/7-87/7654/3-(54)3/6-56/782'3'/7654/3---/
--0//

It was inevitable that someone, someday, would devise a system of music notation using only standard typewriter characters. Although the earliest experiment with a machine that
typed letters and numbers dates back to 1714, it was not until
1867 that the first practical machine was patented. It then
took just under a century for someone to think of using the
modern typewriter as a means of notating music. As happens so
frequently in the area of mechanical inventions, several musicians came forward with notation systems utilizing the typewriter at almost the same time, and Andrew Lotz was one of the
first to publish a full-length book on an individual system.
It is interesting to note that eleven years before Lotz's proposal appeared, the first of several differently designed music typewriters was patented. Invented by Cecil Effinger in
1954, this particular machine used standard notation symbols
rather than numbers and letters.

"One of the great disadvantages of many proposed new systems of notation," Lotz wrote, "has been that those who learned them were illiterate in the standard method, and those who
were literate in the standard method found it easier to stick
with the notation they knew thoroughly than to learn a new
system with no other advantage than as a substitute notation."
Unwittingly, perhaps, Lotz has written the epitaph for his own
method, ingenious as it is. Developed to provide for nearly
every notational requirement -- at least for non-avant garde
music -- it cannot erase basic musical education. Contemporary
musicians are trained from childhood to interpret unchanging
symbological notation: Pitch is always represented vertically,
and duration is depicted horizontally. It is patently impossible to duplicate without equivocation this logical process
by using either numerals, letters, or linguistic symbology.

1965. Oskar Karl Walter Heim, Breakthrough in Music? The Need
    for a Simple Way to Write Music. n.p., the author.
Staff: 4-line, constituted as shown below.
Register symbols:

$\cdot$ 1 - 12 $\cdot\cdot\cdot$ C_1-B_1	1 -12 $\cdot\cdot\cdot$ C-B	1-12 $\cdot\cdot$ $\cdot$ c-b	1-12 $\cdot$ $\cdot$ c^1-b^1	$\cdot$ $\dot{1}$-$\dot{1}2$ c^2-b^2	$\cdot\cdot$ $\dot{1}$ $\cdot\cdot$-$\dot{1}2$ c^3-b^3	$\cdot\cdot\cdot$ $\dot{1}$ $\cdot\cdot\cdot$-$\dot{1}2$ c^4-b^4

Pitch:

1	2	3	4	5	6	7	8	9	10	11	12	1
C	C# Db	D	D# Eb	E	F	F# Gb	G	G# Ab	A	A# Bb	B	C

Key signatures: Indicated by the pitch number; for example:
    4 major = Eb major, 10 minor = A minor.
Duration: Expressed by integers (whole numbers) set in the
    central meter column. The numbers add up to the total of
    the smallest units present in the measure, as prescribed
    by the time signature.

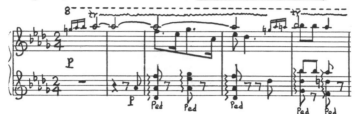

Rests: The symbol - placed after a pitch number and beneath
   the integer in the meter column.
Meter: Expressed as a fraction, set in front of the column
   of integers.
Example 5-42. Franz Liszt, <u>Hungarian Rhapsody</u> no. 12.

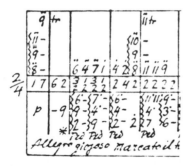

"An unfortunate choice of symbols for music notation in times
past," said Heim, "still impedes music in all its branches.
The old notation inflicts excessive hardship in reading, writing, transposing, copying, printing, learning and playing. . .
The only solution to this dilemma is to base music notation on
numbers. There is no other way -- it's the engineer's, the
mathematician's method." Few musicians are also mathematicians,
and fewer still are engineers; consequently, many may disagree
with Heim that numerical notation -- especially for complex
music -- is the way of the future. The author maintained that
his system was only for the young, the "growing generation,"
as he put it. Older musicians, he went on to say, will be in-
tolerant. True, perhaps, but even young professionals will
dismiss Heim's proposal as inflicting even more hardship on
practicing musicians than the traditional method it was designed to supplant.

1966. John Robbins, <u>Revelations in Music. A Bold and Thorough</u>
   <u>Rewrite of the Art of Music (Computation)</u>. n.p., the author.
Staff: 3-line, arranged vertically.
Clef signs: None; the left-hand column is for the pianist's
   left hand; the right-hand column, for the right hand.

Pitch:

C	1	2
C#/Db	2	1
D	3	0
D#/Eb	4	9
E	5	8
F	6	7
F#/Gb	7	6
G	8	5
G#/Ab	9	4
A	0	3
A#/Bb	1	2
B	2	1

Duration: Each measure beat receives equal vertical space; the number of beats per measure is determined by the meter.

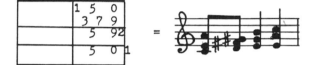

Tied notes are indicated as follows: $\left(\dfrac{4}{4}\right.$

Rests: Designated by blank space.
Meter: Indicated by the number of beat-lines within the measure, for example,

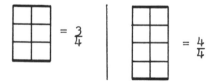

Heim's pamphlet is evidently a further exploration of notational ideas put forward in his 1955 private publication, Music notation simplified; direct reading notation, on file at The Library of Congress.

"The adaptation of Computation as the official language of music will necessitate the translation and reprinting of all theory, harmony, and music books and musical compositions. A challenge to the most ambitious publisher." Can the author of this proposal really be serious? Or is this a put-on, a parody of all the earnest but misguided reforms of notation that have appeared with depressing regularity during the past several hundred years? Let us be charitable and believe the latter.

1970. Christopher Crocker, <u>Digatone: For the Piano</u>. Princeton,
New Jersey: Leisure League of America, Inc.
Staff: 1-line.
Register symbols:

R.H. $\underset{\sim}{..1}$-$\underset{\sim}{..12}$ | $\underset{\sim}{.1}$-$\underset{\sim}{.12}$ | $\underline{1}$-$\underline{12}$ | ① - ⑫ | $\underline{1}$ - $\underline{12}$ | $.\underline{1}$-$.\underline{12}$

L.H. $\underset{\sim}{..1}$-$\underset{\sim}{..12}$ | $\underset{\sim}{.1}$-$\underset{\sim}{.12}$ | $\underline{1}$-$\underline{12}$ | ① - ⑫ | 1 - 12 | $.1$-$.12$

C_1-B_1 | C-B | c-b | c^1-b^1 | c^2-b^2 | c^3-b^3

R.H. $\underline{..1}$-$\underline{..12}$
L.H. $..1$-$..12$
c^4-b^4

Pitch:
1 2   3 4   5 6 7   8   9   10 11 12 1

do #/b re #/b mi fa #/b sol #/b la #/b ti do

Duration: Heavy vertical bars represent conventional barlines;
lighter tactus lines indicate the beats within the measure.
Subdivisions of the beat are shown by shorter tactus lines
(see Example 5-43).
Rests: Indicated by the letter R, its duration extending until
the next pitch numeral.
Meter: The numerator only is given, placed before the first
barline.
Example 5-43. Frédéric Chopin, <u>Prelude in A</u>, op. 28, no. 7.

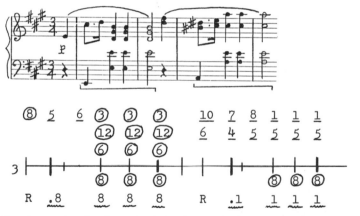

Digatone is designed for the primary teaching of piano. Because of its inherent limitations, it can serve only for music
of the simplest kind, with the most basic of rhythmic patterns
and the most traditional of melodic and harmonic constructions.
The system does not go beyond three-note chords in either hand,
and it is quite unsuited to contrapuntal textures.

1973. Yael Bukspan, <u>Towards a New System of Music Notation</u>.
Tel Aviv, Israel: International Monograph Publishers.

Staff: None; the system is designed solely for typewriter
   characters.
Register symbols:

((	(	(())	()	)	))	)))	))))
A_2-B_2	C_1-B_1	C-B	c-b	c^1-b^1	c^2-b^2	c^3-b^3	c^4-b^4

Pitch:

1	10	11	110	111	1110	1111	0	01	00	001	000	1
C	C#	D	D#	E	F	F#	G	G#	A	A#	B	C
	D♭		E♭			G♭		A♭		B♭		

Duration:

+=   +   =-   =   -.   -   .   ..   .

Irregular rhythmic figures are notated as follows:

3. = | 5- = | 7.. =

Rests:

?+   ?=   ?-   ?.   ?..   ?...

Dynamics:

pp   p   mp   mf   f   ff

Example 5-44.

4/4)1110- 00.001.))1-.10./1= ?-)00. ..))1../
     11- 1- 111-. 0./1110= ?=/

According to the publisher of this typewritten system of notation, the author is an Israeli-born pianist, a teacher of music and rhythmics, and a musicologist. "Dissatisfaction with
the traditional notation," the publisher goes on to say, "and
an interest in analytical mathematics and the new ways of com-
puterized thinking and working have led her to the invention
of a music notation that is basically simple and can be used
for any kind of hitherto conventionally notated composition."
     Although this system is designed for the modern typewriter,
it is markedly different from Andrew Lotz's 1965 proposal of
a typewritten notation (see page 324). Bukspan contends that
her method is monolinear, that the notation of pitch is binary
and the marking of intervals visual, combining absolute and
relative notation. She also points out that there are no duplications of symbols.
     Be that as it may, this particular form of notation would
seem to be most suitable for the same purposes for which the
Barry Brook-Murray Gould alphabetical proposal (refer to page

365) was designed -- card catalogues, various indexes, charts and tabulations, and the like.

1983. Robert Stuckey, <u>Music in Cyclic Twelfths</u>. London: the author.
Staff: 3-line; the outer lines are heavy.
Register symbols:

1 cy	2 cy	3 cy	4 cy	5 cy	6 cy	7 cy
C_1-B_1	C-B	c-b	c^1-b^1	c^2-b^2	c^3-b^3	c^4-b^4

Pitch: One cycle (1 cy) = one octave.

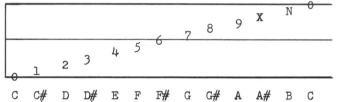

C C# D D# E F F# G G# A A# B C
   Db   Eb   Gb   Ab   Bb

Key signatures: Indicated by the pitch symbol and the mode according to the names of the Greek modes; for example: 3 Ionian = Eb major, 9 Aeolian = A minor.
Duration:

Stems for chords are set to the left of the pitch symbols; for example:

Rests:

, and so on.

Example 5-45. J. S. Bach, "Menuet," from the <u>Little Note Book for Anna Magdalena Bach</u>.

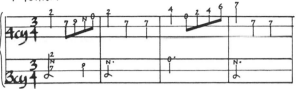

In the words of its inventor, the aim of this most recent numerical proposal in our survey "is to provide the beginner
with a small number of powerful concepts that will enable him
or her to play and invent musically. To this end a set of symbols and a vocabulary has been selected according to the following criteria: a), that they should bear a closer relation
to every day speech [sic] ; b), that they should make links,
wherever possible, with the more general disciplines of math
[ematics], physics, and psychology, and c), that one term
should be chosen from a number of synonyms in order to reduce
the learning load."

Stuckey's "vocabulary" is an extensive list of new or per-
sonally coined terms correlated with the notational elements
of his system; for example, cyclic twelfth, or a semitone;
intersect chord, or a chord common to two or more keys; and
polyradical, or intervals or chords that suggest several roots.
A large part of his proposal is devoted to questions of tonal
and harmonic analysis, acoustical considerations, and the psychological basis of sound itself; notation is often only pe-
ripheral to the discussion.

A communication from the proposer of <u>Music in Cyclic
Twelfths</u> states that his system has undergone at least two
name changes: first, as Figured Semits; a semit is in his
words "the basic unit of interval description;" and second,
Chromatic Digits. The author further states that "we must
accept that further changes of title are a future possibility."

The complex theoretical basis of Stuckey's system is not
reflected in the corresponding notation. All in all, his proposal seems too abstruse for the amateur and too simplistic
for the professional, serving neither in maximum effectiveness.

NOTES

1. John Stainer, "On the Musical Introductions Found in
Certain Metrical Psalters." <u>Proceedings of the Musical Asso-
ciation</u> XXVII, 1900. A critical article by Georg Becker on
Davantes' system appears in the <u>Monatshefte für Musik-
Geschichte</u> I, 11 (1869), pp. 163-178.
2. Athanasius Kircher, <u>Musurgia universalis sive Ars magna
consoni et dissoni in X. libros digesta</u>. Rome: Extypographia
haeredum Francisci Corbelletti, 1650.
3. François-Joseph Fétis, <u>Biographie universelle des mu-
siciens</u>, vol. 5, pp. 35-37. (Paris, 1833-1844).
4. Jean-Jacques Souhaitty, <u>Nouvelle méthode pour apprendre
le plain-chant et la musique</u> (Paris: Thomas Jolly, 1665).

5. Jean-Jacques Souhaitty, <u>Nouveaux élémens de chant ou l'essai d'une nouvelle découverte qu'on à faite dans l'art de chanter</u> (Paris: Pierre le Petit, 1677).

6. Jean-Jacques Rousseau, "Dissertation sur la musique moderne," in his <u>Ecrits sur la musique</u> (Paris: Lefevre, 1819).

7. Etienne Destranges, <u>Le Guide musicale</u> 56, no. 48 (1910), pp. 773-775.

8. Fétis, vol. 3, pp. 385-386.

9. Nicolas Slonimsky, in <u>Baker's Biographical Dictionary of Musicians</u>, fifth edition (New York: G. Schirmer, Inc., 1968), p. 284.

6.
Alphabetical Notations

The proof of the notation is in the reading. Most of
the notational systems which are being devised and
experimentally tried today are too complex to be
practical, too individual or specialized to be of
general application, and inadequate to serve the
composer's needs.

--Peter Yates, Twentieth Century Music, 1967.

Alphabetical letters were used to notate music as early as the
second millenium B.C., when the ancient Greeks wrote down their
instrumental music with a mixture of letters and abstract signs
outlining a three-octave diatonic scale. Mirror forms of the
pitch letters ingeniously indicated raised pitches. Alphabetical notation entered Western music only in the tenth century
A.D., when such prominent theorists as Boethius and Hucbald
employed letter symbols as a teaching tool. By the end of the
Middle Ages -- about the fifteenth century -- neumes had gradually replaced letters as the preferred written record of music. These, in turn, were superseded by mensural notation with
its square and, finally, lozenge-shaped noteheads.
   During the sixteenth century, letter notation was reincar-
nated, so to speak, in the form of tablature. In some tablature
notation, both letters and numbers were present; other forms
combined letters and noteheads. The so-called old German keyboard tablature, prevalent during the first half of the century, favored this combination -- letters in the right-hand
part and noteheads in the left-hand part. By the end of that
century, and persevering into the earliest years of the eighteenth, the new German keyboard tablature employed letters for
both parts.
   Tablature notation, however, was designed for the individualized playing techniques of specific instruments, and it was
not meant to apply to general notation. Hence, the various
tablatures were not reforms or attempts to improve the standard notation of the period and therefore find no place in this
compendium of reforms. Not until the rise of the vocal Tonic-
Sol-fa systems of the early nineteenth century do we encounter
proposals designed to simplify all basic notation by the use

of letters in place of noteheads. This is a process that has
not yet concluded, even though no single letter-system has
ever successfully replaced conventional staff notation, nor
does it seem likely that it ever will.

An esoteric offshoot of letter notation was the musical
cryptography of certain seventeenth- and eighteenth-century
theorists. Secret codes were embedded in a sequence of notes,
with each note representing a predetermined letter of the alphabet. The melodic outline thus formed spelled out a name, a
term, or a message, frequently so arcane that only a fellow
theorist familiar with the game would understand its import.
This unique form of alphabetical notation appears in the ascending and descending scale of notes and the corresponding
letters used by Athanasius Kircher around 1650 in his <u>Parsu
Cryptologia musurgica sive Ars Steganographica</u> (1), as shown
in Figure 6-1.
Figure 6-1.

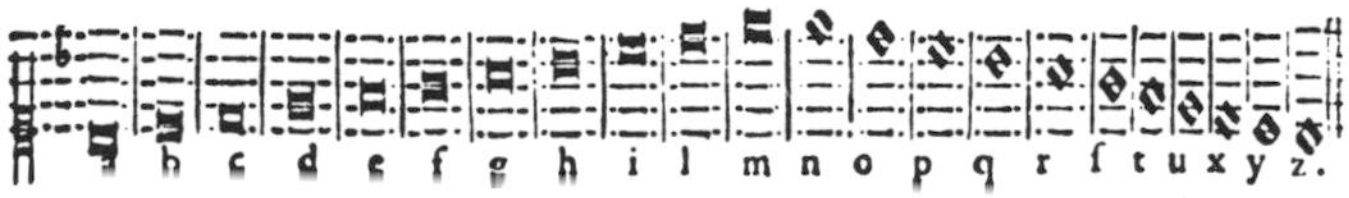

Taking the title of Kircher's famous treatise, the <u>Musurgia
universalis</u>, as the letter code to be deciphered, we find the
solution shown in Figure 6-2.
Figure 6-2.

m u s u r g i a u n i (v) e r s a l i s

Other well-known practitioners of musical cryptography include
Joannes Balthasar Friderici and P. Gaspar Schott (Friderici's
proposal for rhythmic notehead distinction is discussed on
page 272).

The thirty alphabetical notation systems included in this
chapter are interesting not only because they are contemporary
with the full development of modern orthochronic notation, but
also because of the variety of alphabets and printing fonts
that characterized the pitches in different vocal or instrumental registers. Latin, Greek, Italian, Old and Modern German -- all are to be found in the letter systems proposed from
the seventeenth to the twentieth century. In addition, contrasting printing styles -- capitals and lowercase, cursive
and italic, boldface and pica -- all figured in the letter
methodologies put forward by theorists and pedagogues hopeful
of simplifying music reading for the musically illiterate.
This premise is really the only justification for alphabetical
notation, just as it is for numerical and stenographic methods.

General rejection of these alternative ways of notating
music, however, cannot be attributed solely to perversity on
the part of the worldwide musical community -- in spite of the
humorous comment made by a certain Lord Brabazon of Tara:
"Such a thing is worth while trying and not beneath our dig-

nity, but do not expect help from musicians; they revel in the
mysticism of their trade union (2)." Sheer pragmatism, if nothing else, surely accounts for the unwillingness of modern
musicians to embrace the concept of alphabetical notation for
it, like other failed systems, is not the sought-for panacea
for the ailments of our traditional notation.

1612. Johann Lippius, <u>Synopsis musicae novae omnino verae</u>
<u>ataque methodicae universae, in omnis sophiae praegustum</u>
<u>inventae disputatae et propositae omnibus philomusicis</u>
(Synopsis of a new musical technique altogether valid, and
well-constructed in its entirety; in a foretaste of all wis-
dom, moreover, created, publicly debated, and set forth
for all music-lovers) (3). Strassburg: Impensis Pauli Le-
dertz, typis Caroli Kieffer.
Staff: None.
Register symbols:

A̰-G̰ (Italic capital letters)	A̰-G̰ (Boldface capital letters)
C-B	c-b

a - g (Single lowercase letters)	aa-gg (Double lowercase letters)
c^1-b^1	c^2-b^2

aaa-ggg (Triple lowercase letters)
c^3-b^3
Pitch:
  A (a)   B (b)   C (c)   D (d)   E (e)   F (f)   G (g)
  C   D   E   F   G   A   B
Example 6-1.

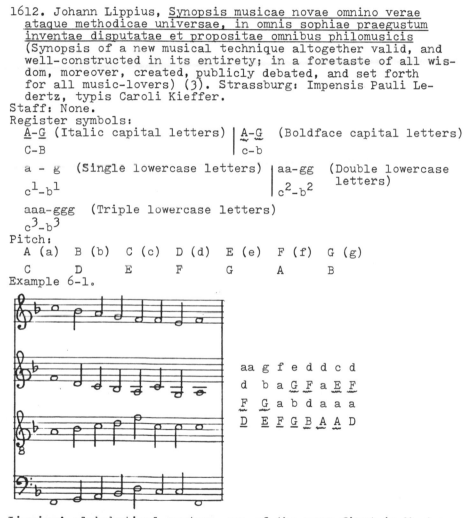

aa g f e d d c d
d b a G̰ F a Ḛ F̰
F̰ G̰ a b d a a a
D̰ Ḛ F̰ G̰ B̰ A̰ A̰ D

Lippius' alphabetical system, one of the very first in Western
music, laid the foundation for many similar notational methods
to come in succeeding centuries. Primarily a philosopher and
theologian, not a theorist or composer, Lippius did write one
composition, which was intended to illustrate the so-called
ornate style of the period. He included his composition, writ-

ten for four voice parts on a single eleven-line staff, in his
<u>Disputatio tertia</u>, delivered at Wittenberg University in 1610.

1636. Le Padre Marin Mersenne, "Expliquer une autre méthode
pour apprendre à chanter et à composer sans les notes ordinaires par le moyen des seules lettres" (Explanation of an
alternative method of learning to sing and to compose without conventional notes, using only letters), <u>Harmonie universelle, contenant la théorie et la pratique de la musique</u>.
Paris: Pierre Ballard.
Staff: None.
Register symbols:

VRM – Z

| | V R M – Z | v r m – z | $\underline{v}$ $\underline{r}$ $\underline{m}$ – $\underline{z}$ |
| G-f | g-f^1 | g^1-f^2 | g^2-f^3 |

Pitch:

V	R	M	F	S	L	Z	V
G	A	B	C	D	E	F	G

ut ré mi fa sol la za ul
Mersenne had originally suggested using the symbol ✳ beneath
the pitch letter to indicate its chromatic inflection up-
wards. Realizing that printers lacked this symbol, he substituted the prime sign after the letter.

V	V'	R	R'	M	F	F'	S	S'	L	Z	Z'	V
G	G#	A	A#	B	C	C#	D	D#	E	F	F#	G

Duration: Each beat is set off by commas.
Example 6-2. Chorale, <u>Ein' feste Burg ist unser Gott</u>.

s, | s,s,rm,f' | sf',m,r,s | f',m,r,mr | vZ',L,S, |

Oddly, Mersenne's letter notation was not as successful in
practice as was his numerical system (see page 285). Although
the letter V was the accepted form of U (representing ut),
the letter Z seems a peculiar choice for F (za).

1707. Andreas Werckmeister, <u>Musikalische Paradoxal-Discourse,
oder ungemeine Vorstellungen wie die musica einen hohen und
göttlichen Uhrsprung habe. . . .</u> (Musical paradoxical dis-
courses, or uncommon ideas on how music has a lofty and di-
vine origin). Quedlinburg, Germany: Theodor Philipp Calvisius.
Staff: None.
Register symbols: Four contrasting printing fonts distinguish
the four vocal octaves.

| Old German capitals | Latin capitals | Old German lowercase |
| C-H (B) | c-h | c^1-h^1 |

Latin lowercase
c^2-h^2
Pitch:
C   D   E   F   G   A   H   C

ut re mi fa sol la si ut
Duration: Expressed by numbers set above the pitch letters.
1   2   4   8   16

Example 6-3. Chorale, <u>Ein' feste Burg ist unser Gott.</u>

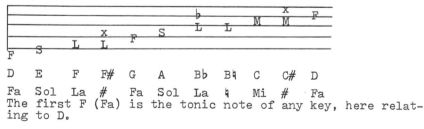

```
4 | 4 4 8 8 4 | 8 8 4 4 4 | 4 4 4 8 8 | 8 8 4 4 |
c | c c g a h | c h a g c | h a g a g | f e d c |
```

A noted organist and an authority on organ tuning, Werckmeister wrote a number of important studies on theoretical subjects, including the earliest known treatise on the science of
equal temperament (4). Because of his extensive knowledge of
the organ and its literature, it is not surprising that he
chose to depict note duration according to the method commonly
used in German organ tablature. Werckmeister did not live to
witness either success or failure of his alphabetical notation,
which was issued posthumously.

1721. Reverend John Tufts, <u>An Introduction to the Singing of</u>
<u>Psalm-Tunes in a Plain and Easy Method</u>, fifth edition.
Boston: Samuel Gerrish.
Staff: 5-line.
Clef signs:
   Canto (G-clef) | Bass (F-clef)

Pitch:

D   E   F   F#   G   A   Bb   B♮   C   C#   D
Fa Sol La #   Fa Sol La   ♮   Mi #   Fa
The first F (Fa) is the tonic note of any key, here relat-
ing to D.

Duration:

F: S.   L   F͡S or ͡SL

Meter: ¢ (common time) and 3 (tripla time) only.
Example 6-4. Hymn, <u>Psalm 100</u>.

Alphabetical notation had been used as a pedagogical tool for
almost 150 years before Tufts published his so-called plain
and easy method. In 1560 the Frenchman Pierre Davantes had
combined the scale syllables with noteheads on the staff (see
page 284), and two years later the English publisher John Day
had put out a psalter in which the notes were duplicated with
syllable letters. It is recorded, incidentally, that the Puri-
tans brought copies of Day's <u>The Whole Booke of Psalms</u> with
them to the newly established Massachusetts Bay Colony.

Whether or not Tufts knew of these previous uses of letter
notation is conjectural; history, as we know, is replete with
examples of the reinvention of systems, notational or otherwise. Certainly Tufts' <u>An Introduction to the Singing of Psalm-
Tunes in a Plain and Easy Method</u> was not the first Fa-Sol-La
method practiced in the United States. It appeared, for instance, in the ninth edition (1698) of the celebrated <u>Bay
Psalm Book</u>, a publication that was surely known to Tufts.

Unfortunately, the earliest editions of Tufts' own book
have been lost; the fifth edition (1726) is the one to which
scholars of the period turn for detailed information. Designed,
as he said, for "Children, or People of the meanest Capaci-
ties," his treatise is an admirable exposition in simple terms
of all the salient elements of music writing and reading, easily grasped by even the most illiterate of students.

1766. Charles DeLusse, Lettre sur une nouvelle dénomination
des sept degrés successifs de la gamme, ou l'on propose de
nouveaux caractères propres à les noter (Comment on a new
designation of the seven scale degrees; proposed new symbols
for correctly notating them). Paris: Mercure.
Staff: 5-line.
Clef signs: Only the C-clef was used by DeLusse.

Pitch:

C	C#	Db	D	D#	Eb	E	F	F#

Gb	G	G#	Ab	A	A#	Bb	B	C

Duration:

A É I   ā è̀ ī   a é   o̲ u̲ w̲   a̲

Example 6-5.

The antecedent of DeLusse's alphabetical system of notation
was that of Michael Altenburg in his 1617 Gaudium Christianum,
a collection of six motets. Altenburg's plan also influenced
a number of other letter systems put forward in the eighteenth
century, in particular his device of using different printing
types for the letters to distinguish register. DeLusse, however, favored representing the pitches with vowels rather than
serialized letters, and his type distinctions characterized
durational differences rather than pitch levels.

1786. Johann Abraham Peter Schulz, Entwurf einer neuen und
leichtverständlichen Musiktabulatur, deren man sich, in Er-

mangelung der Notentypen, in kritschen und theoretischen
Schriften bedienen kann, und deren Zeichen in allen Buch-
druckereyen vorräthig sind, nebst einem Probeexemp__ (Plan
of a new and easily understood notation of music which will
serve if there is a lack of note types in critical and theoretical writings. These are available at all printers, and
a sample follows). Berlin: Verlag der Rellstabschen Musik-
handlung und Musikdruckerey.
Staff: None.
Register symbols: Indicated by five different printing faces.

Cicero antiqua versalia	Cicero Fraktur versalia
C D E F G A H	$\mathcal{L\ D\ E\ F\ G\ A\ H}$
C-B	c-b
Cicero antiqua gemein	Cicero Fraktur gemein
c d e f g a h	$c\ d\ n\ f\ g\ a\ f$
c¹-b¹	c²-b²

Cicero kursiv gemein
c d e f g a h
c³-b³

Pitch:
C *C D *D E F *F G *G A *A H C
C C# D D# E F F# G G# A A# B C
Other accidentals are indicated:
** = ⊠ ; b = ♭; ✝ = ♮.
Key signatures:
*/ = 1 sharp; **/ = 2 sharps; ♭, = 1 flat; b,, = 2 flats,
and so on.
Duration:
C D E F G

o   ρ   ſ   ⌐   ⌐

Rests:
I   1   1   1   1   1
    2   4   8   16 32

—   —   ⌇   7   ⅂   ⅂

Meter: 4∫4, 3∫2, 6∫8, for example.
Articulations:
C D E
(- - -) = legato | F G A (. . .) = staccato | C̈ G⃛ = tremolo
Upside-down letters are used to represent appoggiaturas.
Example 6-6. Chorale, Ein' feste Burg ist unser Gott.

**/4♪4   𝄐♪♪ a h *c♪*c h a ♪*c h a h a|g *f e d|

As a German opera director and a prolific composer of vocal
music, Schulz was obviously influenced in his notational scheme
by the needs of singers. For untrained musicians, the method
just described was fairly easy to comprehend. Like Rousseau,
Schulz wished to simplify not only the reading of vocal music
but also its printing. Having fewer symbols than required by
staff notation, and using much less space, the printing of
scores in alphabetical notation proved to be more economical,
a considerable advantage.

In his proposal title, Schulz pointed out that all printers were equipped with the various signs he required for duration, rests, meters, and articulations, as well as the five
type fonts that designated register. His reform, then, was
entirely feasible from the production standpoint. But feasible
or not, it did not succeed in establishing itself as a potent
innovation.

1789. Johannes Presbyter, "De musica antiqua et moderna" (Con-
    cerning old and new music), <u>Diphthérographie musicale</u> I,
    p. 396.
Staff: 6-line.
Clef signs:

and

Pitch:

    ut re mi   fa sol la
Duration: Not indicated, as the rhythm was based on the plain-
    chant melody, which was well-known to those who used this
    system of notation.
Example 6-7. Plainchant, <u>Ut queant laxis</u>.

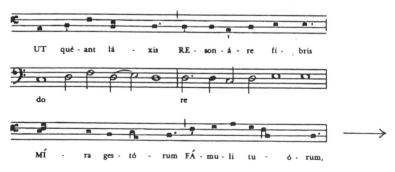

As is evident, Presbyter's system is based on the famous hymn
that formed the framework for Guido d'Arezzo's solmization
syllables. An unusual feature of the present proposal is the
fact that the pitch letters are set only on the staff lines;
also, no provision seems to have been made for the seventh
syllable of the scale, si.

1793. M. R. Patterson, <u>New Notation of Music</u>. Contained in a
   letter to Francis Hopkinson. London.
Staff: None.
Register symbols:

$\bar{A}$-$\bar{G}$	a-g	<u>a-g</u>	<u>A</u>-<u>G</u>
Octave 1	Octave 2	Octave 3	Octave 4

Pitch:

$A^n \quad A^x \quad B^b \quad B^n \quad B^x \quad C^b \quad C^n \quad D^n \quad D^x \quad E^b \quad E^n \quad E^x \quad F^b \quad F^n \quad F^x \quad G^b \quad G^n \quad A^n$

C   C# Db D   D# Eb E   F   F# Gb G   G# Ab A   A# Bb B   C

A = do (tonic) of any key, here applied to C major.
Duration:

A—   B. C: D; E,   F-

$\circ$ $\textstyle\downarrow$ $\textstyle\downarrow$ $\textstyle\downarrow$ $\textstyle\downarrow$ $\textstyle\downarrow$

<u>ACEG</u>: = ♪♪♪♪ | <u>abcd</u>, = ♪♪♪♪ | acbd- = ♪♪♪♪

AC;DFGD, = ♪♪♪♪♪
Rests:

—   •   :   ;   ,   -

Example 6-8.

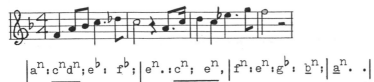

$$|a^n:c^nd^n;e^b: f^b;|e^n.:c^n; e^n,|f^n:e^n;g^b: \underline{b}^n;|\underline{a}^n. .|$$

Patterson pointed out in his letter to Francis Hopkinson that
his system for designating a four-octave span could be applied
to both treble and bass registers individually (as illustrated
above) as well as collectively, thus providing for an eight-
octave total gamut. Unique to Patterson's method among the
alphabetical systems surveyed are the signs for natural (n),
flat (b), and sharp (x), which are placed after the pitch letter rather than before it, or even over it, as might be expected. In many ways this method is visually cluttered and no
simpler in the final analysis than the equivalent in traditional notation.

1805. Pierre Jean Joubert de LaSalette, <u>Sténographie musicale,
ou manière abrégée d'écrire la musique à l'usage des compos-
iteurs et des imprimeries</u> (Musical shorthand, an abbreviated
method of writing music, for composers and printers). Paris:
Chez Goujon.
Staff: None.
Register symbols:

```
  c -b .      |c-b    |c - b    |ċ - b    |c̈ - b̈
  .. ..       | . .   |
  C-B         |c-b    |c¹-b¹    |c²-b²    |c³-b³
```

Pitch:

```
  ʜc  ʟc bd  ʜd  ʟd be  ʜc ʜf  ʟf bg  ʜg  ʟg ba  ʜa  ʟa
   C   C# Db   D   D# Eb   E  F   F# Gb   G   G# Ab   A   A#

  bb  ʜb  ʜc
   Bb  B   C
```

Key signatures: Called "modes" by LaSalette, the various tonalities are identified with the following symbols:

ʟ |ʟʟ |ʟʟʟ |b |bb

 1 sharp |2 sharps |3 sharps |1 flat |2 flats, and so on.

Duration:

```
  c|||      d||      e|      f      g      a̲
```

o   ♩.   ♩   ♩   ♪   ♪

Rests:

```
  0          |0          |0
             |2          |3
  1 beat    |2 beats   |3 beats, and so on.
```

Meter: Indicated by the number of measure beats; barlines
function as in orthochronic notation.
Example 6-9.

Basically, LaSalette's reform has its roots in early German
tablature notation but was also influenced by Rousseau's numerical method, in particular the device of placing dots over
or under the pitch letters to show specific register. Essentially, however, this system was retrogressive rather than
innovative, and it quickly faded into obscurity. This must
have been a truly frustrating experience for LaSalette, who
spent some twenty years developing his notational ideas. But
as we have seen again and again, good intentions and devoted
labor do not guarantee success in the devising of new ways to
notate music.

1808. Johann Michael Haydn, [A notation proposal]. Berlin:
Bliesener.
Staff: None.
Register symbols:
 For tenors | For basses
 (a-(z   )a-)z
Pitch:

 a b c d e f g h i j k l m n o p q r s ß

 G G# Ab A A# Bb B B# cb c c# db d d# eb e e# fb f f#

 ß t u v w x y z

 gb g g# ab a a# bb b

Duration: Large letters designate half-notes and small letters,
quarter-notes; for eighth-notes, the letters are closer together.
Rests:

 ! ? . ; ,

 — — ⚡ 7 ᚵ

Example 6-10. Chorale, Ein' feste Burg ist unser Gott.

(m (m (m (d(g (k (m(k (g (d (m (k (g (d (g(d
(a(s (p (m

Michael Haydn, a younger brother of Franz Joseph Haydn, was
the music director for the Archbishop of Salzburg, and his
notation reform was a natural outgrowth of his responsibility
for choral performances at the cathedral. He also taught composition, and one of his most illustrious pupils was the future pioneer of German romantic opera, Carl Maria von Weber.

A particularly interesting feature of this proposal, and
one seldom encountered in all the letter systems of notation,
is the inclusion of letters for the enharmonic spelling of
each pitch of the chromatic scale from C up to b. Also notable
are the three forms of the letter S in the lowercase old German script used by Haydn.

1810. Charles Guillaume Riebesthal, <u>Nouvelle méthode pour noter</u>
<u>la musique et pour l'imprimer avec des caractères mobiles</u>
(New notational method and printing music with movable type).
Strassburg: Levrault.
Staff: None.
Register symbols: A six-octave span is designated by the fol-
lowing sequence of letters:

		Troisième	⚹	ℓ	μ	φ	γ	λ	σ
Octaves aiguës....	*En montant.*	Deuxième	U	R	M	F	G	L	S
		Première	*u*	*r*	*m*	*f*	*g*	*l*	*s*
		Première	ᴎ	⌐	ᴝ	⟍	σ	⌐	ᵔ
Octaves graves....	*En descendant.*	Deuxième	⊐	⅄	Ⅿ	⌐	⌒	⌐	ꭢ
		Troisième	α	⌒	⅄	⊖	⌵	⋗	⌒

Pitch: The diatonic scale, ut—si, is outlined by the series
   ut ré mi fa sol la si
of letters shown above.
Duration:

U.   r   M   f

♩.   ♩   ♪   ♬

Example 6-11. Contre-danse, <u>La Soliphie</u>.

In theory, Riebesthal's mirror relationship of the lower octave pitch letters with the series for the upper octave is
reasonable; however, requiring the singer to read the letters
placed on their sides is unreasonable. The inventor should
not have been surprised by the early demise of his proposal.

1811. Samuel Rootsey, <u>An attempt to simplify the notation of
music, together with an account of that now in use. Illustrated by examples, both sacred and secular</u>. London: Bald-
win.
Staff: None.
Register symbols:

Men's voices	Women's voices
<u>a-m</u> <u>n-z</u>	a - m n - z
C-B c-b	c^1-b^1 c^2-b^2

Pitch: The letters a to z, omitting j and u, outline a two-
octave span.

a	b	c	d	e	f	g	h	i	k	l	m	n - z
C	C#	D	D#	E	F	F#	G	G#	A	A#	B	C — B
	D♭		E♭			G♭		A♭		B♭		

Duration:

ā b̄ c̄   a b c   (a) (b) (c)   (ab)   (a b)   a; b, (ȧḃċ)

This system uses no barlines and each beat is set off by
a comma.
Rests: All durations are indicated by a period.

Example 6-12. Thomas Tallis, <u>The Evening Hymn</u>.

$$
\left\{
\begin{array}{l}
\text{h,} \quad \text{mm} \quad \text{,mm} \quad \text{gg} \quad \text{, hm} \quad \text{,kk, hh} \quad \text{,hg,h;m,} \quad \text{hh} \quad , \\
\text{c,} \quad \text{hh} \quad \text{,hh,k(kmn),m(kh),nn,m(mnp),kk,h;p,(nm)(kh),} \\
\underline{\text{h}}\text{,(}\underline{\text{vtr}}\text{)(}\underline{\text{pn}}\text{),}\underline{\text{mh}}\text{,} \; \underline{\text{pp}} \quad \text{,} \; \underline{\text{rr}} \; \text{,}\underline{\text{tt}}\text{,} \; \underline{\text{vm}} \quad \text{,}\underline{\text{np}}\text{,}\underline{\text{h}}\text{;}\underline{\text{v}}\text{,} \quad \underline{\text{rp}} \quad ,
\end{array}
\right.
$$

$$
\left\{
\begin{array}{l}
\text{kh,} \quad \text{gg} \quad \text{,k(hg),cc,hk,hg,h.} \\
\text{nm,k(kh),g(ec),eg,hn,mk,h.} \\
\underline{\text{tv}}\text{,} \; \underline{\text{pp}} \quad \text{,} \; \underline{\text{pm}} \quad \text{,}\underline{\text{np}}\text{,}\underline{\text{rn}}\text{,}\underline{\text{pp}}\text{,}\underline{\text{h}}\text{.}
\end{array}
\right.
$$

Rootsey's account of the notation of his time was one of the
first such surveys, predating by a dozen years the better-
known treatises by Georges Marie Raymond and Joseph Raymondi.
Evidently Rootsey was more successful in his analysis of others' notation than he was in establishing his own proposed
alphabetical system.

The two letter methods of Rootsey and Michael Haydn (see
page 344) warrant comparison; both make use of the alphabet,
a to z, complete in Haydn's notation and nearly so in Rootsey's. By duplicating the series of letters used for the bass
voice two octaves higher for soprano voices, Rootsey increased
to four octaves the total range available. There is no question that his choice of type font for both series of letters
is much easier to read than Haydn's old German script -- at
least for non-Germans.

1815. Johann Friedrich Samuel Döring, <u>Vollständiges Alten-</u>
<u>burger Choral-Melodien-Buch in Buchstaben vierstimmung</u>
<u>gesetzt</u> (Complete book of alphabetical chorale melodies in
four parts, for the city of Altenburg). Görlitz, Germany:
Gotthold Heinze.
Staff: None.

Register symbols:

Boldface capitals	Lowercase Latin	Lowercase italics	Cursive
C-H	c-h	$c - h$	c-d-e
C-B	c-b	c^1-b^1	c^2-b^2

Pitch:

C 'C ,D D 'D ,E E F 'F ,G G 'G ,A A 'A ,H H C

C C# Db D D# Eb E F F# Gb G G# Ab A A# Bb B C

Duration:

C= 'D= ,E= f g a c'd,e

Example 6-13. J. S. Bach, "Chorale," from the Saint Matthew Passion.

```
S   h | h h'a'f | h'c d  d e d'c
A   a | g'g'f'c | h'f'f  h |'c h'a
T  'f | e d'c'a | e e de'f | g'f'f
B  'd | e'e'f'f |'g'a h  h |'a h'f
```

In common with nearly all the proposers of either alphabetical or numerical notation systems, Döring aimed to make it easier for the untrained church congregations to sing hymns and chorales. His method, which had much in common with the German organ tablature of the period, is unique only in being designed for use in a specific city. It must be said that although his cursive script for the two-line octave is ingenious, at the same time it is not easy to read or to write.

1833. Antonmaria Nichetti, Prospetto di un nuòvo modo più agevole di scrittura musicale (Prospect of a new and more comfortable method of musical notation). Padua: Tipografia del Seminario.
Staff: 2-line; the lines are widely spaced,
Clef signs: See Example 6-14.

Pitch:

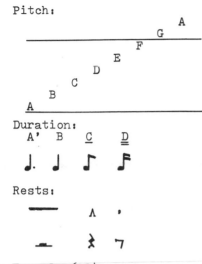

Duration:

A'   B   C   D

♩.   ♩   ♪   𝅘𝅥𝅯

Rests:

▬   ∧   •

▬   𝄽   7

Example 6-14.

It would require a charitable disposition, indeed, to agree
with Nichetti that his system is a "more comfortable method of
musical notation." Specifically, the pitch levels in the example shown are erratic, and the durational indications are
haphazard, to say the least. There is no record of this notation having been used by anyone other than its inventor.

1841. Reverend John Curwen and John Spencer Curwen, <u>How to
Read Music and Understand It. Staff Notation and Tonic Sol-
Fa</u>. London: J. Curwen & Sons, Ltd.
Staff: None.
Register symbols:

d̲ r̲ m̲, or d r m | d r m | d̄ r̄ m̄, or d́ ŕ ḿ
                    | |
c-b | c¹-b¹ | c²-b²

Pitch: The pitch letters of the scale are derived from the
Anglicized spellings of the solmization syllables. Doh (d)
is transferred to a new tonic for all modulations.

d de ra r   re ma m   f   fe sa s   se la l   le ta t   d

C C# Db D   D# Eb E   F   F# Gb G   G# Ab A   A# Bb B   C

doh   ray   me fah   soh   lah   te doh

Key signatures: Indicated by the name of the tonality.
   Key G; Key B♭; Key F♯, and so on.
Duration: The distance between the pitch symbols is propor-
   tional to their duration.
Rests: All values are designated by blank space.
Meter:

| \| | \| | \|\| | \| | \|.d .r | \|,m ,f | \|__s __s |
| primary beat | secondary beats | ½-beat | ¼-beat | held note |

Example 6-15. Chorale, <u>Ein' feste Burg ist unser Gott</u>.

d̄ | d̄ d̄ |.s.l t̄ |.d̄.t̄ l | s d̄ | t̄ l | s .l.s |.f.m r | d

A former minister in the Church of England, and someone completely untrained in music, Curwen had to approach the teaching of sight-singing as a beginner himself. His method was
largely developed from the Norwich Sol-Fa System (sometimes
referred to as the Lancashire System) of Sarah Ann Glover,
first put forward in her <u>Scheme to Render Psalmody Congrega-
tional</u> (1835). Devised solely for the teaching of vocal music
to children and what were then euphemistically called the
"lower classes," Curwen's method had sociological-religious
implications for its inventor.

   Best suited to simple, uncomplicated melodies, his approach
was criticized by professional musicians as actually retarding
the progress of music pedagogy. Be that as it may, Curwen's
system was so successful that his book went through many printings. Furthermore, a Tonic Sol-Fa Association was formed in
England in 1853, followed ten years later by a "College" devoted to the teaching of Curwen's reform. In addition, numerous Tonic Sol-Fa choral societies were established throughout
the country; indeed, many are still active to this day.

   Curwen's <u>How to Read Music</u> was a joint collaboration with
his son, as was his <u>The Standard course of lessons and exercises in the Tonic Sol-Fa Method of Teaching Music</u>, published
in 1872. Seven years later Curwen established the London publishing house of John Curwen & Sons, Ltd., a firm that is still
in existence.

   The Curwen method of solfege, highly successful in its own
right, also motivated a number of subsequent proposals on the
Continent. Related systems were developed by the German teacher
Agnes Hundoegger (1850), the Frenchman Alexander Brody in his
<u>Nouveau systeme de notation</u> (1854), and the Spaniard Julian
Vidales (1856; see page 352). Each largely duplicated the Curwens' method of vocal notation, with only minor, individual
alterations.

1845. Sarah Ann Glover, <u>Norwich Sol-Fa System</u>. Norwich, England: Hamilton & Jarrold.
Staff: None.

Register symbols:

Low	Middle	High
S ` L ` T `	S L T	S´ L´ T´

Pitch:

S   Soy Low L Loy Tow T D Doy Row R Roy Mow M F Foy Sow

G G# Ab A A# Bb B C C# Db D D# Eb E F F# Gb

Sol   La   Ti Do   Re   Mi Fa

D (Do) is the tonic of any key.

Duration:

D R M   d r m   —D   —r

♩   ♪   prolonged note

Rests:

+	+2	+3 2	+4 3 2
1 beat	2 beats	3 beats	4 beats, and so on.

Meter: S = strong beat in simple or compound time; .L = weak
    beat in simple time; !T = weak beat in compound time.

Example 6-16. Chorale, <u>Ein' feste Burg ist unser Gott</u>.

.d´ | d´ .d | s´l´ .t | d´t´ .i | s´ .d | t´ .i | s´ .i´s´ | fm .r   d

The Norwich Sol-Fa System is, in part, an expansion of the
author's notation reform first published in 1835 as the <u>Scheme
to Render Psalmody Congregational</u>. It also represents a modification of John Curwen's solfege methods, which came out four
years before the appearance of the Norwich Sol-Fa System. A
certain amount of cross-fertilization thus took place between
the two methods, both designed to facilitate the sight-reading
of hymns. Both inventors also further refined their individual
approaches to the problem, and in its final form Glover's method emerged under the impressive title of <u>A Development of the
Tetrachordal System, Designed to Facilitate the Acquisition
of Music, by a Return to First Principles</u> (5).
    "The present little treatise," she wrote in her foreword,
"explains a literal notation of music intelligible to the most
infant mind, yet calculated to serve as an introduction to a
scientific use of the customary notation of music." This is
debatable, at best, yet we must credit both Glover and the
Curwens with possessing the true zeal and commitment of the
dedicated reformer.

1855. Juan-Nepomuceno Adorno, <u>Système mélographique absolu</u>
    (Absolute melographic system). Paris: Firmin Didot frères.
Staff: 5-line (2-3), arranged vertically.
Register symbols: The same as used in Adorno's <u>Système mélo-
    graphique relatif</u> (see page 21).
Pitch: Capital letters representing time values are set on
    the appropriate lines and spaces in lieu of conventional
    noteheads.

Duration:

Rests:

Example 6-17.

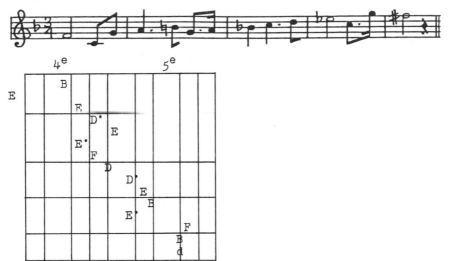

This, the second phase of Adorno's <u>Système mélographique</u>, was aimed primarily at facilitating transposition. Here, he also extended his use of letters by abbreviating certain ornaments and performance directives, as for instance,

 tr = trill   m = mordent   EF⌐ = appoggiatura

It is difficult to see, however, that his letters representing durational values are more effective than the ordinary note-heads on staff lines and spaces, together with the stems, flags, and beams he used previously.

1856. Julian Vidales, <u>Nuevo método para aprender la música por letras</u> (New method of learning music by means of letters) n.p., the author.

Staff: 2-line.

Register symbols:

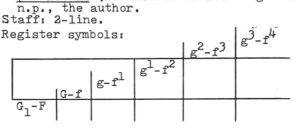

Pitch:
    s s; l! l l; c! c d d; r! r r; m! m f f; s! s

    G G# Ab A A# Bb B C C# Db D D# Eb E F F# Gb G
    A canceling natural sign is designated by a question mark
    following the letter; for example:
    s? = G♮, l? = A♮, m? = E♮, and so on.
Duration:
    s:: l:. c: d. r, m f̄ s̲

Rests: All values are represented by a line through the pitch
    letter; for example:
    s̶, l̶, e̶, and so on.
Meter: The number of beats per measure is shown as follows:

    (..) = $\frac{2}{4}$ |(...) = $\frac{3}{4}$ |(......) = $\frac{6}{8}$, for example.

Example 6-18.

		c:	m:		m:	m:		m.	r,d,r:		
(....)		;s;:			;s. l:	;s.	l:	‡	l.		
		m	m,r,d,c,		d	c	l;:				
		m			m	m	f	;f			

r:		c:	c:
l.	s?,;f,s		m;:
c		r	r
s:.		l,s,	d

Although this method of Vidales was loosely based on the solfege systems of Sarah Ann Glover and John Curwen (see pages
349 and 351), it seems to be designed for instrumental music
as well, because of the wide pitch range it can accommodate.
We may safely assume, however, that few musicians of the period greeted Vidales' proposal with marked enthusiasm.

___

1861. Louis Albert Joseph Danel, Méthode simplifiée pour l'en-
    seignement populaire de la musique vocale (Simplified method
    for teaching elementary vocal music). Lille, France: the
    author.
Staff: None.

Register symbols:

D - B. |D–B |D–B |D̈–B̈ |D̈ - B̈

Octave 1| Octave 2| Octave 3| Octave 4| Octave 5

Pitch:

D   R   M   F   S   L   B   D

ut   re   mi   fa   sol la   si   ut

Chromatic alterations are shown by lowercase letters.

l = ♭, z = #

Duration:

a   e   i   o   u   v(eu)   ᴧ(ou)

𝅝   𝅗𝅥   ♩   ♪   𝅘𝅥𝅯   𝅘𝅥𝅰   𝅘𝅥𝅱

The actual notation consists of a series of syllables comprising the pitch letters, the durational letters, and any
chromatic alterations of the diatonic pitches, as demonstrated in the example below.

Example 6-19.

Del Mi | Fil-o Soz Lo Bo Ruz | Mi Bel | Lo So Mol Ro Si | Del-i|

"Simplified" is surely a misnomer for this proposal; the compound syllables are far more difficult to memorize than are
the standard noteheads and accompanying accidentals. It is
perfectly true that, in his system, Danel combines three elements in one symbol, a highly desirable goal in any notational
reform, but his solution is impractical. Not the least of the
problems engendered in reading Danel's notation are one's in-
voluntary reactions to the implicit humor in certain of the
syllable combinations -- suz, lil, mul, liz, to cite a few
such instances. Listeners to music may not need to keep a
straight face at all times, but performers generally must.

1873. Ebenezer P. Stewart, Improvement in Music-Notation. U.S.
    Patent 138,104.
Staff: 3-line (1-2); the outer lines are printed red and the
    central line is blue.
Clef signs: Not discussed by the author.
Pitch: Three different alternative methods are proposed: 1)
    by pitch letter, 2) by diatonic scale syllable, and 3) by
    numbers, which indicate rhythmic values.

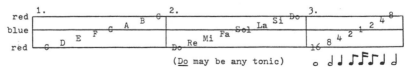

(Do may be any tonic)   𝅝 𝅗𝅥 𝅘𝅥 𝅘𝅥𝅯𝅘𝅥𝅯𝅘𝅥𝅯 𝅘𝅥 𝅗𝅥

Duration: For the first two systems, the note values are shown
by the relative distances of the successive letters or syllables within the barlines. In the third system, the numbers
indicate the rhythmic distinctions, as demonstrated above.
Rests:

System 1	System 2	System 3
~~G~~ ~~D~~ ~~E~~	~~Fa~~ ~~Sol~~ ~~La~~	~~16~~ ~~8~~ ~~4~~ ~~8~~ ~~4~~
all values	all values	▬ ▬ 𝄾 7 ⌐

Example 6-20.

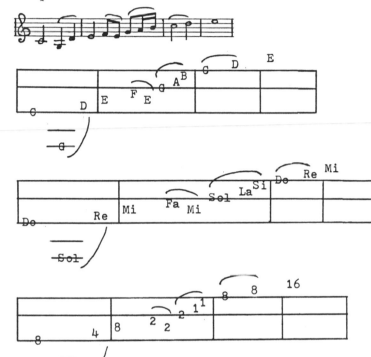

"Be it known that I, Ebenezer P. Stewart, of Cotton Plant, in
the county of Tippah and State of Mississippi, have invented
a new and Improved System of Musical Notation," begins the inventor's description of his proposal. The object, as one can
easily anticipate, was "to simplify the method of writing and
to facilitate the reading of music." Even a citizen of Cotton
Plant can aspire to glory by devising a new and better way of
notating music. History, however, has deemed otherwise, and
Stewart's reform gathered dust on the shelves of the United
States Patent Office until this researcher unearthed it.

1879. D. Agostino Micci, <u>Nuòvo sistèma musicale</u> (New musical
  system). Rome: Tipografia della pace.
Staff: None.
Register symbols: The author makes provision for a nine-octave
  gamut, a span which even the modern orchestra cannot encompass.

D - S	D - S	D - S	D - S	D - S	D̄ - S̄
Octave 1	Octave 2	Octave 3	Octave 4	Octave 5	Octave 6

D̂ - Ŝ	D̿ - S̿	D̂̂ - Ŝ̂
Octave 7	Octave 8	Octave 9

Pitch:

D	A	R	E	M	F	I	S	O	L	U	**S**	D

C	C#	D	D#	E	F	F#	G	G#	A	A#	B	C
	Db		Eb			Gb		Ab		Bb		

Note that the letter S for the pitch of B (si) is thicker
than that for G (sol).

Duration:

| | |	\V/ \V/ 2 2	\\V/ \\V/ 3 3	• •	: :
D A R	E M or I S	O L or U D	R M	S A
1 beat	2 beats	3 beats	½-beat	¼-beat

Rests: Shown by blank space.
Example 6-21.

In one of those odd coincidences that occasionally surface
during research, it was discovered that, in the year 1879, two
musicians proposed alphabetical notation systems, both with
provision for a nine-octave gamut. It is highly unlikely that
Micci, who resided in Rome, and John Russ (next discussed),
who lived in the United States, could have known about each
other's proposal. Clearly, the Italian's method is the more
practical, discounting his unrealistic provision for an unnecessarily extended range. Micci's choice of vowels to char-
acterize the sharped and flatted notes is simple, and he clev-
erly avoids the ambiguity of two letter S's by making one
heavier in outline. Only his symbology for duration is questionable, especially as it relates only to beats and not to
precise orthochronic values.

_____

1879. John D. Russ, <u>Letter Music, or Musical Tones Expressed</u>
  <u>by Letters</u>. Paterson, New Jersey: the author.
Staff: None.

Register symbols: Nine octaves are designated by the following
type fonts for the notes of the diatonic scale:

c^5-b^5 c d e f g a b

c^4-b^4 C D E F G A B

c^3-b^3 C D E F G A B

c^2-b^2 c d e f g a b

c^1-b^1 C D E F G A B

c-b   c d e f g a b

C-B   C D E F G A B

C_1-B_1 C D E F G A B

C_2-B_2 C D E F G A B

Pitch: By letter, as shown above.
Duration:

C   Ď   Ė   (Ḟ)   (G̅)

♩   𝅝   ♩   ♪   𝅘𝅥𝅮

The author also provided a chart of modified pitch letters
for what he termed "high" and "low" half-notes:

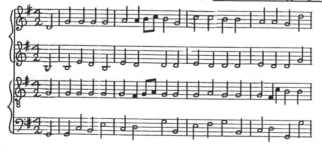

Barlines are shown as inverted semicolons.
Rests: The symbol ⌒ serves for all durations.
Example 6-22. Thomas Tallis, The Evening Hymn.

This author's setting of the Thomas Tallis hymn should be compared with Samuel Rootsey's version on page 347. There are a
number of discrepancies in the present setting, particularly
in the hymn tune proper, given here to the soprano voice. (In
Rootsey's version it is in the tenor part.)

Judging from the example of Letter Music provided by its
inventor, one would naturally assume that his system was intended for vocal music. But considering the nine-octave span
of modified letters, one must believe that Russ also had instrumental writing in mind, even though the very lowest and
highest pitches provided for do not exist on any instrument
known to us today. Even if these notes could be produced elec-
tronically, they would be inaudible as specific pitches to
the human ear -- so what is the point?

1898. Daniel Eyquem, <u>Nouvelle méthode d'écriture musicale avec
application de la théorie des douze sons</u> (New musical nota-
tion and its application to the theory of the twelve tones).
Paris: Henry Lemoine et Cie.
Staff: 2-line; the lines are widely spaced apart.
Clef signs: None.
Pitch:

C C# Db D D# Eb E   F F# Gb G G# Ab A A# Bb B C

do   re   mi fa   sol   la   si do

Duration:

Large majuscule (**D**)   Large majuscule underlined (**R**)
o   ♩

Small majuscule with   Small majuscule with stem
attached stem (**D**)   and flag(s) (**R**)
♩   ♪

Example 6-23. Chorale, <u>Ein' feste Burg ist unser Gott</u>.

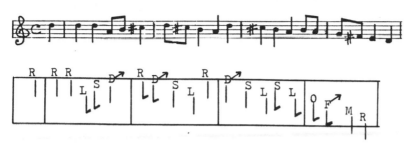

Eyquem's proposal received its impetus from a system that was
published in 1863 under the title <u>Choix de cantiques pour les
missions</u> (Selection of songs for missions). Retaining the
standard pentagram, this notation consisted of the letters
U R M A O L S, representing ut, ré, mi, fa, sol, la, si, the
letters placed on the appropriate lines and spaces of the
staff. This procedure essentially duplicates the method of
Johannes Presbyter (see page 341), who placed his pitch letters on the lines of a six-line staff. Eyquem substituted D
for U (do for ut) and F for A, but retained the O for sol. He
also favored a two-line rather than a five-line staff, the
pitch letters set on different levels between the pair of
lines.

    The use of majuscule letters injects a visual problem, how-
ever, because, for the average reader of music or of prose,
some majuscule type is more difficult to decipher than ordinary type. And, needless to say, majuscule letters are time-
consuming for the copyist to write properly. Eyquem's system
might have proved more durable had he relied on a more basic,
simple typeface.

1900. Pierre DeLaruelle and Louis Cossart, <u>Nouvelle notation
    musicale</u> (New music notation). Paris?: the authors.
Staff: 5-line.
Clef signs:
  G-clef (Sol) | C-clef (Do) | F-clef (Fa)

Pitch:
  D   R   M   F   S   L   s̸   D
  C   D   E   F   G   A   B   C

  do   ré   mi   fa   sol la   si   do
Key signatures: Displayed conventionally.
Duration:
  D   R   M   F   S
  2   1   ½   ¼   ⅛

Rests:

2   1 $\frac{1}{2}$ $\frac{1}{4}$ $\frac{1}{8}$

Meter: A number representing the subdivisions of the primary
beats of the measure takes the place of the customary denominator; for example,

$\frac{4}{2} = \frac{4}{4}$, $\frac{6}{3} = \frac{6}{8}$, $\frac{9}{3} = \frac{9}{8}$.

Example 6-24.

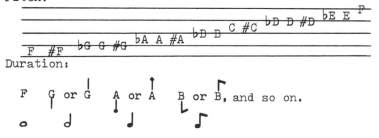

These two notation reformers rather neatly solved the problem
of using two S's in their series of scale syllable letters;
the slash through the lowercase ȿ for si in the scale is easy
to write and obvious in intent. Comparison might be made with
Micci's solution of the same problem (page 356) -- a thicker
S instead of a slash through the letter. As is true for most
of the alphabetical notations already discussed, this joint
venture was designed primarily for vocal solmization and was
not intended to apply to instrumental music.

1900. J. B. Hill and M. W. Hill. The home teacher in Hill's
new notation makes music easy for students of the organ and
piano. Laurens, South Carolina: the authors.
Staff: 5-line.
Clef signs: Standard G- and F-clefs.
Pitch:

Duration:

F   G or G̣   A or Ạ   B or Ḅ, and so on.

Rests: Traditional forms, except for the quarter-rest: ⌠ .

Example 6-25.

The Hills' method departs from traditional notation only in substituting pitch letters for noteheads on the staff. Why this system should be easier for the keyboard student is neither convincingly argued nor conclusively demonstrated by the authors in their explanation and accompanying musical examples. To substitute letters for noteheads on the normal five-line staff is really an exercise in futility. The letters are actually harder to read than are conventional noteheads, especially when they are stacked vertically in chords, as demonstrated in Example 6-25.

1902. José Pereira de Sampaio, <u>Théorie exacte et notation finale de la musique</u> (Correct theory and ultimate musical notation). Porto, Portugal: Empreza editoria da "Historia de Portugal, de Schaefer."
Staff: None.
Register symbols:

d^1-c^1 | d^2-c^2 | d^3-c^3 | d^4-c^4 | d^5-c^5 | d^6-c^6 | d^7-c^7

C_1-B_1 | C-B | c-b | c^1-b^1 | c^2-b^2 | c^3-b^3 | c^4-b^4

Pitch:

d 'd 'r r 'r 'm m f 'f 's s 's 'l l 'l 'c c d

C C# Db D D# Eb E F F# Gb G G# Ab A A# Bb B C
Duration:

Example 6-26. J. S. Bach, "Prelude in C," from <u>The Well-Tempered Clavier</u>, Book I.

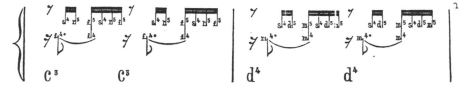

This notation is not, and can never be, the "ultimate notation." For one thing, Pereira de Sampaio's device for pitch
alteration is unclear -- the same mark is used both for raising and lowering a note. Only in context would one know which
was required, and even then one's decision might be open to
question. The numbers attached to the pitch letters, minuscule
in the original notation, are a visual hazard; they are difficult to read, especially when stems and flags are in close
proximity. It is no mystery, therefore, that this proposal has
never become what its inventor so obviously hoped -- a "final"
notational reform.

1908. Joseph A. Shires, <u>Music Notation</u>. U.S. Patent 881,085.
Staff: 5-line.
Clef signs: Standard G-clef only.
Pitch: As the system is designed solely for single-line vocal
   music, the textual words or their component syllables are
   set on the staff lines and spaces in place of noteheads.
Duration:
   1 |2 |3
   the denominator value, |2 beats (♩) |3 beats, and so on.
   or 1 beat (♩)
Example 6-27. Western folksong, <u>Red River Valley</u>.

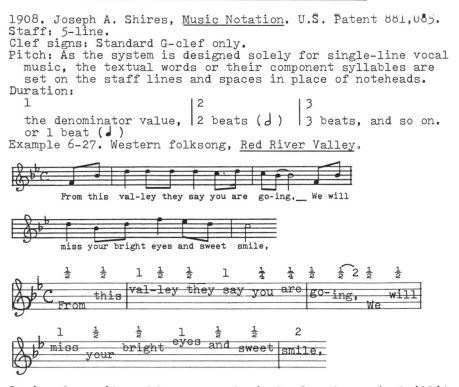

Designed, so it would seem, exclusively for the musical illiterate, Shires' proposal could perhaps serve for very well-known
hymns and secular songs, the relative position of the textual
words on the staff being only a general reminder to the singer.

Otherwise, this notational method is too primitive to have validity in the continuing search for widely applicable new notation.

1925. William B. Glisson, <u>Musical Notation</u>. U.S. Patent
1,551,819.
Staff: 3-line; the top line is broken.
Clef signs:
   Treble (G-clef) | Alto (C-clef) | Bass (F-clef)

Example 6-28.

It was naive of this notation inventor to assume that a person
could easily read letters and numbers placed on their sides.
Though Glisson's system does eliminate accidental signs, to
retain them before the pitch letters would make reading more
comfortable for the performer. Certainly the rest symbols
would be more readily visible standing alone in normal position, rather than laid sideways. But such arguments are aca-

demic when a proposal appears to have no chance of adoption
by present-day notators.

1950. F. Hettiger Verlag, <u>Klavier Selbstunterricht</u> (The piano
self-taught). Lorrach, Germany: Hettiger verlag.
Staff: 3-line; the lines are widely spaced and heavily drawn.
Clef signs: None; the upper space is for the right hand, and
the lower space is for the left hand.
Pitch:

C C̄ D D̄ E F F̄ G Ḡ A Ā B C

C C# D D#E F F# G G# A A# B C
   Db   Eb   Gb   Ab   Bb

Note-letters in the right hand above 1-line b are printed
in red, as are the letters in the left hand below small c.
Letters in the octave from c to b are printed in blue.
Duration:

C--- |D-- |E- |F |g
4 beats |3 beats |2 beats |1 beat |½-beat

Meter: The number of eighth-notes per measure takes the place
of a time signature; for example,

4 beats = $\frac{2}{4}$ (four eighths), 6 beats = $\frac{3}{4}$ (six eighths).

Example 6-29. Franz Schubert, <u>Sonata in C Minor</u>, op. posth.

4					
Right	Ḡ—GGAG	Ḡ— —Ā	C C C̄ C̄	C̄—Ā
hand	C—C̄—	D̄— dfgf D̄D̄	A G A	G—G
			D̄ C C F	D̄——
Left	D̄—D̄—	D̄— —D̄	D̄ E F C̄	D̄——
hand	Ḡ—Ā—	C c CG	G Ḡ F C̄	D̄——

This system, like that of the Sullivan Conservatorium of Music
(see page 65), is the product of a publishing firm rather than
an individual. One assumes, therefore, that the editors joint-
ly arrived at a consensus on its format and symbology. It was
designed for piano music used in teaching children and adult
beginners, evidently of a rather simple harmonic and rhythmic
texture. It is, however, somewhat surprising to find a publisher advocating the use of color printing of certain notes
-- surely an important economic consideration, if nothing else.
As with the Sullivan Conservatorium system, we have no report
on the successful use of this keyboard method.

1964. Barry S. Brook and Murray Gould, "Notating Music with
   Ordinary Typewriter Characters," <u>Fontes Artis Musicae</u> **XI**, 3,
   pp. 142-159.
Staff: None.
Register symbols: None; the G-clef is implied.
Pitch:
   Indicated by capital letters for a note within a 4th of the
   previous pitch: C bE #F B, and so on.
   For a note more than a 4th higher: C ;G bE 'bD.
   More than a 4th lower: bB ,bE, D ,#F, and so on.
   More than an octave higher: C ''E, D ''G#.
   More than an octave lower: C ,,bB, A ,,F.
   Sharps are written as # or x, flats as b, and naturals as n.
   Double-sharps are xx, and double-flats are bb.
Key signatures: #FC = D major; #FCm = B minor; bBEA = Eb
   major; bBEAm = C minor, for example.
Duration:
   1C   2D   4E   8F   6G   3A   5B   7C   9D   0E

   (8CDE) = |(4EGBDF5) =

   1C——4C = |2(D) =

Augmentation dot = . , barline = / , double bar = //.
There is one space between consecutive pitch letters, tie
signs, and rests, except when "beamed" notes are within
parentheses.
Rests:
   1-   2-   4-   8- |4E(-)

             , and so on.

Meter:
   44 = $\frac{4}{4}$, 34 = $\frac{3}{4}$, 68 = $\frac{6}{8}$, and so on.
Tempo:
   2-120 = ♩ = 120 |6-80 = ♪ = 80, for example.
Performance directives:
   Trill (tr) = t, tremolo = w, glissando = j, repeat = /:/.
Example 6-30.

   Mod 4-66 #FCG 34 8-E/8C.6B 8A.6G 8B.6A/8G.6F 4F 8-F/

   8D.6C 8B.6#A 8C.6B/4nA

Somewhat facetiously subtitled <u>A Plaine and Easie Code System</u> <u>for Musicke</u>, this typewriter proposal was devised primarily for library card and thematic catalogues, union catalogues and indexes, research projects requiring tabulations and charts, and musical examples in books and articles. It is not, then, a method of notation for composers or arrangers, and it certainly is not a system for performers to read.

The authors postulated the following "optimum conditions" for the eventual success of their new proposal:

1) "It must be speedy, simple, absolutely accurate as to pitch and rhythm. It should be as closely related mnemonically to musical notation as possible, so that it appears natural and right, avoiding arbitrary symbols. It should require only a single line of typewritten characters without the need of back-spacing or for a second pass over the line. It should be usable by non-musicians with only a few minutes of instruction. It must be easily recognizable as music from the symbols alone and immediately retranslatable, without loss, into conventional notation.
2) It must be applicable to all western music, from Gregorian chant to serial music.
3) It must be universally understandable and internationally acceptable.
4) It must be so devised as to be readily transferable to electronic data-processing equipment for key transposition, fact-finding, tabulating and other research purposes."

Optimum conditions, indeed. One can easily shoot holes in the authors' contentions, such as suggesting that a nonmusician could master the system "with only a few minutes of instruction." And why would a nonmusician use the system anyway? Critics of the proposal have pointed out that no provision was made for key transposition, a lack that is perhaps moot inasmuch as there seems little likelihood that the Brook-Gould system will ever gain the international acceptance its authors desire.

1967. Benke Lajos, "Javaslat a tizenkétfokú hangrendszer új írásmodjára" (Recommendation for a New Way of Notating the Twelve-Tone System), <u>Magyar zene</u> VIII, 4, pp. 401-407.
Staff: 2-line; the lines are widely spaced apart.
Clef signs: As shown in Example 6-31.
Pitch:

d	v	r	p	m	f	n	s	c	l	b	t	d
C	C#	D	D#	E	F	F#	G	G#	A	A#	B	C
	Db		Eb			Gb		Ab		Bb		
do	vu	re	po	mi	fa	ne	so	cu	la	be	ti	do

Duration:

Example 6-31.

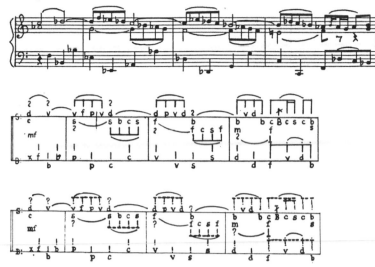

Lajos made three different proposals in his _Magyar zene_ article: The first uses a five-line staff and normal noteheads
with stems alternating in position; this was discussed and
illustrated on page 262. The second and third proposals rely
on letters for the pitches, derived from the syllables for
each note of the chromatic scale. The third system also incorporates some stenographic symbols, such as using the question mark in place of the half-note symbol used in the second
proposal.

One outstanding drawback to both letter systems is that
the different sizes of intervals are the same in relation to
the staff lines, as are the directions of pitch successions.
Lajos' first method of notation is thus the most practical of
his three proposals.

Just as numerical notation will in all probability never supersede the familiar method inherited from the past, neither
will alphabetical systems be ultimately accepted as superior
procedures in committing music to paper. And it is even more
certain that stenographic notation, considered in chapter 7,
will not become the preferred mode of music notation in the
years ahead. So we are left with a time-tested, eminently
logical, and essentially pragmatic system of notating music
that is preferable to all the many reforms advanced during
some three hundred years of musical history.

NOTES

1. Athanasius Kircher, Musurgia universalis sive Ars magna consoni et dissoni in X. libros digesta. Rome: Extypographia haeredum Francisci Corbelletti, 1650.

2. Lord Brabazon of Tara, "Simplification of Music Notation," Nature, vol. 149, no. 3785 (1942), pp. 554-555.

3. English translation by Benito Rivera; issued as Synopsis of New Music (Colorado Springs: Colorado College Music Press, 1977).

4. Andreas Werckmeister, Musikalische Temperatur, in his Hypomnemata musica, oder musikalisches Memorial, welches bestebet in kurzer Erinnerung dessen. . . . (Quedlinburg: Theodor Philipp Calvisius, 1697).

5. Sarah Ann Glover, A Development of the Tetrachordal System, Designed to Facilitate the Acquisition of Music, by a Return to First Principles. Norwich, England: the author, 1850.

7.
Stenographic Systems

An integrated notation involves much more than
merely inventing it; that would be easy, but to
make it immediately comprehensible and translat-
able into physical acts is another thing.

--Harry Partch, Genesis of a Music, 1949.

Stenographic, or shorthand, musical notation may be considered
an inevitable byproduct of experiments with numerical and alphabetical systems. In the search for an efficient notation
easy enough for the musically illiterate, some species of
stenographic symbology was inescapable. For its advocates,
this form of notation was as effective as number and letter
systems, but simpler.
    The science of stenography, we are told, dates back as far
as the first century B.C., when a Roman scribe in Cicero's
household, Marcus Tullius Tiro, invented a shorthand method
he called "brief writing." Tiro's system, with subsequent additions by other calligraphers, eventually contained more than
13,000 characters. Modern stenography, however, appeared only
at the end of the sixteenth century in Timothy Bright's cursive method (1588), based on permutations of the straight line,
the circle, and the half-circle. The science and practice of
stenography, nonetheless, was not universally accepted until
the mid-1800s, when Sir Isaac Pitman published his Stenographic Sound-Hand (1), the first of numerous systems issued by
various inventors.
    Stenographic methodology entered Western musical notation
in the early nineteenth century, when John Austin, Benoît
Auguste Bertini, and Jean Michel Hippolyte Prévost, among others, devised their individual systems. It is significant that
stenographic signs were initially applied to notating vocal
music of conspicuously uncomplicated substance and character.
For plainchant and simple folksong, stenographic notation was
reasonably adequate; for music of melodic, harmonic, or rhythmic complexity, it proved to be woefully deficient.
    In our own time, the typewriter has made a limited kind
of stenographic notation simple and practical, providing the
means of putting down musical ideas without recourse to con-

ventional staff symbology. (See, for instance, the proposals of Barry Brook and Murray Gould, page 365, and Yael Bukspan, page 329.) Typewritten notation is, of course, an amalgam of letters, numbers, and grammatical signs -- a hybrid form of a hybrid system of communication, so to speak.

Being extremely unorthodox, as well as imprecise, stenographic notation has never convinced most composers that it is a viable means of setting down their musical thoughts. Only in the field of electronic and computer-generated music, where symbology must of necessity be highly technical, do stenographic modes offer a useful method of recording in written form such specialized sonic material.

Both implicit and explicit musical graphics, which were widely prevalent forms of experimental notation during the 1950s and 1960s, are visually close to many of the stenographic inventions displayed here. (See, for example, the illustration of Jean Kutahialian's invention on page 397.) The basic purpose of the avant-garde graphics, however, was quite different: merely to suggest free choice of musical components in performance rather than to express specific musical statements in a radically altered format. Still, it is unlikely that either avant-garde graphic notation or any of the twenty-six systems illustrated in these pages will ever supplant the more traditional methods of notating the music of our time.

1799. Michael Woldemar, <u>Tableau mélotachygraphique</u> (A melographic chart). Paris: Cochet.
Staff: 5-line.
Clef signs: Standard G-clef.
Pitch: A combination of small unstemmed black noteheads and stenographic markings which follow the general contour of groupings of successive pitches.
Example 7-1.

As is evident, Woldemar's stenographic system is a compromise between abstract symbology and conventional notation -- a kind of musical shorthand that is general rather than precise. Altered pitches are indicated by a dot beneath or above the affected notehead or pitch sign.

A lengthy article by the historian François Joseph Fétis (<u>Revue Musicale</u> IV, 1832, pp. 270-274) should be of interest to those curious about the reaction of his contemporaries to Woldemar's system. Needless to say, the proposal did not meet with unqualified success.

1802. John Austin, <u>A System of Stenographic Music</u>. Glasgow: the author.

Staff: None.
Register symbols:

Pitch:

Duration:

Rests: Not mentioned by the author.
Meter:

Example 7-2.

The matrices of Austin's signs are a straight line, a curve,
and a small loop; dots are added to those marks that designate
flats and sharps. All in all, the system utilizes a commendable limitation of resources. It is doubtful, however, that
Austin's proposal could have enjoyed much success, in spite
of its logical construction.

1812. Benoît Auguste Bertini, Stigmatographie; ou L'art d'écrire avec des points. Suivie de Mélographie, nouvelle manière
de noter la musique (Stigmatography, the art of writing with
dots. Based on Mélographie, a new way of notating music).
Paris: chez Martinet.
Staff: None.
Register symbols:

Pitch:

| C | C# Db | D | D# Eb | E | F | F# Gb | G | G# Ab | A | A# Bb | B |

Concurrent with his pitch symbology, Bertini devised an unorthodox series of pitch syllables:
do ro né rậi zậi mo bo bế jâi bâi vâi

Duration: Indicated by a series of related stenographic signs
derived from the prevailing meter denominator. Certain values are expressed by a combination of signs, such as,
32 = 3+2, or 16 = 1+6.

1   2   4   8   16   32

Meter: Expressed by a fractional figure; the numerator represents the value of the measure beat and the denominator, the
value of the entire measure. For example,
$\frac{8}{3\,2} = \frac{4}{4}$ or $\frac{2}{2}$. The 8 represents a quarter-note and the 32
stands for a whole-note.

Example 7-3. French folk song, Ah, vous dirai-je, maman.

The following is an explanation of the sequence of stenographic signs in the example above:

Register symbol for c^2-b^2, $\underline{c}^2$, meter signature $\frac{8}{3\,2}$ ($\frac{2}{2}$), $\underline{c}^2|$

$\underline{g}$ $\underline{g}$ $\underline{a}$ $\underline{a}$ | g,16 (♩), $\underline{f}^2$, 8 (♩), $\underline{f}^2$ | $\underline{e}$ $\underline{e}$ $\underline{d}$ $\underline{d}$ | $\underline{c}$,16 (♩), $\underline{c}^2$,

4 (♪), $\underline{d}^2$ $\underline{e}$ $\underline{f}$ | g, 8 (♩), g^2 $\underline{a}$, 4 (♪), $\underline{b}^2$, register symbol

for c^3-b^3, $\underline{c}^3$, register symbol for c^2-b^2, $\underline{a}^2$ | g, 16 (♩).

Bertini employed a peculiar practice in his stenographic notation, demonstrated in Example 7-3, of placing the meter symbol
between the first and second notes of the melody, for reasons
that remain obscure.
    Many years after issuing this proposal, Bertini published
a tract entitled Phonological system for acquiring extraordi-

nary facility on all musical instruments as well as singing
(2). A highly ambitious project, to be sure, but one that
apparently made no greater stir in the world of music than had
his earlier stenographic system of notation.

1834. Jean Marie Michel Hippolyte Prévost, Sténographie musi-
cale, ou l'art de suivre l'exécution musicale en écrivant
(Musical shorthand, or the art of putting musical ideas into
written form). Mainz, Germany: B. Schott Söhnen.
Staff: 9-line, consisting of pairs of dotted lines below and
above a standard pentagram.
Clef signs: Traditional G- and F-clefs.
Pitch:

$$\text{(}\quad|\quad\cap\quad/\quad\cup\quad-\quad\backslash\quad\text{(}$$
C D E F G A B C

A complex system of stenographic markings, based on the
seven pitch symbols, outline the general contour of successive notes. Ascending and descending intervals are designated by the following plan:

Flats are shown by a large loop and sharps by a small loop.

Key signatures: Displayed in the following manner:

Duration: For individual notes not belonging to a note-group,
the signs are related to the staff line or space of the
pitch affected; for example,

Rests:

Meter: With the exception of 2/4 time, only the numerator is
    given, as demonstrated under Key signatures.
The following excerpts illustrate Prévost's stenographic notation for single-line melodic writing and for music with a
chordal texture.
Example 7-4.

Example 7-5.

L'accoutumance ainsi nous rend tout familier:
Ce qui nous paraissait terrible, singulier,
S'apprivoise avec notre vue
Quand ce vient à la continue.
(Custom thus makes everything familiar:
What seems to us dreadful, peculiar,
Is made acceptable in our eyes
When it becomes common practice.)

--La Fontaine

This amusing quotation prefaces the detailed explication of
Prevost's unusual stenographic system of notation. Together
with the method of Rambures, next discussed, it earned the
designation of "bizarre" from Joseph Raymondi in his analytical Examen critique des notations musicales. The fundamental
premise of Prévost's system was to avoid the practice in traditional notation of assigning separate signs for each of the
twelve pitches of the octave by devising multiple signs that
outlined a series of notes, or even an entire measure. Prévost
was convinced that musical stenography should be entirely different from ordinary stenographic methods, so as not to confuse the musician conversant with the current letter system.
It cannot be denied that he did indeed achieve this goal, but
at a cost -- the loss of a broadly based constituency of musicians eager and willing to master his intricate notation. Thus,
Prévost's novel musical shorthand is now only one more item in
the overflowing repository of notational curiosa.

1842. A. de Rambures, Sténographie musicale, ou méthode simplifiée pour l'enseignement la lecture et l'écriture de la musique et du plain-chant, suivie de six grand tableaux (Musical
shorthand, a simplified method for teaching the reading and
writing of instrumental music and plainchant, according to
six master plans). Paris: Hachette.
Staff: 1-line.
Clef signs:

Soprano (high)	(low)	Alto	Tenor (high)	(low)	Bass (high)	(low)

Pitch:

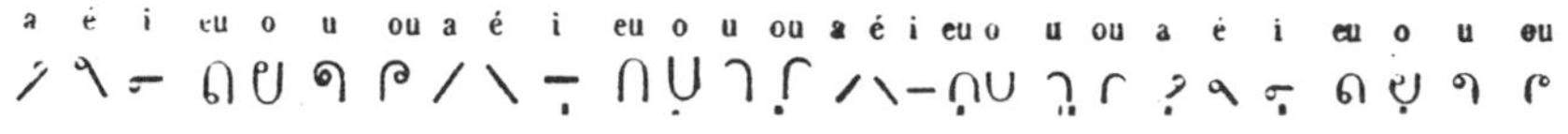

C   D   E F G A B   c ——————— b   c¹ ——————— b¹   c² ——————— b²

Chromatic inflections are designated in either one of the
two ways shown below:

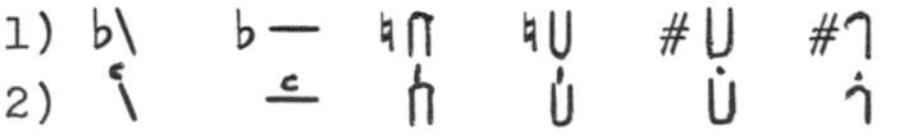

1) b\   b—   ♮⌒   ♮∪   #∪   #⌐
2) \   ⌐   ♭   ∪   ∪   ⌐
   Db   Eb   F♮   G♮   G#   A#

Key signatures: Shown by a combination of symbols: t, for
   tonique; the sign for ♭, ♮, or #, plus that for the tonic
   note; the symbol for register.

t $\frac{\mathsf{c}}{\mathsf{q}}$ = E♭ major,   │   t / = C major,
             low soprano   │   high tenor
             register   │   register

Duration: Expressed by an elaborate series of modified pitch
   symbols, above, on, or below the single staff line. A different series is used for each register; the examples below
   pertain to octaves 2, 3, and 4.

Rests:

Dynamics:

pp   p   mp   mf   f   ff

Example 7-6. French folk song, **O mon pays!**

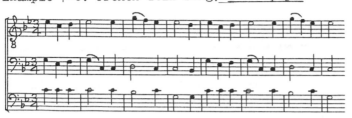

As is evident, all of the pitch symbols in Rambures' system are derived from two basic forms: The three sides of a triangle (/ — \), and a U-shaped sign (∩ ∪).

A prime example of a system with admirable theoretical concepts but lacking in practical application, this first invention of Rambures was followed in 1855 by a second tract, in which he outlined a plan of musical stenography using either standard or mixed stenographic notation (3).

One curious feature of Rambures' notation, illustrated in the example above, is his placing the low bass part above that for the high bass -- for reasons unexplained.

1842. V. D. de Stains, _Phonography; or, The Writing of Sounds._
In two parts . . . Logography; or, Universal Writing of
Speech; and Musicography; or, Symbological Writing of Music;
With a Shorthand for Both. London: E. Wilson.
Staff: 1-line.
Clef signs: A single symbol representing the C-clef: —θ—

Pitch:

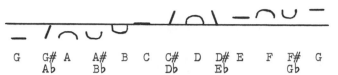

| G | G# Ab | A | A# Bb | B | C | C# Db | D | D# Eb | E | F | F# Gb | G |

Duration: Shown by the spacing and the length of the pitch
  marks. Barlines, however, are evenly spaced.
Rests: Indicated by blank space.
Example 7-7. Plainchant, from the _Liber Usualis_.

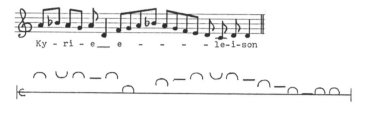

Ky - ri - e__ e - - - - le-i-son

1842. Jules Charles Teule, _Exposition du système de l'écriture
  musicale chiffrée suivie d'une note sur le comparateur des
  tons_ (Explanation of the numerical system of music notation,
  followed by an observation on the comparison of sounds).
  Paris: the author?
Staff: 1-line.
Register symbols: The numbers are placed above or below the
  single staff line.

1	2	3	4	5	6	7
1	2	3	4	5	6	7
A_2-B_2	C_1-B_1	C-B	c-b	c^1-b^1	c^2-b^2	c^3-b^3

Pitch:

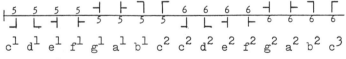

c^1 d^1 e^1 f^1 g^1 a^1 b^1 c^2 c^2 d^2 e^2 f^2 g^2 a^2 b^2 c^3

Example 7-8.

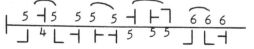

Although it is called a numerical system, Teule's notation is really stenographic by virtue of his matrix of signs for pitch, the numbers referring only to register. The seven diatonic pitches are represented by permutations of two basic symbols: ⌟ ⌐ . Combined with the register numerals, the final numbered note of each octave duplicates the first numbered note of the next higher octave, as shown above. Presumably, sharp and flat signs are placed relative to the pitch symbols as required.

1843. Bartolomeo Montanello, _Intorno allo scrivere la musica: lettera a Marco Beccafichi_ (On the subject of notating music, in a letter to Marco Beccafichi). Milan: G. Ricordi.
Staff: None.
Register symbols: Ancillary markings on the basic pitch signs designate the various octaves.

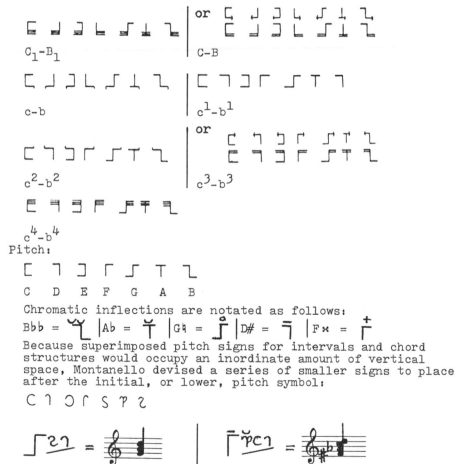

Pitch:

$$C \quad D \quad E \quad F \quad G \quad A \quad B$$

Chromatic inflections are notated as follows:

Bbb = | Ab = | G♮ = | D♯ = | F× =

Because superimposed pitch signs for intervals and chord structures would occupy an inordinate amount of vertical space, Montanello devised a series of smaller signs to place after the initial, or lower, pitch symbol:

Montanello provided a number of examples illustrating his suggested shorthand notation for various melodic and harmonic patterns:

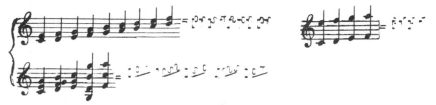

Duration:

The author also included examples of various rhythmic figures with differing values:

Rests:

— — • , √ ∧

▬ ▬ ⟩ ⌐ ⊣ ⊣

Meter:

$\underline{4} = \frac{4}{2}$, $\underline{3} = \frac{3}{4}$, $\underline{6} = \frac{6}{8}$, for example.

Articulations:

————— • • • • • • /////// ∿∿∿∿

   legato staccato spiccato trill

One year following his letter to Signor Beccafichi, Montanello
sent a similar message to the publisher Giovanni Ricordi, which
he headed <u>Di un modo facile ed economico per istampare la musi-</u>
<u>ca</u> (Concerning an easy and economical method of printing music).
Easy and economical the system may have been to print, but to
any composer or copyist it must surely have been something of
a nightmare.

1853. August Baumgartner, <u>Kurzgefasste Anleitung zur musik-</u>
   <u>alischen Stenographie oder Tonzeichenkunst</u> (Short introduction to musical shorthand or tone-symbol art). Munich: G.
   Franz.
Staff: 1-line.
Register symbols: None; each voice or instrument relates the
   four-octave span of stenographic marks to its individual
   range.

Octave 4: g a b c^1 d^1 e^1 f^1 | g^1-f^2

Octave 3: G A B c d e f | g-f^1

Octave 2: G_1 A_1 B_1 C D E F | G-f

Octave 1: G_2 A_2 B_2 C_1 D_1 E_1 F_1 | G_1-F

$$\ell \;\; \sim \;\; \text{₹} \;\; \imath \;\; \sim \;\; / \qquad\qquad \int \;\; \imath \;\; \jmath \;\; o \;\; e \;\; c \;\; /$$

Octave 4: g^2-f^3 | g^3-f^4

Octave 3: g^1-f^2 | g^2-f^3

Octave 2: g-f^1 | g^1-f^2

Octave 1: G-f | g-f^1

$$\ell \;\; \backsim \;\; \gamma \;\; 3 \;\; \jmath \;\; \iota \;\; \int \qquad\qquad \gamma \;\; \ell \;\; \backslash \;\; \frown \;\; \backslash \;\; \jmath \;\; \sim$$

Pitch: The basic marks for the diatonic scale, shown above,
   are modified to distinguish upward and downward melodic
   leaps, as follows:

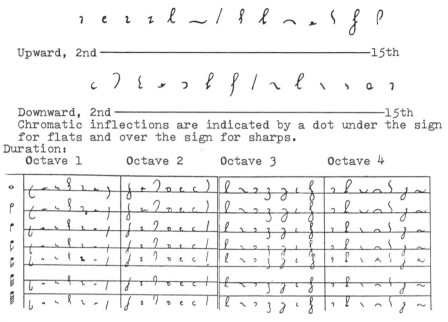

Chromatic inflections are indicated by a dot under the sign
for flats and over the sign for sharps.

Rests:

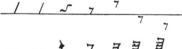

Example 7-9.

As the earliest advocate of notational stenography in Germany,
Baumgartner wrote numerous articles on the subject for various
of the stenography journals published in Munich. He was also
the author of a general history of musical notation, which was
issued in 1856 (4).

1854. C. Hermann, "Über musikalische Stenographie" (Concerning
    musical shorthand), Zeitschrift für Stenographie II, 2.
Staff: 1-line.
Register symbols:
    l, r (bass "region")

2. r (soprano "region")

f^2-e^3

f^1-e^2

$f-e^1$

Pitch:

F G A B C D E F

Chromatic alterations are designated as follows:

$\mathcal{l}$ = ♭ | $\mathcal{l}$ = #

The pitch signs within each measure are joined together in
the manner of cursive writing: *learn* . Repetitions of individual notes or note-groups are enclosed between two semicolons.

Key signatures: The sign /, which represents the tonic pitch
of any tonality, is elaborated, as shown below, to designate
major and minor tonalities on white keys and black keys.

Major, white key | Major, black key

Minor, white key | Minor, black key

Duration: Designated by the relative size and thickness of
the pitch symbol, exemplified below by the sign for C.

o ♩ ♪ ♪ ♪ ♪ ♪ ♪

Rests:

Example 7-10.

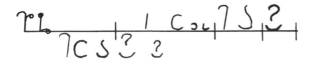

Like the French musician Prévost, whose proposal was discussed
on page 373, Hermann was a committed advocate of all forms of
stenography, but he believed that musical shorthand should be
entirely original in its symbology and not patterned after
other forms of this writing technique. Certainly Hermann's
system is not as elaborately constructed as Prévost's, and
perhaps for that reason was more successful in its application
to this novel form of musical notation.

___

1872. Antonio Aloysio, <u>Nuovo sistema di notazione musicale che
tende a facilitare la lettura, la esecuzione e la stampa della musica a tipi mobili</u> (A new system of musical notation
which facilitates the reading, the playing and the printing
of music, using movable type). Venice: Tipografia di G. Cec-
chini.
Staff: 1-line, dotted.
Register symbols:

C_1-B_1	C-B	c-b	c^1-b^1	c^2-b^2	c^3-b^3	c^4-b^4

Pitch:

C	C# / Db	D	D# / Eb	E	F	F# / Gb	G	G# / Ab	A	A# / Bb	B	C
do	lu	re	na	mi	fa	tu	sol	bi	la	ge	si	do

Duration:

Rests: The standard symbols, positioned as shown below.

Example 7-11.

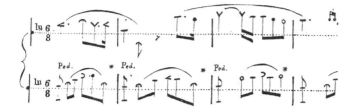

Aloysio's system was loosely based on that formulated by
Maurice Depierre the same year (see below), although he attempted to develop the Frenchman's ideas more logically. His
pitch symbols are derived from but two basic forms: ⌒ and V.
One series outlines the whole-tone scale from C to A#/B♭, the
other, the whole-tone scale from C#/D♭ to B. In so doing,
Aloysio was merely transferring to musical stenography a procedure followed by several notational reformers who altered
notehead shapes or colors to conform to the two scale patterns.

1872. Maurice Depierre, <u>Caractères servant à la notation de
la musique appliquée et étudiée au moyen d'un système nou-
veau de claviers</u> (Symbols serving music notation, applied
and learned by means of a new keyboard method). Annecy,
France: Imprimerie de Bordet.
Staff: None.
Register symbols: Not known.
Pitch:

⌒ ⊙ ⋀ ⋀ ⋀ ⊣) ⑈   ⩾ ⟩ ⟩ ⋃

C   C# D♭ D D# E♭ E E# F♭ F F# G♭
ut   ré   mi   fa

⋃ ⊍ ⩔ V V ⋲ ⟨ ⟨ ⋔ ⌒

G G# A♭ A A# B♭ B B# C♭ C
sol   la   si   ut
Duration:

⋂̈ ⋀̇ ⌒̄
♩ ♩ ♪

Example 7-12.

♪♩♪ ♩♭♪ ♪. ♯♪♯♪ ♩♪ ♩.

⋂⟨ ⟩V ⊍⟨V ⩾⋃⋀ ⋂⋀

Depierre's symbology, like that of Aloysio, was based on two
contrasting signs: ∩ and ∧ . More complex in its permutations
than in Aloysio's notation, however, each pitch symbol assumes
three forms to designate flat, natural, and sharp. His system
also includes signs for less frequently altered pitches: E#,
Fb, and B#. It should be pointed out that <u>ut</u> represents the
tonic of any tonality, the series of stenographic marks then
commencing with the new tonic pitch.

1873. Alex. M. Seymat, <u>Panorama d'un nouveau système de notation pour la musique et le plain-chant, ou méthode stého-
graphique de notation</u> (Survey of a new system of notation
for instrumental music and plainchant; a method of musical
shorthand). Paris: the author.
Staff: 1-line; a second line is superimposed as needed to increase the range.
Register symbols: None; high, middle, and low registers are
indicated by the position of the pitch symbols relative to
the staff line, as shown below.
Pitch: <u>Ut</u> represents the tonic note of any tonality; the series of pitch symbols below begin arbitrarily on C

o ϕ ✗ ＼ ✗   ʮU) ⟩ ⌒

C C# Db D D#   Eb E F   F# Gb

ut   ré   mi fa

∩ ⼐ ⼓ (¢ ⼆ ／ o

G G# Ab A A# Bb   B   C

sol   la   si ut

Key signatures: Indicated by the pitch symbol of <u>ut</u> positioned
above the staff line just before the first barline, as illustrated in Example 7-13.
Duration: The quarter-note is the beat norm; a dot following
a pitch symbol extends its duration by one full beat. — .
Rests: All values are designated by a single symbol: — .
Example 7-13.

This proposal was first published under the title of <u>Nouveau
système de notation pour le plain-chant et la musique sur la
portée adéquate à la gamme</u> (New system of notation for plainchant and music written on the conventional staff). Because
Seymat's method was designed only for single-line vocal music,

a limited gamut suffices. Emulating the procedures of several
other proposers of stenographic notation, Seymat derived the
seven diatonic pitch symbols from three basic signs: o, /,
and ∪ .

1883. J. Leon Riom. Nouveau système de notation pour la mu-
    sique (New system of musical notation). Paris: A. Boyer et
    Cie.
Staff: 1-line.
Register symbols: None.
Pitch:

Duration:

Rests:

Example 7-14. French folk song, Le coucou.

Cou - cou, cou - cou, dis - moi pour - quoi   ta voix tou - chan - te

sou - pi - re et   chan - te, chan - te, chan - te plei - ne d'e - moi?

The virtue of simplicity is evident in Riom's stenographic
system in that all the pitch signs are derived from a single
matrix -- the sides and ends of a rectangle.

1885. Hans Moser, [Proposal for stenographic notation],
  Magazin für Stenographie 6, 19, p. 218.
Staff: 4-line.
Register symbols: A four-octave span is designated by the size
  and form of the pitch signs.

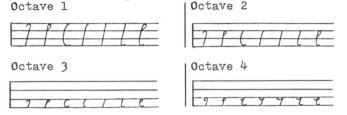

Octave 1 | Octave 2

Octave 3 | Octave 4

Pitch: The diatonic scale C to B is represented by the signs
  shown above.
Duration:

Example 7-15.

1885. Emanuel Zichy-Ferraris, Musikalische Stenographie (Mu-
  sical shorthand). Vienna: the author?
Staff: 4-line; the lines are widely spaced.
Register symbols: None.
Pitch:

/ L ⌐ \ L ⎖ (| L

C C# Db D D# Eb E F F#

∏ ∩ ∏⎍ ⎍ ⎍⎍⎍)) /

Gb G G# Ab A A# Bb B C
Duration:

/ \ (·| ñ̃

o,𝅗𝅥 𝅗𝅥 𝅘𝅥 𝅘𝅥𝅮 𝅘𝅥𝅯 𝅘𝅥𝅰

Rests: Indicated by blank space.
Example 7-16.

As demonstrated in the above example, the pitch signs are
placed in the center staff space to begin, changing to the
higher or lower space to show melodic leaps up or down.

1888. Henri Dupont, <u>Nouvelle sténographie musicale; la stén-
ographie-Duployé appliquée à l'écriture musicale</u> (A new musical shorthand; the Duployé system applied to musical notation). Paris: Institut sténographique.
Staff: None.
Register symbols: None.
Pitch:

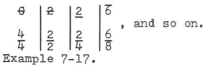

Duration:

Rests: The symbols are added to the adjacent pitch sign.

Meter:

6	2	2	6
4	2	2	6

, and so on.

Example 7-17.

1890. Leon Labutut, Méthode de sténographie musicale, ou la
    musique rendue facile par la suppression des portées et des
    clés (Method of musical shorthand; music made easy by the
    omission of staves and clefs). Condom, France: the author.
Staff: None.
Register symbols: None.
Pitch:

C   C#   C×   Db   D   D#   Ebb   Eb   E   E#   Fb

Γ   Γ#   Γ‖   Gb   G   G#   Ab   A   A#   Bbb   Bb

B   B#   Cb   C

Duration: Not known.

Alerted to the existence of Labutut's system by its reference
in Abdy Williams' historical survey of notation (5), this researcher hoped to track down the original volume by Labutut
in the British Library, only to discover that it had been de-
stroyed in the bombings of London during World War II. Hence,
it was not possible to find out how this inventor expressed
rhythm and duration in his proposal -- vital elements in any
viable method of notating music, whether stenographic or otherwise.

    Labutut's system -- one of the most elaborate in its sym-
bology of all the stenographic notations invented during the
nineteenth century -- is actually derived from only two contrasting signs: a straight and a curved line. What also sets
it apart from other shorthand methods is its provision for
doubly altered pitches (C×,F×,Ebb, and Bbb), which few, if
any other, stenographic systems consider. Finally, it is a
matter of regret that no comparative illustration of this inventor's notation could be provided, lacking information on
his treatment of duration.

1892. Ludwig Rambach, System einer Musik-Stenographie (System
    of musical shorthand). Zurich: Art Institut Orell Füssli.
Staff: 1-line.
Register symbols:

C_1-B_1 │ C-B │ c-b │ c^1-b^1 │ c^2-b^2 │ c^3-b^3 │ c^4-b^4

Pitch: Seven basic signs are devised for the notes of the diatonic scale, each of which is modified to show the various
durational values.

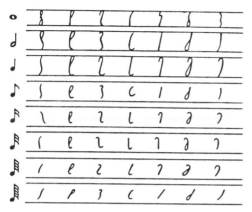

The pitch signs are stacked vertically for chords, the root
at the bottom. For intervallic leaps, up or down, the following signs are used:

	up	down
minor 2nd	⌒	⌣
major 2nd	↖	↙
minor 3rd	(	(
major 3rd	(	(
4th	)	)
5th	—	—
6th	(	)
8va	↗	✕

Example 7-18.

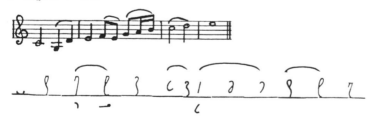

1899. Harry White, Shorthand Music: A New and Altogether
   Unique System of Musical Notation. Windermere, England: the
   author.
Staff: None, although the system was devised solely for piano.

Register symbols: The upper line of the pitch signs represents
the G-clef, the lower line the F-clef.
Pitch:

A	A# B♭	B	C	C# D♭	D	D# E♭	E	F	F# G♭	G	G# A♭

Duration:

Rests:

1	2	4	8	16

, and so on.

Meter:

4/1 = $\frac{4}{4}$ (4 beats in 1 measure)

6/1 = $\frac{6}{8}$ or $\frac{6}{4}$ (6 beats in 1 measure), for example.

Example 7-19.

4/1

1903. Ilmari Henrik Reinhold Krohn, <u>Akzentzeichenschrift</u>
(Stenographic notation). Helsinki: Werner Söderstrom Osakenh-
tiö, Porwoo.
Staff: None.
Register symbols: None; the treble clef is implied.
Pitch: Unlike other stenographic notations, Krohn's proposal
does not assign a separate symbol for each note of the scale
but, instead, for each rising or falling interval following
the initially stated pitch. Chromatic inflections are indicated by a small accidental sign set above the stenographic mark.

F /   G \   A (B♭)

Example 7-20. Chorale, <u>Wenn ich einmal soll scheiden</u>.

A musical scholar as well as a composer, Krohn founded the
music journal <u>Säveletär</u> in Finland in 1906. He was the author
of a study on clef signs entitled <u>Zur Einheitlichkeit der
Notenschlüssel</u> (Concerning the uniformity of clef signs), and
he was also the inventor of a new musical instrument that he
called an acoustic harmonium.

Krohn's stenographic system was devised solely for vocal
melodic writing, which accounts for its very limited symbology.
Provision seems not to have been made by the inventor for interval leaps larger than a fifth, a restriction that would
render his method all but inoperable in music of a more wide-
ranging melodic scheme.

1908. S. E. Hunt, <u>Trichrom Musical Notation. Compend of Tri-
    linear Staff and Chromaneumes</u>. London: the author.
Staff: 3-line.
Clef signs:

Soprano	Alto	Tenor	Bass
S	A	T	B

Pitch:

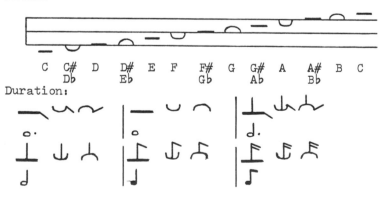

Duration:

Rests:

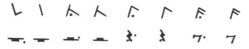

Example 7-21. "Resignation," from <u>The Southern Harmony</u>.

1913. Léopold Frédéric Raab, <u>Stenotic-Klavierschule zumeist</u>
<u>nach Hohmann</u> (Stenographic keyboard system mostly based on
that of Hohmann). Rothenburg, Germany: C. H. Trenkle.
Staff: 1-line.
Register symbols: Indicated by the use of additional staff
lines; a four-octave gamut is encompassed by five lines.

c^3 _____

c^2 _____

c^1 _____

c _____

C _____

Pitch:

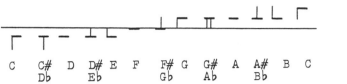

C   C#   D   D#   E   F   F#   G   G#   A   A#   B   C
     Db   Eb   Gb   Ab   Bb

Intervals and chords are notated by a combination of pitch symbols:

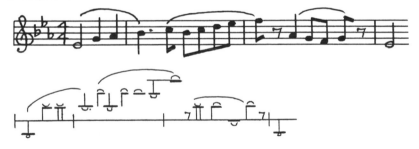

Duration:

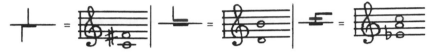

Rests:

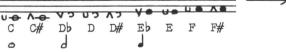

, and so on.

Example 7-22.

1922. Francis Taylor, <u>Musical Shorthand for Composers, Students of Harmony, Counterpoint, etc., easily acquired, can be written very rapidly, is more legible than printed music</u>. London: the author.
Staff: 5-line.
Clef signs: Standard G- and F-clefs.
Pitch:

C   C#   Db   D   D#   Eb   E   F   F#

Gb G G# Ab A A# Bb B C

Diatonic scale in 8ths | Chromatic scale in 16ths

Duration: As indicated in the examples below.
Rests:

Example 7-23.

Example 7-24. Frédéric Chopin, Ballade no. 3, op. 47.

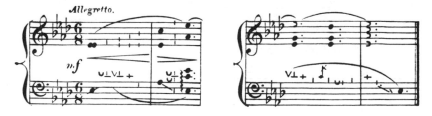

1949. Jean Kutahialian, <u>La sténographie de la musique</u> (Musical
   shorthand). Marseilles: the author.
Staff: None.
Register symbols: None.
Pitch: The signs are derived from the following matrix:

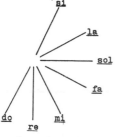

Key signatures:

  / = #, ⌐ = 2 sharps, ⌐ = 3 sharps,

  \ = ♭, ⌐ = 2 flats, ⌐ = 3 flats, for example.

Duration: Shown by the extent of the pitch signs.
Rests:

Example 7-25.

1950. Emile Gouverneur, _Traité complet de sténographie musicale_
(Complete treatise on musical stenography). Brussels: Schott
frères.
Staff: 5-line.
Clef signs:

Pitch:

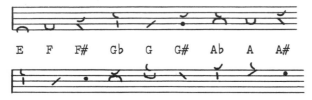

Key signatures: x = a major key; | = a minor key.

Duration:

⌢ ⌒ ⌣ ⌣ ˅ ˎ ˋ | · | ∕ ·

o· o d· d d· d ♪ ♪ ♬ ♬

Rests: The signs are placed after the preceding note-symbol.

⌢ ⌣ ( ) ⊃ ∠

▬ ▬ ⅀ 7 7 ₹

Meter:
34 | 22 | 68
3/4 | 2/2 | 6/8   , for example.

Example 7-26. Wolfgang Amadeus Mozart, _Sonata in D_, K. 576.

In addition to the system just illustrated, Gouverneur proposed a staffless stenographic notation that was far more abstract and elaborate, a sample of which is shown in Example
7-27. Visually, it has much in common with the shorthand method of Jean Kutahialian (page 397). A comparison of Examples
7-25 and 7-27 will reveal many similarities in symbology and
in methodology. And both examples bear a striking resemblance
to certain of the avant-garde graphics that were widely prevalent in the 1950s and 1960s.
Example 7-27.

To affirm that any numerical or alphabetical system of notation is superior to any comparable method remains a personal
assessment; hence, a choice among the foregoing stenographic
procedures is essentially meaningless. All three notational
techniques are outside the mainstream of musical notation.
Therefore this compiler has let stand without comment many of
the stenographic proposals, as none appears likely to influence notational methodology in the future.

To incorporate into present-day notational practice any proposed reform illustrated in this book, the notator would advisedly heed Aristophanes' charge to his fellow Athenian playwrights: "Be clear, and not so clever." When pragmatism and clarity supplant novelty and excessive cleverness, then our system of musical notation can finally achieve the simplification and essential improvement its reformers fervently desire.

NOTES

1. Sir Isaac Pitman, Stenographic Sound-Hand (London: F. Pitman, 1837).
2. Benoît Auguste Bertini, Phonological system for acquiring extraordinary facility on all musical instruments as well as in singing (London: the author, 1830).
3. A. de Rambures, Abrégé de la méthode musicale sténographique, ou manuel pratique pour servir à l'exécution de la musique par la notation usuelle ou par la notation sténographique mixte (Paris: Regnier-Canaux, 1855).
4. August Baumgartner, Kurzgefasste geschichte der musikalischen notation mit einer Übersichtstafel in tableauform und erläutern den notenbeispielen verfasst und entworfen (Munich: Verlag vom verfasser, 1856).
5. Charles Francis Abdy Williams, The Story of Notation (London: The Walter Scott Publishing Co., Ltd., 1903).

Appendixes:
Comparative Tables

A. PROPOSED STAFF REFORMS

1-line

Baumgartner, 381
Carrillo, 314
Cohen, 242
Crocker, 328
Delcamp, 160
Depierre, 385
Fawcett, 251
Fleischhauer, 211
Geisler, 319
Glenn, 261
Hermann, 382
J.F.W. Koch, 297
Maldacker, 254
Menchaca, 206
Miquel, 305
Natorp, 299
Raab, 394
Rambach, 390
Rambures, 375
Riom, 387
Romano, 272
Rousseau, 292
Sauveur, 137
Schmitt, 313
Schulz, 339
Seymat, 386
de Stains, 377

Teule, 306, 378
Waldmann, 304

Aloysio, 384

2-line

Eyquem, 358
Fawcett, 251
Fuller, 98
Harrison, 302
Johannis, 255
Kobelt, 321
Kurcze, 310
Lajos, 366
Naunton, 52
Nichetti, 348
Raymondi, 19
Skapski, 105
Vidales, 352

Clements-Kropp, 312

3-line

J.P. Adams, 199
Arnò, 163
Bässler, 198, 199
Bazin, 57
Beaulieu, 37
Cromleigh, 263
Delau, 128
Delcamp, 160
Frémond, 217
Gambale, 150
Gatting, 123
Gaudard, 212
Groll, 273
Hautstont, 54
Hettiger verlag, 364
Horstig, 294
Hunt, 393
Hyard, 70

Jerichau, 48
Levasseur, 35
Lindorf, 127
Marie, 264
Pum, 268
Rohleder, 142
Russell, 91
Schoenberg, 223
Unbereit, 209
Wallbridge, 156
Weisshappel, 245

Chatillon, 85
Müller-Braunau, 40
Stuckey, 330

Chatillon, 85

Glisson, 363

Perbandt, 210

Naunton, 52

Stewart, 354

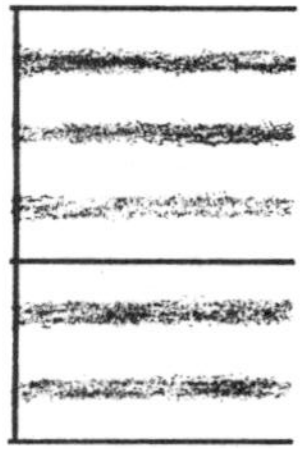

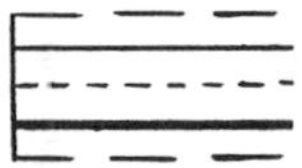

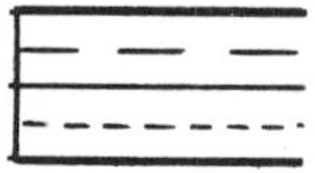

Fee, 68

Cornier, 24

Faunt, 219

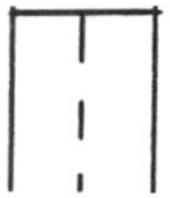

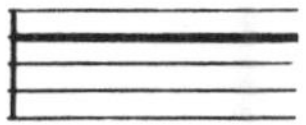

Carozzi, 181

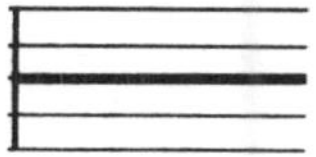

Austman, 174
Schleyer, 318

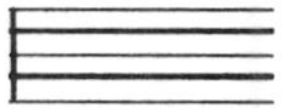

Cogswell, 38

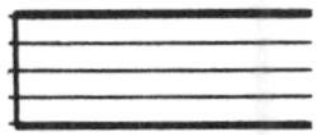

Lundie, 37
Riesen, 46

Stix, 254
Tapley, 109, 267

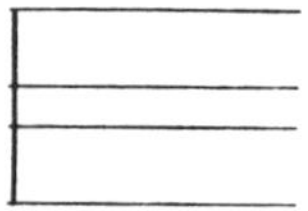

Adsit, 240
Heim, 325

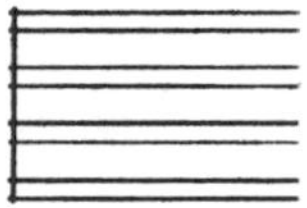

Robberson, 187

5-line

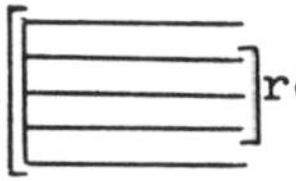

black red

Craig, 27

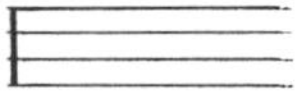

Ailler, 47
Brennink, 107
Cohen, 242
Haines, 246
Klett, 300
Mattheson, 140
Mayrhofers, 189
Moser, 388
Parsons, 319
Robberson, 187
Weisshappel, 245
Zichy-Ferraris, 388

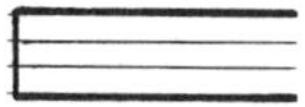

Riesen, 47

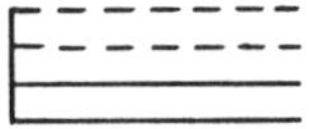

Reed, 101

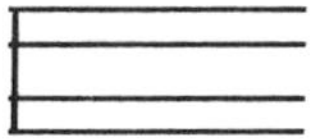

Beunk, 234

Edwards, 82

Robbins, 326

Middlemiss, 236

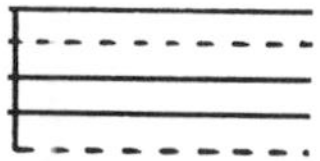

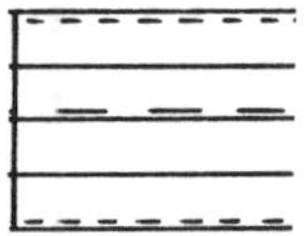

4-line

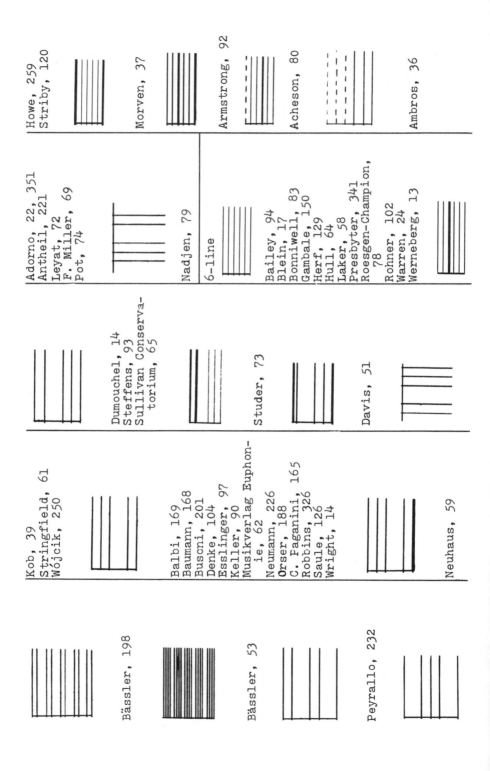

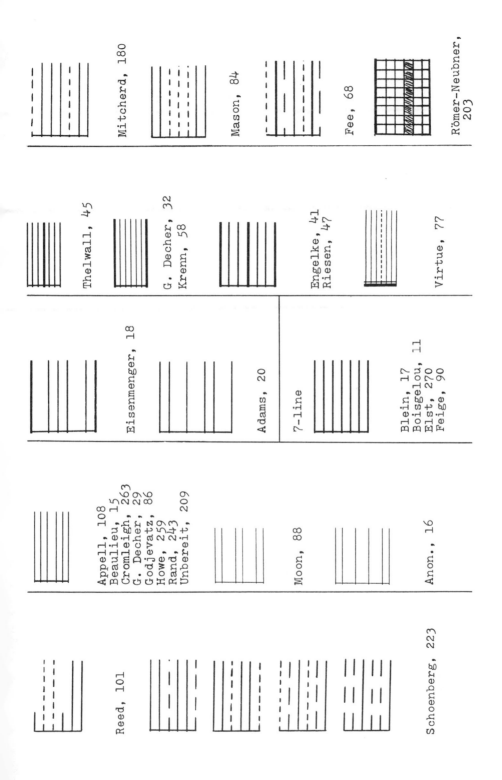

Mitcherd, 180

Mason, 84

Fee, 68

Römer-Neubner, 203

Thelwall, 45

G. Decher, 32
Krenn, 58

Engelke, 41
Riesen, 47

Virtue, 77

Eisenmenger, 18

Adams, 20

7-line

Blein, 17
Boisgelou, 11
Elst, 270
Feige, 90

Appell, 108
Beaulieu, 15
Cromleigh, 263
G. Decher, 29
Godjevatz, 86
Howe, 259
Rand, 243
Unbereit, 209

Moon, 88

Anon., 16

Reed, 101

Schoenberg, 223

405

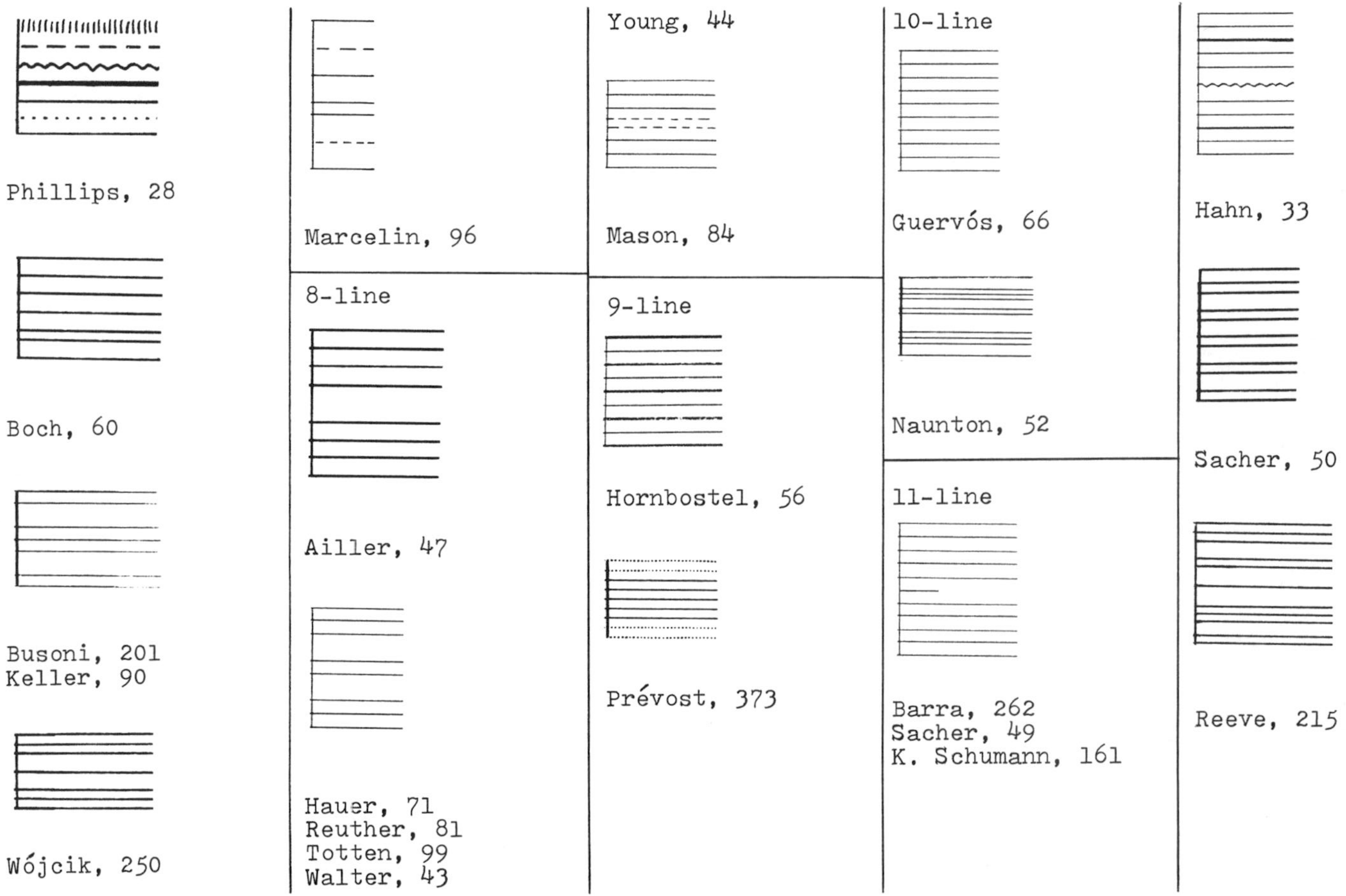

Hahn, 33

Sacher, 50

Reeve, 215

10-line

Guervós, 66

Naunton, 52

11-line

Barra, 262
Sacher, 49
K. Schumann, 161

Young, 44

Mason, 84

9-line

Hornbostel, 56

Prévost, 373

Marcelin, 96

8-line

Ailler, 47

Hauer, 71
Reuther, 81
Totten, 99
Walter, 43

Phillips, 28

Boch, 60

Busoni, 201
Keller, 90

Wójcik, 250

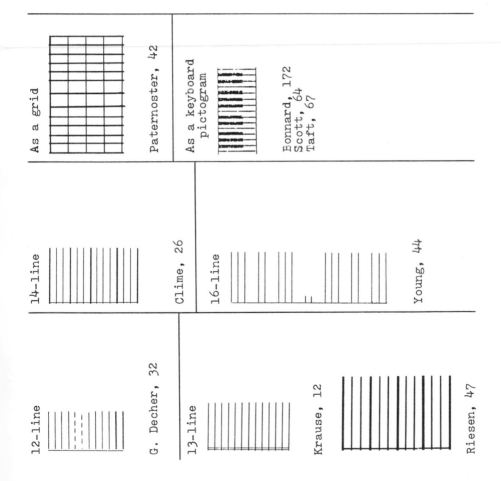

As a grid

Paternoster, 42

As a keyboard pictogram

Bonnard, 172
Scott, 64
Taft, 67

14-line

Clime, 26

16-line

Young, 44

12-line

G. Decher, 32

13-line

Krause, 12

Riesen, 47

407

B. NOVEL CLEF SIGNS

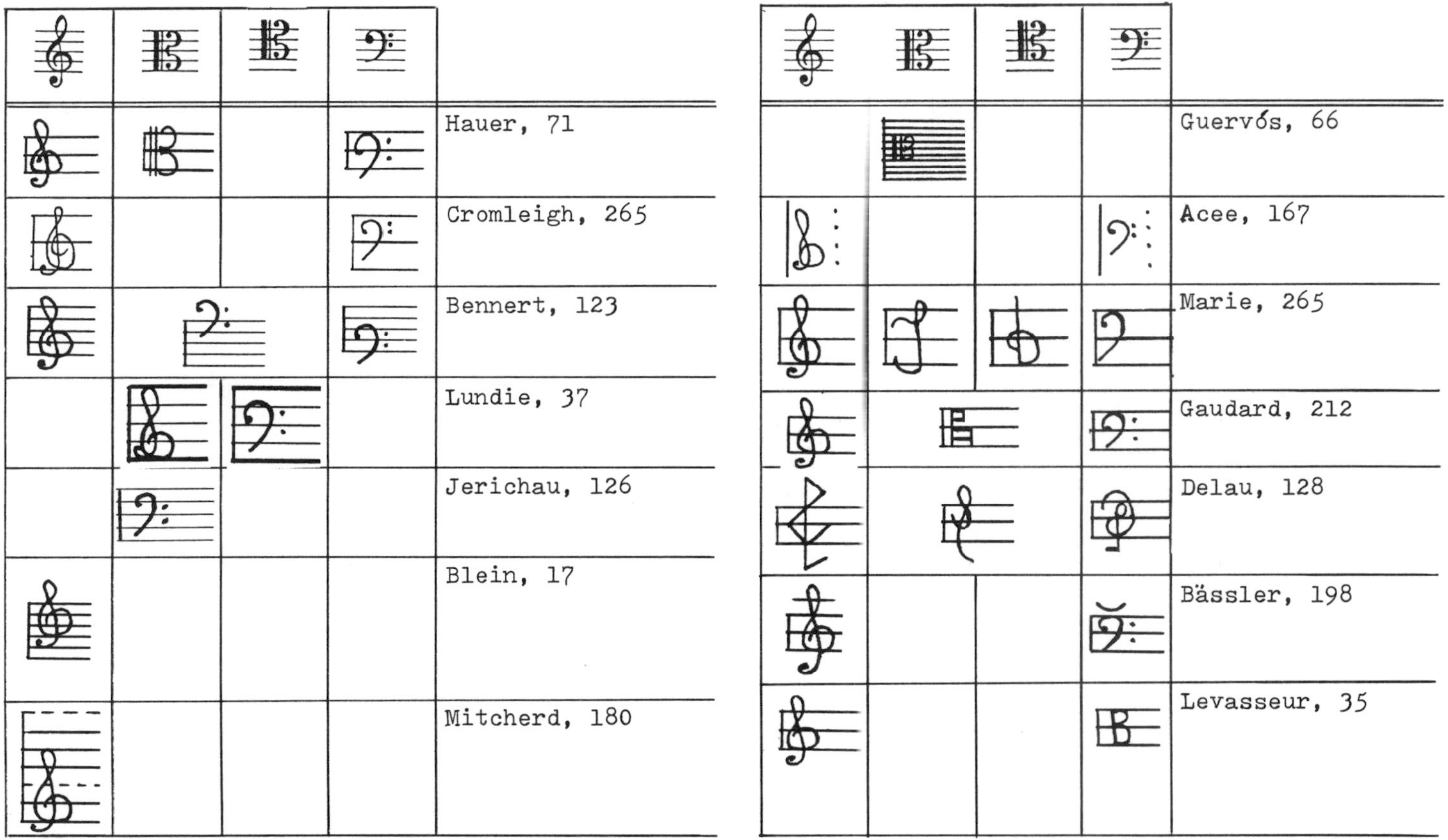

Guervós, 66
Acee, 167
Marie, 265
Gaudard, 212
Delau, 128
Bässler, 198
Levasseur, 35

Hauer, 71
Cromleigh, 265
Bennert, 123
Lundie, 37
Jerichau, 126
Blein, 17
Mitcherd, 180

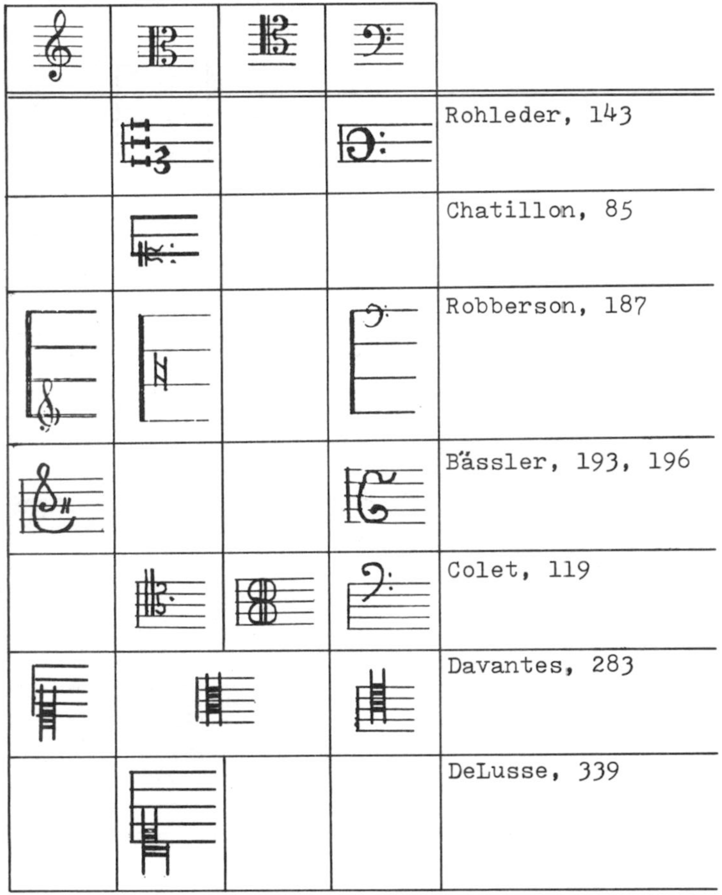
Rohleder, 143
Chatillon, 85
Robberson, 187
Bässler, 193, 196
Colet, 119
Davantes, 283
DeLusse, 339

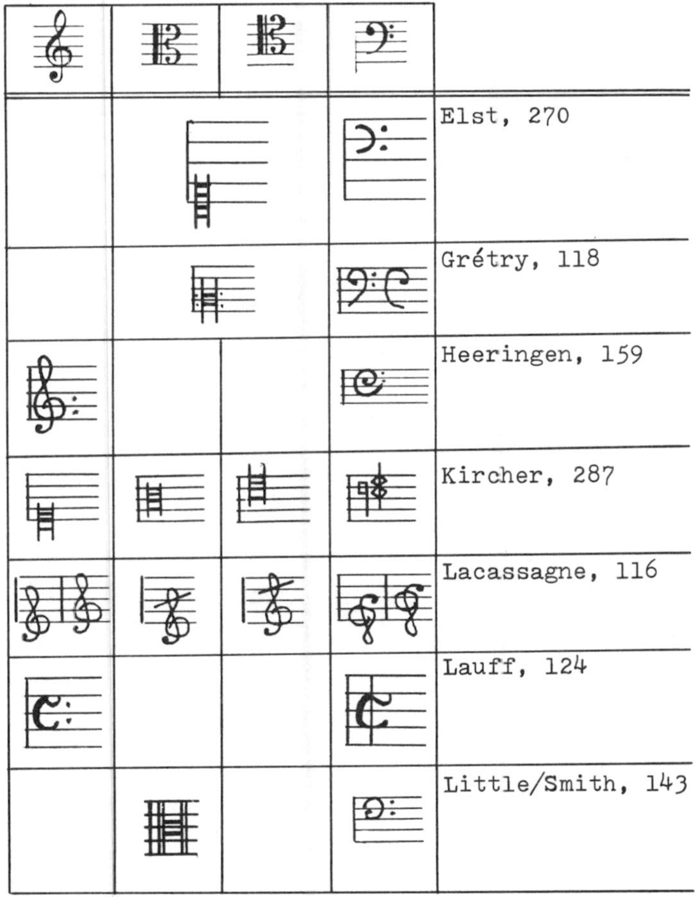
Elst, 270
Grétry, 118
Heeringen, 159
Kircher, 287
Lacassagne, 116
Lauff, 124
Little/Smith, 143

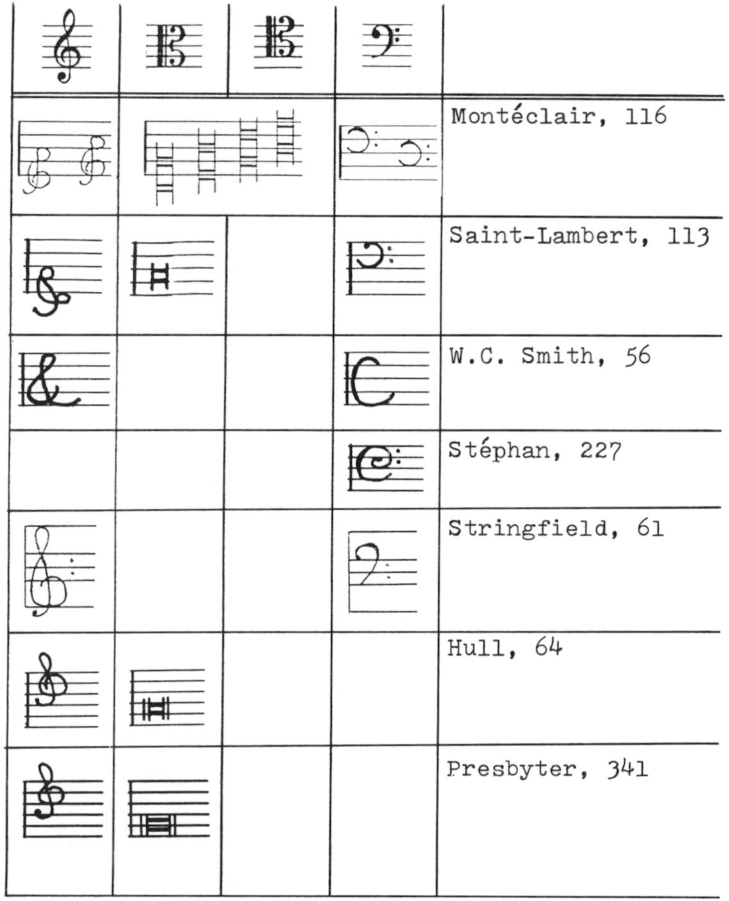

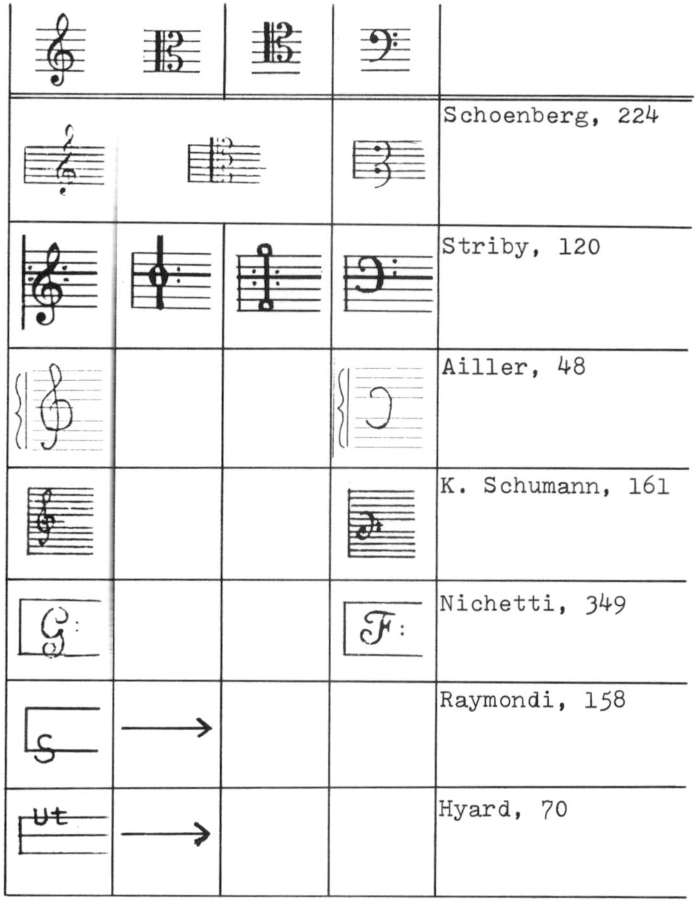

Schoenberg, 224
Striby, 120
Ailler, 48
K. Schumann, 161
Nichetti, 349
Raymondi, 158
Hyard, 70

Montéclair, 116
Saint-Lambert, 113
W.C. Smith, 56
Stéphan, 227
Stringfield, 61
Hull, 64
Presbyter, 341

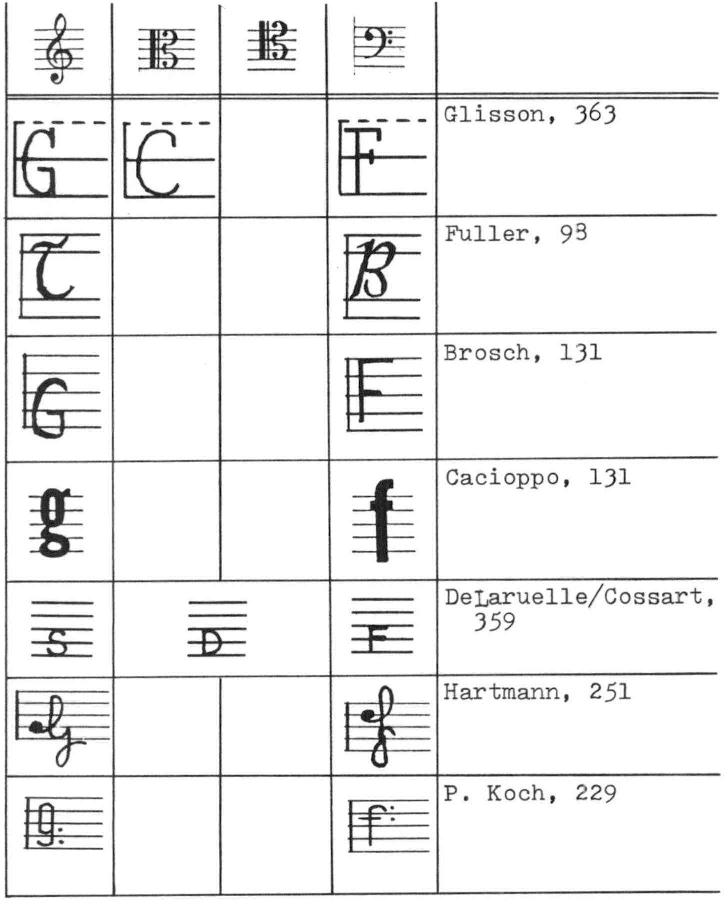
Glisson, 363
Fuller, 93
Brosch, 131
Cacioppo, 131
DeLaruelle/Cossart, 359
Hartmann, 251
P. Koch, 229

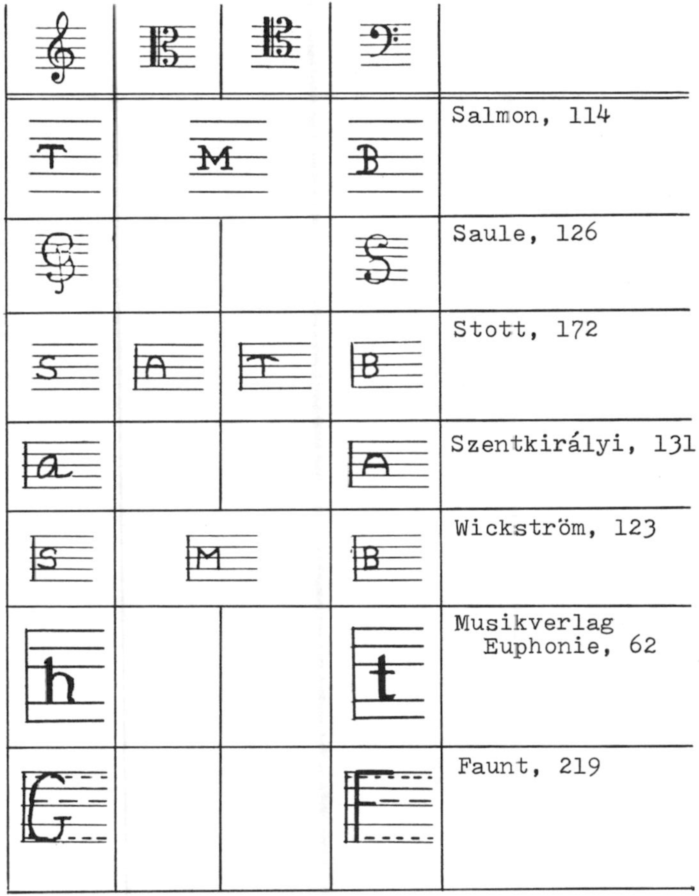
Salmon, 114
Saule, 126
Stott, 172
Szentkirályi, 131
Wickström, 123
Musikverlag Euphonie, 62
Faunt, 219

			Mersenne, 285
			Törnudd, 126
			Tufts, 337
			Wallbridge, 156
			Stix, 254
			Gouverneur, 398
			Krauze, 129
			Otte, 129

			Neuhaus, 59
			Unbereit, 209
			Horstig, 294
			Lajos, 366
			Harrison, 303
			Antheil, 221 / Hettiger verlag, 364
			Avella, 289 / Bontempi, 289 / Kircher, 287
			Busoni, 202
			Hunt, 393

Krause, 12 — de Stains, 377 — Boch, 60 — Hermann, 382 — Rambures, 375 — Huth, 175 — Pot, 74

Schäffer, 129 — Carozzi, 181 — Cogswell, 38 — Denke, 104 — Reed, 101 — Young, 44 — Orser, 188

C. REGISTER SYMBOLOGY

System (author, page)	A_2-B_2	C_1-B_1	$C-B$	$c-b$	c^1-b^1	c^2-b^2	c^3-b^3	c^4-b^4	c^5-
Ailler, 47; Ambros, 36; Delcamp, 160; Guilford, 316; Walter, 43	I	II	III	IV	V	VI	VII	VIII	—
Bazin, 57		0	I	II	III	IV	V	VI	VII
Meerens, 124		I	II	III	IV	V	VI	VII	VIII
A. Decher, 31; G. Decher, 32; Howe, 259; Sacher, 49, 179		I	II	III	IV	V	VI	VII	
Rand, 243; Steinfort, 126			I	II	III	IV	V	VI	
Klett, 300		V	IV	III	II	I			
Bässler, 53; Huntington, 218; Teule, 378; Warren, 24	1	2	3	4	5	6	7	8	
Bässler, 53	1	2	3	4	5	6	7	8	
Meerens, 124		7	8	9	10	11	12	13	14
Hautstont, 54		1	2	3	4	5	6	7	8
Bässler, 192; Engelke, 41; Godjevatz, 87; Mason, 84; Raymondi, 158		1	2	3	4	5	6	7	

	c^5 -	c^4 - b^4	c^3 - b^3	c^2 - b^2	c^1 - b^1	c - b	C - B	C_1 - B_1	A_2-B_2
Robberson, 187			5	4	3	2	1		
Waldmann, 304				6	5	4	3		
Bontempi, 289				18-22	11-17	4-10	(G) 1-3		
Stierlein, 291				19-21	12-18	5-11	(F) 1-4		
Jacob, 291				15-21	8-14	1-7			
Carrillo, 314		$c-b^4$	$\overline{0}$ - $\overline{11}$	$\underline{0}$ - 11	0 - $\overline{11}$	$\underline{0}$ - 0	$\underline{0}$ - $\overline{11}$	0 - $\overline{11}$	
Miquel, 305		$\underline{1}$ - $\underline{\underline{7}}$	$\underline{1}$ - 7	$\underline{1}$ - 7	$\underline{1}$ - 7	$\underline{1}$ - $\overline{7}$	$\underline{\underline{1}}$ - $\overline{7}$	$\underline{\underline{1}}$ - $\overline{7}$	
Rousseau, 292		$\underline{1}$ - $\overline{7}$	$\underline{1}$ - 7	$\underline{1}$ - 7	$\underline{1}$ - 7	$\underline{1}$ - 7	$\underline{1}$ - 7	$\underline{1}$ - 7	
Kobelt, 321			$\underline{1}$ - 7	$\underline{1}$ - 7	$\underline{1}$ - 7	$\underline{1}$ - 7	$\underline{1}$ - 7		
Kuncze, 310				2 - $\underline{1}$	2 - $\underline{1}$	2 - $\underline{1}$	2 - $\underline{1}$		

415

	A_2-B_2	C_1-B_1	$C-B$	$c-b$	c^1-b^1	c^2-b^2	c^3-b^3	c^4-b^4	c^5-
Schmitt, 313				⌐	2	⌐			
J.F.W. Koch, 297 / Natorp, 299 / Waldmann, 304				1 – 7	1 – 7	1 – 7			
Horstig, 294					1 – 7	1 – 7	1 – 7		
Diettrich-Kalkhoff, 208		4	3	2	1 or I	II	III	IV	
Jerichau, 49	5	II	III	IV		2	3	4	
Adorno, 21 / Bailey, 94 / Taft, 67		1e	2e	3e	4e	5e	6e	7e	
C. Paganini, 165		1a	2a	3a	4a	5a	6a	7a	
Stuckey, 330		1 cy	2 cy	3 cy	4 cy	5 cy	6 cy	7 cy	
Hohmann, 309		1 – B	1 – B	1 – B	1 – B	1 – B	1 – B	1 – B	
Acheson, 80		1	2	3	4	5	6	7	
Cromleigh, 264		-3	-2	-1	0	+1	+2	+3	
Esslinger, 97		- 3	- 2	- 1	0	+ 1	+ 2	+ 3	
Crocker, 328	..1-..12	..1-..12	.1-..12	1 – 12	1 – 12	1 – 12	.1 - .12	..1-..12	
Bramsen, 299		**1-**7	**1-**7	*1 -*7	1 – 7	*1 - *7			
	1)	2)	3)	4)	5)	6)	7)	8)	
Sacher, 204		5-2	5-1	5-0	5+1	5+2	5+3		
Sacher, 204		3-2	3-1	3-0	3+1	3+2	3+3		
Armstrong, 92		1-2	1-1	1-0	1+1	1+2	1+3		

Table comparing pitch-notation systems by octave register.

	A₂–B₂	C₁ – B₁	C – B	c – b	c¹ – b¹	c² – b²	c³ – b³	c⁴ – b⁴	c⁵ –
Hahn, 33			1	1'	1''	1'''			
Lotz, 324		1''–7''	1'–7'	1–7	1–7	1'–7'	1''–7''	1'''–7'''	
Souhaitty, 290			1,–7,	1–7	1.–7.	1;–7;			
Heim, 325		1–12	1–12	1–12	1–12	1–12	1–12	1–12	
Chevé, 307 / Clavière, 308 / von Ziwet, 301			1–	1–	1–7	1–7	1*–7*		
Stein, 358			1–7	1–7	1–7	1–7			
Galin, 296 / Pagi, 311			1	1–7	1–7	1–7			
Mathews, 322			1–7	1–7	1–7	1–7			
Richter, 295		1–7	1–7	1–7	1–7	1–7			
Moon, 88		①	②	③	④	⑤			
Sauveur, 137									
Hans, 230					6	7	8		
Eisenmenger, 17		A	B	C	D	E	F	G	
Glenn, 261		c₃	c₂	c₁	c₀	c¹	c²	c³	

	A₂-B₂	C₁ – B₁	C – B	c – b	c¹ – b¹	c² – b²	c³ – b³	a⁴ – b⁴	c⁵ –
Danel, 354			D : B	D – B·	D – B	· D – B	·· D – B		
Micci, 356		D))	D̲ⁱ	D))	D̲	D	D̄	⌒	
Glover, 353			C – H	·D – T̄	D – T	´D – T̄			
Schulz, 340				L – ɣ̌	c – h	ʁ – ɟ	c – h		
Römer-Neubner, 203		a	b	c	d	e	f	ɦ	h
Rousseau, 292		x	a	b	c	d	e		
LaSalette, 348			c·	c·	c	č	č·		
Rootsey, 346			a – m̲	n̲ – z	a – m	n – z			
Curwen, 349				d̲	d	d̄			
Werckmeister, 337			C – H German	C – H Latin	c – h German	c – h Latin			
Lippius, 335			A – G	A – G	a – g	aa – gg	aaa-ggg		
Patterson, 342			A – G	a – g	a – g	A – G			
Brennick, 107		A	A	a	a'	a''	a'''	a''''	
Döring, 348			C – H	c – h	c – h	c d e			
Brody, 350			D – Si	D – Si	D – Si	D̄ – S̄i	o – q		
Miné, 301			1 – 7	8 – 15	a – g	h – n	o – q		
Gatting, 122		X	?	V	C	ℍ	B	W	

418

	A_2–B_2	C_1–B_1	C–B	c–b	c^1–b^1	c^2–b^2	c^3–b^3	c^4–b^4	c^5–	Reference
S	S	R	Q	P	0	1	2	3	4	Reeve, 216
D.	D.	C.	B.	A.	1.	2.	3.	4.		K. Schumann, 161
		C	G	P	1	2	3	4		Lemme, 149
		-3/c	-2/c	-1/c	1/c	2/c	3/c	4/c		Steffens, 93
		1♭	2♭	3♭	4♭	5♭	6♭	7♭		Raymondi, 158
		d^1	d^2	d^3	d^4	d^5	d^6	d^7		Pereira de Sampaio, 361
			C	c	c_1	c_2	c_3			Schroeder, 184
		1.Oct.	2.Oct.	3.Oct.	4.Oct.	5.Oct.	6.Oct.	7.Oct.		Taft, 67 / Vincent, 164
		[symbol]	[symbol]	[symbol]	[symbol]	[symbol]	[symbol]	[symbol]		Austman, 174
	[symbol]	[symbol]	[symbol]	[symbol]	[symbol]	[symbol]	[symbol]	[symbol]		Virtue, 77
[symbol]	[symbol]	[symbol]	[symbol]	[symbol]	[symbol]	[symbol]	[symbol]	[symbol]	[symbol]	Aulnaye, 141
	+	–	/	\	<	.	..	∴		Karlowicz, 313

	Aloysio, 384	Azévedo, 122	Bertini, 371	Bukspan,	Capellen, 200	Fawcett, 252	Groll, 273	Démotz, 139	Frémond, 217	Rambach, 390
c^5 –										
c^4 – b^4										
c^3 – b^3										
c^2 – b^2										
c^1 – b^1										
c – b										
C – B										
C_1 – B_1										
A_2–B_2										

	Johannis, 256	Laker, 58	Lanz, 119	Montanello, 379	Skapski, 105	J.P. Adams, 200	Clements-Kropp, 312	Herf, 130
$c^5 -$								
$c^4 - b^4$								
$c^3 - b^3$								
$c^2 - b^2$								
$c^1 - b^1$								
$c - b$								
$C - B$								
$C_1 - B_1$								
$A_2 - B_2$								

A_2-B_2	C_1 - B_1	C - B	c - b	c^1 - b^1	c^2 - b^2	c^3 - b^3	c^4 - b^4	c^5 -	
									Moser, 388
			1 7	ǀ 7	ʅ 7				Braithwait, 286

A_2-C_1	D_1 - C	D - c	d - c^1	d^1 - c^2	d^2 - c^3	d^3 - c^4	d^4 - c^5	
0-4	0-3	0-2	0-1	01	02	03	04	Pum, 268
A_2-G_1	A_1 - G	A - g	a - g^1	a^1 - g^2	a^2 - g^3	a^3 - g^4	a^4 - c^5	
□ • black	⊐ • brown	⊿ • green	◁ • red	○ • blue	ɔ • orange	ɑ • violet	• tan	Adsit, 240
1	2	3	4	5	6	7	8	Bailey, 94
Oct.1	Oct.2	Oct.3	Oct.4	Oct.5	Oct.6	Oct.7	Oct.8	Cohen, 242
L1—1	L2—2	L3—3	R4—4	R5—5	R6—6	R7—7		Parsons, 320
I	II	III	IV	V	VI	VII	VIII	Roesgen-Champion, 78
C_2-C_1	C_1 - C	C - c	c - c^1	c^1 - c^2	c^2 - c^3	c^3 - c^4	c^4 - c^5	
2	3	4	5	6	7	8	9	Thelwall, 45

System							
Hyard, 70	$C_1 - C$	$C - c$	$c - c^1$	$c^1 - c^2$	$c^2 - c^3$	$c^3 - c^4$	
Teule, 306	Ut 1:	Ut 2:	Ut 3:	Ut 4:	Ut 5:	Ut 6:	
		3	4	5	6		
Beaulieu, 15	$C_1 - c$	$C - c^1$	$c - c^2$	$c^1 - c^3$	$c^2 - c^4$		
	G^0	B_1^2	I_2^3	E_3^4	A_4^5		
Russell, 91	$D_1 - c$	$D - c^1$	$d - c^1$	$d^1 - c^2$	$d^2 - c^3$	$d^3 - c^4$	$d^4 - c^5$
	(1) 55	(2) 110	(3) 220	(4) 440	(5) 880	(6) 1760	(7) 3520
Arellano, 237	$E_1 - E$	$E - e$	$e - e^1$	$e^1 - e^2$	$e^2 - e^3$		
Riemann, 171	a	a	a	⊙	a		
Austin, 371		$c - g^1$	$a^1 - f^3$				
Arnò, 163	$F_1 - E$	$F - e$	$f - e^1$	$f^1 - e^2$	$f^2 - e^3$	$f^3 - e^4$	$f^4 - c^5$
	②	③	④	⑤ or 5	⑥	⑦	
Bremink, 107	A,	A	a	a'	a''	a'''	a''''
	$F_1 - B$	$F - b$	$f^1 - b^2$	$f^2 - b^3$			
Wójcik, 250	0	2	4	6			

423

Bunger, 265

Totten, 100

Mersenne, 336

$G_2 - A_1$	$G - a$	$f - g^1$	$e^1 - f^2$	$e^3 - f^4$
$G_1 - A$	$G - a$	$g - a^1$	$g^1 - a^2$	$g^2 - a^3$
L	B	M	T	U
$G - f$	$g - f^1$	$g^1 - f^2$	$g^2 - f^3$	
V – Z	v – z	v – z	$\underline{v} - \underline{z}$	

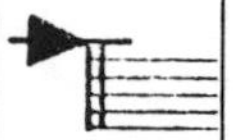

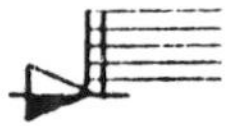

D. PROPOSED NOTEHEAD DESIGNS

1) Pitch

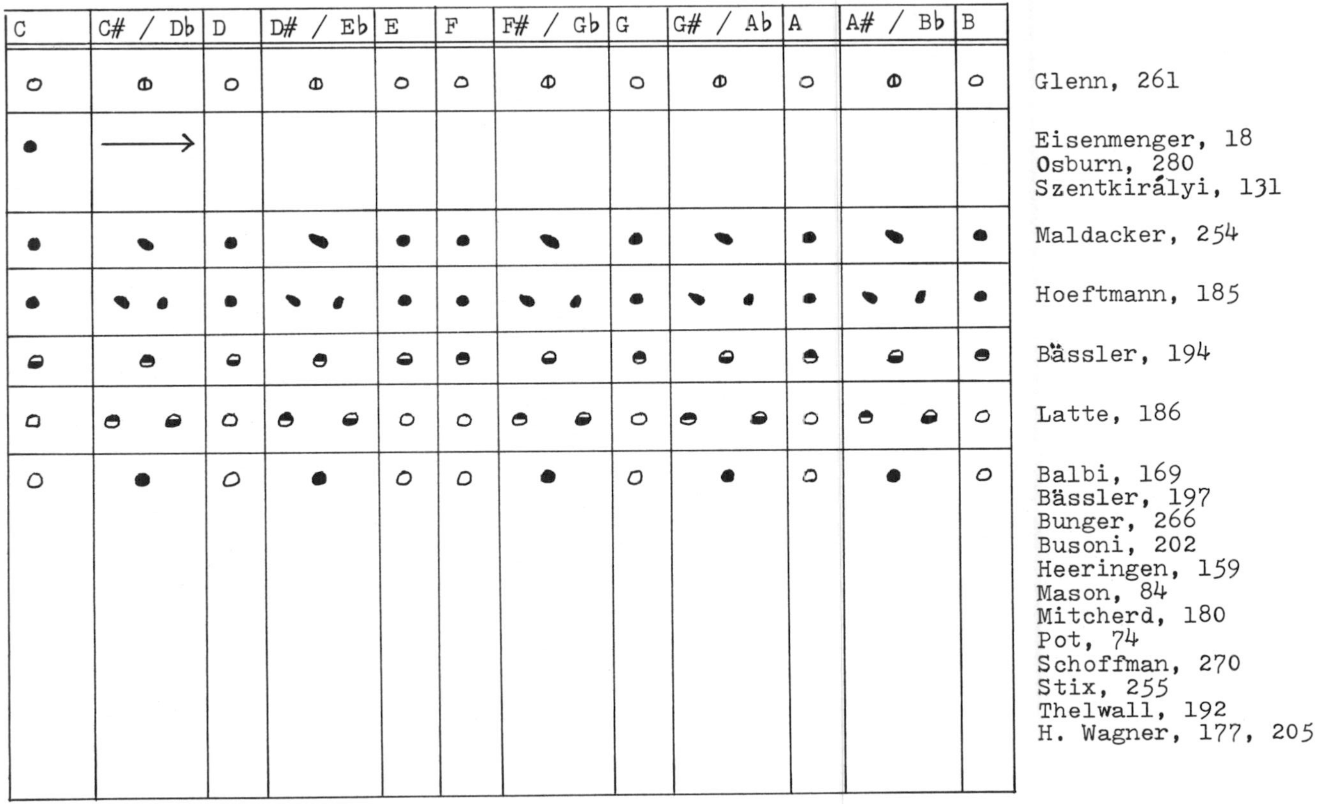

	C	C# / Db	D	D# / Eb	E	F	F# / Gb	G	G# / Ab	A	A# / Bb	B
Glenn, 261	o	e	o	e	o	o	e	o	e	o	e	o
Eisenmenger, 18; Osburn, 280; Szentkirályi, 131	•	↑										
Maldacker, 254	•	◗	•	◖	•	•	◗	•	◗	•	◗	•
Hoeftmann, 185	•	◖	•	◖	•	•	◖	•	◖	•	◖	•
Bässler, 194	◑	◑	◑	◑	◑	◑	◑	◑	◑	◑	◑	◑
Latte, 186	◖	◑	◖	◑	o	o	◑	o	◑	o	◑	o
Balbi, 169; Bässler, 197; Bunger, 266; Busoni, 202; Heeringen, 159; Mason, 84; Mitcherd, 180; Pot, 74; Schoffman, 270; Stix, 255; Thelwall, 192; H. Wagner, 177, 205	o	•	o	•	o	o	•	o	•	o	•	o

425

	F.R. Miller, 69	Beunk, 235	Bässler, 198 / Fawcett, 253 / Frémond, 217 / Gambale, 150 / Grassi-Landi, 170 / Howe, 259 / Lemme, 149 / Weisshappel, 245 / Wójcik, 250	Bässler, 193	Eimert, 223	Bässler, 193 / Mayrhofers, 190 / Rohleder, 142	Fleischhauer, 211	Marcelin, 96	Neumann, 226	Sauveur, 137
B										
A# / Bb										
A										
G# / Ab										
G										
F# / Gb										
F										
E										
D# / Eb										
D										
C# / Db										
C										

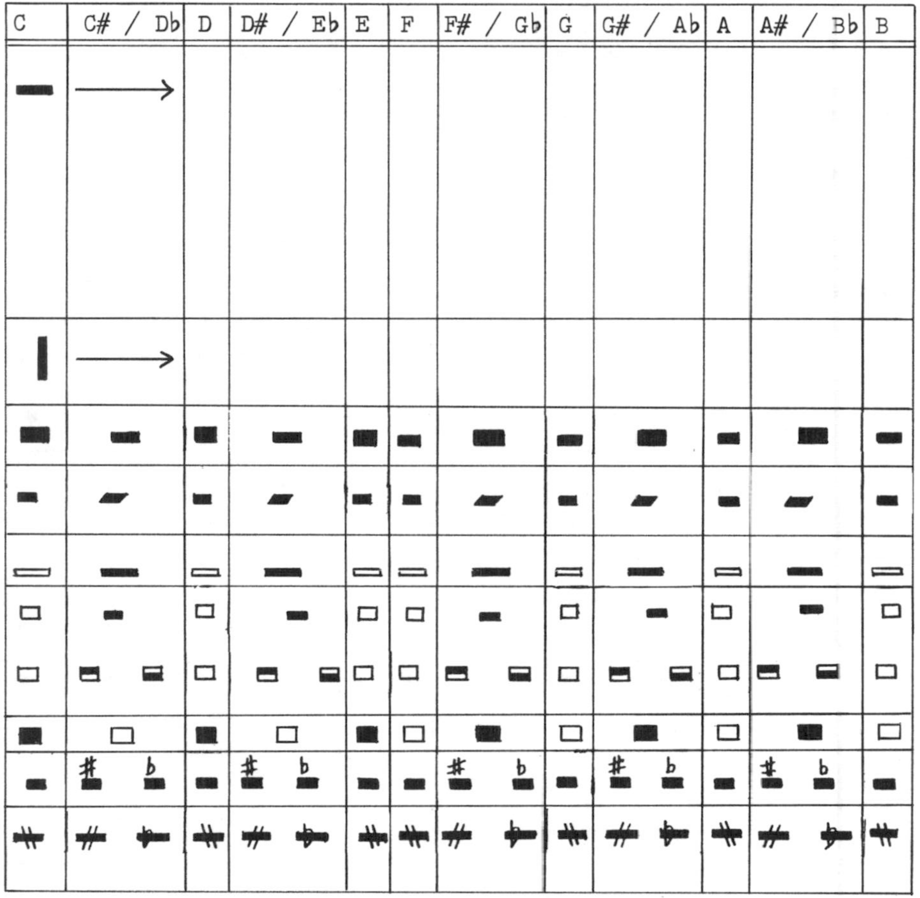

Table of pitch–color (or pitch-association) correspondences by various authors. Column headings (author, page):

- Anon., 16
- Barra, 262
- Baumann, 168
- A. Decher, 31
- Edwards, 82
- Godoy, 249
- Krause, 12
- Lacassagne, 117
- Moon, 89
- Römer-Neubner, 203
- Antheil, 221
- Bonnard, 172
- Leyat, 72
- Engelke, 41
- Wallbridge, 156
- Orser, 188
- Weigand, 178, 185
- Mattheson, 140
- P. Koch, 229
- de Stains, 154

Row labels (pitches), top to bottom: B, A# / Bb, A, G# / Ab, G, F# / Gb, F, E, D# / Eb, D, C# / Db, C

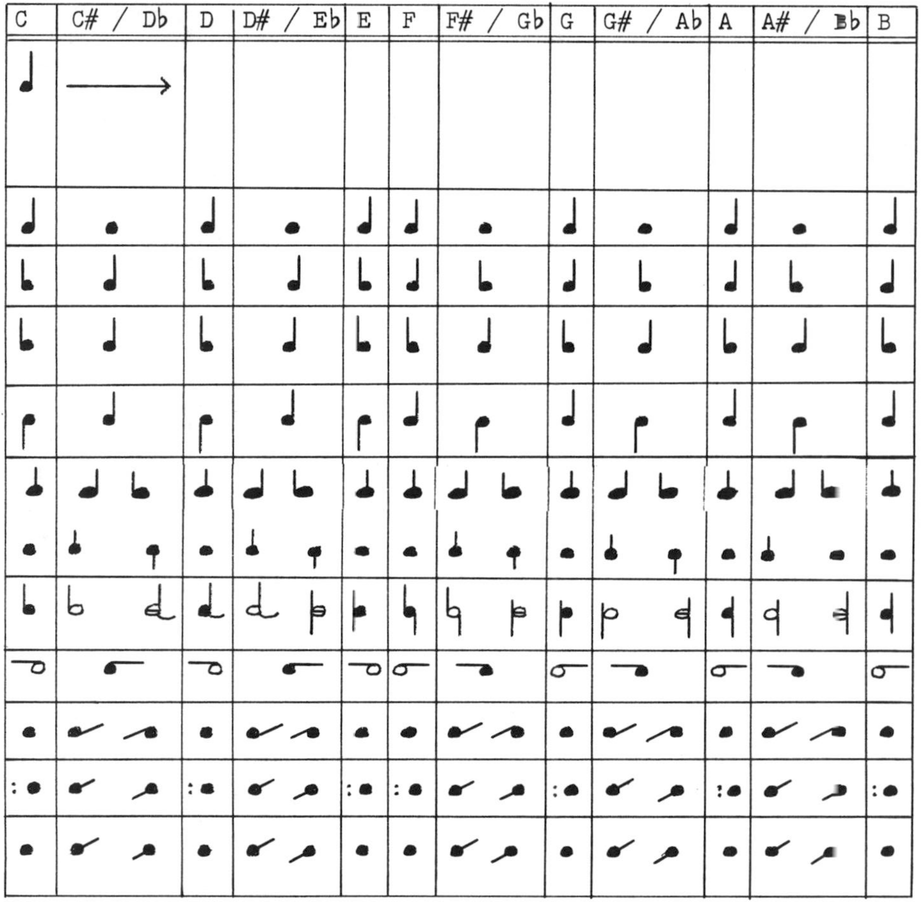

Column headers (left to right):

- Bailey, 94 / G. Decher, 29 / Musikverlag Euphonie, 62 / Skapski, 105 / Warren, 25
- Brisgaloff, 181
- Bässler, 196
- Bässler, 196 / Lajos, 262
- Riesen, 46 / K. Schumann, 161
- Peyrallo, 233
- Pousseur, 257
- Aulnaye, 141
- Nadjen, 79
- Capellen, 201
- Raymondi, 155, 158
- Hartmann, 251 / Studer, 239

Row labels (top to bottom): B | A# / Bb | A | G# / Ab | G | F# / Gb | F | E | D# / Eb | D | C# / Db | C

A table of musical notation symbols by author (columns) and pitch (rows). The cell contents are graphical music notations.

Pitch	Johannis, 256	Démotz, 139	Rand, 243	J.P. Adams, 200	Anderton, 187	Schoenberg, 224	Chailley, 247	Chatillon, 85	Eimert, 248 Kohler, 249	Gaudard, 212	Dwyer, 166	Schäffer, 258	Stehle, 191
B													
A# / Bb													
A													
G# / Ab													
G													
F# / Gb													
F													
E													
D# / Eb													
D													
C# / Db													
C													

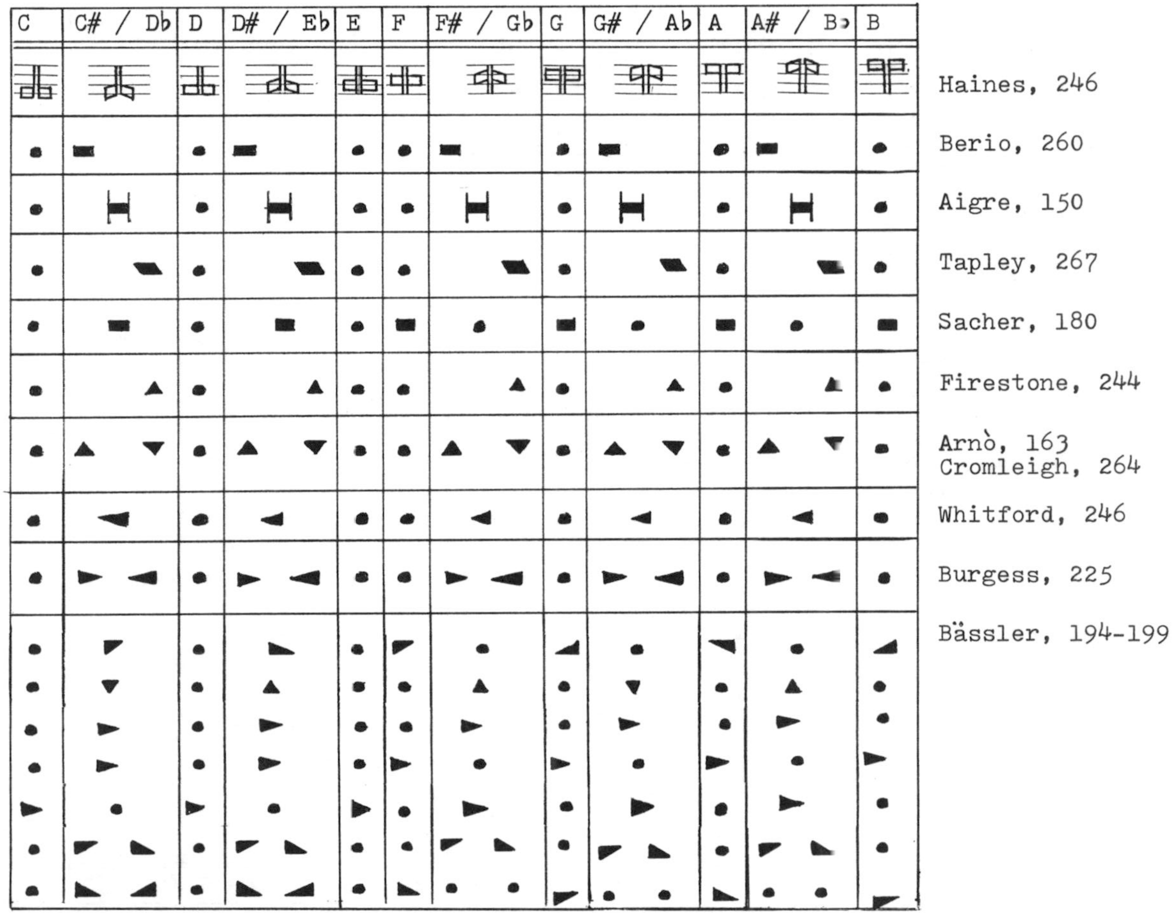
C
C# / Db
D
D# / Eb
E
F
F# / Gb
G
G# / Ab
A
A# / B♭
B
Haines, 246
Berio, 260
Aigre, 150
Tapley, 267
Sacher, 180
Firestone, 244
Arnò, 163
Cromleigh, 264
Whitford, 246
Burgess, 225
Bässler, 194-199

	Marcus, 234	Sacher, 204	Friderici, 272 / Saint-Lambert, 115	Elst, 271	Marie, 265 / Obouhov, 214 / Toch, 229	Diettrich-Kalkhoff, 208 / Hartmann, 252	Pum, 268	Faunt, 219 / Tapley, 267	Sarlit, 240	Hora, 232	Austman, 174	Unbereit, 209	Graaff, 213
B	•	▌		⊞	•	•	⊃	•	•	•	•	•	•
A# / Bb	◆	▲		⊞	×	○	○	□	◢	◣	△	∠	◆
A	•	•		◆	•	•	(	•	•	•	•	×	∨
G# / Ab	◆	◆		◆	×	○	○	□	◢	▼	△	∠	◆
G	•	▌		◇	•	•	⊃	•	•	•	•	×	∨
F# / Gb	◆	▲		⊞	×	○	○	□	◢	▲	△	∠	◆
F	•	•		⊞	•	•	(	•	•	▼	•	×	◆
E	•	◆		⊞	•	•	○	•	•	▲	•	•	•
D# / Eb	◆	▌		⊞	×	○	⊃	□	◢	◣	△	∠	◆
D	•	▲		◆	•	•	○	•	•	■	•	×	∨
C# / Db	◆	•	↑	◆	×	○	(	□	◢	◢	△	∠	◆
C	•	◆	◆	◇	•	•	○	•	•	•	•	×	∨

	Carozzi, 182	Hans, 231	Edition Heinrich, 191	Reeve, 216	Romano, 272	Stéphan, 227	Perbandt, 210	Stott, 173	Tarrant, 279	Robberson, 187	Middlemiss, 236	Arellano, 238	Menchaca, 206	Schroeder, 184
B														
A# / 3b														
A														
G# / Ab														
G														
F# / Gb														
F														
E														
D# / Eb														
D														
C# / Db														
C														

C	C# / Db	D	D# / Eb	E	F	F# / Gb	G	G# / Ab	A	A# / Bb	B

Cohen, 242

Scott, 64
Taft, 67

2) Enharmonic Pitches

	B#	Bbb	F×	Fb	E#	Ebb	C×	Cb
Achtélik, 215	◇	◆	◆	◇	◇	◆	◆	◇
Beunk, 235	●	♭●	#●	●	●	♭●	#●	●
Burgess, 225	▲	▼	▲	▼	▲	▼	▲	▼
Capellen, 201	♪	♫	♫	♪	♪	♫	♫	♪
Carozzi, 182	⊟	◁	◇	◿	⊟	◁	◇	◿
Diettrich-Kalkhoff, 208	×	⊖	※	○	×	⊖	※	○
Faunt, 219	●	◍	●	◉	●	◍	●	◉
Fleischhauer, 211	○	◑	◐	◒	○	◑	◐	◒
Graaff, 213	∨	⋈	×	◇	∨	⋈	×	◇
Keller, 90	♀	♀	♀	♀	♀	♀	♀	♀

	Montanello, 156	Raymondi, 158	Sauveur, 137	Schroeder, 184	Stéphan, 227	Studer, 239	Tapley, 267	Unbereit, 209	H. Wagner, 177	Weisshappel, 245
B#		♪	♪	♪	♦	♪		×	∘	●
Bbb	♪	♪		♪	♪	♪	♪	≈	∘	○
Fx	♪	♪		♪	♦	♪	♪	×	∘	○
Fb		♪	♪	♪	♪	♪	♪	♪	∘	●
E#		♪	♪	♪	♦	♪		×	∘	○
Ebb	♪	♪		♪	♪	♪	♪	≈	∘	●
Gx	♪	♪		♪	♦	♪	♪	×	∘	●
Cb		♪	♪	♪	♪	♪	♪	♪	∘	○

435

3) Diatonic Scale Syllables

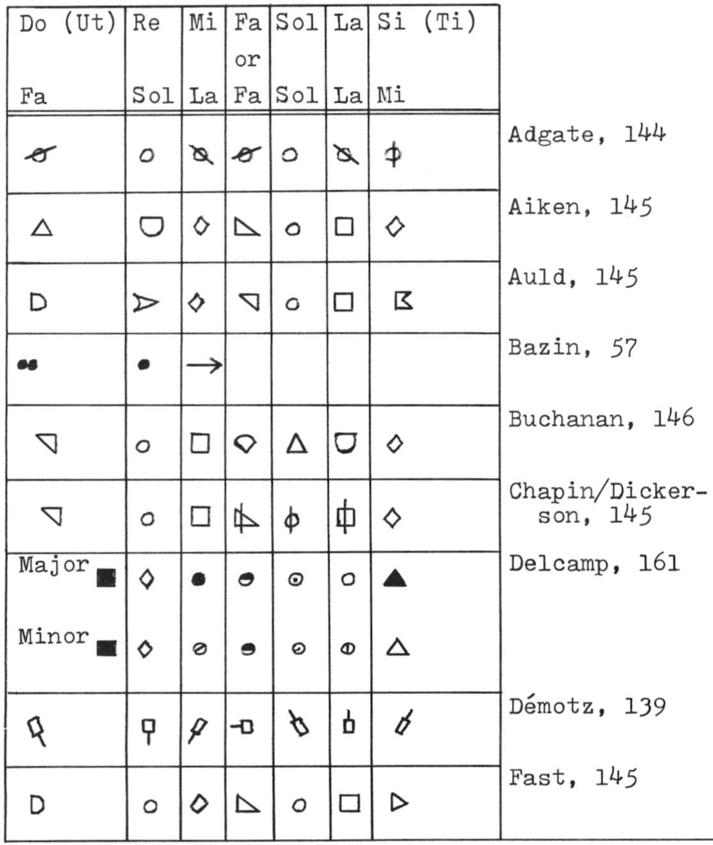
Do (Ut) Fa
Re Sol
Mi La
Fa or Fa
Sol Sol
La La
Si (Ti) Mi
Adgate, 144
Aiken, 145
Auld, 145
Bazin, 57
Buchanan, 146
Chapin/Dickerson, 145
Major
Minor
Delcamp, 161
Démotz, 139
Fast, 145

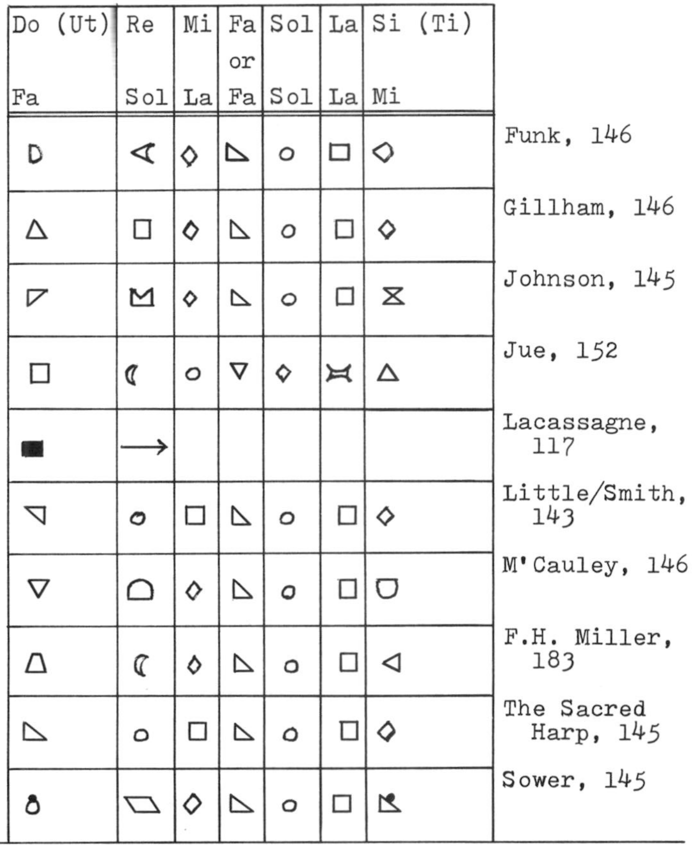
Do (Ut) Fa
Re Sol
Mi La
Fa or Fa
Sol Sol
La La
Si (Ti) Mi
Funk, 146
Gillham, 146
Johnson, 145
Jue, 152
Lacassagne, 117
Little/Smith, 143
M'Cauley, 146
F.H. Miller, 183
The Sacred Harp, 145
Sower, 145

Do (Ut)	Re	Mi	Fa	Sol	La	Si (Ti)	
Fa	Sol	La	Fa or Fa	Sol	La	Mi	
⋈	◻	◁	○	◻	△		Swan, 145
▽	◑	◔	◑	◻	◇		Wakefield, 146
◁	◔	◇	△	◑	▽		Walker, 146
○	⊖	⊡	○	⊖	◠	⊗	Woodward, 145

Do	Ra	Me	Fa	Sol	La	Se	
● green	yellow	red	brown	blue	black	pink	Acee, 167

4) Note Duration

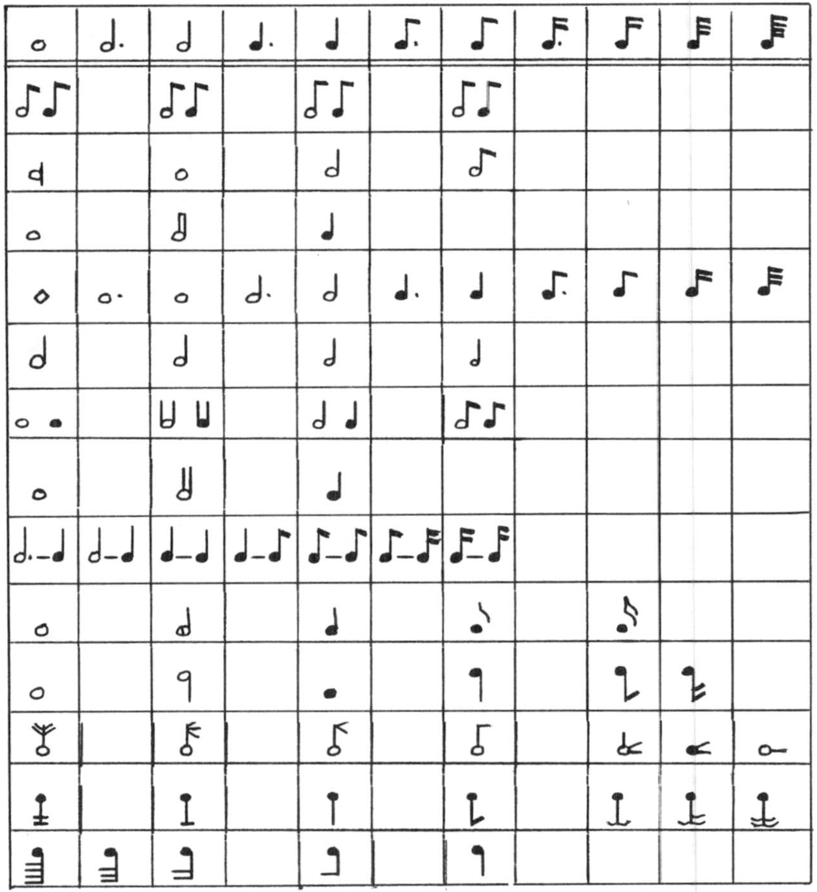

Gambale, 150

Howe, 259

Mason, 84

Raymondi, 158

Rohleder, 142

Schoffman, 270

Tarrant, 279

Studer, 73

Groll, 274

Hautstont, 54

Cohen, 242

Démotz, 139

Stott, 173

	Sauveur, 137	Nadjen, 80	P. Koch, 229	Weigand, 178	Haines, 246	Orser, 188	Middlemiss, 236	Wallbridge, 156	Elst, 270	Busoni, 202	Drieberg, 153	Chailley, 247	Bunger, 266

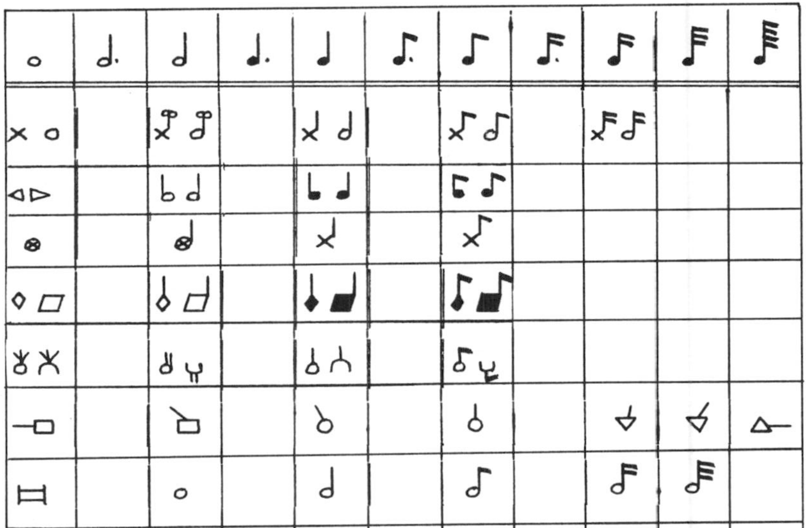

Table of note-value notations (rotated). Columns list the authors and source page references; rows correspond to successive note durations.

Note	Diettrich-Kalkhoff, 208	Lajos, 366	Obouhov, 214 / Toch, 229	Perbandt, 210	Pum, 269	Romano, 272	Weisshappel, 245	Brook/Gould, 365	DeLaruelle/Cossart, 359	Delcamp, 161	Glisson, 363	Stewart, 354	Werckmeister, 337	Dammas, 297 / A.L. Richter, 295
1						◁		5C		$\frac{1}{2}$	64			
2						▷	◻	3C	$\frac{1}{8}$	1	32			
3		◻				▷	◻	6C	$\frac{1}{4}$	2	16	1	16	F 1
4														
5		◻	◻	◼	◻	○	◻	8C	$\frac{1}{2}$	4	8	2	8	1
6									8.					
7		◻	◻	◼	◻	○	◻	4C	1	8	4	4	4	1
8									4.	12				
9		◻	◻	◻	◻	◻	0	2C	2	16	2	8	2	11
10									2.	24				111
11		○	△	⊗	◻	◻	II	1C		32	1	16	1	1111

Davantes, 283 · Hohmann, 309 · J.F.W. Koch, 297 · Mathews, 322 · Miquel, 305 · Parsons, 320 · Schleyer, 318 · Stuckey, 330 · Waldmann, 304 · White, 392 · Adorno, 352 · Danel, 354

	DeLusse, 339	Döring, 348	Eyquem, 358	Glover, 351 M. Haydn, 344	Hill, 360	LaSalette, 343	Nichetti, 349 Riebesthal, 345	Rootsey, 346	Russ, 357	Pereira de Sampaio, 361	Souhaitty, 290	Patterson, 342
𝅘𝅥𝅱												
𝅘𝅥𝅰												A–
𝅘𝅥𝅯	a‖				ⅡC	C‖	u‖	ȧ	(C̄)	dꞆ	a	A'
𝅘𝅥𝅯.												
𝅘𝅥𝅮	a̲		P⅃		LC	C|.	U̲	(a)	(ċ)	dꞀ	b	A;
𝅘𝅥𝅮.											bi	
𝅘𝅥	a	c̲	A⌐	d	•G	e	u	a	G	d◖	e	A:
𝅘𝅥.						U.	a;				ci	
𝅗𝅥	ā̲	c	⌶A	D	—C	c̄|		⎮a̲	ȢC	d	d	A˙
𝅗𝅥.					c̄‖						di	
𝅝	A	C=	Ᵽ	–D	—C	c̄‖‖			c	Ᵽ	e	A—

443

	Aloysio, 384	Austin, 371	Bertini, 372	Bukspan, 329	Depierre, 385	Dupont, 389	Dwyer, 166	Eisenmenger, 18	Gouverneur, 398	Harrison, 303	Hermann, 383	Hunt, 393
♬				⋮		♭					c	
♬		⌐	N	⋮		♩	)·))		▪	∷	ι	
♪		⌐	∴	∷		♩·	)))	▪	＼	∷	c	⨏
♪·								＼				
♩	⌐	ρ	‖	·	ǀ	⌣	))	∷	—	·	⌐	4
♩·		ℓ		⋮				ǀ	∸			
♩	—	ꟼ	⁒	ˌ	·	ꙅ	()	⌐	／		⌐	4
♩·		ϙ		⁝					∠			
♩	=	ℓ	N	⹀	∷	ℓ·	‿	⋮	⊃	·	⌐	⊥
♩·		ℓ	⹀						Ɔ			⊥
o	≡	ϭ	N	+		ℂ			(	∷	⌐	ǀ

444

	Kabala, 278	Natorp, 299	Menchaca, 207	Montanello, 380	Morrell, 276	Moser, 388	Prévost, 374	Raab, 395	Rambures, 376	Riom, 387	Schmitt, 314	Schulz, 340	Stein, 308

445

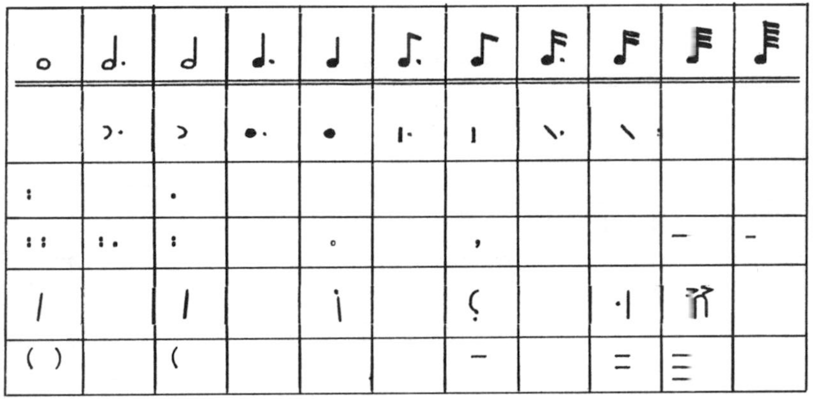

Taylor, 396

Tufts, 338

Vidales, 353

Zichy-Ferraris, 388

von Ziwet, 301

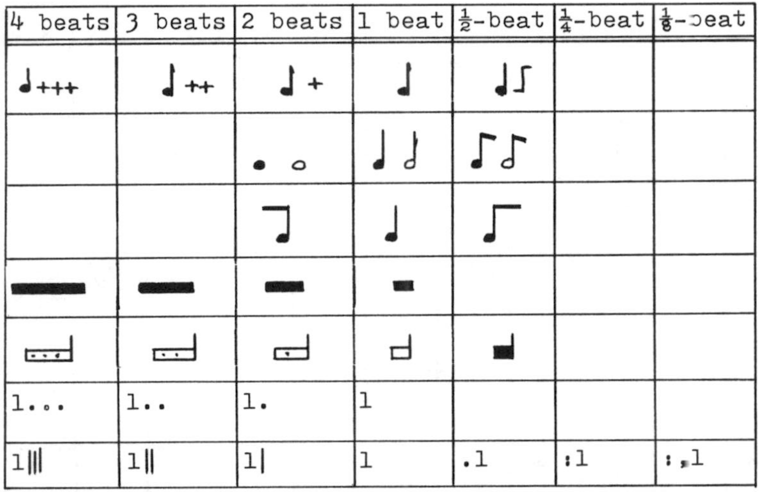
4 beats
3 beats
2 beats
1 beat
½-beat
¼-beat
⅛-beat
1...
1..
1.
1
1|||
1||
1|
1
.1
:1
:,1

G. Decher, 30

Fleischhauer, 211

Skapski, 106

Edwards, 82

Haines, 246

Chevé, 307
Galin, 296

Guilford, 316

	4 beats	3 beats	2 beats	1 beat	½-beat	¼-beat	⅛-beat
Lotz, 324	1---	1--	1-	1	(1	((1	(((1
Rousseau, 292			,1.	,1,			
Shires, 362	4	3	2	1	½	¼	
Hettiger Verlag, 364	C---	C--	C-	C	c		
Micci, 356		ᴡ‑D	ᴠ‑D	‑D	·D	··D	
Clements-Kropp, 312	---	--	-				
Gambale, 151	⌐4	⌐3	⌐2	⌐1			
Musikverlag Euphonie, 62	♩♩♩♩	♩♩♩	♩♩	♩	♪·		
Pagi, 311	xx	x-	x	-	·|	·|	
Warren, 25	||||	|||	||					

E. NOVEL REST SYMBOLS

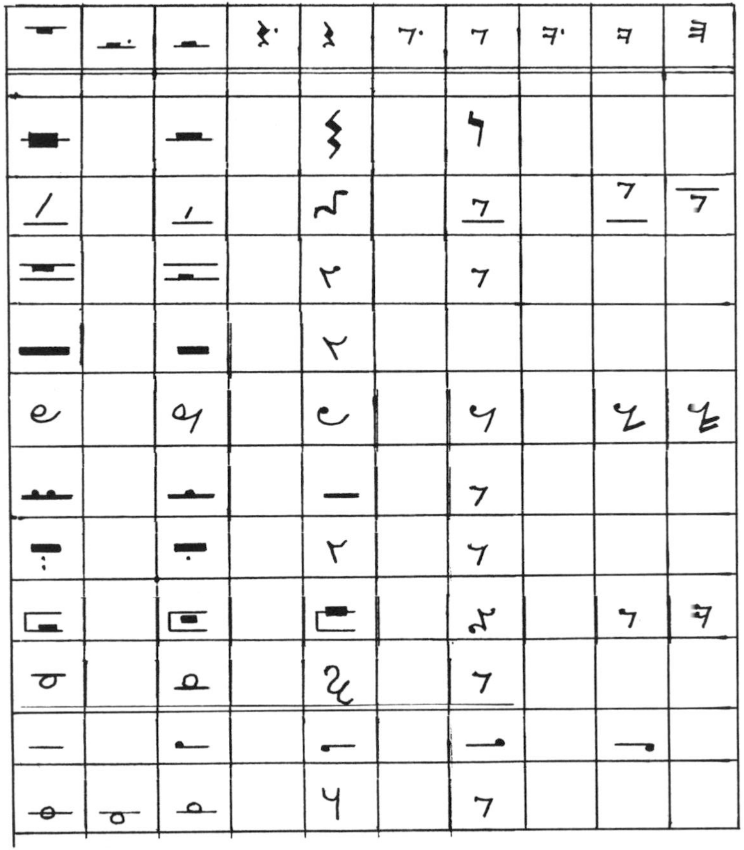
Arellano, 238
Baumgartner, 382
Beunk, 235
Gaudard, 212
Hautstont, 54
Hohmann, 309
Middlemiss, 236
Raymondi, 158
Engelke, 41
Menchaca, 207
Raab, 395

Rambures, 376	Sauveur, 137	Brook/Gould, 365	Delcamp, 161	Faunt, 219	Glisson, 363	Schleyer, 318	Schulz, 340	Stewart, 355	White, 392	Adorno, 352	Harrison, 303
♩	)•	3-	♪		32		1/32		32	g	R;;
♩	‖•	6-	♪	[2]	16		1/16	♪	16	f	R;
					16.						
♩	│•	8-	♪	[1]	8		1/8	♪	8	e	R,
♩			♪		8.						
│•	•	4-	♪	—	4		$\frac{1}{4}$	♪	4	d	R
│			♪		4.						
│	♩	2-	16	▭	2	$\frac{1}{2}$	$\frac{1}{2}$	♪	2	b	.R
┊	♩		24		2.						
▌	♩	1-	32	▢	1	1	I	♪	1	a	:R

	Braithwait, 286	Bukspan, 329	Démotz, 139	Dupont, 389	Dwyer, 166	Firestone, 244	Gouverneur, 398	M. Haydn, 344	Hermann, 383	Hunt, 394	Kutahialian, 397	Mathews, 322

	Montanello, 381	Nadjen, 80	Nichetti, 349	Orser, 189	Patterson, 342	Perbandt, 210	Prévost, 374	Rambach, 391	Riebesthal, 148	Riom, 387	Romano, 273	Russell, 91

451

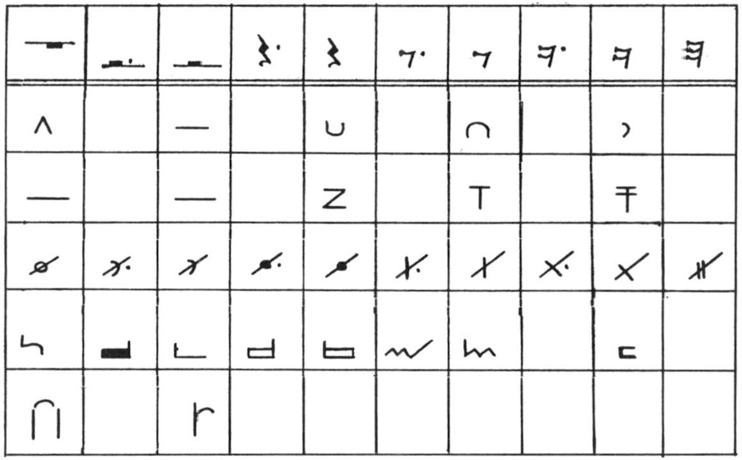

	Souhaitty, 291	Stuckey, 330	Taylor, 396	Wallbridge, 157	Weigand, 178

Quarter-rest symbol only

Heeringen, 160	Hill, 360	Lajos, 362	Little/Smith, 144	Waldmann, 305

452

Rest symbol for all durations

Symbol	Sources	Symbol	Sources	Symbol	Sources
S	Aulnaye, 141	■	Neumann, 226	ʒ	Frémond, 217
O	Klett, 300 Miquel, 306 Rousseau, 292 Waldmann, 305	⌐	H. Wagner, 178, 206	long / short	Orser, 188
R	Crocker, 328 Toch, 229	*	Guilford, 316 Kobelt, 321	V >	Pot, 75 Wójcik, 250
θ or Đe	Stewart, 355	·°	Davantes, 283		Russ, 357
⌿	Vidales, 353 Arnò, 163	–	Heim, 326 Seymat, 386	C	Osburn, 280
▄	Fawcett, 252 Skapski, 106	φ	Fleischhauer, 211	‖‖‖	
		•	Rootsey, 346		

	4 beats	3 beats	2 beats	1 beat	½-beat	¼-beat	⅛-beat
Chevé, 307 / Galin, 296	0000	000	00	0			
Glover, 351	+432	+32	+2	+			
LaSalette, 343	0/4	0/3	0/2	0			
Lotz, 324	0---	0--	0-	0	(0	((0	(((0
Pagi, 311	xx	x-	x	-	•	••	
G. Decher, 30	♪						
Gambale, 151							
Musikverlag Euphonie, 63							
Warren, 25	≡≡≡	≡≡	≡	—			

454

F. PITCH SYLLABLES

Source	C	C#/Db	D	D#/Eb	E	F	F#/Gb	G	G#/Ab	A	A#/Bb	B
Acee, 167	do		ra		me	fa		sol		la		se
Aloysio, 384	do	lu	re	na	mi	fa	tu	sol	bi	la	ge	si
Bertini, 372	do	ro	né	râi	zâi	mo	bo	lo	bé	jâi	bâi	vâi
Cogswell, 38	do	di ra	re	ri me	mi	fa	fi se	sol	si le	la	li se	si
Frémond, 217	do	ta	ro	pa	mo	fa	co	sa	vo	la	bo	ga
Glisson, 363	do	di rah	re	ri me	mi	fa	fi se	sol	si le	la	li te	ti
Glover, 350	do	doy row	re	roy mow	mi	fa	foy sow	sol	soy low	la	loy tow	ti
Kob, 39	do	d di	re	ri	mi	fa	fi	sol	sil	la	li	si
Lajos, 262	do	vu	re	po	mi	fa	ne	so	cu	la	be	ti
Menchaca, 206	do	du	re	ro	mi	fa	fe	sol	nu	la	se	si
Roesgen-Champion, 78	Do	dé	Ré	ré	Mi	Fa	fé	Sol	sé	La	lé	Si
Virtue, 77	do	di	re	me	mi	fa	fi	so	le	la	te	ti
Curwen, 351	doh	de ra	ray	re ma	me	fah	fe sa	soh	se la	lah	le ta	te
Totten, 99	doh	de	ray	re	me	fa	fe	sol	se	la	le	te
Heeringen, 159	doe	dee	ray	ree	me	fa	fee	sole	see	la	lee	pa
F.H. Miller, 183	doe	dee raw	ray	ree may	mee	faw	fee say	sole	see lay	law	lee say	see
Aigre, 150	ut	da	ré	bo	mi	fa	di	sol	fi	la	ri	si
Blein, 17	ut	dé	ré	bé	mi	fa	da	sol	lé	la	di	si
Elst, 270	ut	it ra	ré	ri ma	mi	fa	fi sal	sol	sil lae	la	li	at
Mersenne, 285	ut		ré		mi	fa		sol		la		za
Gambale, 150	ba	ca	da	fa	la	ma	na	pa	ra	sa	ta	va
Grassi-Landi, 170	ba	be	bi	bo	da	de	di	do	la	le	li	lo

C	C#/Db	D	D#/Eb	E	F	F#/Gb	G	G#/Ab	A	A#/Bb	B	
ba	be	do	du	da	de	go	gu	ga	ge	bo	ba	Pum, 268
da	de	ga	ge	ma	me	fa	fe	la	-e	sa	se	Engelke, 41
bé	bi	cé	ci	dé	di	fé	fi	lé	-i	mé	mi	Lemme, 149
bé	bo la	lé	10 pa	pé	fa	fé fo	ma	mé mo	ra	ré da	ba	Sarlit, 240
pa	pi ro	ra	ri go	ga	so	fa be	bo	ba le	-o	la de	do	Sauveur, 138
a		é		i	eu		o		u		ou	Rambures, 375

456

Reference	C / VII	C# /Db / VIII	D / IX	D# /Eb / X	E / XI	F / XII	F# /Gb / I	G / II	G# /Ab / III	A / IV	A# /Bb / V	B / VI
Thelwall, 45; Avella, 289; Kircher, 287; Klett, 300; Mersenne, 285; Teule, 306	1 8		2		3	4		5		6		7
Braithwait, 286; Galin, 296; Kobelt, 321; Richter, 295; Rousseau, 292; Stein, 308; von Ziwet, 301	1		2		3	4		5		6		7
Carrillo, 314	0	1	2	3	4	5	6	7	8	9	10	11
Crocker, 328; Guilford, 316; Heim, 325; Schleyer, 318	1	2	3	4	5	6	7	8	9	10	11	12
Stierlein, 291	5 12 19		6 13 20		7 14 21	1 8 15		2 9 16		3 10 17		4 11 18
Bukspan, 329	1	10	11	110	1110	11110	1111	0	01	00	001	000
Clements-Kropp, 312	□	10	2		3	4		5		6		7
Miné, 301	1 8 ~~15~~	~~7 8 15~~	2 9	~~2 8~~	3 10	4 11	~~4 11~~	5 12	~~8 12~~	6 13	~~6 13~~	7 14
Bramsen, 299	1	2	2	3	3	4	5	5	6	6	2	7

C	C# /Db	D	D# /Eb	E	F	F# /Gb	G	G# /Ab	A	A# /Bb	B	
1	1̸ 2⃥	2	2̸ 3⃥	3	4	4̸ 5⃥	5	5̸ 6⃥	5	6̸ 7⃥	7	Chevé, 307 Rousseau, 292
1	1̄ 2̲	2	2̄ 3̲	3	4	4̄ 5̲	5	5̄ 6̲	5	6̄ 7̲	7	Geisler, 319
1	1̸ 2̶	2	2̸ 3̶	3	4	4̸ 5̶	5	5̸ 6̶	5	6̸ 7̶	7	Busby, 308
4	#4	5	#5	6	7	#7	1	#1	2	#2	3	Bontempi, 289
1	#1 b2	2	#2 b3	3	4	#4 b5	5	#5 b6	5	#6 b7	7	Horstig, 294 Miquel, 305 Natorp, 299 Vincent, 305 Waldmann, 304
4	#4 b4	4	#4 b4	4	4	#4 b4	4	#4 b4	4	#4 b4	4	Parsons, 320
1	# b 1 2	2	# b 2 3	3	4	# b 4 5	5	# b 5 6	6	# b 6 7	7	Pagi, 311
1.	.2	2.	.3	3.	4.	.5	5.	.6	6.	.A	B.	Davantes, 283
0	1	2	3	4	5	6	7	8	9	X	N	Stuckey, 330
1	V	2	W	3	4	X	5	Y	6	Z	7	Mathews, 322
V	D	2	R	3	4	F	5	A	6	H	7	Karlowicz, 313
1	1s. s.2	2	2s. s.3	3	4	4s. s.5	5	5s. s.6	6	6s. s.7	7	Harrison, 303
1	2	3	4	5	6	7	8	9	♉	u	s	Schmitt, 314
1	2	3	4	5	6	7	8	9	✢	0	B	Hohmann, 309
1	s1 f2 B1 b2	2	s2 f3 B2 b3	3	4	s4 f5 B4 b5	5	s5 f6 B5 b6	6	s6 f7 B6 b7	7	Lotz, 324

	C	C# /Db	D	D# /Eb	E	F	F# /Gb	G	G# /Ab	A	A# /Bb	B
Nichetti, 349 / Russ, 357	C		D		E	F		G		A		B
Lippius, 335	A		B		C	D		E		F		G
Werckmeister, 337	C		D	E	E	F		G		A		H
Micci, 356	D	A	R	E	M	F	I	S	O	L	U	S
Glisson, 363	D	Я	R	R	M	F	S/F	S	S/I	L/I	I/L	T
DeLaruelle/Cossart, 359	D		R		M	F		S		L		B̷
Stewart, 354	⊘	'C ,D	D	'D ,E	E	F	'F ,G	⊘	'G ,A	A	'A ,H	B
Döring, 348	C	D→Я	D	R→M	E	F	F→O	G	O→L	A	L→S	H
Eyquem, 358	D	C̄	D	D̄	E	F	F̄	G	Ḡ	L	Ā	S
Hettiger verlag, 364	C	C̄	D	D̄	E	F	F̄	G	Ḡ	A	Ā	B
Mersenne, 336	F	F'	S	S'	L	Z	Z'	V	V'	R	R'	M
Schulz, 340	C	*C	D	*D	E	F	*F	G	*G	A	*A	H
Tufts, 337	F	x/F	S	x/S	L	F	x/F	S	x/S	L	x/L	M
Brook/Gould, 365	xC	bD	D	xD bE	E	F	xF bG	G	xG bA	A	xA bB	B
Patterson, 342	An	Ax	Bn	Bx	Cn	Dn	Dx	En	Ex	Fn	Fx	Gn
Hill, 360	C	#C bD	D	#D bE	E	F	#F bG	G	#G bA	A	#A bB	B
Danel, 354	D	Dz R1	R	Rz M1	M	F	Fz S1	S	Sz L1	L	Lz B1	B
Glover, 351	D	Doy Row	R	Roy Mow	M	F	Foy Sow	S	Soy Low	L	Loy Tow	T
Lippius, 335	a		b		c	d		e		f		g

	C	C#/Db	D	D#/Eb	E	F	F#/Gb	G	G#/Ab	A	A#/Bb	B
Presbyter, 341	u		r		m	f		s		l		–
Riebesthal, 345	u	l	r	n	m	f		g		l		s
M. Haydn, 344	j	k	m	o	p	s	s	t, a	u, b	v, c	x/y, e/f	z, g
Lajos, 366	d	v	r	p	m	f	n	t, a	u, c	l	b, e	t
Rootsey, 346	a	b, o	c, p	d, q	e, r	f, s	g, t	h, v	i, w	k, x	l, y	m, z
Weisshappel, 245	d	e	f	g	h	i	k	l	m	a	b	c
Curwen, 349	d	de, ra	r	re, ma	m	f	fe, sa	s	se, la	l	le, ta	t
Miné, 301	g	♯g	a, h	♯a	b, i	c, j	♯c	d, k	♯d	e, l	♯e	f, m
Pereira de Sampaio, 361	d	'd, 'r	r	'r, 'm	m	f	'f, 's	s	's, 'l	l	'l, 'c	c
Vidales, 353	d	d:, r:	r	r:, m	m	f	f:, s:	s	s:, l:	l	l:, c:	c
DeLusse, 339	a	✳ a, bé	é	✳ é, bè	è	i	✳ i, bo	o	✳ o, bu	u	✳ u, bw	w
LaSalette, 343	ⱶ	db	ⱶ	eb	ⱶ	ⱶ	gb	ⱶ	ab	ⱶ	hb	ⱶ

460

I. STENOGRAPHIC PITCHES

Source	C	C# / Db	D	D# / Eb	E	F	F# / Gb	G	G# / Ab	A	A# / Bb	B
Hermann, 383												
Moser, 388												
Prévost, 373												
Rambach, 391												
Teule, 378												
Aloysio, 384												
Bertini, 372												
Hunt, 393												
Raab, 395												
de Stains, 378												
White, 392												

	Austin, 371	Depierre, 385	Dupont, 389	Gouverneur, 398	Labutut, 390	Montanello, 379	Rambures, 375	Riom, 387	Seymat, 386	Taylor, 395	Zichy-Ferraris, 388
B											
A# / Bb											
A											
G# / Ab											
G											
F# / Gb											
F											
E											
D# / Eb											
D											
C# / Db											
C											

Select Bibliography

ARTICLES

Bailey, Marshall. "Duodecuple Notation." American Composers Alliance Bulletin 10, no. 3 (1962): 12-14.

Bartolozzi, Bruno. "Proposals for Changes in Musical Notation." Journal of Music Theory 5, no. 2 (1961): 297-301.

Bent, Ian D.; Hiley, David; Bent, Margaret; and Chew, Geoffrey. "Notation." In New Grove Dictionary of Music and Musicians, vol. 13, 333-420. London: Macmillan, Ltd, 1981.

Brenn, Franz. "Equiton." Parts 1, 2, Schweitzerische Musikzeitung 101 (1961): no. 2, 78-87; no. 3, 23-27.

Cowell, Henry. "Our Inadequate Notation." Modern Music 4, no. 3 (1927): 29-33.

Dart, Thurston. "Notation." In Grove's Dictionary of Music and Musicians, fifth edition, 121-124. New York: St. Martins Press, 1964.

Destranges, Etienne. "L'écriture octavinale." Le Guide musicale 56, no. 48 (1910): 773-775.

Hull, Arthur Eaglefield. "Notations, Musical." In A Dictionary of Modern Music and Musicians, 351-353. New York: E. P. Dutton & Co., Inc., 1924.

Marrocco, W. Thomas. "The Notation in American Sacred Music Collections." Acta Musicologica 36, no. 1 (1964): 136-142.

Rongnon, Paul. "Origines de la notation musicale moderne." In Encyclopédie de la musique et Dictionnaire du Conservatoire, Deuxième Partie, 364-404. Paris: Delagrave, 1913-1930.

Rousseau, Jean-Jacques. "Projet conçernant de nouveaux signes pour la musique." In Ecrits sur la musique, Paris: Académie royale des sciences de Paris, 1742.

Scholes, Percy. "Notation and Nomenclature." In The Oxford Companion to Music, tenth edition, 690-692. London: Oxford University Press, 1970.

Sitsky, Larry. "Ferruccio Busoni's 'Attempt at an Organic Notation for the Pianoforte' and a Practical Adaptation of It." The Music Review 29, no. 1 (1968): 27-33.

Stainer, John. "On the Musical Introductions Found in Certain Metrical Psalters." Proceedings of the Musical Association 27 (13 November 1900).

Stone, Kurt. "Notation." In Dictionary of Contemporary Music, edited by John Vinton, 517-526. New York: E. P. Dutton & Co, 1974.

Szentkirályi, Andras. "An Attempt to Modernize Notation." The Music Review 34, no. 2 (1973): 100-123.

Yates, Peter. "The Proof of the Notation." In Twentieth Century Music, 221-238. New York: Pantheon Books, 1967.

BOOKS

Acland, Arthur H. Dyke. Letters on Musical Notation and the Present State of Musical Education. London: Darton & Clark, 1841.

Anon. Chromatic Notation. Victoria, B.C. & Montreux: Edition Chroma, 1983.

Baumgartner, August. Kurzgefasste geschichte der musikalischen notation mit einer übersichtstafel in tableauform und erläutern dem notenbeispielen verfasst und entworfen. Munich: Verlag von verfasser, 1856.

Bunger, Richard. The Diatonic Staff. Carson, California: the author, 1980.

Chailley, Jacques. Les notations musicales nouvelles. Paris: Leduc et Cie., 1950.

Cole, Hugo. Sounds and Signs. London: Oxford University Press, 1974.

Comettant, Oscar. Les musiciens, les philosophes et les gaités de la musique en chiffres. Paris: E. Dentu, Ed., 1870.

Cope, David. New Music Notation. Dubuque, Iowa: Kendall/Hunt Publishing Company, 1976.

Cowell, Henry. New Musical Resources. New York: Something
    Else Press, Inc., 1969.

David, Ernest, and Mathis Lussy. Histoire de la notation
    musicale depuis ses origines. Paris: Imprimerie nationale,
    Heugel et fils, 1882.

Diettrich-Kalkhoff, Franz. Geschichte der Notenschrift. Jauer
    in Schlesien: Verlag von Oskar Hellmann.

Ergo, Emile. L'acte final de la tragi-comédie musicale les
    "aveugles-réformateurs" de la notation actuelle et les
    belles (!) perspectives du système à dix-neuf sons dans
    l'octave. Anvers: Libraire néerlandaise, 1911.

Fétis, François-Joseph. La musique mise à la portée de tout
    le mond, third edition. Brussels: Hawman et Cie., 1839.

Gilson, F. H. The History of Shaped or Character Notes.
    Boston: the author, 1889.

Gouverneur, Emile. Traité complet de sténographie musicale.
    Brussels: Edition Schott Frères, 1949.

Huys, Bernard, ed. De Gregoire le Grand à Stockhausen.
    Brussels: Biblioteque royale de Belgique, 1966.

Johannis, Carl. Notenschriftreform. Stuttgart: Schuler Ver-
    lagsgesellschaft, 1961.

Karkoschka, Erhard. Notation in New Music. Translated by Ruth
    Koenig. New York: Praeger Publishers, Inc., 1972.

LaFond, John Francis. A New System of Music both Theoretical
    and Practical, and yet not Mathematical. London: the au-
    thor, 1725.

Lippius, Johann. Synopsis of New Music. Translated by Benito
    V. Rivera. Colorado Springs: Colorado College Music Press,
    1977.

Pagès, Alphonse. La méthode musicale Galin-Paris-Chevé. Paris:
    Libraire de l'Echo des Feuilletons, 1860.

Partch, Harry. Genesis of a Music. Madison: University of
    Wisconsin Press, 1949.

Pot, Cornelis. What is Klavarskribo? Slikkerveer, Holland:
    The Klavarskribo Institute, 1968.

Quantz, Otto. Zur Geschichte der neuen chromatischen Klaviatur
    und Notenschrift. Berlin: Georg Stilke, 1877.

Rambures, A. de. Abrégé de la méthode musicale sténographie.
    Paris: Regnier-Canaux, 1855.

Rambures, A. de. Notations comparées et art d'écrire le chant
à la dictée aussi vite qu'il est émis ou sténographie
musicale. Second edition. Paris: Blanchet, 1855.

Raymond, Georges Marie. Des principaux systèmes de notation
musicale usités ou proposés chez divers peuples tant an-
ciens que modernes, ou Examen de cette question: l'écriture musicale generalement usitée en Europe est-elle
vicieuse au point q'une réforme complete soit devenue indispensable? Turin: De l'Imprimerie royale, 1824.

Raymondi, Joseph. Essai de simplification musicographique,
avec un précis analytique des principaux systèmes de notation musicale proposés depuis le sixieme siecle. Paris:
Bernard-Latte, 1843.

___. Examen critique des notations musicales proposées depuis
deux siècles. Paris: Libraire Encyclopédique de Roret,
1856.

___. Les principaux systèmes de notation musicale. Turin:
Memoires de l'Académie de Turin XXX, 1825.

Read, Gardner. Music Notation: A Manual of Modern Practice.
Second edition. New York: Taplinger Publishing Co., Inc.,
1969.

Riemann, Hugo. Studien zur Geschichte der Notenschrift.
Leipzig: Breitkopf & Härtel, 1878.

Sacher, Hans. Unsere Tonschrift. Kurzer Rückblick auf deren
Werdegang sowie auf die Vorschläge zu deren Verbesserung,
ferner ein neuer Vorschlag für Tonbenennung und Notenschrift. Vienna: A. Pichlers Witwe & Sohn, 1903.

Sachs, Melchior Ernst. G. Decher's Tonschrift für das gleichstufige Tonsystem in ihrer anwendung für die chromatische
Klaviatur. Munich: Verlag des vereins "Chroma," 1877.

Stefan, Emil. Unsere Tonschrift und die Bestrebungen, sie zu
vereinfachen. Vienna: Erste Wiener vereins-buchdruckerei,
1899.

Stone, Kurt. Music Notation in the Twentieth Century. New
York: W. W. Norton and Company, 1980.

Tappolet, Willy. La notation musicale et son influence sur
la pratique de la musique du moyen âge à nos jours.
Zurich: Editions de la Baconniere à Boudry, 1947.

Wickström, August. Die Vereinfachung der Tonbezeichnung.
Leipzig: Belaieff, 1880.

Williams, Charles Francis Abdy. The Story of Notation. London:
The Walter Scott Publishing Co., Ltd., 1903.

Winternitz, Emmanuel. <u>Musical Autographs from Monteverdi to Hindemith</u>. 2 vols. Princeton: Princeton University Press, 1955.

Wolf, Johannes. <u>Handbuoh dor Notationokundo</u>. Vol. 2: III, IV. Hildesheim: Georg Olms Verlagsbuchhandlung, 1919.

Index of Names

About the Author

GARDNER READ is Professor Emeritus at Boston University School for the Arts and a well-known composer, lecturer, and writer. His earlier books include *Music Notation: A Manual of Modern Practice, Twentieth Century Notation, Style and Orchestration, Modern Rhythmic Notation, Contemporary Instrumental Techniques,* and *Thesaurus of Orchestral Devices* (Greenwood).